Handbook of Brief Cognitive Behaviour Therapy

Handbook of Brief Cognitive Behaviour Therapy

Edited by

Frank W. Bond
Goldsmiths College, University of London, UK

Windy Dryden
Goldsmiths College, University of London, UK

JOHN WILEY & SONS, LTD

Published in paperback August 2004

Reprinted July 2005

Email (for orders and customer service enquiries): cs-books@wiley.co.uk
Visit our Home Page on www.wileyeurope.com or www.wiley.com

Other Wiley Editorial Offices

John Wiley & Sons Inc., 111 River Street, Hoboken, NJ 07030, USA

Jossey-Bass, 989 Market Street, San Francisco, CA 94103-1741, USA

Wiley-VCH Verlag GmbH, Boschstr. 12, D-69469 Weinheim, Germany

John Wiley & Sons Australia Ltd, 33 Park Road, Milton, Queensland 4064, Australia

John Wiley & Sons (Asia) Pte Ltd, 2 Clementi Loop #02-01, Jin Xing Distripark, Singapore 129809

John Wiley & Sons Canada Ltd, 22 Worcester Road, Etobicoke, Ontario, Canada M9W 1L1

Wiley also publishes its books in a variety of electronic formats. Some content that appears
in print may not be available in electronic books.

Library of Congress Cataloging-in-Publication Data

Handbook of brief cognitive behaviour therapy / edited by Frank W. Bond, Windy Dryden.
    p.   cm.
Includes bibliographical references and index.
ISBN 0-470-02132-2 (pbk. : alk. paper)
1. Cognitive therapy—Handbooks, manuals, etc.   2. Brief psychotherapy—Handbooks, manuals, etc.
I. Bond, Frank. W.   II. Dryden, Windy.
RC489.C63H357   2004
616.89′14—dc22   2004008518

British Library Cataloguing in Publication Data

A catalogue record for this book is available from the British Library

ISBN 10: 0-470-02132-2 (P/B)
ISBN 13: 978-0-470-02132-3 (P/B)
ISBN 10: 0-471-49107-1 (H/B)
ISBN 13: 978-0-471-49107-1 (H/B)

Typeset in 10/12pt Times by TechBooks, New Delhi, India
Printed and bound in Great Britain by Antony Rowe Ltd, Chippenham, Wiltshire
This book is printed on acid-free paper responsibly manufactured from sustainable forestry
in which at least two trees are planted for each one used for paper production.

Contents

About the Editors

Frank W. Bond, BA (Honours), DipPsych, MSc, PhD, C Psychol, is Senior Lecturer in the Department of Psychology at Goldsmiths College, University of London. His research and practice centre around occupational health psychology and, in particular, how work redesign and cognitive behaviour therapies can independently, and together, help to improve workers' psychological health, absenteeism levels, and productivity. Dr Bond also maintains a private practice in cognitive behaviour therapy.

Windy Dryden, BSc, DipPsych, MSc, PhD, C Psychol, is Professor of Counselling at Goldsmiths College, University of London. He is the editor or author of over 125 books in the area of counselling and psychotherapy. His primary interests are rational emotive behaviour therapy and disseminating its theory and techniques to the general public, through writing short, accessible, self-help books.

List of Contributors

Donald H. Baucom, *Department of Psychology, University of North Carolina, Chapel Hill, 258 Davie Hall, Chapel Hill, North Carolina 27599-3270, USA*

F. Michler Bishop, *Director, Alcohol and Substance Abuse Services, Albert Ellis Institute, 45 East 65th Street, New York, New York 10021-6593, USA*

Frank W. Bond, *Department of Psychology, Goldsmiths College, University of London, New Cross, London SE14 6NW, UK*

Alan Carr, *Department of Psychology, Room 232 Science Building, University College Dublin, Belfield, Dublin 4, Ireland*

Michelle G. Craske, *Department of Psychology, UCLA, Franz Hall, 405 Hilgard Avenue, Los Angeles, California 90095-1563, USA*

Albert Ellis, *Albert Ellis Institute, 45 East 65th Street, New York, New York 10021-1593, USA*

Norman B. Epstein, *Department of Family Studies, University of Maryland, College Park, Maryland 20742, USA*

Paul E. Flaxman, *Department of Psychology, Goldsmiths College, University of London, New Cross, London SE14 6NW, UK*

Steven C. Hayes, *Department of Psychology /296, University of Nevada, Reno, Nevada 89557-0062, USA*

Holly Hazlett-Stevens, *Department of Psychology, UCLA, Franz Hall, 405 Hilgard Avenue, Los Angeles, California 90095-1563, USA*

Nina Heinrichs, *Center for Anxiety and Related Disorders, Boston University, 648 Beacon Street, 6th Floor, Boston, Massachusetts 02215, USA*

Stefan G. Hofmann, *Department of Psychology, Boston University, 648 Beacon Street, 6th Floor, Boston, Massachusetts 02215, USA*

Wendy Hunt, *Department of Family Studies, University of Maryland, College Park, Maryland 20742, USA*

Kelly L. Jarvis, *Department of Psychology and Social Behavior, University of California, Irvine, Irvine, California 92697-7085, USA*

Edmund Keogh, *Department of Psychology, University of Bath, Claverton Down, Bath BA2 7AY, UK*

Follin Armfield Key, *Department of Psychiatry and Human Behavior, Brown University, Providence, Rhode Island 02912, USA*

Jaslean J. La Taillade, *Department of Family Studies, University of Maryland, College Park, Maryland 20742, USA*

Raymond W. Novaco, *Department of Psychology and Social Behavior, University of California, Irvine, Irvine, California 92697-7085, USA*

David A. Spiegel, *Center for Anxiety and Related Disorders, Boston University, 648 Beacon Street, 6th Floor, Boston, Massachusetts 02215, USA*

Adrian Wells, *Academic Division of Clinical Psychology, University of Manchester, Rawnsley Building, Manchester Royal Infirmary, Oxford Road, Manchester M13 9WL, UK*

Robert D. Zettle, *Department of Psychology, Wichita State University, 410 Jabara Hall, Wichita, Kansas 67260, USA*

Preface

This handbook discusses issues concerning the definition, the assessment, and, in particular, the practice of brief cognitive behaviour therapy (CBT). We believe it is unique, in that it shows practitioners how they can use brief CBT to treat a *wide variety* of problems, including those of a clinical, academic/evaluative, and occupational stress/performance nature. This book also considers the differences between brief and "regular" CBT, identifies contraindications for the former, and summarises the empirical evidence of the efficacy of brief CBT. Finally, this book discusses an important professional issue in brief CBT: therapist burnout and how to avoid it.

Certainly, the time seems ripe for a handbook on brief CBT. The UK National Health Service and managed care in the USA are now influential, and difficult to ignore, advocates for the use of brief psychotherapeutic interventions. Furthermore, even before these powerful proponents, therapists were commenting that many individual clients were seeking brief psychotherapy for their problems (Wells, 1993); and, in response to these wishes, books have been published that detail brief therapies from psychodynamic (e.g., Book, 1998), eclectic (Garfield, 1998), and multiple perspectives (e.g., Wells & Giannetti, 1993). These books do not, however, provide CBT-oriented psychologists with knowledge about how to treat a wide range of problems from their own perspective. One aim of this volume is to provide this currently needed knowledge.

Another distinctive goal of this handbook, as briefly mentioned above, is to detail how brief CBT can be used to treat problems in several different settings. Today, CBT is employed in the traditional consulting room, hospital wards, and even organisations. Clinical and counselling psychologists are often the people who administer CBT in these diverse settings, but work and health psychologists are now receiving training in this psychotherapy and employing it in their specialist areas. It does not appear that one book on CBT has described how this approach to treatment can be employed in the different contexts in which it is currently used. Thus, we hope that this book can make a timely, unique, and useful contribution by describing how brief CBT is used to treat ubiquitous problems such as emotional disorders, pain, test (or evaluative) anxiety, and work-related stress.

Frank W. Bond
Windy Dryden
London, 2004

REFERENCES

Book, H.E. (1998). *How to practice brief psychodynamic psychotherapy: The core conflictual relationship theme method*. Washington, DC: American Psychological Association.
Garfield, S.L. (1998). The *practice of brief psychotherapy*. Chichester: Wiley.
Wells, R.A. (1993). Clinical strategies in brief psychotherapy. In R.A. Wells & V.J. Giannetti (Eds.), *Casebook of the brief psychotherapies* (pp. 3–17). New York: Plenum Press.
Wells, R.A., & Giannetti, V.J. (1993). *Casebook of the brief psychotherapies*. New York: Plenum Press.

CHAPTER 1

Brief Cognitive-Behavioral Therapy: Definition and Scientific Foundations

Holly Hazlett-Stevens and Michelle G. Craske

Department of Psychology, UCLA, Los Angeles, CA, USA

Over the past 50 years, cognitive-behavioral therapies (CBT) have become effective mainstream psychosocial treatments for many emotional and behavioral problems. Behavior therapy approaches were first developed in the 1950s when experimentally based principles of behavior were applied to the modification of maladaptive human behavior (e.g., Wolpe, 1958; Eysenck, 1966). In the 1970s, cognitive processes were also recognized as an important domain of psychological distress (Bandura, 1969). As a result, cognitive therapy techniques were developed and eventually integrated with behavioral approaches to form cognitive-behavioral treatments for a variety of psychological disorders. In this paper, we review the evidence for brief forms of CBT across various disorders. First, we consider the basic principles of CBT that render such therapies well suited for abbreviated formats.

BASIC PREMISES OF CBT

Although a number of different cognitive-behavioral techniques have been developed to address a variety of specific clinical problems, a set of basic principles and assumptions underlies all of these techniques. First, psychological dysfunction is understood in terms of mechanisms of learning and information processing. Basic learning theory incorporates findings from laboratory research on classical and operant conditioning. For example, certain phobic symptoms may represent a classically conditioned fear response that persists long after the removal of the original unconditioned stimulus. In this event, repeated, unreinforced exposure to the conditioned stimulus without the unconditioned stimulus is assumed to extinguish the conditioned fear response. In a similar vein, operant conditioning explains how undesired symptoms or behaviors are maintained as a function of the consequences that follow. For example, chronic pain behaviors are believed to be maintained in large part by attention from others. Therapies that teach persons to operate in their environment, so as to maximize positive reinforcement for adaptive behaviors and minimize such

Handbook of Brief Cognitive Behaviour Therapy. Edited by Frank W. Bond and Windy Dryden.
© 2002 John Wiley & Sons, Ltd. ISBN 0-470-02132-2.

reinforcement for problematic behaviors, have developed from early operant conditioning research. Cognitive research has shown that distortions in processing information about oneself and the environment are integral to many behavioral and psychological problems. For example, biases toward attending to threatening information or toward interpreting ambiguous situations as threatening contribute to excessive or unnecessary anxiety. Similarly, memory biases for distressing events or negative details of events may contribute to depressed mood. Learning to shift appraisals, core beliefs, and associated biases in attention and memory forms the basis of cognitive therapies.

Second, the cognitive-behavioral approach to treatment is guided by an experimental orientation to human behavior, in which any given behavior is seen as a function of the specific environmental and internal conditions surrounding it (Goldfried & Davison, 1994). Behavior is therefore lawful and can be better understood and predicted once its function is revealed. Because cognitive processes as well as overt behavior are viewed as adaptive and subject to change, the cognitive domain is also appropriate for therapeutic intervention (Goldfried & Davison, 1994). CBTs are therefore designed to target specific symptoms and behaviors that are identified as a part of the diagnosis or presenting problem for treatment. The cognitive-behavioral therapist approaches treatment with the assumption that a specific central or core feature is responsible for the observed symptoms and behavior patterns experienced (i.e., lawful relationships exist between this core feature and the maladaptive symptoms that result). Therefore, once the central feature is identified, targeted in treatment, and changed, the resulting maladaptive thoughts, symptoms, and behaviors will also change. For example, a CBT therapist treating panic disorder might discover that the patient holds the erroneous belief that a rapid heartbeat indicates a heart attack. Treatment would therefore aim to challenge this misconception with education and cognitive restructuring while encouraging the patient to experience intentionally the sensation of a rapid heartbeat in order to learn that a heart attack does not occur.

Third is the premise that change is effected through new learning experiences that overpower previous forms of maladaptive learning and information processing. For example, facing feared objects or situations without escape or avoidance enables new approach behaviors and judgments of safety to be learned. Change can therefore occur in the short term as a result of learning these new thoughts and behaviors, and be maintained over the long term as these newly acquired responses generalize across situations and time. CBT also often involves the teaching of new coping skills (such as assertiveness, relaxation, or self-talk) for more effective response to environmental situations. This is expected to lead to improved outcome over time as the new skills are practiced and repeatedly implemented. Clinical improvement can therefore result from two different pathways. First, as previous maladaptive thoughts and behaviors are replaced with more adaptive responses, new learning occurs as the result of new experiences. Second, the individual may learn effective coping skills that lead to improved functioning over time as these skills are practiced and developed.

Fourth is the value of scientific method for CBT, as reflected in the therapist's ongoing evaluation of change at the level of the individual patient. From their experimental orientation, CBT therapists generate hypotheses about an individual's cognitive and behavior patterns, intervene according to that hypothesis, observe the resulting behavior, modify their hypothesis on the basis of this observation, and so on. Thus, the CBT therapist is not simply bound to a set of techniques, but practices from a basic philosophical position consistent with scientific methods (Goldfried & Davison, 1994). This experimental approach is also apparent in the large number of randomized, controlled psychotherapy outcome research studies of the efficacy of CBT. In 1995, a Task Force of the American Psychological Association's Division of Clinical Psychology reviewed the psychotherapy outcome research literature to determine which treatments were considered effective, according to certain research criteria. By their 1996 update (Chambless et al., 1996), 22 different treatments were deemed "well-established," meeting the most rigorous research criteria for efficacy, while an additional 25 treatments met the less stringent criteria of "probably efficacious treatments." The great majority of these "empirically supported therapies" were cognitive-behavioral treatments for a variety of problems, including anxiety disorders, depression, physical health problems, eating disorders, substance abuse, and marital problems. Thus, much research evidence is available to support the use of CBT to treat a number of specific symptoms and behavioral problems.

The cognitive-behavioral conceptualization of psychological dysfunction, the specific nature of the target of CBT, the hypothesized mechanisms of therapeutic change, and the value of the scientific method all render CBT suitable for brief formats. That is, once the critical maladaptive learning and information processing is understood, crucial therapeutic learning experiences can be structured and coping skills can be taught in a very short period of time. Similarly, continuous evaluation of the efficacy of CBT enables variations in its delivery to be examined. One such variation is the length of treatment.

BRIEF CBT

As a result of the problem-focused approach, CBT treatments are typically brief and time-limited in nature. Many CBT treatments lead to significant clinical improvement and symptom reduction, relative to other forms of psychotherapy, in as few as 10–20 sessions. However, treatment researchers are now working to streamline existing effective CBTs to make them even more efficient, cost-effective, and affordable. Some approaches to increase the efficiency of CBT treatments include adapting individual treatments to a group format, self-help materials and bibliotherapy, and computer-assisted therapy programs. The most common approach for enhancing efficiency, however, is to abbreviate existing CBT treatments by reducing the number of treatment sessions. Not only is this trend a pragmatic response to external pressures such as the rise of managed health care in the USA, but it also reflects the underlying assumption (already stated) that effective CBT results from identifying and changing specific cognitions and behaviors that are responsible for the presenting problem. As CBT treatment research progresses, more powerful therapies containing only those techniques that lead to significant change are developed. Similarly, as additional research further pinpoints the likely cause of a particular disorder, treatments become better targeted at the maladaptive features in need of intervention.

Brevity has many clear advantages. Increased cost-effectiveness could make treatment accessible to more individuals in need of assistance. Patients enjoy rapid treatment gains, and this may also improve the credibility of the treatment and increase the motivation for further change. However, this approach may be disadvantageous in some circumstances. Abbreviated CBT approach assumes that the target for change is clearly defined and circumscribed. Patients presenting with more diffuse symptoms or with particular comorbid conditions that interfere with directly targeted programs (such as Axis II disorders) may need more lengthy treatment. The abbreviated approach also assumes that the patient is motivated to participate in the treatment and is ready to make cognitive and behavioral changes. Therefore, patients who are ambivalent about change and unwilling to comply with necessary homework assignments may not benefit from treatments with very limited durations. Similarly, brief CBT puts a greater burden on the patient to engage actively in treatment both during and between sessions. The CBT patient assumes much responsibility for learning necessary therapeutic material and practice of related exercises and skills, significantly more so when such treatment is abbreviated. Finally, the brief CBT approach demands that the therapist be able to keep the patient focused on the specific goals and tasks of treatment. This requires the therapist to be skilled at redirecting patients quickly while maintaining a strong therapeutic alliance. Not all therapists may be suitable for brief CBT. These potential disadvantages clearly warrant empirical investigation.

In the next section, we provide a brief overview of the empirical research evidence that supports the practice of brief CBT. Although there is no clear, standard definition of "brief" CBT, we considered CBT interventions consisting of fewer than 10 sessions. This cutoff was based on the observation that current standard CBT treatments typically span 10–20 sessions. We located empirical studies of the efficacy of brief CBT by asking experts in a variety of areas about available research and by searches of Psychological Abstracts. This section is not an exhaustive review of the current literature, but an overview with a focus on studies that employed randomized controlled group psychotherapy outcome research designs. We structured our review by diagnostic category, as there has been no empirical investigation of the efficacy of brief CBT across different disorders.

In evaluating the research to date for brief CBT, several issues become noteworthy. The first issue, to which we already alluded, is that certain disorders may be more amenable to brief CBT than other disorders. Specifically, more circumscribed disorders with more readily definable lawful relationships, such as specific phobias, seem most suitable for brief CBT. In accord, the specific phobias have been studied more than any other disorder vis-à-vis brief CBT. The remaining issues have to do with the quality of research to date regarding brief CBT; they are summarized in Table 1.1. For example, how should the efficacy of brief CBT be evaluated? We found very few studies that directly compared abbreviated to unabbreviated CBT, and those that did were often "confounded" by the incorporation of self-help adjunct materials for the abbreviated CBT only. Unconfounded studies were found in the treatment of specific phobias only. The majority of studies compare brief CBT to another type of therapy (e.g., nondirective), an attention placebo control, or waiting list control. While important, these designs do not directly assess the relative merits of brief CBT versus unabbreviated CBT.

A third issue concerns the dimensions along which to compare abbreviated and unabbreviated CBT: is abbreviated CBT as effective as unabbreviated CBT in terms of acute response, long-term response, and nontargeted symptoms or conditions? Most studies evaluate short-term or acute response as well as long-term status. Despite the reasoning that relapse *may* be elevated after brief CBT relative to unabbreviated CBT, particularly if skills and new learning are not repeated and reinforced after the end of treatment, the evidence generally suggests good long-term response to brief CBT. With respect to nontargeted symptoms and comorbid conditions, evidence for the benefits of unabbreviated CBT is growing, at least with respect to anxiety disorders. For example, targeted treatment for panic disorder leads to significant improvements in other comorbid anxiety disorders, depressive disorders, and Axis II features (e.g., Brown & Barlow, 1995; Tsao et al., 1998). Some studies have investigated the effects of brief CBT on measures that are not specific to the particular disorder (e.g., depression,

Table 1.1 Empirical issues addressed by the reviewed research for each Disorder

Disorder	Research features						
	Brief vs standard CBT, unconfounded by adjunct materials	Acute response	Long-term response	Generalization to nontargeted symptoms and conditions	Therapeutic mechanisms	Individual difference predictors of outcome	Therapist variables related to outcome
Panic disorder	X	X	X	X		X	
Specific phobia		X	X	X		X	
GAD		X	X	X		X	
Social phobia		X	X	X		X	
PTSD prevention		X	X	X			
Depression		X	X	X		X	
Bulimia nervosa/BED		X	X	X		X	
Obesity		X	X	X		X	
Couples therapy		X					
Alcohol use		X	X	X		X	
Headache		X	X	X	X	X	X
Low-back pain		X	X	X	X		

general anxiety, and overall psychological functioning), but yet to be evaluated is whether brief CBT has the same broad-based effect on diagnosed comorbid conditions.

A fourth consideration is whether the process of therapeutic change is the same in brief CBT as in unabbreviated CBT. Rachman & Whittal (1989) compared fast and slow responders to exposure therapy for fears of spiders and snakes. They hypothesized that steady and slow reductions in fear reflect a type of trial and error learning, whereas fast reductions in fear reflect insight and reasoning, akin to a "flashbulb" effect. Obviously, the goal of brief CBT is to structure the learning experiences in order to maximize this second type of learning. Very rarely have therapeutic mechanisms been studied, to date.

A final issue concerns individual difference variables that predict outcome from brief CBT, such as attitudes to treatment, chronicity, severity, and ongoing life stressors. Some available research suggests that, as with standard CBT, positive attitudes toward treatment predict treatment response to brief CBT. Other findings suggest that brief CBT may be more effective with less severe populations. However, some studies found no significant predictors of outcome. More research is needed to elucidate which individual characteristics lead to improved treatment outcome under what treatment conditions. Finally, the relationship between therapist variables, such as level of experience, and therapeutic outcome is also of importance and has been rarely studied.

PANIC DISORDER AND AGORAPHOBIA

A number of advances have been made to reduce the number of treatment sessions for panic disorder and agoraphobia. Traditional CBT is provided over 10–20 sessions and includes several treatment components (Craske, 1999). Education and cognitive restructuring address faulty beliefs and misconceptions about the meaning of bodily sensations. Corrective breathing techniques are sometimes incorporated to regulate breathing. Finally, various forms of interoceptive and in vivo exposure are designed to reduce fear and avoidance of physical sensations and agoraphobic situations. Several investigations support the use of abbreviated CBT to treat panic disorder and agoraphobia.

One series of studies compared brief therapist-administered CBT to self-help treatment approaches. Lindren et al. (1994) found that an eight-session group CBT treatment effectively reduced panic and agoraphobia symptoms on a number of outcome measures when compared to a waiting-list condition. They also found that an eight-week, self-help, bibliotherapy treatment was equally effective. In a later study, this research group found that a self-administered, bibliotherapy treatment was comparable to an eight-session individual treatment consisting of education, breathing and relaxation training, cognitive restructuring, and imaginal and in vivo exposure (Gould et al., 1993). Similarly, Ghosh & Marks (1987) reduced treatment to a minimum of three and a maximum of 10 sessions in their self-directed exposure program for agoraphobia. Results showed that this psychiatrist-instructed treatment led to substantial improvement in agoraphobic avoidance at six-month follow-up. The fact that their other treatment conditions that included a self-help book or computer instructions only were just as effective suggests that an exposure program with no therapist contact is an effective mode of treatment. However, recent evidence questions the effectiveness of purely self-help treatments for panic attacks in the absence of any therapist contact (Febbraro et al., 1999). Notably, none of these studies compared abbreviated to unabbreviated CBT, and effects on comorbid conditions were not reported.

A few studies have investigated the use of telephone contacts to reduce the number of therapy sessions. Côté et al. (1994) provided panic disorder patients with either 17 individual CBT sessions (including education, breathing retraining, relaxation, cognitive therapy, and interoceptive and situational exposure) or the same treatment delivered over seven sessions and eight brief telephone contacts. The results indicated that both treatments were effective, with significant and equivalent improvements at six-month follow-up. For housebound agoraphobic patients or those who are isolated from treatment facilities, guided exposure treatment involving only telephone contact may also be effective when provided over eight (Swinson et al., 1995) or 10 (McNamee et al., 1989) telephone sessions. This last study, however, reported a high dropout rate for the group receiving telephone-guided exposure.

Direct comparisons between abbreviated and unabbreviated CBT include a study by Botella & García-Palacios (1999), who compared a standard 10-session CBT for panic disorder to an abbreviated five-session treatment in a community sample with an overall low level of education (average of 9.7 years). The results suggested that the treatments were effective and comparable, with both groups maintaining gains at 12-month follow-up. Such results are similar to those of Newman et al. (1997), who compared standard 12-session individual CBT to an abbreviated four-session, computer-assisted CBT. Both treatment groups demonstrated significant improvement at post-treatment and at six-month follow-up. Analyses of clinical significance suggested the superiority of the 12-session condition, but only at post-treatment. Finally, Clark et al. (1999) compared standard 12–15-session cognitive therapy for panic disorder to a brief five-session version of the same treatment. Both of these treatments were highly effective and superior to a waiting-list control condition, and there were no significant differences between the two treatments. It is noteworthy, and in contrast to lengthier CBT trials, that the brief versions of treatment mentioned in the previous three studies all included self-help material as an adjunct to treatment. Botella & García-Palacios (1999) provided a self-help manual and audiotape to their brief treatment participants, while Clark et al. (1999) also provided self-study written materials and exercises to patients in the brief cognitive therapy condition. Likewise, Newman et al. (1997) included a computer-assisted therapy component to all participants receiving the four-session treatment. Thus, it is unclear whether the results would have differed had unabbreviated CBT included the same self-help material.

A final approach abbreviates the length of treatment by administering intensive treatment over a brief period of time. Evans et al. (1991) provided 18 hours of intensive group CBT over two days. Significant reductions in symptoms were found for this group when compared to a waiting-list control group, and the clinically significant improvement found for 85% of these patients was maintained at one-year follow-up. However, these results should be interpreted with caution because this was not a randomized trial. In another open trial, Spiegel & Barlow (2000) are evaluating an eight-day intensive treatment program for panic disorder with moderate to severe agoraphobia that incorporates therapist-directed and self-directed exposure. The preliminary findings are very positive.

A few studies reported an individual difference variable of relevance to outcome from brief CBT. We (Craske et al., 1995) found that four weekly sessions of abbreviated CBT were superior to four sessions of nondirective counseling of panic disorder patients seeking pharmacological treatment. However, the results were not as effective as typically found with 10–15 sessions of CBT, and less severe patients improved most with this particular abbreviation of CBT. Febbraro et al. (1999) found that, among their sample of individuals experiencing panic attacks with or without panic disorder, the presence of a panic disorder diagnosis did not predict outcome. The Clark et al. (1999) study described above found that belief that treatment would be successful at the end of the first session predicted outcome at post, and a measure of beliefs about bodily sensations predicted outcome at one-year follow-up. However, Evans et al. (1991) reported that none of their 11 pretreatment variables predicted outcome.

SPECIFIC PHOBIA

Much work has been done to develop brief and effective CBT for various specific phobias. Treatment typically includes education about the nature of fear, cognitive restructuring of thoughts and misconceptions about the feared object or situation, and systematic imaginal and in vivo exposure to the feared object or situation (Craske, 1999). These procedures are employed for all types of phobias, although applied tension is used in the treatment of blood, injury, and injection phobias (Öst, 1996a). In 1996, Öst reviewed the specific phobia treatment outcome research and found rates of clinical improvement ranging between 77% and 90% after only one to eight sessions. Treatment studies for acrophobia; animal phobia; blood, injury, and injection phobias; claustrophobia; dental phobia; and flying phobia were included. Öst also examined the long-term outcome of these studies and concluded that these gains are generally maintained for up to 10 years after successful treatment.

A number of studies support the use of single-session treatments for specific phobias. For example, Öst et al. (1991) found that one session of therapist-directed exposure lasting a maximum of three hours effectively reduced fear and avoidance in spider-phobic patients. This treatment was superior to a two-week, self-directed exposure program. These researchers later demonstrated that this single-session, therapist-directed treatment is also superior to self-help manual treatment programs that involved unsupervised patient-directed exposure exercises either at home or in the clinic (Hellström & Öst, 1995). Therapist-directed single-session exposure treatment is also effective when provided in a group format (Öst et al., 1997b), especially when provided in smaller (i.e., three to four people) groups (Öst, 1996b).

Single-session CBT for other phobias is supported when compared to longer-length treatments. Hellström et al. (1996) compared a single two-hour session to five sessions of an applied tension treatment that taught patients to prevent the fainting response with muscle tension upon exposure to feared blood and injury stimuli. A third treatment group received a single two-hour session of tension only without the exposure. All three groups improved significantly at post-treatment and one-year follow-up. Although the five-session applied tension treatment was superior to the one-session applied tension treatment at post-treatment, no differences were found at follow-up. They also found that individuals classified as "fainters" improved as much as (and on two measures even more so than) those classified as "non-fainters." This research group also concluded that a single session of therapist-directed exposure is the treatment of choice for injection phobia (Öst et al., 1992). One treatment session that did not exceed three hours in length was highly effective at both post-treatment and at one-year follow-up. Furthermore, this single-session treatment was just as effective as the same treatment delivered over five sessions. Recent evidence also suggests that one session of CBT for claustrophobia is comparable to five sessions of the same treatment (Öst et al., 2001). Similarly, one three-hour session of exposure and cognitive restructuring was just as effective as five sessions of the same treatment for flying phobia at post-treatment and at one-year follow-up (Öst et al., 1997a). However, some loss in treatment gains at follow-up was reported for both groups in this study. Clearly, this body of research suggests that circumscribed phobias are well suited for brief CBT; and it appears to be as effective in the short term as the long term.

OTHER ANXIETY DISORDERS

Of all the anxiety disorders, abbreviated treatments for panic disorder (with and without agoraphobia) and for specific phobia have the most empirical support. A few studies support brief CBT for other anxiety disorders. A growing body of controlled research supports the efficacy of cognitive-behavioral treatments for generalized anxiety disorder (GAD) (Borkovec & Whisman, 1996). Standard CBT treatments include anxiety monitoring, relaxation training, cognitive therapy, and imagery exposure, and are typically conducted over approximately 12 sessions. However, one study compared only eight sessions of CBT to nondirective counseling and to a waiting-list control condition (Blowers et al., 1987). Results showed that while CBT resulted in modest clinical improvements that were consistently superior to the waiting-list condition at post-treatment and at six-month follow-up, few differences emerged between the CBT and nondirective counseling groups. Another study demonstrated that a six-session, large-group course was effective in the treatment of GAD when compared to waiting-list control, but improvements were comparable to a "placebo" version of the treatment (White et al., 1992). Additional research suggests that CBT for GAD can be effective in as few as 4–7 sessions, appearing to be comparable to active medication and superior to medication placebo (Power et al., 1990). A recently developed CBT treatment for GAD was successfully administered over six group sessions with the adjunct use of a palmtop computer program (Newman et al., 1999). However, this report consisted of an uncontrolled case design with a single group of three participants. Lacking in the studies to date is a direct comparison between abbreviated and unabbreviated CBT for GAD.

Social phobia can be effectively treated over approximately 12 sessions of either individual or group CBT, and such treatments typically include psychoeducation, cognitive restructuring, and exposure to anxiety-provoking social situations (Heimberg & Juster, 1995). While there is good controlled psychotherapy outcome research to support this practice, little information is available regarding the efficacy of abbreviated treatments. In an uncontrolled study, Rapee (1993) provided an abbreviated version of the cognitive-behavioral group treatment (CBGT) outlined by Heimberg et al. (1990). Treatment consisted of six 90-minute sessions. The results indicated significant improvement at post-treatment and at three- and six-month follow-up on most outcome variables. However, data were available from only 30 of the original 52 participants, and only one-third of the remaining participants met stringent "responder" clinical criteria at post and follow-up assessments. Although this rate of improvement falls within the estimated 20–95% reported range (Feske & Chambless, 1995), Heimberg and colleagues have reported improvement rates of 75% post-treatment and 81% at six-month follow-up after unabbreviated CBGT (Heimberg et al., 1990).

Foa et al. (1995) investigated the efficacy of a brief intervention to prevent the onset of post-traumatic stress disorder (PTSD) in female recent assault victims. This research group adapted their effective CBT treatment for PTSD into a brief prevention program consisting of four individual two-hour sessions. Results indicated significant improvement on a variety of measures post-treatment and at 5.5 months after the assault. Improvements on some measures were also greater than those found for a matched repeated assessment control group. Finally, only 10% of the CBT group later met diagnostic criteria for PTSD, whereas 70% of the matched control group met PTSD criteria. These results should be interpreted with caution, however, as participants were not randomly assigned. No studies were found for brief CBT treatment for obsessive-compulsive disorder (OCD). Standard CBT for OCD is quite intensive, typically consisting of 15 two-hour sessions that occur daily over a three-week period (Riggs & Foa, 1993). Such intensive treatment may be necessary for an individual to gain adequate exposure to feared situations without engaging in a compulsive response that would reinforce the fear.

DEPRESSION

Substantial empirical evidence supports the use of CBT in the treatment of major depressive disorder. Two such widely studied approaches include Beck's cognitive therapy and behavioral programs based on the work of Lewinsohn (Craighead et al., 1998). Behavior therapy programs aim to increase pleasurable activity while reducing aversive experiences, while CBT also targets negative thoughts regarding oneself and the world with cognitive restructuring. These treatments are administered over 12–20 individual or group sessions, and much research is available to support this practice (Craighead et al., 1998).

A few studies have investigated whether these highly effective treatments can be abbreviated for use in primary care and other community settings. Scott et al. (1997) provided six weekly CBT sessions (lasting approximately 30 minutes each) and written educational material to primary care patients diagnosed with major depression. Patients were randomly assigned to either this treatment condition or to treatment as usual in the primary care clinic. The results indicated that the treatment participants recovered at significantly higher rates than the control group immediately after treatment, and these gains were maintained at one-year follow-up. Similarly, Katon et al. (1996) provided a collaborative care treatment for depressed patients in a primary care medical setting. Treatment included four to six individual CBT sessions. In addition, therapists and physicians consulted with study psychiatrists to optimize effective medication treatment and improve medication adherence. Patients were randomized to either the collaborative condition or treatment as usual. The results demonstrated significant improvement for those treatment patients diagnosed with major depression when compared to the treatment as usual control condition. Finally, a brief six-session group CBT appears to be effective when administered in a non-research community mental health treatment setting (Peterson & Halstead, 1998), but this study was an uncontrolled trial. While these studies support the efficacy of brief treatment, they do not elucidate how these gains compare to lengthier CBT. If depression is a less circumscribed disorder with less specific core features to target in treatment, brief treatments may not be as effective. However, if therapists can successfully identify and challenge core maladaptive thoughts over a brief period of time, this approach may prove beneficial. Further research that directly compares standard CBT to brief CBT would be needed to answer this empirical question.

Brief CBT may be effective for childhood depression. Wood et al. (1996) provided five to eight sessions of either CBT or relaxation only control to child and adolescent patients (aged 9–17) with diagnosed depressive disorders. At post-treatment, CBT was clearly superior to relaxation control, but the two treatments were similar on most measures by six-month follow-up. Weisz et al. (1997) provided an eight-session CBT for childhood depression that aimed to enhance reward and reduce punishment by teaching children to assert control over their environment as well as to adjust their subjective reactions to undesired events. Elementary school pupils (mean age of 9.6 years) with mild to moderate levels of depression received either eight sessions of this group CBT or no treatment control. Results indicated significant improvements on depression measures for the treatment group compared to the control group both at post-treatment and at nine-month follow-up.

EATING DISORDERS

Although CBT for anorexia nervosa is widely used, few randomized controlled studies have been published, and treatment typically spans a one- to two-year period (Garner et al., 1997). In contrast, CBT for bulimia nervosa is supported by a number of well-controlled research studies (Wilson et al., 1997), and this treatment has been effectively adapted to treat binge eating disorder as well (Wilfley & Cohen, 1997). Abbreviated versions of CBT for bulimia nervosa and for binge eating disorder have been developed.

Standard CBT for bulimia nervosa is often based on the manual of Fairburn et al. (1993). This treatment package includes education, self-monitoring, changes in eating patterns, problem-solving and self-control strategies, and cognitive restructuring, and is typically administered over 19 sessions (Wilson et al., 1997). In a small, uncontrolled trial, this treatment was abbreviated to a maximum of eight 20-minute sessions in a primary care setting, and 55% of patients showed significant improvement (Waller et al., 1996). These results are consistent with a randomized controlled study that found eight sessions of CBT to be highly effective through six-month follow-up and superior to an attention placebo self-monitoring treatment (Thackwray et al., 1993).

A few studies suggest that brief interventions that emphasize the educational component might also be helpful to some bulimic patients. For example, Olmstead et al. (1991) compared a five-session educational group treatment for bulimia nervosa to 19 sessions of individual standard CBT. The results demonstrated equal effectiveness in symptom reduction for the least severe 25–45% of the sample, whereas standard CBT was associated with greater improvement for the more severe participants. This replicates our finding with panic disorder and agoraphobia (Craske et al., 1995). This five-session psychoeducation treatment has also proven more effective than waiting-list control (Davis et al., 1990) and equivalent to a 12-session CBT group process intervention (Davis et al., 1997), although this last study employed a sequential cohort design without random assignment. In a follow-up study, however, Davis et al. (1999) compared a six-session educational treatment to this same treatment combined with 16 additional sessions of CBT, and found some advantage of the lengthier treatment. Although this study compared a brief CBT treatment to a longer treatment, the additional sessions in the standard CBT condition contained elements other than those found in the brief psychoeducational treatment.

A second line of research has found the number of treatment sessions for bulimia nervosa and binge eating disorder to be reduced with the aid of self-help materials. In 1994, Treasure et al. compared eight sessions of CBT following the provision of a self-help manual to 16 sessions of standard CBT for bulimia nervosa. Results at post-treatment and at 18-month follow-up yielded no differences between the two treatment groups, and both were superior to a waiting-list control group. Similarly, uncontrolled research suggests that this guided self-help approach can be effective when provided over as few as four sessions (Cooper et al., 1994; Cooper et al., 1996). In a large randomized controlled trial, Carter & Fairburn (1998) compared pure self-help and non-specialist facilitator-guided self-help treatment to a waiting-list control condition. Both self-help groups were given a book based on the CBT treatment for binge eating disorder (Fairburn, 1995), and the guided self-help participants met with a facilitator for six to eight brief sessions to discuss the content of the materials. The results indicated that both treatment conditions led to significant changes when compared to the waiting-list group, and treatment gains were maintained at six-month follow-up. However, later research has demonstrated the advantages of therapist-guided self-help treatment for binge eating when compared to an unguided version of this treatment (Loeb et al., 2000).

A related condition, obesity, can be effectively treated with CBT in 16–20 sessions (Brownell & O'Neil, 1993), and a few studies suggest that this treatment can be reduced with the aid of a computer therapy program. Agras et al. (1990) randomized mildly to moderately overweight women to a single-session plus computer treatment, a five-session plus computer treatment, or standard CBT provided over 10 group sessions. The results indicated that the *modest* treatment effects were equivalent for the three groups at one-year follow-up. This research group later demonstrated that two different computer therapy treatments combined with four group sessions led to significant weight reduction, although one of the computer groups was superior to the other (Taylor et al., 1991). These computer-assisted treatment programs appear to be most effective when participants are instructed to use them seven days a week, and the addition of a brief support group component does not appear to enhance outcome (Burnett et al., 1992).

COUPLES THERAPY

A few studies have investigated the efficacy of reducing standard 10–20-session CBT in the treatment of couple dysfunction. Halford & Osgarby (1996) conducted a quasi-experimental study comparing a three-session brief CBT to standard 12–15-session CBT. Both treatments yielded significant and equivalent post-treatment effects. Davidson & Horvath (1997) provided either three sessions of brief CBT emphasizing cognitive reframing or delayed treatment to 40 couples. Treatment led to significant improvement compared to delayed treatment on some outcome measures, and the treatment gains were maintained at six-month follow-up. Finally, a three-session assessment-feedback treatment led to small positive changes and was superior to a written-assessment only condition in a sample of non-treatment-seeking college student couples (Worthington et al., 1995).

ALCOHOL USE

A large number of treatment approaches for alcoholism have been developed, and CBT is regarded as one of the more effective treatments (Longabaugh & Morgenstern, 1999). CBT treatments for alcohol use and dependence disorders typically target problem drinking behaviors by improving cognitive and behavioral coping skills. Patients are taught to cope with both internal events, such as alcohol cravings, and external events, such as social pressures to drink and environmental cues that trigger the urge to drink (Fuller & Hilles-Sturmhofel, 1999).

Standard CBT for problem drinking is provided over approximately 12 sessions (Longabaugh & Morgenstern, 1999). A number of brief interventions have been developed and investigated, but these brief interventions typically involve only self-help materials or advice sessions delivered by primary health-care providers. In a review of brief interventions for alcohol problems, Bien et al. (1993) found that physician advice interventions were comparable to standard CBT and to other extensive treatments. They also reported that brief motivational induction treatments appear to be effective in motivating alcoholic patients to seek further treatment. CBT often has served as an extensive treatment against which other forms of brief treatment (e.g., minimal physician advice) are compared (Hall & Heather, 1991). However, one study compared a self-help bibliotherapy intervention to three different therapist-directed brief group interventions (Skutle & Berg, 1987). The first therapist-directed treatment group received six sessions of a guided self-help version of the bibliotherapy intervention. The second treatment group received six sessions of coping skills training, in which ways to cope with high-risk situations were taught and practiced. The final therapist-directed treatment group received a combination of these two treatments delivered over eight sessions. The results indicated that the weekly alcohol consumption decreased significantly for all four groups, and these gains were maintained at one-year follow-up. No significant differences were found among the groups.

CBT for problem drinking has also been abbreviated by Sobell & Sobell (1993). Their guided self-management treatment program aims to motivate behavior change and to provide suggestions and strategies for accomplishing behavioral goals. Treatment procedures include setting drinking behavior treatment goals, alcohol education, self-monitoring, identification of the triggers and consequences related to drinking, and the development of behavioral strategies to attain established goals. Although the length of treatment is flexible to meet the needs of the individual, this guided self-management treatment can be effectively implemented in only two sessions (Sobell & Sobell, 1993). A randomized outcome investigation of this treatment compared two 90-minute sessions of the behavioral components only to two 90-minute sessions of the behavioral components plus cognitive relapse prevention (Sobell et al., 1995). The results indicated that both groups exhibited significant reductions in reported drinking behavior. These outcomes were maintained at six- and 12-month follow-up. However, no differences were found between the two treatments.

Marlatt and colleagues have developed a single-session intervention for the prevention of drinking problems in high-risk college students. Marlatt et al. (1998) randomly assigned college freshmen to receive either an individual interview session or no treatment during the winter term of their first year. Participants considered to be at the highest risk of developing alcohol-related problems (on the basis of reported high-school drinking behavior) were selected. The intervention session consisted of reviewing the participants' self-monitoring of drinking; individualized feedback about observed drinking patterns, associated risks, and beliefs about alcohol; discussion of information and misconceptions regarding the effects of alcohol; and suggestions for risk reduction. This intervention was designed to increase motivation, and confrontational or judgmental comments were avoided. The results indicated decreases in drinking rates and harmful consequences for both groups over the two-year follow-up period, but the treatment gains were significantly greater for the intervention group.

PAIN MANAGEMENT

While effective CBT-oriented treatments are available for a variety of chronic pain conditions, this section will focus on the brief treatment research for headache and low-back pain. CBT programs are widely used, effective approaches for the management of headache pain (Blanchard & Seymour, 1996). Treatment typically employs education, some form of relaxation training (e.g., progressive muscle relaxation, autogenic training, and meditation) and/or biofeedback, and cognitive coping techniques (Holroyd & Penzien, 1994). Over the past decade, researchers have developed brief "minimal therapist contact" treatments, in which CBT is administered in only three to five sessions. In 1996, Rowan & Andrasik systematically reviewed the available controlled outcome research to examine the efficacy of minimal therapist contact CBT for headache pain. For adult tension-type headache, two studies showed that three sessions were comparable to 10 sessions of relaxation training (Teders et al., 1984; Blanchard et al., 1985). Equivalent efficacy was also demonstrated for three sessions of relaxation when compared to five sessions of relaxation plus cognitive therapy (Attanasio et al., 1987; Appelbaum et al., 1990) and to 11 sessions of relaxation and cognitive therapy (Attanasio et al., 1987). However, one study did show some advantage of a three-session treatment including both relaxation and cognitive therapy over three sessions of relaxation alone (Tobin et al., 1988). Minimal therapist contact CBT for tension headache has also proven superior to waiting-list control (Appelbaum et al., 1990) and comparable to amitriptyline medication (Holroyd et al., 1991). Rowan & Andrasik (1996) concluded that these brief tension headache treatments, largely consisting of progressive muscle relaxation training, are as effective as longer, clinic-based relaxation training treatments, with 37–50% of participants meeting stringent clinical improvement post treatment and up to two-year follow-up.

Rowan & Andrasik (1996) also identified several studies that support minimal therapist contact CBT for vascular (migraine and migraine combined with tension-type) headaches. For example, Williamson et al. (1984) found that four sessions of group relaxation training were equivalent to eight group sessions, with both treatments yielding significant improvements compared to an attention placebo. Similarly, three sessions of individual relaxation training were found comparable to 16 sessions for both pure migraine and migraine combined with tension-type headache participants (Blanchard et al., 1985). Three-session individual relaxation plus thermal biofeedback appears to be equivalent to 16 sessions of the same treatment (Jurish et al., 1983), to three sessions of an abortive medication and compliance intervention (Holroyd et al., 1988), and to five sessions of the same treatment plus cognitive therapy (Blanchard et al., 1990). This treatment was also superior to a headache-monitoring condition (Blanchard et al., 1990). Finally, Richardson & McGrath (1989) found that only two sessions of CBT produced the same effects as an eight-session CBT, both of which were superior to waiting-list control. From these studies, Rowan & Andrasik (1996) concluded that brief relaxation interventions, either with or without thermal biofeedback, are as effective as longer treatments, leading to clinically significant improvement in 40–79% of patients.

A few studies support the use of minimal therapist contact treatments for headaches in children and adolescents. Three sessions of relaxation training were found superior to both nine sessions of an attention placebo condition and a headache monitoring only condition in the treatment of adolescent tension headache (Larsson et al., 1987). For the treatment of vascular headaches, three and four-session thermal biofeedback treatments appear to be equivalent to 10 sessions in children aged 8–16 years (Burke & Andrasik, 1989; Guarnieri & Blanchard, 1990). Finally, a single session of CBT with additional therapist telephone contact was comparable to eight sessions of CBT and superior to waiting-list control in a group of 11–18-year-old migraine patients (McGrath et al., 1992).

Judith Turner and colleagues have developed effective, brief CBT interventions for the treatment of chronic low-back pain in adults. Early research demonstrated that five 90-minute sessions of group CBT were comparable to five sessions of relaxation only on most measures post-treatment, with some advantages of the CBT group up to two years after treatment (Turner, 1982). When an eight-session group behavioral treatment aimed at altering problematic "pain behaviors" was compared to an eight-session group CBT treatment, both treatments yielded significant and equivalent improvement by one-year follow-up, unlike the waiting-list control condition (Turner & Clancy, 1988). This eight-session behavioral treatment was also effective when combined with an exercise component, showing greater improvement than eight sessions of either component alone post-treatment (Turner et al., 1990). However, all three treatments were better than waiting-list control, and all three were equivalent at six-month and one-year follow-up. Similarly, six-session relaxation training, six-session cognitive therapy, and a six-session CBT combining these elements all led to significant and equivalent reductions in pain intensity when compared to waiting-list control (Turner & Jensen, 1993). These gains were maintained for all three treatment groups at both six-month and one-year follow-up.

SUMMARY

A number of controlled research studies support the use of abbreviated CBT for the treatment of panic disorder (with and without agoraphobia) and a number of specific phobias. Preliminary research suggests that brief CBT treatments might also be useful in the treatment of GAD and social phobia, as well as in the prevention of PTSD after assault. Early efforts to reduce the length of treatment for depression have been identified for both adult and child populations. In the area of eating disorders, reduced session treatments are effective for both bulimia nervosa and binge eating disorder, with a few studies supporting the use of brief computer-assisted therapy for obesity and weight reduction. Some research also suggests that couples therapy CBT can be abbreviated and produce positive outcomes. While much research supports the efficacy of CBT for alcohol use disorders, brief treatments generally do not include CBT therapy components. One CBT treatment, however, has been abbreviated to as few as two sessions, and the outcome data are promising. A similar single-session intervention appears to be useful in the prevention of alcohol-related problems in college students. Finally, a large body of research supports the use of minimal therapist contact treatment for headache, and a recent meta-analysis shows that these treatments are consistently comparable to longer, clinic-based treatments (Haddock et al., 1997). Minimal therapist contact headache treatment also appears to be effective for children and adolescents. The use of abbreviated CBT for chronic low-back pain is supported in a series of research investigations as well.

These findings generally support the practice of abbreviating standard CBT. However, some conditions have been studied far more than others. The conditions with specific, circumscribed, maladaptive features and symptoms may be better suited to this approach. In fact, specific phobias are the only disorders in which unconfounded comparisons have supported the use of brief CBT versus unabbreviated CBT. When the source of the maladaptive behavior can be readily identified and targeted in treatment, brief methods are appropriate. If the patient suffers from a diffuse set of complex maladaptive thoughts and behaviors, then longer treatment may be indicated. This may explain why clinical problems such as panic disorder, specific phobia, and pain can be effectively treated in a few sessions, while other disorders, such as depression and GAD, warrant further study. We need more research that directly compares standard and brief CBT (unconfounded by adjunct materials), especially across different disorders so that we are better able to identify those most likely to benefit from an abbreviated approach, and that identifies the therapeutic mechanisms of change and assesses the impact of therapist variables on outcome.

REFERENCES

Agras, W.S., Taylor, C.B., Feldman, D.E., Losch, M., & Burnett, K.F. (1990). Developing computer-assisted therapy for the treatment of obesity. *Behavior Therapy, 21*, 99–109.

American Psychological Association Division of Clinical Psychology Task Force on Promotion and Dissemination of Psychological Procedures (1995). Training in and dissemination of empirically-validated psychological treatments: Report and recommendations. *The Clinical Psychologist, 48*, 3–23.

Appelbaum, K.A., Blanchard, E.B., Nicholson, N.L., Radnitz, C., Kirsch, C., Michultka, D., Attanasio, V., Andrasik, F., & Dentinger, M.P. (1990). Controlled evaluation of the addition of cognitive strategies to a home-based relaxation protocol for tension headache. *Behavior Therapy, 21*, 293–303.

Attanasio, V., Andrasik, F., & Blanchard, E.B. (1987). Cognitive therapy and relaxation training in muscle contraction headache: Efficacy and cost-effectiveness. *Headache, 27*, 254–260.

Bandura, A. (1969). *Principles of behavior modification.* New York: Holt, Rinehart, and Winston.

Bien, T.H., Miller, W.R., & Tonigan, J.S. (1993). Brief interventions for alcohol problems: A review. *Addiction, 88*, 315–336.

Blanchard, E.B., Andrasik, F., Appelbaum, K.A., Evans, D.D., Jurish, S.E., Teders, S.J., Rodichok, L.D., & Barron, K.D. (1985). The efficacy and cost-effectiveness of minimal-therapist-contact, non-drug treatments of chronic migraine and tension headache. *Headache, 25*, 214–220.

Blanchard, E.B., Appelbaum, K.A., Nicholson, N.L., Radnitz, C.L., Morrill, B., Michultka, D., Kirsch, C., Hillhouse, J., & Dentinger, M.P. (1990). A controlled evaluation of the addition of cognitive therapy to a home-based biofeedback and relaxation treatment of vascular headache. *Headache, 30*, 371–376.

Blanchard, E.B., & Seymour, D. (1996). Psychological treatment of benign headache disorders. *Professional Psychology: Research and Practice, 27*, 541–547.

Blowers, C., Cobb, J., & Mathews, A. (1987). Generalised anxiety: A controlled treatment study. *Behaviour Research and Therapy, 25*, 493–502.

Borkovec, T.D., & Whisman, M.A. (1996). Psychosocial treatment for generalized anxiety disorder. In M.R. Mavissakalian & R.F. Prien (Eds.), *Long-term treatments of anxiety disorders* (pp. 171–199). Washington, DC: American Psychiatric Press.

Botella, C., & García-Palacios, A. (1999). The possibility of reducing therapist contact and total length of therapy in the treatment of panic disorder. *Behavioural and Cognitive Psychotherapy, 27*, 231–247.

Brown, T.A., & Barlow, D.H. (1995). Long-term outcome in cognitive-behavioral treatment of panic disorder: Clinical predictors and alternative strategies for assessment. *Journal of Consulting and Clinical Psychology, 63*, 754–765.

Brownell, K.D., & O'Neil, P.M. (1993). Obesity. In D.H. Barlow (Ed.), *Clinical handbook of psychological disorders* (2nd ed., pp. 318–361). New York: Guilford Press.

Burke, E.J., & Andrasik, F. (1989). Home- versus clinic-based biofeedback treatment for pediatric migraine: Results of treatment through one-year follow-up. *Headache, 29,* 434–440.

Burnett, K.F., Taylor, C.B., & Agras, W.S. (1992). Ambulatory computer-assisted behavior therapy for obesity: An empirical model for examining behavioral correlates of treatment outcome. *Computers in Human Behavior, 8,* 239–248.

Carter, J.C., & Fairburn, C.G. (1998). Cognitive-behavioral self-help for binge eating disorder: A controlled effectiveness study. *Journal of Consulting and Clinical Psychology, 66,* 616–623.

Chambless, D.L., Sanderson, W.C., Shoham, V., Johnson, S.B., Pope, K.S., Crits-Christoph, P., Baker, M., Johnson, B., Woody, S.R., Sue, S., Beutler, L., Williams, D.A., & McCurry, S. (1996). An update on empirically validated therapies. *The Clinical Psychologist, 49,* 5–18.

Clark, D.M., Salkovskis, P.M., Hackmann, A., Wells, A., Ludgate, J., & Gelder, M. (1999). Brief cognitive therapy for panic disorder: A randomized controlled trial. *Journal of Consulting and Clinical Psychology, 67,* 583–589.

Cooper, P.J., Coker, S., & Fleming, C. (1994). Self-help for bulimia nervosa: A preliminary report. *International Journal of Eating Disorders, 16,* 401–404.

Cooper, P.J., Coker, S., & Fleming, C. (1996). An evaluation of the efficacy of supervised cognitive behavioral self-help for bulimia nervosa. *Journal of Psychosomatic Research, 40,* 281–287.

Côté, G., Gauthier, J.G., Laberge, B., Cormier, H.J., & Plamondon, J. (1994). Reduced therapist contact in the cognitive behavioral treatment of panic disorder. *Behavior Therapy, 25,* 123–145.

Craighead, W.E., Craighead, L.W., & Ilardi, S.S. (1998). Psychosocial treatments for major depressive disorder. In P.E. Nathan & J.M. Gorman (Eds.), *A guide to treatments that work* (pp. 226–239). New York: Oxford University Press.

Craske, M.G. (1999). Anxiety disorders: Psychological approaches to theory and treatment. Boulder, CO: Westview Press.

Craske, M.G., Maidenberg, E., & Bystritsky, A. (1995). Brief cognitive-behavioral versus nondirective therapy for panic disorder. *Journal of Behavior Therapy and Experimental Psychiatry, 26,* 113–120.

Davidson, G.N.S., & Horvath, A.O. (1997). Three sessions of brief couples therapy: A clinical trial. *Journal of Family Psychology, 11,* 422–435.

Davis, R., McVey, G., Heinmaa, M., Rockert, W., & Kennedy, S. (1999). Sequencing of cognitive-behavioral treatments for bulimia nervosa. *International Journal of Eating Disorders, 25,* 361–374.

Davis, R., Olmstead, M., & Rockert, W. (1990). Brief group psychoeducation for bulimia nervosa: Assessing the clinical significance of change. *Journal of Consulting and Clinical Psychology, 58,* 882–885.

Davis, R., Olmstead, M., Rockert, W., Marques, T., & Dolhanty, J. (1997). Group psychoeducation for bulimia nervosa with and without additional psychotherapy process sessions. *International Journal of Eating Disorders, 22,* 25–34.

Evans, L., Holt, C., & Oei, T.P.S. (1991). Long term follow-up of agoraphobics treated by brief intensive group cognitive behavioural therapy. *Australian and New Zealand Journal of Psychiatry, 25,* 343–349.

Eysenck, H.J. (1966). Personality and experimental psychology. *Bulletin of the British Psychological Society, 19,* 1–28.

Fairburn, C.G. (1995). *Overcoming binge eating.* New York: Guilford Press.

Fairburn, C.G., Marcus, M.D., & Wilson, G.T. (1993). Cognitive-behavioral therapy for binge eating and bulimia nervosa: A comprehensive treatment manual. In C.G. Fairburn & G.T. Wilson (Eds.), *Binge eating: Nature, assessment, and treatment* (pp. 361–404). New York: Guilford Press.

Febbraro, G.A.R., Clum, G.A., Roodman, A.A., & Wright, J.H. (1999). The limits of bibliotherapy: A study of the differential effectiveness of self-administered interventions in individuals with panic attacks. *Behavior Therapy, 30,* 209–222.

Feske, U., & Chambless, D.L. (1995). Cognitive-behavioural versus exposure only treatment for social phobia: A meta-analysis. *Behavior Therapy, 26,* 695–720.

Foa, E.B., Hearst-Ikeda, D., & Perry, K.J. (1995). Evaluation of a brief cognitive-behavioral program for the prevention of chronic PTSD in recent assault victims. *Journal of Consulting and Clinical Psychology, 63,* 948–955.

Fuller, R.K., & Hilles-Sturmhöfel, S. (1999). Alcoholism treatment in the United States: An overview. *Alcohol Research and Health, 23,* 69–77.

Garner, D.M., Vitousek, K.M., & Pike, K.M. (1997). Cognitive-behavioral therapy for anorexia nervosa. In D.M. Garner & P.E. Garfinkel (Eds.), *Handbook of treatment for eating disorders* (2nd ed., pp. 94–144). New York: Guilford Press.

Ghosh, A., & Marks, I.M. (1987). Self-treatment of agoraphobia by exposure. *Behavior Therapy, 18*, 3–16.

Goldfried, M.R., & Davison, G.C. (1994). *Clinical behavior therapy* (2nd ed.). New York: John Wiley.

Gould, R.A., Clum, G.A., & Shapiro, D. (1993). The use of bibliotherapy in the treatment of panic: A preliminary investigation. *Behavior Therapy, 24*, 241–252.

Guarnieri, P., & Blanchard, E. (1990). Evaluation of home-based thermal biofeedback treatment of pediatric migraine headache. *Biofeedback and Self-Regulation, 15*, 179–184.

Haddock, C.K., Rowan, A.B., Andrasik, F., Wilson, P.G., Talcott, G.W., & Stein, R.J. (1997). Home-based behavioral treatments for chronic benign headache: A meta-analysis of controlled trials. *Cephalalgia, 17*, 113–118.

Halford, W.K., & Osgarby, S. (1996). Brief behavioural couples therapy: A preliminary evaluation. *Behavioural and Cognitive Psychotherapy, 24*, 263–273.

Hall, W., & Heather, N. (1991). Issue of statistical power in comparative evaluations of minimal and intensive controlled drinking interventions. *Addictive Behaviors, 16*, 83–87.

Heimberg, R.G., Dodge, C.S., Hope, D.A., Kennedy, C.R., Zollo, L.J., & Becker, R.E. (1990). Cognitive behavioural group treatment for social phobia: Comparison with a credible placebo control. *Cognitive Therapy and Research, 14*, 1–23.

Heimberg, R.G., & Juster, H.R. (1995). Cognitive-behavioral treatments: Literature review. In R.G. Heimberg, M.R. Liebowitz, D.A. Hope, & F.R. Schneier (Eds.), *Social phobia: Diagnosis, assessment, and treatment* (pp. 261–309). New York: Guilford Press.

Hellström, K., Fellenius, J., & Öst, L.-G. (1996). One versus five sessions of applied tension in the treatment of blood phobia. *Behaviour Research and Therapy, 34*, 101–112.

Hellström, K., & Öst, L.-G. (1995). One-session therapist directed exposure vs two forms of manual directed self-exposure in the treatment of spider phobia. *Behaviour Research and Therapy, 33*, 959–965.

Holroyd, K.A., Holm, J.E., Hursey, K.G., Penzien, D.B., Cordingly, G.E., Theofanous, A.G., Richardson, S.C., & Tobin, D.L. (1988). Recurrent vascular headache: Home-based behavioral treatment versus abortive pharmacological treatment. *Journal of Consulting and Clinical Psychology, 56*, 218–223.

Holroyd, K.A., Nash, J.M., Pingel, J.D., Cordingley, G.E., & Jerome, A. (1991). A comparison of pharmacological (amitriptyline HCL) and nonpharmacological (cognitive-behavioral) therapies for chronic tension headache. *Journal of Consulting and Clinical Psychology, 59*, 387–393.

Holroyd, K.A., & Penzien, D.B. (1994). Psychosocial interventions in the management of recurrent headache disorders 1: Overview and effectiveness. *Behavioral Medicine, 20*, 53–63.

Jurish, S.E., Blanchard, E.B., Andrasik, F., Teders, S.J., Neff, D.F., & Arena, J.G. (1983). Home- versus clinical-based treatment of vascular headache. *Journal of Consulting and Clinical Psychology, 51*, 743–751.

Katon, W., Robinson, P.,Von Korff, M., Lin, E., Bush, T., Ludman, E., Simon, G., & Walker, E. (1996). A multi-faceted intervention to improve treatment of depression in primary care. *Archives of General Psychiatry, 53*, 924–932.

Larsson, B., Melin, L., Lamminen, M., Ullstedt, F. (1987). A school-based treatment of chronic headaches in adolescents. *Journal of Pediatric Psychology, 12*, 553–566.

Lindren, D.M., Watkins, P.L., Gould, R.A., Clum, G.A., Asterino, M., & Tulloch, H.L., (1994). A comparison of bibliotherapy and group therapy in the treatment of panic disorder. *Journal of Consulting and Clinical Psychology, 62*, 865–869.

Loeb, K.L., Wilson, G.T., Gilbert, J.S., & Labouvie, E. (2000). Guided and unguided self-help for binge eating. *Behaviour Research and Therapy, 38*, 259–272.

Longabaugh, R., & Morgenstern, J. (1999). Cognitive-behavioral coping-skills therapy for alcohol dependence: Current status and future directions. *Alcohol Research and Health, 23*, 78–85.

Marlatt, G.A., Baer, J.S., Kivlahan, D.R., Dimeff, L.A., Larimer, M.E., Quigley, L.A., Somers, J.M., & Williams, E. (1998). Screening and brief intervention for high-risk college student drinkers: Results from a 2-year follow-up assessment. *Journal of Consulting and Clinical Psychology, 66*, 604–615.

McGrath, P.J., Humphreys, P., Keene, D., Goodman, J.T., Lascelles, M.A., Cunningham, S.J., & Firestone, P. (1992). The efficacy and efficiency of a self-administered treatment for adolescent migraine. *Pain, 49*, 321–324.

McNamee, G., O'Sullivan, G., Lelliott, P., & Marks, I. (1989). Telephone-guided treatment for house-bound agoraphobics with panic disorder: Exposure vs. relaxation. *Behavior Therapy, 20*, 491–497.

Newman, M.G., Consoli, A.J., & Taylor, C.B. (1999). A palmtop computer program for the treatment of generalized anxiety disorder. *Behavior Modification, 23*, 597–619.

Newman, M.G., Kenardy, J., Herman, S., & Taylor, C.B. (1997). Comparison of palmtop-computer-assisted brief cognitive-behavioral treatment to cognitive-behavioral treatment for panic disorder. *Journal of Consulting and Clinical Psychology, 65*, 178–183.

Olmstead, M.P., Davis, R., Garner, D.M., Rockert, W., Irvine, M.J., & Eagle, M. (1991). Efficacy of a brief group psychoeducational intervention for bulimia nervosa. *Behaviour Research and Therapy, 29*, 71–83.

Öst, L.-G. (1996a). Long-term effects of behavior therapy for specific phobia. In M.R. Mavissakalian & R.F. Prien (Eds.), *Long-term treatments of anxiety disorders* (pp. 171–199). Washington, DC: American Psychiatric Press.

Öst, L.-G. (1996b). One-session group treatment of spider phobia. *Behaviour Research and Therapy, 34*, 707–715.

Öst, L.-G., Alm, T., Brandberg, M., & Breitholtz, E. (2001). One vs. five sessions of exposure and five sessions of cognitive therapy in the treatment of claustrophobia. *Behaviour Research and Therapy, 39*, 167–183.

Öst, L.-G., Brandberg, M., & Alm, T. (1997a). One versus five sessions of exposure in the treatment of flying phobia. *Behaviour Research and Therapy, 35*, 987–996.

Öst, L.-G., Ferebee, I., & Furmark, T. (1997b). One-session group therapy of spider phobia: Direct versus indirect treatments. *Behaviour Research and Therapy, 35*, 721–732.

Öst, L.-G., Hellström, K., & Kåver, A. (1992). One versus five sessions of exposure in the treatment of injection phobia. *Behavior Therapy, 23*, 263–282.

Öst, L.-G., Salkovskis, P.M., & Hellström, K. (1991). One-session therapist-directed exposure vs. self-exposure in the treatment of spider phobia. *Behavior Therapy, 22*, 407–422.

Peterson, A.L., & Halstead, T.S. (1998). Group cognitive behavior therapy for depression in a community setting: A clinical replication series. *Behavior Therapy, 29*, 3–18.

Power, K.G., Simpson, R.J., Swanson, V., Wallace, L.A. (1990). A controlled comparison of cognitive-behaviour therapy, diazepam, and placebo, alone and in combination, for the treatment of generalised anxiety disorder. *Journal of Anxiety Disorders, 4*, 267–292.

Rachman, S., & Whittal, M. (1989). Fast, slow and sudden reductions in fear. *Behaviour Research and Therapy, 27*, 613–620.

Rapee, R.M. (1993). Recent advances in the treatment of social phobia. *Australian Psychologist, 28*, 168–171.

Richardson, G.M., & McGrath, P.J. (1989). Cognitive-behavioral therapy for migraine headaches: A minimal-therapist-contact approach versus a clinic-based approach. *Headache, 29*, 352–357.

Riggs, D.S., & Foa, E.B. (1993). Obsessive compulsive disorder. In D.H. Barlow (Ed.), *Clinical handbook of psychological disorders* (2nd ed., pp. 189–239). New York: Guilford Press.

Rowan, A.B., & Andrasik, F. (1996). Efficacy and cost-effectiveness of minimal therapist contact treatments of chronic headaches: A review. *Behavior Therapy, 27*, 207–234.

Scott, C., Tacchi, M.J., Jones, R., & Scott, J. (1997). Acute and one-year outcome of a randomized controlled trial of brief cognitive therapy for major depressive disorder in primary care. *British Journal of Psychiatry, 171*, 131–134.

Skutle, A., & Berg, G. (1987). Training in controlled drinking for early-stage problem drinkers. *British Journal of Addiction, 82*, 493–501.

Sobell, M.B., & Sobell, L.C. (1993). *Problem drinkers: Guided self-change treatment*. New York: Guilford Press.

Sobell, M.B., Sobell, L.C., & Gavin, D.R. (1995). Portraying alcohol treatment outcomes: Different yardsticks of success. *Behavior Therapy, 26*, 643–669.

Spiegel, D.A., & Barlow, D.H. (2000). *8-Day treatment of panic disorder with moderate to severe agoraphobia: Preliminary outcome data.* Poster presented at Annual Conference of the Association for Advancement of Behavior Therapy, New Orleans.

Swinson, R.P., Fergus, K.D., Cox, B.J., & Wickwire, K. (1995). Efficacy of telephone-administered behavioral therapy for panic disorder with agoraphobia. *Behaviour Research and Therapy, 33,* 465–469.

Taylor, C.B., Agras, W.S., Losch, M., Plante, T.G., & Burnett, K. (1991). Improving the effectiveness of computer-assisted weight loss. *Behavior Therapy, 22,* 229–236.

Teders, S.J., Blanchard, E.B., Andrasik, F., Jurish, S.E., Neff, D.F., & Arena, J.G. (1984). Relaxation training for tension headache: Comparative efficacy and cost-effectiveness of a minimal therapist contact versus a therapist delivered procedure. *Behavior Therapy, 15,* 59–70.

Thackwray, D.E., Smith, M.C., Bodfish, J.W., & Meyers, A.W. (1993). A comparison of behavioral and cognitive-behavioral interventions for bulimia nervosa. *Journal of Consulting and Clinical Psychology, 61,* 639–645.

Tobin, D.L., Holroyd, K.A., Baker, A., Reynolds, R.V.C., & Holm, J.E. (1988). Development and clinical trial of a minimal contact, cognitive-behavioral treatment for tension headache. *Cognitive Therapy and Research, 12,* 325–339.

Treasure, J., Schmidt, U., Troop, N., Tiller, J., Todd, G., Keilen, M., & Dodge, E. (1994). First step in managing bulimia nervosa: Controlled trial of therapeutic manual. *British Medical Journal, 308,* 686–689.

Tsao, J.C.I., Lewin, M.R., & Craske, M.G. (1998). The effects of cognitive-behavior therapy for panic disorder on comorbid conditions. *Journal of Anxiety Disorders, 12,* 357–371.

Turner, J.A. (1982). Comparison of group progressive-relaxation training and cognitive-behavioral group therapy for chronic low back pain. *Journal of Consulting and Clinical Psychology, 50,* 757–765.

Turner, J.A., & Clancy, S. (1988). Comparison of operant behavioral and cognitive-behavioral group treatment for chronic low back pain. *Journal of Consulting and Clinical Psychology, 56,* 261–266.

Turner, J.A., Clancy, S., McQuade, K.J., & Cardenas, D.D. (1990). Effectiveness of behavioral therapy for chronic low back pain: A component analysis. *Journal of Consulting and Clinical Psychology, 58,* 573–579.

Turner, J.A., & Jensen, M.P. (1993). Efficacy of cognitive therapy for chronic low back pain. *Pain, 52,* 169–177.

Waller, D., Fairburn, C.G., McPherson, A., Kay, R., Lee, A., & Nowell, T. (1996). Treating bulimia nervosa in primary care: A pilot study. *International Journal of Eating Disorders, 19,* 99–103.

Weisz, J.R., Thurber, C.A., Sweeney, L., Proffitt, V.D., & LeGagnoux, G.L. (1997). Brief treatment of mild-to-moderate child depression using primary and secondary control enhancement training. *Journal of Consulting and Clinical Psychology, 65,* 703–707.

White, J., Keenan, M., & Brooks, N. (1992). Stress control: A controlled comparative investigation of large group therapy for generalized anxiety disorder. *Behavioural Psychotherapy, 20,* 97–114.

Wilfley, D.E., & Cohen, L.R. (1997). Psychological treatment of bulimia nervosa and binge eating disorder. *Psychopharmacology Bulletin, 33,* 437–454.

Williamson, D.A., Monguillot, J.E., Jarrell, M.P., Cohen, R.A., Pratt, J.M., & Blouin, D.C. (1984). Relaxation for the treatment of headache: Controlled evaluation of two group programs. *Behavior Modification, 8,* 407–424.

Wilson, G.T., Fairburn, C.G., & Agras, W.S. (1997). Cognitive-behavioral therapy for bulimia nervosa. In D.M. Garner & P.E. Garfinkel (Eds.), *Handbook of treatment for eating disorders* (2nd ed., pp. 67–93). New York: Guilford Press.

Wolpe, J. (1958). *Psychotherapy by reciprocal inhibition.* Stanford: Stanford University Press.

Wood, A., Harrington, R., & Moore, A. (1996). Controlled trial of a brief cognitive-behavioural intervention in adolescent patients with depressive disorders. *Journal of Child Psychology and Psychiatry, 37,* 737–746.

Worthington, E.L., McCullough, M.E., Shortz, J.L., Mindes, E.J., Sandage, S.J., & Chartrand, J.M. (1995). Can couples assessment and feedback improve relationships? Assessment as a brief relationship enrichment procedure. *Journal of Counseling Psychology, 42,* 466–475.

CHAPTER 2

Assessment Issues in Brief Cognitive-Behavioral Therapy

Follin Armfield Key
Department of Psychiatry and Human Behavior,
Brown University, Providence, RI, USA
and
Michelle G. Craske
Department of Psychology, UCLA, Los Angeles, CA, USA

As reviewed in Chapter 1, brief cognitive-behavioral therapy (CBT) has been used with some success for a variety of problems, including anxiety disorders, depression, eating disorders, headaches, and chronic low-back pain. It has also been applied to couples therapy and to problem drinking. Brief therapy, however, is unlikely to be optimal for every person or for every problem. In this chapter, we focus on assessment issues for brief CBT. In particular, we address assessment of outcome and suitability of brief CBT from the standpoint of the diagnosis, the patient, and the therapist.

Brief CBT is defined as therapy that is presented in fewer sessions than the average 10–20 that are typically offered in targeted CBT, and/or presentation over a limited time period. The latter refers to massed delivery of CBT, such as the treatment of panic disorder and agoraphobia over 7–10 consecutive days (Spiegel & Barlow, 2000). Ten years ago, the consensus was that short-term or brief therapy comprised 20 or fewer sessions (Hoyt, 1990). Many current protocols of CBT would meet this particular criterion for brevity. Given the advances since the time of that definition, and given that "standard" CBT is widely considered to be 10–20 sessions, brief CBT is defined as fewer than 10 sessions for the purposes of our discussion.

Understanding the nature of brief CBT is necessary before examining assessment issues. First, in its purest sense, brief CBT refers to a condensing of CBT material. However, many versions of brief CBT minimize the amount of therapist contact without reducing the amount of material to be covered. In these cases, therapist contact is augmented by self-help in the form of books, workbooks, audiotapes, or even computer programs. Patients study on their own to obtain the necessary psychoeducation and complete cognitive and/or behavioral skills training and tasks that might otherwise be accomplished with the therapist. In other words, "the brief psychotherapy patient or client is expected to act rather than

Handbook of Brief Cognitive Behaviour Therapy. Edited by Frank W. Bond and Windy Dryden.
© 2002 John Wiley & Sons, Ltd. ISBN 0-470-02132-2.

suffer and to become an involved participant in the therapeutic process" (Wells & Phelps, 1990: p. 4).

Second, as with all unabbreviated CBT, but particularly so with brief CBT, the guiding principles of intervention are "a clear focus on the patient's complaints, devising specific treatment for specific problems, relatively brief periods of treatment, and systematic appraisals of outcome" (Wells & Phelps, 1990: p. 6). The notion of specific treatment for specific problems requires a clear and precise assessment of the nature of the problem, and recognition that some problems may be more amenable to brief CBT than other problems.

WHICH PROBLEMS ARE MOST AMENABLE TO BRIEF CBT?

We believe that there are several factors that will determine the suitability of brief CBT and, hence, should be assessed. The first is problem and treatment definition—or, how well defined is the problem, and how well targeted is CBT? As the "active ingredients" in CBT have been identified, treatments have become far more focused on the disorders they target. The result has been more effective treatments, as indicated by the number of cognitive-behavioral therapies that have been classified as "empirically supported treatments" by the APA Division 12 Task Force report (Chambless et al., 1996). Specificity of treatment is presumed to be even more necessary when therapy time is very limited. MacKenzie & Livesley (1986) wrote, "As the length of treatment is decreased, it becomes increasingly important that the application of the most effective ingredients be optimized." (p. 715).

Understanding of the core cognitive feature of certain disorders has provided one avenue for tailoring treatments to specific targets. For example, because fear of bodily sensations has been identified as central to panic disorder, targeting misinterpretations of sympathetic arousal and systematic exposure to the sensations to obtain disconfirming evidence for misinterpretations ultimately leads to change (e.g., Clark, 1986). In posttraumatic stress disorder (PTSD), the core cognitions have been identified as the world as alienated and dangerous, and oneself as incompetent and helpless (Foa et al., 1995). In their brief intervention to prevent PTSD, Foa et al. (1995) targeted the first element by having patients repeatedly relive the traumatic memories, and addressed the second by having patients realize that they can tolerate the memories of the event and by teaching them new coping skills.

We have not been as successful in identifying a core cognitive feature for all psychological disorders. Effecting change—much less very rapid change—in disorders that are pervasive or diffuse is likely to be more challenging. It is probably for this reason that most evidence for brief CBT pertains to specific phobias (e.g., Arntz & Lavy, 1993; Öst et al., 1997a; Öst et al., 1997b; Öst et al., 1998). In contrast, an eight-session, anxiety-management intervention (relaxation and modification of upsetting thoughts) was no more successful than nondirective counselling in reducing generalized anxiety disorder (GAD) (Blowers et al., 1987). However, as reviewed in Chapter 1, there are some recent, more promising findings regarding brief CBT for GAD (Power et al., 1989, 1990).

There are other disorders for which specifically targeted treatments are yet to be tested, although continuing research is likely to yield such treatments. For example, currently, no agreed-upon treatment for anorexia nervosa exists (Wilson, 1999). Until recently, the prevailing theory about the maintenance of anorexia was broad: overvalued ideas about the personal implications of body shape and weight, combined with individual characteristics

such as perfectionism, asceticism, difficulties in regulation of affect, and "eccentric reinforcement contingencies" (Vitousek, 1996). The treatment based on this theory was equally
broad; it targeted interpersonal and family difficulties, low self-esteem, and identification
and expression of emotions. Often it was lengthy. A newer theory has, as the defining
feature of anorexia nervosa, an extreme need to control eating (Fairburn et al., 1999).
These researchers do not discount other features of the disorder, but do not believe they
are essential targets of intervention. The treatment that follows this theory is simpler, focusing on the issue of self-control, and eliminating other issues unless they present an
obstacle to change. Should this theory and its treatment offspring gain support, the treatment may eventually be deliverable in fewer sessions. Fairburn and colleagues point to
the success of bulimia treatments, where "a wide range of problems could be the target of treatment, including most of those addressed by the current cognitive behavioural
treatment for anorexia nervosa, yet the cognitive-behavioural treatment for bulimia nervosa focuses almost exclusively on the concerns about shape and weight and disturbed
eating" (p. 10).

Related to the issue of problem and treatment definition is the possibility that generalized,
widespread disturbances in relating with others (i.e., Axis II disorders) may be less suitable
for brief CBT. This is not to be confused with circumscribed interpersonal problems such
as conflict between partners, which may be targeted efficiently by a short intervention. For
example, a brief intervention for couples significantly improved dyadic-adjustment target
complaints and conflict-resolution skills, albeit without affecting relationship beliefs and
spousal attributions, relative to a no-treatment control (Davidson & Horvath, 1997). More
generalized and marked interpersonal difficulties, however, typically require lengthier treatment. The most effective treatment for an Axis II condition—dialectical behavior therapy
(DBT)—was developed by Linehan for borderline personality disorder. As designed, this
treatment is intensive and lasts about one year (Linehan, 1993). That being said, one investigation (Evans et al., 1999) of a brief derivation of DBT suggests some benefit within limited
domains. Patients with cluster B personality disorders who had a recent history of recurrent and deliberate self-harm received an average of 2.7 sessions, along with six self-help
booklets that contained elements of DBT. Results at follow-up indicated significantly lower
depressive symptoms and nonsignificantly lower rates of suicidal acts per month among
the experimental group than for those who received treatment as usual. This suggests that
a focused approach may have some impact on the most destructive behaviors of Axis II
disorders. Interpersonal functioning was not a target of this intervention, and we believe it
is less likely than discrete behaviors to respond to such a brief approach.

Another factor to consider is the context of the problem. A study that targeted depression
among men with HIV found that eight sessions of group social support yielded greater
reductions in psychiatric symptoms and anxiety for more participants than did equal-length
group CBT (Kelly et al., 1993). The authors concluded that the existential nature of the
issues confronting young adults facing a shortened future, stigmatized by both society and
their families, made the opportunity to gain support from others in the same situation most
helpful. CBT was superior only in reducing illicit drug use. Thus, when the lack of social
support is the primary problem, a process-oriented intervention may be more effective
than CBT.

In summary, disorders most appropriate for brief CBT—areas where we can bring about
significant change quickly—are those for which the problem and the treatment are well
defined and circumscribed.

FUNCTIONAL ASSESSMENT

Given that a well-defined problem with a well-targeted treatment is considered to be essential to the success of brief CBT, a detailed functional analysis of the presenting problem becomes even more essential. The importance of the functional analysis derives from the underlying assumption that lawful relationships exist among behaviors and outcomes. Thus, the functional assessment goes well beyond a description of form—symptoms and the resulting diagnosis. A functional assessment performs the task its name implies; it describes the function of the behavior, including the specific situation (cognitive, physiological, and environmental) and the events that precede, co-occur with, and follow the target behavior (O'Brien & Haynes, 1993). Ideally, the behavior is assessed in a wide range of settings, and with various modalities including standardized self-reports, self-report diaries (e.g., of panic attacks, binge episodes, marital arguments, or negative thoughts), interviews, and collateral reports, as well as observational data. To put these data in context, the therapist should be reasonably informed of the empirical literature about the given problem.

Goldfried (1982) described four levels of analysis in a functional assessment: antecedents of behavior, the organismic level, the behavior itself, and the consequences of the behavior. Detailed information is required for each. To understand antecedents, the therapist should enquire about the precise nature of the stimuli that elicit the behavior, the setting in which the behavior occurs, and how that setting differs from others in which it does not occur. The organismic level focuses on the cognitive features, including how patients interpret the events, what expectations exist, and the labeling of their own behavior (e.g., "I am going crazy"). Analysis of the behavior itself should elucidate situation-specific examples, duration, frequency, and pervasiveness. Finally, the therapist should obtain information about the consequences of the behavior—the content (e.g., praise, attention, or avoidance of pain), timing (e.g., positive short-term and negative long term, as in drug abuse), and frequency. From this analysis, the lawful relationships and areas at which to intervene can be pinpointed.

Some level of functional analysis already exists in many manualized CBT treatments, such as those for specific phobia, panic disorder, agoraphobia, social phobia, eating disorders, pain management, and so on. Because the anxiety disorders form relatively cohesive subgroups, the treatments are tailored specifically to the unique aspects of each anxiety disorder. Thus, CBT for social phobia targets fears of negative evaluation whereas CBT for panic disorder targets misappraisals of bodily sensations. Nevertheless, there is still a need for individual case formulation. For example, within the "fear of fear" conceptualization that underlies CBT for panic disorder, individuals differ significantly in terms of their interoceptive and exteroceptive triggers, perceived catastrophic outcomes, the logic used to arrive at those outcomes, and their safety signals. Tailoring of CBT to each individual's profile is assumed to lead to more effective outcomes. Hence, a careful functional analysis of the antecedents; the thoughts, behaviors, and physiological features; and the reinforcing consequences is essential even when manualized treatments exist.

Functional analyses sometimes shift or become more refined as more information is gathered over the course of unabbreviated CBT. In the case of brief CBT, there is less time for data gathering and little time for error in functional analysis. Thus, we recommend that for every presenting problem for brief CBT, a template be available for the areas to be assessed in order to hone the functional analysis as quickly as possible. Again, manualized unabbreviated CBTs will provide the overarching framework or template within which to conduct an individualized functional analysis. For example, manualized CBTs for anxiety disorders will guide the clinician to assess lawful relationships among catastrophic cognitions, avoidance behaviors, and safety signals. Similarly, manualized CBTs for chronic pain will guide the clinician to assess lawful relationships among pain behaviors, analgesics, and secondary reinforcements.

The exact task of treatment hinges on a thorough functional assessment. A case in point is exposure, which is considered de rigueur in many treatments for anxiety, but would be unlikely to benefit the patient if not appropriately designed. For example, therapist-directed exposure to "contaminants" is unlikely to be beneficial to the person with obsessive-compulsive disorder whose fear of spreading contamination is restricted to conditions of spreading contamination inadvertently when alone. The therapist views the patient's problem behavior as a dependent variable, and uses data from the functional assessment to determine the independent variable—in other words, to decide what can best be manipulated in order to bring about change (Goldfried, 1982). The therapist can choose to modify variables at any level(s) delineated above. If the functional analysis does not yield clearly specified variables to manipulate, brief CBT may not be suitable.

ASSESSING THE PATIENT

Aside from assessing whether the problem itself is suitable for brief CBT, there may be individual difference variables to consider. Overall, issues that impede traditional CBT are likely to pose even more difficulties in brief CBT. In selecting whom to treat with brief CBT, a strong motivation to change is the first characteristic to assess. Even more than most patients, those who participate in brief CBT will have to make the most of the very limited session time they have. In addition, having fewer sessions with the therapist probably requires a greater time commitment by the patient outside the clinic. In their review of minimal-contact treatments of chronic headaches, Rowan & Andrasik (1996) pinpoint the need for a higher level of patient motivation as one of the few drawbacks of such approaches.

One reasonable index for motivation is the level of distress that results from the specific problem being targeted relative to other problem areas. Thus, a patient who is most wanting meaningful interpersonal relationships may derail a therapist's efforts to implement a specific problem-focused treatment program because, for that patient, emotional support may be most important. However, a patient whose distress springs largely from the aftereffects of a trauma, or from problems associated with binge eating, is likely to be most interested in achieving relief from these symptoms. Establishing the target goals and principal diagnosis is essential in this case. Structured or semistructured interviews are valuable in differentiating principal from secondary diagnoses based on the current levels of distress and disablement associated with each disorder.

Treatment credibility ratings obtained after explanation of the therapy are another method of assessing motivation. Because brief CBT offers so little time for the patient to be convinced of the benefits of the approach, those who start off confident of its potential are likely to put more effort into the treatment. The finding that treatment credibility at the end of the first session of brief CBT for panic disorder predicted improvement (Clark et al., 1999) supports this hypothesis. Patients with panic disorder and agoraphobia who had unfavorable attitudes toward the treatment condition to which they were assigned were more likely to drop out of treatment (Grilo et al., 1998), although this was in reference to unabbreviated CBT. Öst et al. (1998) found that treatment credibility and motivation were the only significant predictors of outcome in their brief treatment of specific phobia.

Second, patients who are not contending with too many stressful life events will probably be more likely to benefit from brief CBT than will those whose lives are currently filled with major changes and stressors. While stressors may interfere with all therapies, any distraction from treatment in brief CBT results in the loss of a greater percentage of the therapy. In addition, patients enduring stressful living conditions, whether they result from aversive life events or general socioeconomic pressures, are likely to have difficulty finding time to conduct the self-study or cognitive or behavioral between-session tasks so essential to brief treatment. Low education and low income were found to impede unabbreviated treatment of panic disorder (Grilo et al., 1998), probably as a result of its effect on the discretionary time to devote to treatment.

Third, cognitive functioning is likely to predict the success of brief CBT (Rowan & Andrasik, 1996). Many examples of brief CBT include supplemental bibliotherapy to master material that typically would be covered in session (Clark et al., 1999; Scott et al., 1997). Patients unable to comprehend this material on their own need more time with therapists who can explain it in simple terms. Even without the requirement of outside-session reading, patients in brief CBT must be able to grasp material presented in session quickly and to apply it to their own condition. Thus, studies of brief as well as unabbreviated CBT often exclude illiterate individuals (e.g., Foa et al., 1995; Scott et al., 1997).

Fourth, educational level may contribute to a patient's suitability for brief CBT in several ways. Patients with little formal education may lack the background to benefit from treatments where they are responsible for mastering much, if not all, of the material independently. Education may serve as an overall index of persistence. Finally, lower education is frequently correlated with lower incomes, which can result in many of the difficulties discussed above regarding stressful life events, and associated with greater problems with treatment retention in general (Grilo et al., 1998).

Fifth, severity of psychopathology has been shown to predict outcome in brief interventions. A CBT self-help manual for binge eating was tested, comparing therapist-guided self-help with unguided self-help (Loeb et al., 2000). A significant predictor of poorer outcome was more severe baseline symptomatology (eating, depressive, and overall psychiatric symptoms). Likewise, among individuals who received four sessions of treatment for panic disorder, there was a trend for the less depressed to respond more favorably (Craske et al., 1995). Moreover, chronicity may be relevant to the degree that a well-established and intensively rehearsed behavior is possibly more difficult to extinguish. It is perhaps for this reason that a brief intervention for PTSD was implemented only with women who had recently (mean = 15 days) experienced an assault (Foa et al., 1995). There have been no applications of brief CBT for chronic PTSD. However, research on brief CBT for specific phobias suggests that duration of the phobia does not significantly predict outcome (Öst et al., 1998). Further empirical evaluation is needed to determine the importance of severity and chronicity for brief CBT.

Related to severity of problems is comorbidity, which may hinder response to brief CBT, especially when the comorbid problems fall on the Axis II spectrum. That is, given that Axis II disorders are less amenable to treatment overall, their comorbid presence is likely to interfere with treatment of the targeted problem. For example, in traditional CBT, patients without any personality disorder have been found to benefit more from treatment for panic disorder than those with a personality disorder (Marchand et al., 1998).

An additional factor to consider is the patient's attitude toward seeking help. Mental illness continues to be stigmatized, and those ashamed by their problems may prefer to minimize their contact with psychologists. For example, Loeb et al. (2000) suggest that individuals with bulimia may avoid seeking treatment because of the perceived embarrassing nature of their disorder. In such cases, a greater reliance on self-help methods may be more comfortable than many weekly meetings with a mental health professional. An advantage of self-help methods, delivered either alone or as adjuncts, is the resulting increase in patients' sense of mastery and control (Newman et al., 1997) that may lead to a greater presence of self-efficacy (Bandura, 1982). Thus, hesitation about therapy may be a positive predictor for brief CBT.

Other characteristics to consider when selecting patients for brief CBT include the ability to establish quickly a trusting and collaborative relationship with the therapist, the willingness to assume personal responsibility for change, and two characteristics important for any cognitive therapy: the ability to identify intrusive negative thoughts and an awareness of emotional fluctuations (Moretti et al., 1990). Finally, depending on the population from which the brief therapy patient is drawn, additional characteristics may optimize treatment outcome. For example, if the patient is a child, parental support—e.g., helping the child with monitoring and other homework—has been found to be important (Allen & McKeen, 1991).

ASSESSING THE THERAPIST

Therapists implementing brief treatments may need to be highly skilled to effect change in little time (Scott et al., 1997). Several areas are especially important. First, therapists must be able to establish a reasonably strong working relationship with the patient almost immediately. Little time can be dedicated solely to building rapport. Second, such therapists must know the treatment intimately to make the most of each moment with the patient. Third, they must be skilled at structuring the therapy, both within sessions to ensure material is covered, and across sessions to ensure that all presenting problems are addressed. Fourth, they need to be good teachers, able to present material clearly and concisely, to come up with specific examples as needed, and to apply them to the patient's situation. Fifth, the ability to communicate positive expectancies about the treatment could prove helpful, especially with limited time (Whisman & Jacobson, 1990).

Therapist variables that have been shown to predict positive outcome from unabbreviated CBT may become even more relevant to the success of brief CBT. From their review of the extant literature on this topic in 1995, Keijsers et al. concluded that empathy, warmth, positive regard, and genuineness assessed early in treatment predict positive outcome; that patients who viewed their therapists as understanding and respectful improved the most; and that patient perceptions of therapist expertness, self-confidence, and directiveness related positively to outcome, although not consistently. In their own study of junior therapists who provided CBT for panic disorder and agoraphobia, Keijsers et al. (1995) found advantages of different interactional styles at different points in therapy; directive statements and explanations in session 1 predicted poorer outcome, whereas such statements towards the end of treatment predicted better outcome; empathic listening in session 1 related to better behavioral outcome, whereas empathic listening in session 3 related to poorer behavioral outcome. Given the short duration of brief CBT, the tipping of the balance from initial empathy to directiveness happens quickly, and further evaluation is needed of the relationship between therapist process variables and outcome.

ASSESSING THE OUTCOME

Obviously, the intended goal of the therapy dictates the outcome that will be assessed. The goal of brief CBT is not necessarily the same as unabbreviated CBT. For example, sometimes brief CBT aims to teach skills rather than reduce symptoms. In that case, outcome measures assess whether the patient has acquired the skills. These measures can range from multiple-choice or fill-in-the-blank tests, to the presentation of relevant scenarios to which the patient must apply concepts learned in the treatment, to the in vivo demonstration of the skill at the end of therapy. For example, Burke and Andrasik (1989) taught parents and children 2to administer thermal feedback over three sessions (supplemented by take-home manuals) to reduce headache activity. Parents and children were tested pre- and post-treatment about their knowledge of the treatment procedures they had been taught. The test showed that children's knowledge increased significantly during treatment, suggesting the skills had been learned. In a seven-session structured group treatment that aimed to increase adaptive and coping behaviors among adolescent girls who had experienced sexual abuse, a primary outcome measure was a skills mastery test (Kruczek & Vitanza, 1999). This multiple-choice test was given before and after treatment, and included such items as, "Which of the following is one of the basic ways people respond to stress?" "To cope with angry feelings, I should first ask myself____?" Similarly, in our brief one-day workshop intervention for persons at risk of panic disorder (Gardenswartz & Craske, 2001), the primary outcome measure at the end of the workshop was retention of the educational material. Only at the six-month assessment was symptom status re-evaluated.

Sometimes the goal is symptom reduction, even with brief CBT. For example, we evaluated change in panic frequency per week after our four-week CBT for panic disorder (Craske et al., 1995). In headache-treatment research, a reduction of 50% in headache activity has become the standard (Rowan & Andrasik, 1996). One-session treatments for phobias (e.g., Öst, 1989; Öst et al., 1997a; Öst et al., 1997b; Öst et al., 1998) measures outcome via various scales, including the Spider Questionnaire (Klorman et al., 1974) and the Fear Survey Schedule–III (Wolpe & Lang, 1964). A more important measure, however, is the patient's accomplishment of behavioral approach tasks—such as an injection phobic being able to receive an injection or a spider phobic being able to catch a spider with a drinking glass and piece of paper and throw it out—without undue anxiety.

Behavioral approach tasks are clearly valuable measures of improvement. However, performance in the situation treated may not generalize to more naturalistic settings; and performance with a specific stimulus (e.g., small, fast spiders) may not generalize to other stimuli (e.g., large, hairy spiders). Öst (1989) encourages generalization by assigning homework to be completed as soon as possible after the one-session treatment: Patients are asked to seek out and confront the phobic object in their natural environments. Assessment of generalization can be conducted via behavioral approach tasks with stimuli that were not directly targeted in treatment (e.g., Williams & Kleifield, 1985) and by contacting patients for a brief verbal or written report shortly after the treatment's end regarding generalization to the natural context.

Another alternative to behavioral approach tasks is an ongoing log of behavior—e.g., number of drinks consumed or amount of food eaten per day; self-rating of activities, mood, or pain intensity daily for a circumscribed time period. Compliance with such requirements is likely to be a major issue, however (see Craske & Tsao, 1999).

Symptom and behavioral measures can be used immediately after brief and massed CBT, because they assess how the patient responds to a given stimulus at a given time. Most standardized self-report scales refer to a block of time, such as Beck Depression Inventory (Beck et al., 1961) and the Beck Anxiety Inventory (Beck et al., 1988), which refer to mood state over the last week. These latter kinds of measures would be suitable for brief, but not massed, CBT.

ASSESSING OUTCOME IN THE LONG TERM

In research, outcome is assessed to provide data about the effectiveness of a standardized treatment. In the clinical setting, where the number of sessions is not predetermined, treatment response is assessed in order to determine when to terminate therapy. Brief CBT is typically constrained to a limited amount of therapist contact, but some patients may require further intervention or benefit from booster sessions. Therefore, at the end of brief CBT, the therapist should determine whether treatment gains are incomplete or whether the patient is at risk of relapse. Such indicators include scores on outcome questionnaires that fail to meet a predetermined target, the presence of symptoms such as panic attacks or binge eating that are still distressing or interfering, or the failure of the patient to acquire the knowledge that the treatment attempted to impart.

Post-treatment status does not always predict long-term outcome, however, so follow-up assessment is important. This can be accomplished either at the therapist's or the patient's initiative. The former would entail a therapist-directed plan to contact all patients treated via brief CBT at some point—e.g., monthly for several months—after treatment's end. At these follow-up contacts, patients can report on the presence or absence of the symptoms that were targeted in treatment and generally describe how they are doing. Such information would enable the patient and therapist together to decide about the need for booster sessions. Alternatively, patients can use self-report methods, such as daily or weekly diaries monitoring the targeted symptoms, to assess their own status, and contact the therapist for follow-up treatment as needed. This latter technique would be analogous to a relapse-prevention plan.

Clearly, in many cases, changes in symptomatic measures may not be apparent until some time after brief CBT treatment is over. For example, changes in quality of life and interference with functioning are not likely to be observed in the week after a one-day workshop for panic disorder and agoraphobia (Gardenswartz & Craske, 2001). In this case, the value of follow-up assessments becomes even greater. For example, Evans et al. (1999) took baseline measures and then waited until six months after the end of treatment to assess outcome from their treatment for deliberate self-harm. They were targeting a particularly severe problem, parasuicidal behavior, in an extremely high-risk population, so measurement of change immediately after the average 2.7 sessions of treatment was not meaningful. The assumption, of course, is that change will occur in the weeks and months following a very brief intervention, in terms of specific symptoms but especially in terms of traits, life functioning, and personality characteristics. This contrasts somewhat with lengthier CBT, where change is expected to occur both throughout CBT and in the following weeks and months.

Another area to assess is generalizability of effects to nontargeted conditions, or comorbid conditions. Targeted traditional-length CBT has been found not only to decrease substantially the problem that was the target, but also comorbid disorders (Brown & Barlow, 1992; Tsao et al., 1998). We do not yet know whether this pattern holds true for briefer versions of CBT, although, as reviewed in Chapter 1, there is consistent evidence to suggest that brief CBT has effects on nontargeted symptom measures, as in the case of changes in measures of depressed mood after a brief intervention for anxiety disorders. Many studies of brief interventions exclude comorbid disorders—for example, in treating panic disorder, Clark et al. (1999) excluded severe agoraphobia and depression that needed immediate treatment; Scott et al. (1997) targeted depression and excluded those with depression secondary to a nonaffective psychiatric illness, dysthymia, and bipolar disorder. In an eight-session treatment of GAD, individuals with any other diagnosable disorder were excluded (Blowers et al., 1987). In addition, those comorbid disorders not excluded were not tracked, so we have no data on whether the brief intervention had any impact on the severity of nontargeted disorders.

Finally, if brief treatments require unwieldy assessment procedures, the purpose of the brevity is defeated. One of the many reasons that research treatment protocols seldom are used by practising clinicians is the large number of instruments involved, some of which require complicated scoring (Sobell, 1996). Short paper-and-pencil measures provide high return for low investment. They are simple for clinicians to administer and score, and are too aversive for patients to complete. One study, for example (Davidson & Horvath, 1997), gave patients who received three sessions of couples therapy five brief clinical measures (e.g., the Dyadic Adjustment Scale [Spanier, 1976]) and also asked them to report their compliance with homework.

CONCLUSIONS

The goal should be to have a clear sense in the beginning as to which problems, which patients, and which therapists are appropriate for brief CBT. Then, as in any good CBT, a thorough functional analysis should provide information necessary to conduct the treatment, as well as offer the patient important feedback that itself will probably effect some change. Outcome measures will be guided somewhat by the goal of brief CBT (skills or educational attainment versus symptom reduction), and whether the intervention was massed or not. Follow-up assessment is recommended to determine whether further intervention may be required, as well as to gain information to improve treatments for the future.

REFERENCES

Allen, K. D., & McKeen, L. R. (1991). Home-based multicomponent treatment of pediatric migraine. *Headache*, **31**(7), 467–472.

Arntz, A., & Lavy, E. (1993). Does stimulus elaboration potentiate exposure in in vivo treatment? Two forms of one-session treatment of spider phobia. *Behavioural Psychotherapy*, **21**(1), 1–12.

Bandura, A. (1982). Self-efficacy mechanism in human agency. *American Psychologist*, **37**(2), 122–147.

Beck, A. T., Epstein, N., Brown, G., & Steer, R. A. (1988). An inventory for measuring clinical anxiety: Psychometric properties. *Journal of Consulting and Clinical Psychology*, **56**(6), 893–897.

Beck, A. T., Ward, C. H., Mendelson, M., Mock, J., & Erbaugh, J. (1961). An inventory for measuring depression. *Archives of General Psychiatry*, **4**, 561–571.

Blowers, C., Cobb, J., & Mathews, A. (1987). Generalised anxiety: A controlled treatment study. *Behaviour Research and Therapy*, **25**(6), 493–502.

Brown, T. A., & Barlow, D. H. (1992). Comorbidity among anxiety disorders: Implications for treatment and DSM-IV. *Journal of Consulting and Clinical Psychology*, **60**(6), 835–844.

Burke, E. J., & Andrasik, F. (1989). Home- vs. clinic-based biofeedback treatment for pediatric migraine: Results of treatment through one-year follow-up. *Headache*, **29**(7), 434–440.

Chambless, D. L., Sanderson, W. C., Shoham, V., Johnson, S. B., Pope, K. S., Crits-Cristoph, P., Baker, M., Johnson, B., Woody, S. R., Sue, S., Buetler, L., Williams, D. A., & McCurry, S. (1996). An update on empirically validated therapies. *The Clinical Psychologist*, **49**, 5–18.

Clark, D. M. (1986). A cognitive approach to panic. *Behaviour Research and Therapy*, **24**(4), 461–470.

Clark, D. M., Salkovskis, P. M., Hackmann, A., & Wells, A. (1999). Brief cognitive therapy for panic disorder: A randomized controlled trial. *Journal of Consulting and Clinical Psychology*, **67**(4), 583–589.

Craske, M. G., Maidenberg, E., & Bystritsky, A. (1995). Brief cognitive-behavioral versus nondirective therapy for panic disorder. *Journal of Behavior Therapy and Experimental Psychiatry*, **26**(2), 113–120.

Craske, M. G., & Tsao, J. C. I. (1999). Self-monitoring with panic and anxiety disorders. *Psychological Assessment*, **11**(4), 466–479.

Davidson, G. N. S., & Horvath, A. O. (1997). Three sessions of brief couples therapy: A clinical trial. *Journal of Family Psychology*, **11**(4), 422–435.

Evans, K., Tyrer, P., Catalan, J., & Schmidt, U. (1999). Manual-assisted cognitive-behaviour therapy (MACT): A randomized controlled trial of a brief intervention with bibliotherapy in the treatment of recurrent deliberate self-harm. *Psychological Medicine*, **29**(1), 19–25.

Fairburn, C. G. (1981). A cognitive behavioural approach to the treatment of bulimia. *Psychological Medicine*, **11**(4), 707–711.

Fairburn, C. G., Shafran, R., & Cooper, Z. (1999). A cognitive behavioural theory of anorexia nervosa. *Behaviour Research and Therapy*, **37**(1), 1–13.

Foa, E. B., Hearst-Ikeda, D., & Perry, K. J. (1995). Evaluation of a brief cognitive-behavioral program for the prevention of chronic PTSD in recent assault victims. *Journal of Consulting and Clinical Psychology*, **63**(6), 948–955.

Gardenswartz, C. A., & Craske, M. G. (2001). Prevention of panic disorder. *Behavior Therapy*, **32**(4), 725–737.

Goldfried, M. R. (1982). Behavioral assessment: An overview. In A. S. Bellack, M. Hersen, & A. E. Kazdin (Eds.), *International handbook of behavior modification and therapy* (1st ed.). New York: Plenum Press.

Grilo, C. M., Money, R., Barlow, D. H., Goddard, A. W., Gorman, J. M., Hofmann, S. G., Papp, L. A., Shear, M. K., & Woods, S. W. (1998). Pretreatment patient factors predicting attrition from a multicenter randomized controlled treatment study for panic disorder. *Comprehensive Psychiatry*, **39**(6), 323–332.

Hoyt, M. F. (1990). On time in brief therapy. In R. A. Wells & V. J. Giannetti (Eds.), *Handbook of brief psychotherapies* (pp. 115–143). New York: Plenum Press.

Keijsers, G. P. J., Schaap, C. P. D. R., Hoogduin, C. A. L., & Lammers, M. W. (1995). Patient-therapist interaction in the behavioral treatment of panic disorder with agoraphobia. *Behavior Modification*, **19**(4), 491–517.

Kelly, J. A., Murphy, D. A., Bahr, G. R., Kalichman, S. C., Morgan, M. G., Stevenson, Y., Koob, J. J., Brasfield, T. L., & Bernstein, B. M. (1993). Outcome of cognitive-behavioral and support group brief therapies for depressed, HIV-infected persons. *American Journal of Psychiatry*, **150**(11), 1679–1686.

Klorman, R., Weerts, T. C., Hastings, J. E., Melamed, B. G., & Lang, P. (1974). Psychometric description of some specific-fear questionnaires. *Behaviour Therapy*, **5**, 401–409.

Kruczek, T., & Vitanza, S. (1999). Treatment effects with an adolescent abuse survivor's group. *Child Abuse and Neglect*, **23**(5), 477–485.

Linehan, M. M. (1993). *Skills training manual for treating borderline personality disorder*. New York: Guilford Press.

Loeb, K. L., Wilson, G. T., Gilbert, J. S., & Labouvie, E. (2000). Guided and unguided self-help for binge eating. *Behaviour Research and Therapy*, **38**(3), 259–272.

MacKenzie, K. R., & Livesley, W. J. (1986). Outcome and process measures in brief group psychotherapy. *Psychiatric Annals*, **16**(12), 715–720.

Marchand, A., Goyer, L. R., Dupuis, G., & Mainguy, N. (1998). Personality disorders and the outcome of cognitive-behavioural treatment of panic disorder with agoraphobia. *Canadian Journal of Behavioural Science*, **30**(1), 14–23.

Moretti, M. M., Feldman, L. A., & Shaw, B. F. (1990). Cognitive therapy: Current issues in theory and practice. In R. A. Wells & V. J. Giannetti (Eds.), *Handbook of brief psychotherapies* (pp. 217–237). New York: Plenum Press.

Newman, M. G., Consoli, A., & Taylor, C. B. (1997). Computers in assessment and cognitive behavioral treatment of clinical disorders: Anxiety as a case in point. *Behavior Therapy*, **28**(2), 211–235.

O'Brien, W. H., & Haynes, S. N. (1993). Behavioral assessment in the psychiatric setting. In A. S. Bellack & M. Hersen (Eds.), *Handbook of behavior therapy in the psychiatric setting* (pp. 39–71). New York: Plenum Press.

Öst, L.-G. (1989). One-session treatment for specific phobias. *Behaviour Research and Therapy*, **27**(1), 1–7.

Öst, L.-G., Brandberg, M., & Alm, T. (1997a). One versus five sessions of exposure in the treatment of flying phobia. *Behaviour Research and Therapy*, **35**(11), 987–996.

Öst, L.-G., Ferebee, I., & Furmark, T. (1997b). One-session group therapy of spider phobia: Direct versus indirect treatments. *Behaviour Research and Therapy*, **35**(8), 721–732.

Öst, L.-G., Stridh, B.-M., & Wolf, M. (1998). A clinical study of spider phobia: Prediction of outcome after self-help and therapist-directed treatments. *Behaviour Research and Therapy*, **36**(1), 17–35.

Power, K. G., Jerrom, D. W. A., Simpson, R. J., Mitchell, M. J., & Swanson, V. (1989). A controlled comparison of cognitive-behaviour therapy, diazepam and placebo in the management of generalised anxiety. *Behavioural Psychotherapy*, **17**, 1–14.

Power, K. G., Simpson, R. J., Swanson, V., & Wallace, L. A. (1990). A controlled comparison of cognitive-behaviour therapy, diazepam, and placebo, alone and in combination, for the treatment of generalised anxiety disorder. *Journal of Anxiety Disorders*, **4**, 267–292.

Rowan, A. B., & Andrasik, F. (1996). Efficacy and cost-effectiveness of minimal therapist contact treatments of chronic headaches: A review. *Behavior Therapy*, **27**(2), 207–234.

Scott, C., Tacchi, M. J., Jones, R., & Scott, J. (1997). Acute and one-year outcome of a randomised controlled trial of brief cognitive therapy for major depressive disorder in primary care. *British Journal of Psychiatry*, **171**, 131–134.

Sobell, L. C. (1996). Bridging the gap between scientists and practitioners: The challenge before us. *Behavior Therapy*, **27**(3), 297–320.

Spanier, G. B. (1976). Measuring dyadic adjustment: New scales for assessing the quality of marriage and similar dyads. *Journal of Marriage and the Family*, **38**(1), 15–28.

Spiegel, D. A., Barlow, D. H. (November, 2000). Eight-day treatment of panic disorder with moderate to severe agoraphobia: Preliminary outcome data. Poster presented at the 34th Annual Convention of the Association for Advancement of Behavior Therapy, New Orleans, LA.

Tsao, J. C. I., Lewin, M. R., & Craske, M. G. (1998). The effects of cognitive-behavior therapy for panic disorder on comorbid conditions. *Journal of Anxiety Disorders*, **12**(4), 357–371.

Vitousek, K. M. (1996). The current status of cognitive-behavioral models of anorexia nervosa and bulimia nervosa. In P. M. Salkovskis (Ed.), *Frontiers of cognitive therapy* (pp. 383–418). New York: Guilford Press.

Wells, R. A., & Phelps, P. A. (1990). The brief psychotherapies: A selective overview. In Richard A. Wells & V. J. Giannetti (Eds.), *Handbook of brief psychotherapies* (pp. 3–6). New York: Plenum Press.

Whisman, M. A., & Jacobson, N. S. (1990). Brief behavioral marital therapy. In R. A. Wells & V. J. Giannetti (Eds.), *Handbook of brief psychotherapies* (pp. 325–349). New York: Plenum Press.

Williams, S. L., & Kleifield, E. (1985). Transfer of behavioral change across phobias in multiply phobic clients. *Behavior Modification, 9*(1), 22–31.

Wilson, G. T. (1999). Cognitive behavior therapy for eating disorders: Progress and problems. *Behaviour Research and Therapy, 37*, S79–S95.

Wolpe, J., & Lang, P. (1964). A fear survey schedule for use in behaviour therapy. *Behavioural Research and Therapy, 2*, 27–30.

CHAPTER 3

Brief ACT Treatment of Depression

Robert D. Zettle
Department of Psychology, Wichita State University, Wichita, KS, USA
and
Steven C. Hayes
Department of Psychology, University of Nevada, Reno, NV, USA

The purpose of this chapter is to discuss the short-term treatment of depression with acceptance and commitment therapy (ACT—pronounced as one word, "act," not A-C-T). We will first consider the psychological contexts that seem to relate to the initiation, exacerbation, maintenance, and alleviation of depression. We will then present a brief overview of the principles and techniques of ACT, and show how they attempt to modify the contexts within which depression occurs. Finally we will review the literature on the impact of ACT on depression.

AN ACT VIEW OF DEPRESSION

The theory and technology of ACT are grounded philosophically in functional contextualism (Biglan & Hayes, 1996; Hayes, 1993; Hayes et al., 1988), which has as its core analytic unit the ongoing act-in-context (Pepper, 1942). The central components of contextualism include (a) a focus on the whole event, (b) an understanding of the nature and function of the event within a context, and (c) a pragmatic truth criterion. In applying these components to therapy, ACT is characterized by a thoroughgoing functionalism in which the content of client complaints is not taken too literally, but the function of them is examined continuously.

The usual view of depression is content driven. Persons complaining of depressive "symptoms" are diagnosed with a mood or affective disorder, and efforts are then made to change the form, frequency, or situational sensitivity of these symptoms by manipulating their purported causes, be they dysfunctional cognitions (e.g., Beck et al., 1979), a low rate of pleasurable activities (e.g., Lewinsohn et al., 1980), or disordered brain processes (Delgado & Moreno, 1999). Conversely, in ACT, the problematic nature of depression and its varied symptoms are assumed to be entirely functionally based and contextually determined. Stated another way, the root problem in depression is not depressed mood or negative thoughts, nor even the behavioral impact of such events, but the way that specific contexts link mood, thought, and behavior into an overall pattern of ineffective living.

Handbook of Brief Cognitive Behaviour Therapy. Edited by Frank W. Bond and Windy Dryden.
© 2002 John Wiley & Sons, Ltd. ISBN 0-470-02132-2.

One major contextual factor appears to be the human language community itself. ACT is a verbal psychotherapy explicitly based on basic research in the nature of language and cognition (Hayes et al., 1999; Kohlenberg et al., 1993). Within an array of verbal contexts, depression may be viewed as problematic because it is believed to be "bad", it is seen as reflective of the quality of one's life, because depression is held to be a cause for behavior or its absence, and can be justified through reason-giving, and because these verbal constructions suggest that depression must be avoided and/or eliminated before more effective living is possible. In this way, depression comes to "cause" a life restriction, but only because a social/verbal context supports this feeling–action relationship. ACT treatment of depression accordingly focuses on changing the contextual features that are thought to link depressed content to problems in living rather than on depression per se. When depressed mood and thought are no longer tightly linked to behavior, the self-amplifying downward spiral of depression is eliminated, without ever targeting mood or thought for direct change efforts.

In an ACT perspective on depression, the pathological links between emotion, cognition, and behavior are produced particularly by experiential avoidance and cognitive fusion. Experiential avoidance is the tendency to attempt to modify the form, frequency, or situational sensitivity of private events (thoughts, feelings, memories, and behavioral predispositions) even when this effort produces behavioral harm. An example would be avoiding feeling sad or hurt, or trying not to think of a dead loved one, even when this effort deflects from living in accord with valued goals (e.g., raising a family, maintaining an intimate relationship, or working). Cognitive fusion is the tendency for the stimulus functions of verbal/cognitive events to dominate over other sources of behavioral regulation. Both features come from human language itself.

The specific theory of language and cognition on which ACT is based is called relational frame theory (RFT) (Hayes et al., 2001). It is simply beyond the scope of this chapter to provide an account of RFT (see Hayes, 1989; Hayes & Hayes, 1989, 1992, for early summaries of this literature, or Hayes et al., [2001] for a book-length version). The core process can be expressed simply, however. A normal child taught to relate stimulus A to stimulus B will now also relate B to A. Even human infants (Lipkens et al., 1993) learn to relate stimuli in such a bidirectional fashion—so far as we know, unlike any other species. The source of this process is the subject of considerable theoretical debate—RFT is only one account—but the basic performance is a fact.

We have argued elsewhere (e.g., Hayes et al., 1999) that it is the bidirectionality of human language that leads directly to experiential avoidance and cognitive fusion. For example, verbal knowledge of a painful history itself becomes painful through bidirectionality. A person remembering past abuse feels upset because the verbal events and the original abuse are bidirectionally related. Without bidirectionality, reports would have to precede and predict, not just follow, painful events to acquire painful functions themselves. Thus, humans may be tempted to avoid painful memories of abuse the way animals would avoid abuse itself. This shows that experiential avoidance is built into human language itself.

Cognitive fusion is as well. The stimulus functions of verbal events arise due to their bi-directional nature (among other processes that would require more time than we have here to discuss). Stated loosely, because words and events stand in a bidirectional relation, humans can deal with the world by dealing with referents to it. As humans interact verbally with the world, they become more focused on thinking, evaluating, and categorizing it. Humans become "fused" with their own cognitions in the sense that this verbal source of behavioral regulation becomes more and more dominant. As a consequence, the behavioral functions of our world increasingly originate from derived stimulus relations and rules rather than from direct contact with contingencies and with what works.

If these processes are often pathological, and yet are built into human language itself, in what sense is the pathological process contextually determined? The answer is that it is possible to manipulate the social/verbal community in therapy itself in such a way that the normal effects of language are challenged and transformed. Examples of how this is attempted in ACT will be given later in the chapter.

Consistent with ACT assumptions, experiential avoidance has been implicated in a large number of behavioral disorders (Hayes et al., 1996). The publications on thought suppression, coping, and reason-giving provide good examples of the ways aspects of experiential avoidance participate in the creation of psychopathology. We will cover each in the following sections.

Thought Suppression

The preponderance of negative thoughts that typifies the thinking of depressed individuals has been well documented (see Haaga et al., 1991; Mathews & MacLeod, 1994, for reviews). In a survey among the general population, suppressive strategies (e.g., "think about something else," "use willpower; forget it," and "avoid thinking about it") were common responses to the question, "What's the thing to do when you're feeling depressed?" (Rippere, 1977a). The "common-sense belief" that suppression is effective in eliminating intrusive, depressive thoughts, furthermore, is one that is apparently widely practiced. For example, the use of thought suppression has been reported by both subclinically (Wenzlaff & Bates, 1998) and clinically depressed (Brewin et al., 1998) populations. Brewin et al. found that depressed cancer patients reported significantly more intrusive memories than nondepressed cancer patients and that greater numbers of intrusive memories were associated with efforts to suppress them.

The literature on thought suppression, in general (Wegner, 1994), and as it applies to depression, in particular (Beevers et al., 1999; Wenzlaff, 1993), is consistent in documenting the ineffectiveness of this coping strategy. Subclinically depressed individuals especially are ineffective in suppressing negative material, as documented through a series of experiments by Wenzlaff et al. (1988). Subclinically depressed and nondepressed participants read a story depicting either a very positive or a very negative event. Immediately afterwards, all participants were asked to write down their thoughts, with half of them instructed not to think about the story while doing so. An analysis of the participants' protocols indicated that all groups thought less of the story over a nine-minute period, with the exception of depressed individuals who were attempting to suppress negative thoughts. These subjects reported a decrease of thoughts during the first two-thirds of the nine-minute period, but an abrupt increase in negative thoughts during the final three minutes.

Not only does thought suppression result in a relative increase in depressing thoughts, but it may also increase depressed mood. Wenzlaff et al. (1991) found that reinstating a musically induced mood that nondepressed participants were in while suppressing a target thought resulted in a return of the suppressed thought. Conversely, instructing subjects not to think about the target thought reinstated the original mood. In effect, a vicious circle is established between thoughts and mood, such that efforts to suppress negative thoughts associated previously with a dysphoric mood result in increased dysphoric mood, which in turn, leads to a re-emergence of the suppressed thought.

Although it has not been subjected to a similar experimental analysis, various bodily states (e.g., sad facial expressions and stooped body posture) have also been cited as cues that may reinstate depressive thinking (Teasdale & Barnard, 1993). For example, depressed individuals may assume a slumping, "defeated" body posture while experiencing negative thoughts and dysphoric mood. Resuming the posture at a later time may reinstate the depressing thoughts and mood, thus making the suppression of negative thoughts even more difficult. The impact of thought suppression on bodily states is also well documented, including even negative immunological effects (Petrie et al., 1998).

Depressed individuals use characteristic distraction patterns as methods of thought suppression. In attempting to rid themselves of one depressing thought, depressives typically focus on other dysphoric thoughts, while nondepressed individuals rely upon positive thoughts (Wenzlaff et al., 1988). This difference cannot be attributed to the failure of depressives to recognize the effectiveness of positive distracting thoughts, but is apparently due to the greater accessibility of negative thoughts for use as distracters. Even when subclinically depressed participants are provided with positive distracters, however, they are unable to use them as effectively as nondepressed participants in suppressing a negative thought.

Summary

Thought suppression as a way of experientially avoiding and escaping from unwanted negative thoughts appears to be at least temporarily effective for individuals who are not in significant psychological difficulty. This same strategy appears to be ineffective for those experiencing symptoms of depression.

The degree to which these findings can be generalized to psychotherapy clients experiencing severe levels of clinical depression, however, remains unclear. Most of the research investigating the suppression of negative thoughts (e.g., Wenzlaff et al., 1991) has used college student participants experiencing what must be regarded as a subclinical level of depression (e.g., a score of 7 or above on the short form of the Beck Depression Inventory [Beck & Beck, 1972]). While it does not seem unreasonable to think that clinical depressives may find it even more difficult to suppress successfully highly emotionally laden self-referential thoughts (e.g., "I can't do anything right"), empirical support for such a conclusion must await the results of systematically extending work in thought suppression to psychiatric populations. However, additional research investigating avoidant coping styles and reason-giving by clinically depressed clients, to which we now turn, provides ample support for the dysfunctional roles played by experiential avoidance in depression.

Ineffective Coping Styles

Several ineffective coping styles have been implicated in depression (Cronkite & Moos, 1995). Unfortunately, different terms and concepts, in some cases by the same research group, have been used to denote these coping styles, including "emotion-focused coping" (Billings et al., 1983; Coyne et al., 1981; DeGenova et al., 1994), "avoidance coping" (Krantz & Moos, 1988), "emotional discharge coping" (Swindle et al., 1989), "ineffective escapism" (Rohde et al., 1990), and "ruminative coping" (Nolen-Hoeksema et al., 1994; Nolen-Hoeksema & Morrow, 1991). However, it is our contention, despite their apparent differences, that all such coping styles can be meaningfully regarded as functioning in the service of experiential avoidance.

Emotion-focused coping, for instance, has been characterized as "regulating an individual's emotional response to a problem" (DeGenova et al., 1994: p. 656), in contrast to problem-focused coping, which is directed at resolving problems that cause depression (Lazarus & Folkman, 1984). One example of emotion-focused coping is "tried to forget the whole thing," whereas "made a plan of action and followed it" is cited as illustrating a problem-focused strategy (DeGenova et al., 1994: p. 656). Items that make reference to unsuccessful attempts to suppress ("Quite often I cannot overcome unpleasant thoughts that bother me") and avoid depressing thoughts ("I cannot avoid thinking about mistakes I have made in the past") load on the empirically derived coping factor of "ineffective escapism" (Rohde et al., 1990).

Perhaps the one coping style that on the surface might appear to be unrelated to experiential avoidance is rumination (Nolen-Hoeksema, 1993). Depressives who engage in ruminative coping worry excessively but passively about their depression. Ruminative coping includes focused brooding about the self (e.g., "I think back to other times I have been depressed"), one's depressive symptoms (e.g., "I think about how hard it is to concentrate"), and the implications of one's depression (e.g., "What does it mean that I feel this way?") and its possible causes (e.g., "I go away by myself and think about why I feel this way"). Clearly, ruminative coping is not problem-focused in the sense already mentioned, and, with its focus on determining the causes of depression, it may contribute to the type of dysfunctional reason-giving (to be discussed in the section that follows) that has also been implicated in depression. While rumination may thus precede reason-giving, it has been suggested that ineffective thought suppression, in turn, may precede rumination. That is, depressives may initially but unsuccessfully try to suppress their negative thoughts and emotions before turning to rumination (Nolen-Hoeksema et al., 1994). Nolen-Hoeksema and Morrow (1991) found that college students who tended to avoid negative emotions were also more likely to ruminate about them. Similarly, widows who avoided talking with others about their husbands' suicides were found to be more likely to ruminate about it than widows who talked about their loss (Pennebaker & O'Heeron, 1984). Thus, it appears to be useful to regard thought suppression, rumination, and reason-giving as different forms of experiential avoidance lying on a temporal continuum.

It also seems meaningful to view depression itself within the context of a process affected throughout by avoidant coping. Comparisons between depressed and nondepressed individuals consistently have found that depressives are more likely to use emotion-focused and other types of avoidant coping styles and less likely to employ problem-solving coping than their nondepressed counterparts (Billings et al., 1983; Billings & Moos, 1981; Coyne et al., 1981; DeGenova et al., 1994; Folkman & Lararus, 1980; Pearlin & Schooler, 1978). At least two prospective studies suggest not only that avoidant coping is correlated with current depression, but also that it may function as an independent risk factor in predicting the onset of depression. Within a community sample of older adults, the coping factor of ineffective escapism was found to be associated with current depression and also to have a direct and interactive effect of stress on future depressive episodes over a two-year period (Rohde et al., 1990). Nolen-Hoeksema and Morrow (1991) documented similar findings among college students after an earthquake. Specifically, students who displayed a ruminative style in coping with depressed mood were more likely to be depressed seven weeks after the earthquake than their peers with less ruminative response styles.

An avoidant coping style is not only a risk factor for those who becomes depressed in the first place, but is also predictive of who is likely to experience an exacerbation and continuation of mood disorder. Nolen-Hoeksema et al. (1994) found that bereaved adults with a ruminative style were more likely to experience higher levels of depression six months later, even after controlling for initial depression levels. In another longitudinal study, Moos and his colleagues examined the relationship between avoidance coping assessed at intake and the long-term outcome of treatment for depression. One year after the start of treatment, 41% of clients who relied heavily on avoidance coping at intake were still depressed, compared to 26% of clients who did not resort to avoidance coping (Krantz & Moos, 1988). At four-year follow-up, a similar pattern was maintained, as clients who displayed emotional discharge coping at intake experienced more depression and physical symptoms (Swindle et al., 1989). The negative relationship between reliance on avoidant coping and responsivity to treatment for depression may, in part, be attributable to a poor client–therapist relationship. Depressed clients who relied more heavily on avoidance coping found it harder to form a positive relationship with their therapist in short-term psychotherapy (Gaston et al., 1988).

Summary

A wide array of investigations consistently have found that coping styles emphasizing experiential avoidance are associated with the initiation, exacerbation, and maintenance of depression, as well as poor responsivity to its treatment. That such convergent findings have been accumulated despite divergent populations (college students, HIV-infected patients, bereaved adults, older adults, depressed clients, etc.) and differing ways of assessing depression and evaluating coping styles attests to the robust and powerful role of experiential avoidance in depression.

Reason-Giving

Depressed clients ruminate, at least in part, in order to arrive at the reasons or causes for their depression. Unfortunately, many of the "causes" that are discovered involve private events that cannot be successfully suppressed, avoided, or escaped. The process of reason formulation or reason-giving itself can become dysfunctional, in that it expends time and energy that could be more productively channeled elsewhere (i.e., problem-focused coping), as is the control that its byproducts may exert upon behavior. Reasons that make reference to private events would not be problematic were it not for the fact that they are seen by the verbal-social community and clients themselves as causes of their depression that presumably must themselves be changed in order to overcome depression (Zettle & Hayes, 1986).

Said another way, clients begin to believe their own stories about why they are depressed and unfortunately those stories involve internal rather than external "causal" events. Investigations of common-sense beliefs about depression have found that a high percentage of individuals hold that depression is causally unrelated to external events (79% as reported by Bloor [1983] and 92% by Rippere [1977b]) and that "feeling depressed is not the same thing as feeling depressed about something." Individuals who give more reasons for depression not surprisingly also ruminate more in response to depressed mood (Addis & Carpenter, 1999). Among depressed clients, those who can offer "good reasons" for their depressed behavior tend to be both more depressed and more difficult to treat than other depressives. Additionally, they differentially respond to treatment compared to depressed clients who do not give as many reasons for their depression (Addis & Jacobson, 1996).

Summary

Reason-giving is a form of experiential avoidance: it is part of the process of figuring out how to get rid of something. Although it has not been as extensively investigated as some other facets of experiential avoidance, reason-giving is an integral part of the contextual mosaic supporting depression. It has been both indirectly, through its relationship with ruminative coping, and directly associated with nonresponsivity to treatment for depression.

Given the powerful data on thought suppression, coping, and reason-giving, the success of *any* approach to psychotherapy for depression may be contingent upon its ability to undermine these forms of experiential avoidance. It is a sobering thought, because most forms of psychotherapy for depression pay little overt attention to this factor at all. ACT is an exception.

OVERVIEW OF ACT

This portion of the chapter summarizes the major approach and goals of ACT. No attempt is made to provide an extensive coverage of such matters, and interested readers are advised to consult Hayes et al. (1999) for a more in-depth treatment of them.

Application of ACT

Strategically, ACT attempts to create a special verbal/social community within therapy in order to undermine experiential avoidance, cognitive fusion, reason-giving, and other verbal contexts and constructions that help support psychopathology. In doing so, it frequently uses metaphors, paradox, and experiential exercises to point out the traps created by language. ACT does not necessarily seek to eliminate the personal distress experienced by clients. Rather, one of its goals is to enable clients to distinguish between circumstances in which direct behavioral change is possible (*commitment*) and those in which psychological *acceptance* is a more viable alternative. Most importantly, ACT actively undermines clients' efforts to rid themselves of what are seen as impeding and unwanted private events that stand in the way of acting in accordance with values in life.

The following sections are brief illustrations of some of the key components that comprise ACT.

Creative Hopelessness

The first objective of ACT is for clients to realize that whatever they have been seeing as possible solutions to their problems, including entering therapy itself, may instead be part of the problem. The various efforts and strategies that clients have attempted to get rid of depression are examined dispassionately and in some detail. Clients are asked to consider the possibility that perhaps they are still depressed, not because they haven't tried hard enough or have lacked sufficient motivation to rid themselves of depression, but because their efforts to do so are simply making the problem worse. The goal is not for clients to *feel* hopeless, but for them to see the hopelessness of their previous agenda: avoiding or escaping from depression as a means to effective living. Seeing the hopelessness of the agenda is called *creative* hopelessness, because it commonly carries a sense of opening up. The client does not know what to do, but knows, that, whatever it is, it will have to be new. Throughout this process, a distinction is made between blaming oneself for having a problem such as depression in the first place and being "creatively responsible" (literally, having the ability to respond—"response-able"—differently) in reaction to it.

The "quicksand metaphor" is commonly used early in ACT to encourage clients to disband previous efforts at experiential avoidance and open themselves up to alternatives. Clients are told the following:

> It would be like if you were caught in quicksand. Of course, you'd try what you know how to do to get out, but almost everything you know about how to get out will only get you deeper into the quicksand. If you pushed down with one foot to get out, your foot would only sink in. The safest thing to do with quicksand is to spread out and try to get yourself fully in contact with the quicksand. Maybe your situation is like that. It may not make logical sense, but maybe what you need to do is stop struggling and instead get fully into contact with what you have been struggling with.

The purposes of this first phase of ACT are to undermine reason-giving, to block experiential avoidance, and to disconnect language from its normal, literal functions. If everything that can be thought of to "solve" a problem is itself an aspect of the problem, then language itself may be seen in a slightly different way. Language becomes a behavioral process to notice, but not one to use to deal with troubles. This is an example of what we mentioned earlier in the chapter: using the social/verbal community in therapy to change the context in which language has its problematic functions. There are many other examples of this in ACT, but we will not be able to go into many of these in any detail in the present chapter due to space limitations (see Hayes et al., 1999).

The Problem of Control

If the goal of engendering creative hopelessness is successful, clients are ready to appreciate more fully why their agenda of experiential avoidance has failed. Instead of explicitly interpreting the difficulty as one of experiential avoidance, the central problem is presented as one of deliberate attempts to control. It is pointed out that deliberate attempts to control or get rid of unwanted circumstances work quite well when such events lie outside ourselves. In short, the operative rule is "If you don't like something (e.g., a messy house), figure out what you need to do in order to get rid of it, and do it (clean the house)." By contrast, an experiential appeal is made to clients about the futility of extending the control agenda to private events. While deliberate efforts to control depressive thoughts, for example, may appear to work in the short term, the suppression literature and, more importantly, the direct experience of depressed clients suggest that this strategy is actually harmful in the long run.

Instead, the operative rule involving direct control of private events appears to be "If you aren't willing to have it, you've got it."

A series of "thought experiments" and exercises are presented to underscore how deliberate attempts to control private events typically "backfire." With regard to the control of feelings, something like the following commonly is presented:

> Let's imagine you were hooked up to the world's most sensitive polygraph and in such a way that both of us could clearly see its readings and thereby immediately know how anxious or relaxed you were. Now suppose I presented you with the following task—all you have to do is remain relaxed. Furthermore, to increase your motivation on the task, I take out a loaded revolver, point it to your head, and tell you I will pull the trigger if you fail at the task by becoming anxious. What will happen?

After clients acknowledge that they would be unable to remain relaxed under such circumstances, the presentation continues:

> Do you see in this situation that it is very important for you to avoid becoming anxious? But what happens when you deliberately try to avoid becoming anxious? Do you see that now anxiety itself becomes something to be anxious about? Isn't it true in your own experience that a very similar thing happens with other unwanted emotions as well—that if you're depressed and have struggled to get rid of it, depression itself can be something to be depressed about, so that now you are even more depressed. Sure, you don't go through life hooked up to a polygraph, but we all have something that serves the same purpose—our own nervous systems. We don't need a machine to tell us when we are anxious or depressed; our own body and nervous system will tell us. We also don't have guns pointed at our heads either, but you must be motivated to get rid of your depression or why would you be here? You won't be shot if you become even more depressed, but what do you think will happen to you and your life if you don't successfully rid yourself of it? Notice that deliberately trying to control feelings doesn't work with positive emotions either. Suppose I offered you a million dollars if you could fall in love within 24 hours with the first stranger you encounter upon leaving here. Could you do it?

To underscore the futility of trying to control unwanted thoughts, clients are typically asked to suppress a specific thought; e.g., "For example, whatever you do right now, don't think of jelly doughnuts! Especially jelly doughnuts that are so big around, are all covered with powdered sugar, and are all sugary and gooey when you bite into them. Whatever you do, don't think of them." In our experience, this phase of ACT is the one most clients readily relate to, as they have had the experience of being unable to get rid of a thought or feeling that they did not want.

Willingness

Once clients more fully understand the counterproductive nature of their control agenda, it is useful to present willingness as an alternative. The "two scales metaphor" is used to differentiate deliberate control from willingness:

> Imagine there are two scales, like the knobs on a stereo. One is right out here in front of us and it is called "depression." It can go from 0 to 10. In the posture you're in, what brought you in here, was this: "My level of depression is too high." In other words, you have been trying to turn the knob down on this scale. But now there's also another scale. You may not have even known it's there because it's hidden and hard to see. This other scale can also go from 0 to 10. What we have been doing is gradually preparing the way

so that we can see this other scale. We've been bringing it around to look at it. It's really the more important of the two, because it's the one that makes the difference, and it's the only one of the two that you can control. This second scale is called "willingness." It refers to how open you are to experiencing your own experience when you experience it—without trying to control it, avoid it, escape from it, and so on. When depression is up here at 10, and you're wrestling with it to make it go down or go away, then you're unwilling to feel and experience the depression. In other words, the willingness scale is down at 0. But that is a terrible combination. It's like a ratchet or something. You know how a ratchet wrench works? When you have a ratchet set one way, no matter how you turn the handle on the wrench, it can only tighten the bolt. It's like that. When depression is high and willingness is low, the ratchet is in and depression can't go down. That's because if you are really, really unwilling to have depression, then depression itself is something to be depressed about. It's as if when depression is high, and willingness drops down, the depression kind of locks into place. So, what we need to do in this therapy is shift our focus from the depression scale to the willingness scale. You've been trying to control depression for some time and it just doesn't work. Don't believe me when I say this, but look at your own experience. It's not that you weren't clever enough; it simply doesn't work. Instead of doing that, we will turn our focus to the willingness scale. Unlike the depression scale, which you can't move around at will, the willingness scale is something you can set anywhere. It's not a reaction—not a feeling or a thought—it's a choice. You've had it set low. You came in here with it set low—in fact, coming in here at all may initially have been a reflection of its low setting. What we need to do is get it set high. If you do this, I can guarantee that if you stop trying to control depression, your level of depression will be low—or—it will be high. I promise you! And when it is low, it will be low, until it's not low and then it will be high. And when it's high it will be high until it isn't high anymore. Then it will be low again—I'm not teasing you. There just aren't good words for what it is like to have the willingness scale set high.

The shift from an agenda of deliberate control to willingness is critical but also tricky for several reasons. For one, willingness cannot be subverted into a form of emotional control:

CLIENT: OK, so if I am willing to be depressed, then it'll go away?

THERAPIST: It may or it may not. If you're willing to be depressed, your depression is free to seek its own level. But you can't trick yourself. If you're willing to experience depression only in order to get rid of it, then you're not willing to have it. And remember, if you're not willing to have it, you've got it.

It's also not uncommon for clients to experience other types of confusion surrounding willingness. From an ACT perspective, willingness is not a concept or a feeling, but a strategy clients can adopt in order to gain control of their lives. Control over one's life, however, is not achieved through controlling unwanted private events. They are uncontrollable and attempts to do so only results in one's life being out of control. As a strategy, willingness most usefully is thought of as an activity, or in some instances, not acting. For example, depressed clients might not feel willing to get out of bed and go to work in the morning, but could be willing in the sense that they show up for work.

A final difficulty clients may experience at this phase of ACT is in distinguishing between being willing and wanting. They are not the same. One can be willing to experience depression in the service of achieving an important goal without wanting to experience the emotion. Similarly, willingness is not the same as "gutting it out," tolerating, or ignoring certain thoughts and feelings. Most importantly, willingness must occur simultaneously at the levels of overt behavior and private events. Clients must not only be willing to put themselves in situations that are likely to occasion depression, but also not engage in activities to reduce or escape from it when it does occur.

Defusion

Willingness is facilitated through other components of ACT, particularly "cognitive defusion." By the use of this term we mean the disruption of the usual meaning functions of language. Defusion weakens the tight equivalence classes and verbal relations that establish stimulus functions through verbal processes (Hayes et al., 1999). Words are usually seen as equivalent to the things they describe, even when applied to one's life (e.g., "My life is hopeless"). However, through defusion, a thought may come to be not just understood, but also heard as a sound or simply observed as an automatic verbal relation.

Several means are used within ACT to promote defusion and, by doing so, change the stimulus functions of language for clients. These include the use of mindfulness exercises, paradox, and metaphor, as well as several "verbal conventions." One such convention has to do with use of the words "but" and "and." What "but" literally means is that what follows the word, "but," contradicts what went before the word. What is really the case, though, is that one's got whatever precedes and follows the "but." The convention that ACT adopts as part of the language of therapy is to replace "but" with "and." For example, a client who says, "I wanted to go out with my friends, but I was too depressed," would be prompted to reformulate the statement with an "and"—"I wanted to go out with my friends *and* I was depressed." Both things are true and one doesn't negate the other. The client might be asked, "Is it possible that you could have gone out with your friends *and* be depressed?"

A second verbal convention consists of distinguishing between evaluation and description. This is important because all of us commonly make almost no distinction between the primary properties of events themselves (the description with which most others would agree) and their secondary properties derived from the emotional responses and evaluations we have to the events (evaluations that may be unique to each individual). This is problematic when clients react to a subjective property of some event as an objective, external property of it. For instance, depressed clients may believe the thought, "I am a worthless human being." While all would agree that clients are human beings, the adjective "worthless" is a subjective evaluation that clients are making of themselves. The ACT therapist would help the client to separate descriptions from evaluations, perhaps by saying something like the following: "Aren't what you really saying or thinking is that you are a human being and right now that you have the evaluation that you are worthless? So, let's have you try saying it that way—'I am a human being and I am having the evaluation that I am worthless.'" More generally, clients are encouraged to label all verbal processes for what they are. For example, ACT works with clients to say, "I'm having the thought (or feeling, evaluation, urge) that_____." This helps clients to see that their private events are things that they are experiencing rather than taking the thoughts and evaluations literally.

Self as Distinct from Private Events

Especially in depression, negative thoughts and feelings that clients experience are about themselves. It becomes important therapeutically not only to help clients distinguish between verbal descriptions and evaluation, but also to distinguish between themselves and private events that are experienced as self-evaluations. Loosely speaking, clients may identify too closely with self-referential thoughts and feelings (e.g., "I think I'm worthless, so I must be worthless").

In order to undermine attachment to verbal content as a matter of personal identity, ACT helps clients find a sense of self that transcends the literal and is defined by the continuity of consciousness over the course of one's lifetime (Hayes, 1984). The sense of observing from "here now" is one that all verbally able humans experience under certain conditions (e.g., when meditating). ACT highlights this naturalistic sense of spirituality through metaphors and experiential exercises designed to recontact clients with their "observing self." This sense of self appears to be critical, as it provides clients with at least one stable, immutable fact about themselves that has and can be experienced directly, and that will not be threatened by a willingness to experience previously avoided private events. It seems less threatening to clients to face depression and other types of psychological pain in life if they know that no matter what happens, the "I," in at least one important sense of that word, will not be at risk.

Another metaphor, that of "house and furniture," is used to help clients distinguish between their sense of self and undesirable psychological content:

> It's as if you were a house filled with furniture. The furniture is not, and can never be, the house. Furniture is the content of the house, or what's inside it. The house merely holds or contains the furniture and provides the context in which furniture can be furniture. Notice that whether the furniture is thought to be good or bad says nothing about the value of the house. Suppose you are more like the house than the furniture. Just as the furniture is not the house, suppose in some deep sense that your thoughts and feelings are not you.

Values and Commitment

The phases of ACT that have been presented to this point primarily are designed to increase willingness and undermine experiential avoidance and cognitive fusion. The acceptance of previously avoided depressive thoughts, feelings, and memories, however, is not a goal in its own right, but is sought in the service of enabling clients to move their lives in a valued direction. Helping clients identify valued life goals and to make and keep commitments consistent with these values, even in the face of psychological obstacles, is the focus of the final phase of treatment within ACT.

ACT defines values as verbally constructed, globally desired life directions. Values manifest themselves over time and unfold as an ongoing process rather than an outcome (like heading west). Thus, values are more like choosing a direction (valuing the direction of west), while concrete goals are more like selecting an attainable destination (getting to California). Importantly, values are chosen, and not decided upon. On this point, ACT holds that it is useful to draw a distinction between choosing a course of action and deciding upon one. Another metaphor is used to make this distinction:

> Suppose you commit yourself to drive a small busload of children to an outing at the state fair. You were planning on going to the state fair anyway and thought you'd help out. Imagine, though, that after you commit yourself to the trip, its organizer informs you that little Johnny Boogernose, the meanest, nastiest kid in the bunch, will be riding with you. Still, you said you'd transport a load of children, so you head off to the state fair, several miles away. Imagine, though, that just a few miles out the kids start fighting,

squawking, and hollering uncontrollably. So you pull off to the side of the road and inform them that you won't go any further until they shut up and behave themselves. Notice, though, what happens when you do that—who is now in control of whether or not *you* make it to the fair? Is it you or the rowdy kids? What if they never shut up? You're stuck. Are you prepared to spend the rest of your life pulled over to the side of the road? Do you see that your choice to go to the fair has now been transformed into a decision that is out of your hands? Imagine further that the rowdy kids, even little Johnny Boogernose himself, are thoughts, feelings, and memories that you wish you could shut up. And you're not just on a trip to the fair but on life's journey. Are you going to choose the direction you take or are you going to let your thoughts and feelings decide for you?

Because thoughts and feelings, as pointed out earlier, are typically cited as reasons for actions and held as behavioral causes, an effort also is often made at this point in ACT to undermine any dysfunctional control exerted by reason-giving. For example, clients are asked to choose between two imaginary dishes of ice cream, one chocolate and the other vanilla. Once the choice is announced, the client is repeatedly asked "Why?" until all possible reasons to justify the choice have been exhausted. Usually, three or four why questions will exhaust the reason-giving repertoire in this area. Exasperated clients usually finally say something like, "I don't know why I choose it, I just do," and that precisely is the point. Choices are to be made not because of a proper alignment of thoughts and feelings nor because of all the right reasons. Choices and commitments are to be made because they move us in a direction consistent with our values. In this regard, the final critical question presented to clients by ACT is the following:

Given a distinction between you and the things you've been struggling with and trying to change, are you willing to experience those things, fully and without defense, as they are, and not as they say they are, *and* do what takes you in a valued direction in the situation?

If the client can answer "yes" to this question, then life itself opens up just a bit. If the answer is no, then, psychologically speaking, the client becomes a bit smaller.

Summary

ACT is a comprehensive approach to verbal psychotherapy that is philosophically grounded in functional contextualism and based upon basic behavior analysis developments in language and cognition. It is designed, and normally implemented, as a brief (10–20 sessions) outpatient therapy that employs the use of metaphor, paradox, and experiential exercises to undermine cognitive fusion, experiential avoidance, and other forms of verbal/social support for psychopathology. Research investigating the degree to which ACT can successfully treat depression through processes consistent with its model of psychopathology will be considered in the next section.

TREATMENT OF DEPRESSION WITH ACT

Although the total number of published reports investigating the treatment of depression with ACT is rather modest, ACT, to our knowledge, is the only brief, behaviorally based intervention that has been evaluated by both efficacy and effectiveness research (Seligman, 1995).

Efficacy Research

Efficacy research, in general, is more common than effectiveness research and has been used to "validate empirically" a number of psychological treatments (American Psychological Association Task Force on Promotion and Dissemination of Psychological Procedures, 1995), including cognitive (Beck et al., 1979) and interpersonal therapy (Klerman et al., 1984) for depression. In an initial randomized clinical trial (Zettle & Hayes, 1986), 18 depressed women received 12 weekly sessions of either cognitive therapy (Beck et al., 1979) or an early version of ACT. Participants in both conditions improved significantly from pretreatment through the end of a two-month follow-up. However, those receiving ACT were judged by a blind, independent evaluator using the Hamilton Rating Scale for Depression (Hamilton, 1960) to be significantly less depressed at follow-up than women treated with cognitive therapy.

An analysis of several process measures also detected differences between ACT and cognitive therapy in the mechanisms through which therapeutic change was apparently effected. At pretreatment, posttreatment, and follow-up, participants completed the Automatic Thoughts Questionnaire (ATQ) (Hollon & Kendall, 1980) and a Reasons Questionnaire specifically developed to assess reason-giving for dysfunctional behavior. The ATQ assesses separately the frequency and degree of believability of negative thoughts associated with depression. Participants in both therapy conditions reported significant, but equivalent, reductions in frequency scores across the course of the study. A different pattern of findings, however, was found on ATQ believability scores. Participants treated with ACT reported significantly greater reductions than those receiving cognitive therapy in their belief in depressive thoughts at posttreatment. In short, significantly lower believability scores for ACT clients were not associated with similar differential reductions in ATQ frequency ratings. Stated somewhat differently, changes in the believability of depressive thoughts occurred independently of reductions in their frequency, consistent with ACT's emphasis on undermining experiential avoidance. The goal of ACT in this regard can be cast as one of reducing the dysfunctional control exerted by depressive thoughts, as reflected by reductions in believability ratings, but not by merely eliminating such private events. Through ACT, depressed clients may still have depressive thoughts, but learn how to react differently to them.

Further evidence that ACT works by weakening verbal/social support for psychopathology is offered by findings from the Reasons Questionnaire. Participants initially were asked to provide separate reasons for their overeating and being suicidal, and subsequently, to rate "how good" each reason was. Judges reliably categorized reasons as "external," referring to environmental events as the cause of the dysfunctional behavior, or "internal," referring to private events. The participants treated with ACT showed a significant reduction in validity ratings for internal reasons from pretreatment to follow-up. By contrast, those receiving cognitive therapy showed only a slight and nonsignificant reduction in the extent to which they viewed private events as "good reasons" for dysfunctional behavior.

A second comparative outcome study investigating the efficacy of ACT relative to cognitive therapy evaluated both treatments when delivered in a group, rather than individual, format (Zettle & Rains, 1989). A total of 31 depressed women were randomly assigned to ACT or to one of two variants of cognitive therapy. All three groups showed significant, but equivalent, reductions in depression over 12 weeks of treatment and two-month follow-up. While ACT was found to be equivalent in efficacy to cognitive therapy when both were delivered in a group, as opposed to individual, format, other discrepant findings again suggested that the two interventions may operate through different processes. Specifically, participants treated with cognitive therapy reported significant reductions from pretreatment through follow-up in their agreement with depressive beliefs as assessed by the Dysfunctional Attitude Scale (DAS) (Weissman & Beck, 1978). By contrast, participants receiving ACT showed only slight, nonsignificant reductions in DAS scores.

Upon first consideration, these results may appear to be directly opposite to the earlier findings of Zettle and Hayes (1986) in which ACT clients, relative to those receiving cognitive therapy, showed greater reductions in ATQ believability scores. One possible explanation of these seemingly discrepant findings may involve differences in the wording used in the two instruments and in the type of cognitive activity each purportedly assesses. The ATQ asks participants to "indicate how strongly, if at all, you tend to believe that thought, when it occurs," while the DAS instructs respondents to decide how much they "agree or disagree" with each listed belief. It is not inconsistent with the conceptualization we have offered for ACT to posit that depressed clients treated with it may continue to agree with "depressogenic beliefs," provided that any associated dysfunctional emotional and behavioral control is effectively weakened. For example, a depressed client successfully treated with ACT may still totally agree that "people will probably think less of me if I make a mistake," but stop avoiding situations in which possible social censure and any resulting embarrassment might occur as a consequence of making mistakes. In other words, "feeling that others think less of me" is no longer a psychological event to be avoided. At the very least, process data from the two efficacy studies are consistent in strongly suggesting that ACT initiates therapeutic change through a mechanism that differs from that of cognitive therapy. This seems especially noteworthy in light of other research that has documented significant reductions in DAS scores when depression is successfully treated with pharmacotherapy (Reda et al., 1985; Simons et al., 1984; Simons et al., 1986).

Most recently, a Swedish study compared ACT to treatment-as-usual (TAU) with 24 unemployed individuals on sick leave suffering from depression (Folke & Parling, 2004). The 11 participants in the TAU condition received governmental interventions available to the unemployed on sick leave, while those randomly assigned to the ACT condition received these services as well as one individual and five weekly group sessions of treatment. After treatment, the ACT group showed significantly lower levels of depression and reported a higher quality of life, general health, and perceived level of functioning compared to the TAU group.

Effectiveness Research

Effectiveness research can be distinguished from efficacy research in several important respects (Seligman & Levant, 1998). While efficacy research typically evaluates manualized therapies delivered for a fixed number of sessions to homogeneous volunteers meeting various selection criteria, effectiveness research investigates the impact of interventions as they are applied in "the field" for varying lengths of time in serving clients actively seeking therapy for a diverse array of presenting problems. A recent study by Stroshal et al. (1998) meets the defining criteria for effectiveness research (Seligman, 1995) and provides further empirical support for the clinical impact of ACT. Because effectiveness research does not screen out participants with multiple interacting problems and "dual diagnoses," it should be noted that only 12% of the participating clients were diagnosed with a mood disorder. However, its results appear to be relevant to an evaluation of brief ACT in treatment of depression. No findings varied as a function of client diagnosis, and mood disorder was the second most common Axis I diagnosis after adjustment disorder. Accordingly, it seems reasonable that the study's general findings would extend more specifically to the effectiveness of brief ACT with depression.

Therapists at mental health centers in a health maintenance organization (HMO) setting were offered training in ACT. The training consisted of an initial introductory ACT workshop, followed by an "intensive" clinical workshop, as well as dissemination of a detailed therapy manual and monthly supervisory consultations over the course of the one-year project. All new clients of ACT-trained therapists over a one-month period, as well as those for a control group of therapists who did not receive the training, were evaluated prior to training and again the following year after the completion of training.

In effect, the design of the study simultaneously evaluated the acquisition of ACT skills through training and their relevance and impact. If ACT were effective with only a few clients, it might have high impact, but low relevance, and no overall difference in outcomes would be expected. Furthermore, if ACT seemed to apply, but was ineffective, no outcome differences would be obtained. Finally, if the training did not reliably lead to the acquisition of ACT skills, differences would not be found even if ACT might otherwise be effective. This appears to be a fairly bold way to evaluate therapeutic impact in the real world, especially given an extensive literature showing that therapist training generally does not improve client outcomes (Dawes, 1994), and, consequently, easily obtained placebo effects are unlikely.

Among other findings, the clients of ACT-trained therapists reported significantly better coping than the clients of untrained therapists and were more likely to have completed treatment within five months of starting therapy. In addition, clients of ACT-trained therapists were more likely to agree with their therapists about the ongoing status of therapy (whether it was still continuing) and less likely to be referred for pharmacotherapy. Finally, evidence also suggested that increasing client acceptance was instrumental to ACT's effectiveness. Specifically, clients of ACT-trained therapists showed increased levels of acceptance after training, while the acceptance scores of clients of untrained therapists did not change.

Summary

Evaluations of the relative efficacy of ACT suggest that it compares favorably with cognitive therapy in the treatment of depression. Although there have only been two comparative outcome studies, evaluating ACT against cognitive therapy appears to provide a fairly rigorous test of its efficacy, given the large body of literature establishing the empirical validity of cognitive therapy. Obviously additional research is necessary for further evaluation and determination of the relative efficacy of brief ACT in treating depression, and if efficacy research provided the only empirical support of ACT's clinical impact, our evaluation of its potential would be even more tempered. However, our overall assessment of ACT is bolstered considerably by evidence for its effectiveness when applied in the field to a variety of clients.

In our view, promising evaluations of the efficacy and effectiveness of ACT are additionally exciting and noteworthy given findings about the processes and mechanisms through which it may initiate therapeutic change. Both efficacy and effectiveness research are consistent in suggesting that ACT facilitates therapeutic change through unique processes consistent with the model upon which it is based. Whether such processes can be more optimally addressed and exploited through further strategic and technical refinements of ACT, possibly thereby resulting in increased levels of efficacy and effectiveness, is a question that also merits additional research.

CONCLUSION

The development and evaluation of ACT is an ongoing process. We have attempted in this chapter to provide a "snapshot" of ACT as it exists at the time of this writing. In some sense, ACT is still in its infancy and will undoubtedly continue to grow and evolve in both unforeseen and more predictable ways.

The strategy of treatment development that has been followed with ACT is unusual. After its earliest applications showed positive effects, over a decade of research was dedicated to basic philosophical, theoretical, and process research. Only in the last few years have additional randomized controlled trials appeared (e.g., Bond & Bunce, 2000), but now with a technology that is on a firmer scientific footing. Whether ACT as a technology will survive we do not know, but it does seem clear that the issues of experiential avoidance, cognitive fusion, and mindfulness and acceptance, are here to stay within the empirical clinical literature. We like to think that expansion of the empirical clinical tradition is good both for the field and for the suffering humanity it serves.

REFERENCES

Addis, M. E., & Carpenter, K. M. (1999). Why, why, why?: Reason-giving and rumination as predictors of response to activation- and insight-oriented treatment rationales. *Journal of Clinical Psychology*, **55**, 881–894.

Addis, M. E., & Jacobson, N. S. (1996). Reasons for depression and the process and outcome of cognitive-behavioral psychotherapies. *Journal of Consulting and Clinical Psychology*, **64**, 1417–1424.

American Psychological Association Task Force on Promotion and Dissemination of Psychological Procedures. (1995). Training in and dissemination of empirically validated psychological treatments: Reports and recommendations. *The Clinical Psychologist*, **48**, 3–23.

Beck, A. T., & Beck, R. (1972). Screening depressed patients in family practice: A rapid technique. *Postgraduate Medicine*, **52**, 81–85.

Beck, A. T., Rush, A. J., Shaw, B. F., & Emery, G. (1979). *Cognitive therapy of depression*. New York: Guilford Press.

Beevers, C. G., Wenzlaff, R. M., Hayes, A. M., & Scott, W. D. (1999). Depression and the ironic effects of thought suppression: Therapeutic strategies for improving mental control. *Clinical Psychology: Science and Practice*, **6**, 133–148.

Biglan, A., & Hayes, S. C. (1996). Should the behavioral sciences become more pragmatic? The case for functional contextualism in research on human behavior. *Applied and Preventive Psychology: Current Scientific Perspectives*, **5**, 47–57.

Billings, A. G., Cronkite, R. C., & Moos, R. H. (1983). Social-environmental factors in unipolar depression: Comparisons of depressed patients and nondepressed controls. *Journal of Abnormal Psychology*, **92**, 119–133.

Billings, A. G., & Moos, R. H. (1981). The role of coping responses and social resources in attenuating the impact of stressful life events. *Journal of Behavioral Medicine*, **4**, 139–157.

Bloor, R. (1983). "What do you mean by depression?"—A study of the relationship between antidepressive activity and personal concepts of depression. *Behaviour Research and Therapy*, **21**, 43–50.

Bond, F. W., & Bunce, D. (2000). Mediators of change in emotion-focused and problem-focused worksite stress management interventions. *Journal of Occupational Health Psychology*, **5**, 156–163.

Brewin, C. R., Watson, M., McCarthy, S., Hyman, P., & Dayson, D. (1998). Intrusive memories and depression in cancer patients. *Behaviour Research and Therapy*, **36**, 1131–1142.

Coyne, J. C., Aldwin, C., & Lazarus, R. S. (1981). Depression and coping in stressful episodes. *Journal of Abnormal Psychology*, **90**, 439–447.

Cronkite, R. C., & Moos, R. H. (1995). Life context, coping processes, and depression. In E. E. Beckham & W. R. Leber (Eds.), *Handbook of depression* (2nd ed., pp. 569–587). New York: Guilford Press.

Dawes, R. M. (1994). *House of cards: Psychology and psychotherapy built on myth*. New York: Free Press.

DeGenova, M. K., Patton, D. M., Jurich, J. A., & MacDermid, S. M. (1994). Ways of coping among HIV-infected individuals. *Journal of Social Psychology*, **134**, 655–663.

Delgado, P., & Moreno, F. (1999). Antidepressants and the brain. *International Clinical Psychopharmacology*, **14** (Suppl 1): S9–S16.

Folke, F., & Parling, T. (2004). *Acceptance and commitment therapy in group format for individuals who are unemployed and on sick leave suffering from depression: A randomized controlled trial*. Unpublished thesis, University of Uppsala, Uppsala, Sweden.

Folkman, S., & Lazarus, R. S. (1980). An analysis of coping in a middle-aged community sample. *Journal of Health and Social Behavior*, **21**, 219–239.

Gaston, L., Marmar, C. R., Thompson, L. W., & Gallagher, D. (1988). Relation of patient pretreatment characteristics to the therapeutic alliance in diverse psychotherapies. *Journal of Consulting and Clinical Psychology*, **56**, 483–489.

Haaga, D. A., Dyck, M. J., & Ernst, D. (1991). Empirical status of cognitive theory of depression. *Psychological Bulletin*, **110**, 215–236.

Hamilton, M. (1960). A rating scale for depression. *Journal of Neurology, Neurosurgery, and Psychiatry*, **23**, 56–61.

Hayes, S. C. (1984). Making sense of spirituality. *Behaviorism*, **12**, 99–110.

Hayes, S. C. (1989). *Rule-governed behavior: Cognition, contingencies, and instructional control*. New York: Plenum.

Hayes, S. C. (1993). Analytic goals and the varieties of scientific contextualism. In S. C. Hayes, L. J. Hayes, H. W. Reese, & T. R. Sarbin (Eds.), *Varieties of scientific contextualism* (pp. 11–27). Reno, NV: Context Press.

Hayes, S. C., Barnes-Holmes, D., & Roche, B. (2001) (Eds.) *Relational frame theory: A post-Skinnerian account of human language and cognition*. New York: Plenum Press.

Hayes, S. C., & Hayes, L. J. (1989). The verbal action of the listener as a basis for rule-governance. In S. C. Hayes (Ed.), *Rule-governed behavior: Cognition, contingencies, and instructional control* (pp. 153–190). New York: Plenum.

Hayes, S. C., & Hayes, L. J. (1992). Verbal relations and the evolution of behavior analysis. *American Psychologist*, **47**, 1383–1395.

Hayes, S. C., Hayes, L. J., & Reese, H. W. (1988). Finding the philosophical core: A review of Stephen C. Pepper's "World hypotheses." *Journal of the Experimental Analysis of Behavior*, **50**, 97–111.

Hayes, S. C., Stroshal, K. D., & Wilson, K. G. (1999). *Acceptance and commitment therapy: An experiential approach to behavior change*. New York: Guilford Press.

Hayes, S. C., Wilson, K. W., Gifford, E. V., Follette, V. M., & Stroshal, K. (1996). Emotional avoidance and behavioral disorders: A functional dimensional approach to diagnosis and treatment. *Journal of Consulting and Clinical Psychology*, **64**, 1152–1168.

Hollon, S. D., & Kendall, P. C. (1980). Cognitive self-statements in depression: Development of an automatic thoughts questionnaire. *Cognitive Therapy and Research*, **4**, 383–395.

Klerman, G. L., Weissman, M. M., Rounsaville, B. J., & Chevron, E. S. (1984). *Interpersonal psychotherapy of depression.* New York: Basic Books.

Kohlenberg, R., Hayes, S. C., & Tsai, M. (1993). Behavior analytic psychotherapy: Two contemporary examples. *Clinical Psychology Review,* **13**, 579–592.

Krantz, S. E., & Moos, R. H. (1988). Risk factors at intake predict nonremission among depressed patients. *Journal of Consulting and Clinical Psychology,* **56**, 863–869.

Lazarus, R. S., & Folkman, S. (1984). *Stress, appraisal, and coping.* New York: Springer.

Lewinsohn, P. M., Sullivan, J. M., & Grosscup, S. J. (1980). Changing reinforcing events: An approach to the treatment of depression. *Psychotherapy: Theory, Research, and Practice,* **47**, 322–334.

Lipkens, G., Hayes, S. C., & Hayes, L. J. (1993). Longitudinal study of derived stimulus relations in an infant. *Journal of Experimental Child Psychology,* **56**, 201–239.

Mathews, A., & MacLeod, C. (1994). Cognitive approaches to emotion and emotional disorders. *Annual Review of Psychology,* **45**, 25–50.

Nolen-Hoeksema, S. (1993). Sex differences in control of depression. In D. M. Wegner & J. W. Pennebaker (Eds.), *Handbook of mental control* (pp. 306–324). Englewood Cliffs, NJ: Prentice-Hall.

Nolen-Hoeksema, S., & Morrow, J. (1991). A prospective study of depression and posttraumatic stress symptoms after a natural disaster: The 1989 Loma Prieta earthquake. *Journal of Personality and Social Psychology,* **61**, 115–121.

Nolen-Hoeksema, S., Parker, L. E., & Larson, J. (1994). Ruminative coping with depressed mood following loss. *Journal of Personality and Social Psychology,* **67**, 92–104.

Pearlin, L. I., & Schooler, C. (1978). The structure of coping. *Journal of Health and Social Behavior,* **19**, 2–21.

Pennebaker, J. W., & O'Heeron, R. C. (1984). Confiding in others and illness rates among spouses of suicide and accidental-death victims. *Journal of Abnormal Psychology,* **93**, 473–476.

Pepper, S. C. (1942). *World hypotheses: A study in evidence.* Berkeley, CA: University of California Press.

Petrie, K. J., Booth, R. J., & Pennebaker, J. W. (1998). The immunological effects of thought suppression. *Journal of Social and Personality Psychology,* **75**, 1264–1272.

Reda, M. A., Carpiniello, B., Secchiaroli, L., & Blanco, S. (1985). Thinking, depression, and antidepressants: Modified and unmodified depressive beliefs during treatment with amitriptyline. *Cognitive Therapy and Research,* **9**, 135–143.

Rippere, V. (1977a). "What's the thing to do when you're feeling depressed?"—A pilot study. *Behaviour Research and Therapy,* **15**, 185–191.

Rippere, V. (1977b). Common-sense beliefs about depression and antidepressive behaviour: A study of social consensus. *Behaviour Research and Therapy,* **15**, 465–473.

Rohde, P., Lewinsohn, P. M., Tilson, M., & Seeley, J. R. (1990). Dimensionality of coping and its relation to depression. *Journal of Personality and Social Psychology,* **58**, 499–511.

Seligman, M. (1995). The effectiveness of psychotherapy: The Consumer Reports Study. *American Psychologist,* **50**, 965–974.

Seligman, M. E. P., & Levant, R. F. (1998). Managed care policies rely on inadequate science. *Professional Psychology: Research and Practice,* **29**, 211–212.

Simons, A. D., Garfield, S. L., & Murphy, G. E. (1984). The process of change in cognitive therapy and pharmacotherapy of depression: Changes in mood and cognition. *Archives of General Psychiatry,* **41**, 45–51.

Simons, A. D., Murphy, G. E., Levine, J. L., & Wetzel, R. D. (1986). Sustained improvement over one year after cognitive and/or pharmacotherapy of depression. *Archives of General Psychiatry,* **43**, 43–48.

Strosahl, K. D., Hayes, S. C., Bergan, J., & Romano, P. (1998). Assessing the field effectiveness of acceptance and commitment therapy: An example of the manipulated training research method. *Behavior Therapy,* **29**, 35–63.

Swindle, R. W., Cronkite, R. C., & Moos, R. H. (1989). Life stressors, social resources, coping, and the 4-year course of unipolar depression. *Journal of Abnormal Psychology,* **98**, 468–477.

Teasdale, J. D., & Barnard, P. J. (1993). *Affect, cognition, and change: Re-modeling depressive thought.* Hillsdale, NJ: Erlbaum.

Wegner, D. M. (1994). *White bears and other unwanted thoughts.* New York: Guilford Press.

Weissman, A., & Beck, A. T. (1978, November). *Development and validation of the Dysfunctional Attitude Scale*. Paper presented at the annual meeting of the Association for Advancement of Behavior Therapy, Chicago.

Wenzlaff, R. M. (1993). The mental control of depression: Psychological obstacles to emotional well-being. In D. M. Wegner & J. W. Pennebaker (Eds.), *Handbook of mental control* (pp. 239–257). Englewood Cliffs, NJ: Prentice-Hall.

Wenzlaff, R. M., & Bates, D. E. (1998). Unmasking a cognitive vulnerability to depression: How lapses in mental control reveal depressive thinking. *Journal of Personality and Social Psychology*, **75**, 1559–1571.

Wenzlaff, R. M., Wegner, D. M., & Klein, S. B. (1991). The role of thought suppression in the bonding of thought and mood. *Journal of Personality and Social Psychology*, **60**, 500–508.

Wenzlaff, R. M., Wegner, D. M., & Roper, D. W. (1988). Depression and mental control: The resurgence of unwanted negative thoughts. *Journal of Personality and Social Psychology*, **55**, 882–892.

Zettle, R. D., & Hayes, S. C. (1986). Dysfunctional control by client verbal behavior: The context of reason giving. *The Analysis of Verbal Behavior*, **4**, 30–38.

Zettle, R. D., & Rains, J. C. (1989). Group cognitive and contextual therapies in treatment of depression. *Journal of Clinical Psychology*, **45**, 436–445.

CHAPTER 4

Panic Disorder with Agoraphobia

Nina Heinrichs and **David A. Spiegel**

Center for Anxiety and Related Disorders, Boston University, Boston, MA, USA

and

Stefan G. Hofmann

Department of Psychology, Boston University, Boston, MA, USA

Panic disorder with agoraphobia (PDA) is a prevalent and chronic condition associated with a substantial reduction in quality of life (Keller et al., 1994; Kessler et al., 1994; Robins & Regier, 1991), intensive use of general medical services including emergency rooms (Klerman et al., 1991), and high social and economic costs (Hofmann & Barlow, 1999). The core feature of panic disorder is the experience of recurrent panic attacks—sudden episodes of fear accompanied by distressing physical sensations such as dizziness, heart racing, palpitations, shortness of breath, choking sensations, sweating, or nausea. The fear is often of dying, losing control, or going crazy. Patients with panic disorder worry persistently about the potential adverse implications or consequences of these attacks. As a result, they often feel vulnerable in places or situations that would be difficult to leave, or where help might not be readily available in the event of sudden need. Examples include open spaces, unfamiliar or unpopulated areas, crowds, public transportation, elevators, bridges, and limited-access highways. If such situations are avoided or cause significant distress, the person is said to have agoraphobia.

Cognitive-behavior therapy (CBT) is a well-established treatment for panic disorder with limited agoraphobia (see the Practice Guideline for the Treatment of Panic Disorder by the American Psychiatric Association [1998], and the Task Force on Promotion and Dissemination of Psychological Procedures of the American Psychological Association, Division of Clinical Psychology [1993]). Standard forms of CBT (e.g., Barlow & Craske, 2000) typically are administered in 10–12 sessions over a period of several months. When agoraphobia is more severe, a situational exposure component (e.g., Craske & Barlow, 2000) is added, which extends the treatment duration (see Hofmann & Spiegel [1999] for a review).

An early meta-analysis of treatment outcome studies for panic disorder with or without mild agoraphobia found that the greatest improvement occurred during the first eight sessions (Howard et al., 1986). Subsequently, Sokol and colleagues showed that panic attacks could be reduced significantly after only a few sessions (Sokol et al., 1989). Based on

Handbook of Brief Cognitive Behaviour Therapy. Edited by Frank W. Bond and Windy Dryden.
© 2002 John Wiley & Sons, Ltd. ISBN 0-470-02132-2.

those findings, several workers have investigated whether the number of CBT sessions or amount of therapist contact can be reduced without substantial loss of efficacy (Clark et al., 1999; Côté et al., 1994; Hecker et al., 1996). These approaches typically have substituted patient self-study materials for therapist contact, although the overall duration of treatment has been the traditional 3–4 months. The results of these trials have been encouraging. For example, Clark et al. (1999) found that a five-session version of CBT combined with self-study modules was comparable to a standard 12-sessions treatment and superior to a wait-list control.

In the preceding studies, participants were panic disorder patients with no more than mild agoraphobia. There are few data available on the efficacy of CBT for patients with higher levels of agoraphobia, although our clinical experience suggested that it was less effective as agoraphobia increased, even when situational exposure instructions were incorporated. That impression was bolstered by an early trial involving PDA patients with moderate to severe agoraphobia, in which it was found that adding graded situational exposure instructions, based on individually constructed fear and avoidance hierarchies, to standard CBT did not significantly enhance improvement of avoidance (Turovsky et al., 1994; Vitali et al., 1996). Patients in both groups (CBT with or without exposure instructions) had considerable residual agoraphobic avoidance at posttreatment.

To address that problem, several years ago two of the current authors (D.A.S. and S.G.H.) and our colleagues began a series of experiments to develop a more effective form of CBT for PDA patients with moderate to severe agoraphobia. The treatment described here is a product of that effort and represents a work in progress. In developing it, we drew heavily upon the work cited above as well as work by Fiegenbaum and his colleagues at the Christoph Dornier Foundation in Germany (Ehlers et al., 1995; Fiegenbaum, 1988; Fiegenbaum & Tuschen, 1996). A major feature of this treatment is its focus on internal sensations as sources of anxiety and fear reactions. Because of that, we have referred to it as "sensation-focused therapy" or, when administered in its intensive form, "sensation-focused intensive therapy" (S-FIT).

TREATMENT OVERVIEW

The treatment consists of three components, which are described in detail later: a brief, largely self-study CBT component; an intensive in vivo situational and interoceptive exposure component; and a skill consolidation and relapse prevention component. The exposure component includes two days of therapist-accompanied, ungraded massed exposure and two or more days of self-administered exposure practice. Therapist contacts are supplemented by a patient workbook (Spiegel, submitted for publication) containing readings and exercises that patients complete prior to therapy sessions. The first installment of the workbook is sent to patients before therapy begins.

The treatment is administered in two formats. In one, patients are treated in groups of 4–6 members over a period of approximately three months. The CBT component is delivered in four weekly $1^1/_2$-hour group sessions. Patients then work individually with a therapist (an average of 8–10 hours of therapist time per patient) for the two-day therapist-accompanied portion of the exposure component, after which they continue with self-administered exposure practices until the group reconvenes. When all the members have completed the exposure component, they meet again as a group for two further bi- or tri-weekly $1^1/_2$-hour sessions for the skill consolidation and relapse prevention component.

Table 4.1 Outline of S-FIT sessions

Session number(s)	Treatment day(s)	Session duration	Treatment component
1–3	1–3	2 hours	CBT
4, 5	4, 5	Variable	Intensive exposure with initial therapist accompaniment
–	6, 7	–	Continued exposure, patient working independently
6	8	2 hours	Skill consolidation and relapse prevention

In the second format (S-FIT), treatment is delivered to patients individually in a highly intensive fashion over a period of eight days. During that period, patients are expected to devote full time to therapy. As S-FIT is typically administered, the CBT component is conducted during Monday through Wednesday and includes three daily two-hour sessions with the therapist. Therapist-accompanied exposure is done on Thursday and Friday. By Saturday, the patient is working independently of the therapist and continues exposure practices alone throughout the weekend. The skill consolidation and relapse prevention component is delivered in a single two-hour session on Monday (see Table 4.1). To date, treatment has averaged 19 hours of therapist time per patient. This format has been very helpful for people who live in a region where no health-care provider specializing in PDA is available, or who have exhausted local treatment options; for those in urgent need of treatment (e.g., in danger of losing their jobs or dropping out of school); and for those who prefer a concentrated therapy. For the remainder of this chapter, we will specifically focus on the intensive treatment format.

Features of Sensation-Focused Therapy for PDA

As noted previously, the current treatment represents our attempt to combine the active in-gredients of existing evidence-based therapies for panic disorder (e.g., panic control therapy, Barlow & Craske, 2000) and agoraphobia (e.g., ungraded massed exposure, Fiegenbaum, 1988; Hahlweg et al., 2001), along with relapse-prevention techniques, in a package that makes efficient use of therapist time. Many of the elements are therefore similar to those of other treatments. Cognitive restructuring, for example, is done as in standard CBT. Symptom-induction procedures are conducted as described in panic control therapy. Re-cent research has shown that repeated trials of mild panic provocation procedures (e.g., hyperventilation, physical exercise, and caffeine consumption) can lead to a decrease in anxiety in some individuals with panic disorder (Hofmann et al., 1999). In addition, the treatment consists of basic components of Fiegenbaum's exposure treatment; i.e., cognitive preparation for exposure, followed by a decision period before exposure is begun, has been adopted. However, the current treatment, especially as administered in its intensive form, differs from existing therapies in several ways.

First, it specifically addresses both the cognitive (fear of panic and related sensations) and behavioral (avoidance and safety behaviors) dimensions of PDA. Unlike other therapies, which focus preferentially on one or the other of these, the current treatment gives them roughly equal weight. This is accomplished without a substantial increase in therapist time by providing the entire content of the program in the self-study workbook, which patients complete prior to sessions. Although some existing CBT treatments have companion patient workbooks, generally the books are used to reinforce and extend material presented in session. The therapy as delivered by the therapist is complete on its own. In the current treatment the reverse is true.

Second, the primary focus of treatment, even during situational exposure, is on the frightening somatic manifestations of anxiety and fear. As conducted in this treatment, the goal of exposure is not habituation to agoraphobic situations, but rather confrontation of the most frightening internal sensations that can be elicited. In that regard, agoraphobic situations provide a useful context for exposure, but they must be combined with aggressively conducted symptom-induction procedures.

Third, patients are guided to experience scary sensations maximally, including full panic attacks. In that regard, any behaviors that reduce the intensity of the sensations or the patient's awareness or fear of them are considered counter-therapeutic. In contrast to therapies that teach management of fear and related somatic symptoms (e.g., slow breathing or relaxation techniques) or use exposure manipulations, such as graded sequencing of tasks, to limit distress, the current treatment emphasizes the deliberate provocation and maximal intensification of feared symptoms. Arousal reduction procedures are not taught, and their use during treatment is proscribed.[1] In fact, anything a patient does to reduce distress or feel safer is meticulously stripped away (with the active collaboration of the patient). In addition, patients are encouraged to accept risk and uncertainty. For example, the search for triggers of panic attacks as a means of making them more predictable or avoidable, which is common in conventional CBT, is de-emphasized in favor of stressing that, whether or not triggers are apparent, all fear reactions (including panic attacks) are essentially the same.

The conduct of the ungraded massed exposure component also presents some unique challenges for patients and therapists. Unlike conventional exposure treatments, where patients work gradually up their fear and avoidance hierarchies, in the current treatment every effort is made to get patients to the top of their hierarchies by the first exposure day. The intensity of this work and the accompanying emotions leave patients, and often therapists, exhausted. This requires special skills on the part of therapists, who must learn how to motivate patients to push themselves to extremes and how to deal compassionately with dependency, refusal, and anger. Patients must learn to remain rational in the face of overwhelming fear, resist the powerful urge to escape, and observe their behaviors, thoughts, and feelings with scientific detachment. Patients and therapists may develop strong emotional attachments during this phase of treatment, which must not be allowed to detract from the goals of therapy. If the therapist shows too much concern for the patient's obvious distress or backs off too easily, the patient will seize upon that as a means of avoidance.

The uniqueness of the therapeutic relationship is especially evident in S-FIT. Many of the patients we have treated with that format have come from other states or countries at considerable financial and emotional cost. Often, they have had numerous unsuccessful attempts at treatment and view our program as a "last-ditch effort." When such patients experience dramatic improvement in as little as a week, they often regard the outcome as miraculous and the therapist as the miracle worker. Termination may be more difficult for

---

[1] There is little evidence that relaxation or breathing procedures add anything of benefit to in vivo exposure for agoraphobia. Moreover, the few studies that have examined different components of CBT suggest that breathing retraining is less important than interoceptive or situational exposure (Craske et al., 1997; Rijken et al., 1992).

these patients than for individuals treated with traditional therapies and may require special handling.

Patient Selection

Several considerations pertain to the selection of patients for this treatment. First, the treatment was designed as an alternative to standard CBT for patients with moderate to severe agoraphobia. In our center, that group constitutes slightly more than one-third of all patients diagnosed with panic disorder or PDA. Those patients typically have been excluded from the development and testing of CBT treatments and are the individuals for whom conventional forms of CBT are presumed to be least effective. Because half of the therapy described here is devoted to exposure, it would not be appropriate for patients with low levels of agoraphobia, who constitute the majority of panic disorder patients. Those patients would be better treated with standard CBT.

Second, because of the brevity and highly focused structure of the treatment, there is little flexibility to address issues other than those directly related to PDA. This treatment has been used in patients with numerous additional diagnoses. Nevertheless, a careful diagnostic assessment is essential before this treatment is offered to ensure that the principal diagnosis is PDA. Particular attention should be paid to differentiating PDA from other phobias, especially social phobia, and from posttraumatic stress disorder. Although we have not yet systematically evaluated the possible predictors of treatment outcome, our clinical experience also suggests that patients with strong hypochondriacal fears may not respond as well as others. Other factors that may be associated with poorer outcome are comorbid personality disorders, mental retardation or other forms of cognitive impairment, psychotic features, and severe depression.

Because of the strong emphasis placed on symptom-induction procedures (e.g., hyperventilation, spinning, straw-breathing, and vigorous exercise), the patient's medical history should be carefully reviewed to ensure that there is no medical contraindication to these procedures (e.g., pregnancy, heart disease, epilepsy, and asthma). The presence of such conditions does not necessarily preclude treatment; however, the procedures may need to be modified (see Feldman et al. [2000] for suggested modifications for patients with asthma). Patients often have exaggerated beliefs about their physical limitations, so consultation and collaboration with the patient's physician are recommended if a medical condition is present.

There is evidence that concurrent use of psychotropic medication during CBT (e.g., Otto et al., 1996) or situational exposure (Marks et al., 1993) increases the risk of relapse. Concurrent medication use limits the development of a sense of self-efficacy by patients and, to the extent that the drugs suppress PDA symptoms, also prevents the patient from experiencing the full severity of the symptoms. Intermittent (as-needed) medication use as a means of coping with intense anxiety or panic is particularly problematic in that regard. Because of this, if possible, we prefer patients not to be taking medications for anxiety or panic during treatment, and we specifically disallow as-needed drug use. When the longer treatment format is used, it may be possible to discontinue pharmacotherapy gradually during the early weeks of treatment. For patients receiving the eight-day treatment format, we recommend that medications be discontinued prior to treatment. When that is not possible (e.g., the patient is unable to work or travel to Boston without medication), we initiate dose reductions at the start of treatment and encourage the patient to complete drug taper after treatment concludes. Therapists should collaborate with the prescribing physician on this plan.

Finally, patients must be willing to experience high anxiety and even panic attacks during the exposure portion of the treatment. Potential patients should be advised of this when treatment options are discussed, and those who are unwilling to do it should probably be steered to conventional graded exposure treatment or standard CBT followed by exposure. However, patients rarely can make an unequivocal commitment to intensive exposure. If they are willing to try, we accept them. The details of the exposure component (e.g., that the patient will be asked to confront the most feared situation by the second day) are not discussed prior to treatment, because at that point it would unnecessarily raise the patient's anticipatory anxiety and increase the likelihood of treatment refusal. Surprisingly few patients who begin treatment under these conditions refuse exposure later. Only one out of approximately 23 patients from our pilot study refused the exposure component.

CASE EXAMPLE

In the remainder of this chapter, we present a case example to illustrate how sensation-focused therapy for PDA is conducted. A detailed therapist manual is forthcoming (Spiegel & Baker, submitted for publication). The example patient was treated in the intensive treatment format, that is, over an eight-day period by one of the current authors (N.H.).

The Patient

Josh was a 25-year-old, married man with a one-year-old child. He contacted the Center for Anxiety and Related Disorders at Boston University in 1999, requesting treatment for panic attacks and marked agoraphobic fear and avoidance. Josh had learned about the panic disorder treatment program from a television program that featured it. Prior to accepting Josh for treatment, we conducted a diagnostic assessment using a semi-structured clinical interview, the brief version of the Anxiety Disorders Interview Schedule for DSM-IV (ADIS-IV, Di Nardo et al., 1994). The assessment was conducted by telephone, because Josh lived out of state.

Josh stated that he had been experiencing panic attacks since the summer of 1992. He said that during a full-blown panic attack he experienced shortness of breath, choking sensations, dizziness, unsteady feelings, and feelings of unreality. A feeling of unreality was usually the first symptom he would notice. Josh reported that during the past six months he had 20 full-blown and 60 "limited-symptom" attacks with three or fewer symptoms. He indicated that during a panic attack he worried about fainting, dying, and "going crazy." Due to his fear of panic attacks, he avoided long-distance and interstate driving, air travel, bridges, open spaces, elevators, and leaving town. In fact, he reported being unable to travel beyond a self-imposed safety zone of approximately 20 miles around his house. When he left his house, he carried a cellular phone and medication with him "just in case." Josh also reported having marital and family difficulties due to his anxiety. He was not able to visit his parents or grandparents, who lived outside his safety zone, or go on family vacations. Several times, he got as far as the airport with his family but was unable to board the plane. He stated that he took a low-paid job because it was located only five miles from his home. At the time of the interview, Josh had been taking paroxetine (40 mg/day) for four months and alprazolam (up to 3 mg/day), as needed.

Josh decided to participate in the intensive treatment program. He made travel plans, including plane tickets and lodging in Boston. His wife expressed concern that he would not be able to fly without sedation and might medicate himself with pills or alcohol. The therapist discussed this with Josh by telephone and strongly urged him to talk to his psychiatrist about appropriate medication options. In fact, Josh did sedate himself to the extent that he was almost barred from the flight by the pilot. Through the efforts of his wife, he was finally taken aboard the plane in a wheelchair, and the couple arrived safely in Boston. Josh stated that he could not recall anything about the trip.

The Treatment

Josh's treatment followed the outline in Table 4.1. Approximately one week before his departure for Boston, Josh was sent the first installment of the patient workbook and was asked to study it and complete the exercises.

Session 1

Content

The reading assignments for session 1 describe the nature and physical basis of anxiety, fear, and panic, including the neurobiological networks that are believed to be involved in those emotions. Anxiety and fear are presented as normal and generally protective states that enhance one's ability to survive and compete in life. Panic attacks are conceptualized as fear reactions that are excessive for a situation or for which triggers are not always apparent. Three maintaining mechanisms for panic attacks are introduced: anxious thoughts (i.e., misinterpretation of panic sensations and worry about the consequences of panic), conditioning (i.e., associations between fear and stimuli that were present when the fear response previously occurred), and anxiety and fear behaviors (i.e., behaviors a person shows or intentionally omits in order to reduce discomfort). The first of these maintaining mechanisms—anxious thoughts—is then discussed in detail. The concept of core anxious thoughts (the ultimate feared catastrophe) is introduced, and techniques are presented to assist patients to identify their own core anxious thoughts. That task is assigned as an exercise.

Process

During the first part of the session, the therapist reviews the treatment format and ensures that the patient is prepared to proceed with it, confirming that the patient has done the assigned reading and completed the exercises. Through Socratic questioning, the therapist assesses the patient's comprehension of the material, clarifies concepts as needed, and assists the patient to apply the concepts to himself. No new material is introduced. The remainder of the session focuses on the patient's attempt to identify his core anxious thoughts. In reviewing the patient's work, the therapist stresses the link between the experience of a scary sensation and the specter of the ultimate feared catastrophe. That generally is easy when the thoughts involve misinterpretation of benign somatic sensations (e.g., an increase in heart rate) as signs of a serious physical or mental event (e.g., a heart attack). However, core anxious thoughts about possible consequences of panic may be more difficult for the patient to identify. The excerpt from Josh's first session (next paragraph) illustrates this.

Irrational anxious thoughts are not restructured during the first session. That is the content of the readings for session 2. The goal of this session is to send the patient home with a set of personally relevant core anxious thoughts to use in the homework exercises. At the conclusion of session 1, the patient is given the second installment of the patient workbook and is asked to study it and complete the exercises prior to session 2.

Josh's First Session

Josh had read the material for session 1 several times and had completed the assigned exercises. His understanding of the material was generally good; however, he had some difficulty in identifying a core anxious thought related to the experience of dizziness, which was a prominent somatic manifestation of his panic and limited symptom attacks. This sensation was particularly distressing if it occurred when Josh was driving. The therapist assisted him to apply the self-questioning techniques described in the workbook to this situation.

THERAPIST: Suppose that you are in your car, driving, and you begin to feel dizzy. What are you afraid will happen?

JOSH: I don't know.

T: Some patients who experience scary sensations while driving say they are afraid of crashing or causing an accident. Is that true for you?

J: No, I don't think so. I'm a good driver. I just hate feeling that way, you know.

T: Yes. Dizziness can be quite uncomfortable. Do you get any other sensations along with that?

J: An unreal feeling! Yeah, I get upset about that. I feel totally dizzy and unstable and my head just feels like it's blowing off.

T: All right. Now I'd like you to imagine that you are driving on the highway right now. You are far away from home, and you start noticing the dizziness and unreality. What do you think?

J: Oh no, there it is. I need to go back. I can't do this.

T: What are you imagining might happen if you keep going?

J: It will get worse.

T: And then what?

J: I don't know. I never let it get worse. I'm afraid I would lose my mind.

T: So, you think you might lose your mind if you don't stop the sensation from getting worse?

J: Yeah.

T: What would losing your mind look like? Would I know? Could I see that from the outside?

J: Yes, definitely. I will be sitting in a chair, babbling, not reacting to anything. I will not recognize Jane [his wife]. And I won't be able to take care of myself anymore.

In this example, Josh's core anxious thought was not of dying or causing someone else's death in an accident, which are more typical when patients begin to panic while driving, but of severe mental incapacity. It turned out that the stimulus for his dizziness was the sight of open spaces, which he encountered when driving. The driving itself was a contributing factor only in that it meant he was away from the safety of home and consequently felt more vulnerable. The therapist assisted Josh to examine several other anxious thoughts, many of which led to the same fear.

Session 2

Content

This session is dedicated to cognitive restructuring. The readings begin with a description of the bodily changes that are orchestrated by activation of the autonomic nervous system, a part of the body's normal preparation for defense. Understanding those changes provides a non-threatening explanation for the somatic sensations that accompany panic attacks, and this is useful in generating alternatives to catastrophic misinterpretations of the sensations. The readings also describe two common evaluative errors PDA patients make regarding the possible adverse consequences of panic attacks—overestimating the likelihood and the seriousness of the consequences—and demonstrate procedures for correcting those errors. In assigned exercises, patients are asked to test their evaluations of the likelihood and seriousness of the core anxious thoughts that were identified in session 1, and revise them as needed for consistency with their experience and logical reasoning.

Process

Most of this session is spent reviewing the assignments and assisting the patient to restructure irrational thoughts. It is important to elicit specific details about the feared consequences of a panic attack (e.g., what exactly the patient thinks would happen if he went "crazy"). The patient's evaluation of the seriousness of an event will depend to a great extent upon his confidence in his ability to cope with it. In addition, some events may be regarded as catastrophic if they occur as a result of a panic attack but are viewed as manageable if they occur for another reason (e.g., throwing up because of panic compared to throwing up due to food poisoning).

During the last 15 minutes of the session, the therapist conducts a voluntary hyperventilation exercise with the patient, for the purpose of demonstrating how symptom-induction procedures should be done. The patient will be asked to do several such procedures for homework. At the conclusion of the session, the patient is given the third installment of the patient workbook and is asked to study it and complete the exercises prior to session 3.

Josh's Second Session

The therapist reviewed Josh's understanding of cognitive restructuring and his work on restructuring his own anxious thoughts. Josh had difficulty in realistically evaluating the likelihood and seriousness of the feared event of "going crazy" as a result of panic attacks, which, as Josh described it in session 1, he imagined as " sitting in a chair, babbling, not reacting to anything," and being unable to recognize his wife or take care of himself. The following excerpt from the session illustrates how the therapist guided Josh to examine this.

THERAPIST: So the core anxious thought that is triggered when you suddenly feel dizzy and things seem unreal is that you will go crazy in the way you described and have to be hospitalized in a mental institution?

JOSH: Yeah. I think that's pretty accurate.

T: How likely do you think that is?

J: I don't know. I think it is probable.

T: On a percentage scale between 0 and 100, "0" meaning it is not possible at all and "100" meaning it will happen for sure, what do you think the probability is?

J: 80%.

T: OK, now let's see if the evidence supports that estimate. How many episodes have you had in your life when you felt dizzy or things seemed unreal?

J: A lot. Probably over 1000 when I felt that to some extent.

T: Let's just consider the episodes when you had those feelings really strongly and thought that you might go crazy.

J: Maybe 400.

T: And out of those 400 times, how many times did your wife admit you to a mental hospital?

J: None.

T: Why not? Did you not behave weird?

J: No, not really weird. I mean I felt out of control, but I knew that the sensations would stop at some point.

T: So how many times did you actually begin to babble like a baby or not recognize your environment?

J: Well, never. But it still think it could happen.

T: Possibly, but, based on your past experience, the likelihood seems pretty low, doesn't it?

J: Yes, but how do I know that it won't happen the next time?

T: You don't. Nothing in life is 100% certain. But it hasn't happened to you in 400 times when you thought it would. Possibly other people with panic disorder have a different experience. Do you think that could be the case?

J: I don't know. Do they?

T: Well, I can only speak from my own experience and my knowledge of patients treated by my colleagues or reported in publications. But I am not aware of any cases in which a person went crazy as a result of having panic attacks.

J: Really? That is interesting. Then I guess it must be pretty unlikely.

T: How likely do you think, between 0 and 100%?

J: Less than 1%, probably 0%.

T: All right. Let's shift our attention now to how serious it would be in the realistically very, very unlikely event that you do go crazy as a result of panic. We need to do this hypothetically, because it has not happened to you. But imagine that during your next panic attack it does. You suddenly start to babble like a baby, you can't think rationally, and you don't recognize Jane when she comes to help you. What do you think would happen next?

J: She would probably take me to a hospital where all the other psychos are.

T: All right. And then what would happen next?

J: I don't know. I would sit in a locked unit and stare at a wall talking to myself.

T: Would anyone take care of you?

J: Yes, the nurses, and I guess there would be a doctor, or something like that.

T: And what would the doctor do?

J: I don't know. He would probably give me some kind of medication.

T: And would that help?

Josh was unsure about the last question. He didn't know anyone who had been hospitalized in a mental unit and again asked the therapist for information. She was able to provide sufficient basic information about prognostic factors and treatment outcomes for Josh eventually to conclude that, in all likelihood, he would recover sufficiently with treatment to return home. Although he still thought the event would be horrible, he concluded that it would be preferable to death and that there was a possibility of his recovering enough to lead a normal life. Had he not been able to restructure this thought, the therapist would have focused on the unlikeliness of the event and guided Josh to view it as he does other, more common catastrophic events (e.g., getting cancer, being murdered).

Session 3

Content

This last CBT session focuses on the second maintaining factor for panic attacks, fear conditioning. The readings describe how conditioning occurs and how it can lead to unexpected panic attacks. Conditioning to somatic sensations (interoceptive conditioning) is emphasized, and it is conceptualized as a non-cognitive learning process through which a

Table 4.2 Symptom induction procedures

Procedure	Examples of target symptom(s) induced
Hyperventilation	Dizziness, dry mouth, sweating, cold hands
Running in place	Heart racing, sweating
Head shaking	Dizziness
Head between knees, lift quickly	Seeing spots, lightheadedness, faintness
Breath holding	Shortness of breath, heart pounding
Breathing through a thin straw	Breathing difficulties, choking or suffocating feelings
Staring at a spot or in a mirror	Derealization, detachment from oneself
Total body muscle tension	Weakness, heaviness in limbs
Staying in a hot place	Feeling hot, sweating
Spinning or twirling	Dizziness

sensation the patient experienced just prior to or during a panic attack acquires the ability to trigger a fear reaction on its own, without the need for cognitive mediation. Because conditioning occurs without conscious awareness, the resulting fear reactions (panic attacks) seem spontaneous.

In order to address this cause of panic attacks, it is essential that all sensations that have become capable of triggering fear reactions are identified. The readings present symptom induction tests as a way to identify individual sensitivities. Symptom induction tests are brief procedures that provoke specific sensations—for example, breathing through a thin straw, hyperventilating, spinning in a chair, or running in place (see Table 4.2). The patient is assigned to conduct these procedures prior to the session. Having thus identified salient sensations, the patient is asked to choose a highly anxiety-provoking procedure and repeat it several times in succession, as a means of illustrating the concepts of interoceptive exposure and habituation.

Process

In session, the therapist reviews the results of the homework exercises and ensures that they were done correctly. The therapist also checks the patient's understanding of the method by which conditioned reactions can be reduced—that is, through repeated interoceptive exposure. In reviewing the patient's interoceptive exposure trial, the therapist considers the duration and number of repetitions performed, the strength of the sensations elicited, and the patient's use of avoidance or safety behaviors (e.g., distraction and holding on to the chair while spinning). If the patient did not experience habituation of anxiety during the exposure assignment, one or more of those factors might account for that. The therapist then has the patient do a series of interoceptive exposures in session, again using a procedure that elicits a high level of anxiety.

The last part of the session is dedicated to preparing the patient cognitively for the upcoming exposure phase of treatment. This represents a departure from the general rule that all content is presented to the patient initially in the form of reading assignments. Because the patient's anxiety about exposure is likely to be high, it is crucial to maximize his motivation. This is best done face-to-face. In addition, doing cognitive preparation at the end of session 3 gives the patient until the next day to confirm his decision to proceed with therapy (see below).

During cognitive preparation, the rationale for ungraded massed exposure is provided and the patient's fears about it are addressed. Unless the patient fully understands and embraces the rationale, he is likely to avoid exposure when his fear increases and may even drop out of treatment. Central assumptions the patient holds about why he has panic disorder need to be included in the model, to decrease future resistance and increase motivation (for further information about specific factors that need to be considered in cognitive preparation, see Fiegenbaum & Tuschen, 1996).

The rationale for situational exposure is based on Hofmann et al. (1996) and is provided in the following way. A specific situation that is perceived as extremely anxiety provoking by the patient is chosen. By Socratic questioning, the patient is assisted to construct a graph of his predicted anxiety level (rated in subjective units of discomfort [SUDS], between 0 and 8) as a function of time as the situation is approached and entered (Figure 4.1). Patients usually predict that they will experience considerable anticipatory anxiety (e.g., SUDS = 5) before they enter the situation, and this will jump to the top of the scale when the situation is entered. The patient is then asked how he has dealt with his intense anxiety so far. Patients usually report that they would not even enter the situation in the first place, and if they did, they either escaped or engaged in a variety of behaviors to reduce anxiety. The patient is made to realize that upon engaging in these behaviors, anxiety reduces in the short term, an effect which reinforces these behaviors that eventually lead to the maintenance or worsening of the problem. The patient is then asked to predict what will happen to his anxiety if he remains in the situation for various periods of time (e.g., 1 hour, 5 hours, 10 hours, and 24 hours) without engaging in avoidance or safety behaviors. Through this process, the patient is guided to acknowledge that his anxiety will eventually decrease, even if he does nothing to reduce it. The next time that he enters the same situation his anxiety will be less intense because he has learned "it is just a matter of time" until his anxiety reduces. The therapist then briefly explains how exposures will be done and challenges

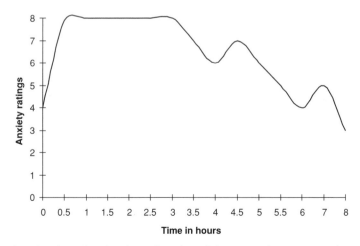

Figure 4.1 A patient's anxiety level as a function of time spent in an extremely anxiety-provoking situation

the patient to decide to commit himself to do it. This is presented in words such as the following:

> Repeatedly facing your fears is a very powerful technique for overcoming agoraphobic fear and avoidance. Moreover, it is the *only* known way to do it. If there were an easier or less painful way, we would use it. Facing avoided situations can be very anxiety provoking and often trigger panic attacks. However, experiencing those emotions and the associated physical sensations is crucial to the effectiveness of the therapy, because unless you learn that you can survive them you will always fear and avoid them. In that regard, the more panic attacks you will have and the stronger the anxiety will be, the more confidence you will gain and the better you will be able to re-program your brain in order to learn that the sensations are not harmful.
>
> The next several days are the most important days of treatment, the days for which we have been preparing and during which you will make the greatest gains. We will not start with easy things. You will face some of the most difficult situations that can be arranged. It will be hard and exhausting, but it will also be short, and I will be there to guide you. You can think of it as like surgery; it will be painful but fast. Also like surgery, you have a choice. You can choose to keep a cancerous organ or live a life crippled by fear, or you can choose to courageously endure the pain in order to break the back of your panic disorder and most likely recover your health and freedom. This is a unique opportunity, and one you are not likely to have again, but you must decide whether the benefit is worth the cost. If you are not willing to do it, we can stop treatment now. Do not decide right now. I want you to think about it.

Our experience is that, when confronted with that choice in the way described, almost all patients later agree to proceed with exposure. The patient is given the next installment of the workbook and told to come back in the morning with the exercises completed and a decision made. If he chooses to continue treatment, he should plan to spend the entire day.

Josh's Third Session

Josh stated that he had done the symptom-induction tests, and some of them did not bother him at all. He said running in place was not scary, because he exercises almost every day. The therapist used this statement to illustrate how a person's thoughts can modify his reactions to physical sensations. Josh was most scared by breathing through a straw and spinning with his eyes closed. Therefore, interoceptive exposures using those procedures were conducted in session. After four trials of breathing through a straw, Josh reported that the sensations no longer made him anxious. The task was then switched to spinning with eyes closed, and, again, he habituated to the sensations after several repetitions. Figure 4.2 depicts the intensity of Josh's sensations and his anxiety during the repeated spinning exposures. The therapist guided Josh to realize that if he consciously attempted to provoke sensations under any given circumstances, his anxiety would diminish.

During the cognitive preparation component of the session, Josh chose "driving on a highway with several lanes and open spaces on either side" as an extremely anxiety-provoking situation. He predicted that, upon entering the highway, he would experience a full-blown panic attack. When the therapist asked him what would happen to his anxiety if it were impossible for him to leave the highway or engage in any avoidance or safety behaviors, Josh acknowledged that it might decrease at "some point". He doubted that his body could physically maintain a maximum panic level for more than 45 minutes. Josh grasped the rationale very quickly, and subsequently he expressed a strong belief that his anxiety would diminish. He was given the next workbook installment and asked to complete the exercises prior to session 4.

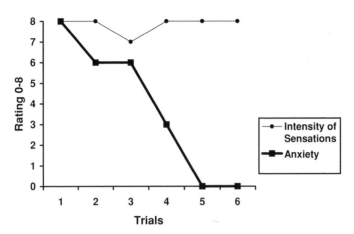

Figure 4.2 Josh's ratings of anxiety and intensity of bodily sensations as a function of number of trials during the interoceptive exposure exercise "spinning while standing and with eyes closed"

Sessions 4 and 5

Content

The readings for sessions 4 and 5 focus on the last of the three maintaining factors for panic attacks, anxiety and fear behaviors. Principal among those are avoidance and safety behaviors. Avoidance is described as any behavior the patient engages in to reduce anxiety or fear. It is the natural consequence of the urge to flee that is an inherent part of the fight-or-flight fear response. Overt (e.g., not going into a feared situation) versus covert (e.g., doing something to reduce scary sensations while in a feared situation) avoidance behaviors are discussed. Safety behaviors are described as things a person does to protect himself from a feared event or to make it easier to escape or get help if needed (e.g., holding on to a wall, carrying a cellular phone). The short- and long-term consequences of these behaviors are discussed, as well as how they act to maintain or even increase fear, and thus panic attacks.

The workbook also contains instructions for constructing a fear and avoidance hierarchy (FAH) and a list of avoidance and safety behaviors, which are assigned to be done prior to session 4. A FAH is a list of situations, activities, and places that the patient fears or avoids because of concerns about panic attacks, ranked according to difficulty. The patient is also asked to specify variations of each item that would make it easier or harder to do. The workbook also presents the rationale for exposure therapy as well as the cognitive preparation arguments that the therapist made at the end of session 3. Finally, instructions are given for conducting exposure practices.

Process

At the beginning of session 4, the therapist confirms that the patient is committed to proceeding with exposure. The patient's FAH and list of avoidance and safety behaviors are then reviewed and expanded. The rationale for ungraded massed exposure is briefly reviewed, and the therapist reminds the patient that the goal for the next two sessions is for the patient to experience anxiety and related sensations to the fullest in a variety of scary situations. To keep anticipatory anxiety from escalating, situations are not specified. The patient is reminded to refrain from using any avoidance or safety behaviors during exposures. He should observe the sensations he experiences and note his thoughts but should refrain from restructuring his thoughts until *after* the exposure. The therapist also informs the patient that s/he will talk to him only as needed during exposures, so as not to serve as a distraction. Exposure then begins.

Exposures are conducted similarly during sessions 4 and 5, the primary difference being the amount of therapist accompaniment that is provided (typically 4–6 hours the first day and 2–4 hours the second day). The patient's FAH and list of avoidance and safety behaviors are used as guides for planning exposures. In the beginning, the therapist chooses tasks that leave the patient little opportunity for avoidance (e.g., taking the patient on a non-stop elevator or a non-stop bus). To make avoidance more difficult, means of escape are removed to the extent possible (e.g., money, car keys, or cellular phone taken away), along with all other safety objects. In addition, the therapist uses commands rather than questions (e.g., "Please step into the elevator" rather than "Are you ready to step into the elevator?"). As soon as the patient is able to do tasks this way, sensation-induction procedures are incorporated, to maximize scary sensations (e.g., the patient is instructed to hyperventilate while on the subway train). A concerted effort is made to get the patient to the top of his FAH by the first exposure day.

During exposures, the therapist obtains periodic SUDS ratings, so that habituation can be monitored. One of the most challenging tasks for the therapist is to recognize subtle avoidance and safety behaviors that may interfere with habituation (e.g., patient's standing by the door of the subway train for easy exit, unnecessarily holding on, or looking at the floor or at a friendly face). These behaviors are pointed out to the patient and he is instructed to stop them. In addition, after each exposure, the patient is asked whether he did anything to reduce his anxiety. After each task, the patient's experiences are briefly discussed and processed. Unless the patient was unable to complete the task, this should be kept to a minimum, so as not to take time from exposures.

Therapist accompaniment is faded out as soon as the patient has done a task with the therapist. At first, the therapist may just withdraw from sight, and then move to a greater distance. Again, this is done initially in situations that would be difficult for the patient to escape. For example, a patient may be left in a shopping mall for a specified period of time without any money or car keys. Later, when the therapist is confident of the patient's ability to follow through, more complex tasks are assigned (e.g., sending the patient on an errand or trip). This is particularly the case during session 5. Because the patient will be assigned to continue exposures on his own over the weekend, he must be able to work independently by then.

At the conclusion of session 5, the therapist assists the patient to develop an exposure plan for the weekend. The patient is also given the final installment of the workbook (covering relapse prevention), but is instructed not to read it before Sunday evening.

Josh's Fourth Session

Josh decided to continue treatment and brought his FAH and list of avoidance and safety behaviors. Driving on unknown roads and on wide-open highways with several lanes was most anxiety provoking for him (SUDS = 8), followed by flying and being in large open spaces (SUDS = 7). Crossing bridges and being in unfamiliar places also were rated as very anxiety provoking (SUDS = 6), while attending church services was rated lower (SUDS = 4).

The therapist decided to begin by having Josh drive on wide-open highways to an unfamiliar place. En route to the car rental office, they passed the Prudential Tower (a 52-story building with a restaurant at the top), and Josh commented that he would never be able to get up to that. The therapist decided to postpone the highway driving and take Josh up. He had little difficulty entering or ascending in the elevator; however, he experienced a strong anxiety reaction when it arrived at the 52nd floor and the doors opened. He retreated to a back corner of the elevator, shaking, and would not disembark. The therapist strongly encouraged Josh to face his fear.

THERAPIST: Please step out of the elevator.

JOSH: [No response. He looks at the floor and assumes a body position that makes him feel more stable (i.e., crouches slightly and widens his stance).]

T: [In a firm voice] Please step out of the elevator now. The longer you wait, the more difficult it will get. Step out now.

J: [He timidly steps out of the elevator but continues to crouch and to look at the floor.]

T: Very good. Now, I want you to stand up and face me. [She gives him her hands and helps him up. He is now standing straight but is still looking at the floor.] Good, now elevate your eyes. Look at me.

J: [He looks at her and then over her shoulder, where windows can be seen. He realizes how high he is.] Oh my God! [He lowers his eyes immediately.]

T: [Gently lifting his chin] Don't avoid it. Look at the windows. Let your anxiety wash over you. It won't hurt you. See how high up you are! What sensations are you experiencing?

J: I feel dizzy and lightheaded. I feel faint and unstable. Shaky. I might vomit.

T: That's great. You are experiencing pretty much all of your typical sensations. Super. Now focus on each of those sensations. How intense are they? Where exactly do you feel them?

J: My legs are wobbly. I think that's what I meant by "shaky." That's an 8. My head— whoa! everything is spinning. It is all over my head. That's an 8, too. My stomach feels like a rock, maybe a 6.

T: Very good. You are doing great.

J: [He begins to hold on to the wall.]

T: Don't hold on to the wall. That's a safety behavior. Don't do anything to protect yourself. Feel the sensations fully. Keep focusing on them. They are a normal part of your fear reaction, and they will go away on their own if you let them.

Josh stood there looking toward the windows for another 10 minutes, during which time most of his sensations gradually abated. The therapist then told him to walk up to the windows and around the perimeter of the restaurant. As soon as his symptoms abated, she asked him to hyperventilate and spin in place, to increase his symptoms of dizziness. Josh complied. After 45 minutes of repeated hyperventilation and spinning and looking out the windows, he reported that he no longer felt afraid, despite feeling completely dizzy. Josh and his therapist then left the Prudential Tower and rented a car.

The therapist had Josh drive to Cape Cod on a highway that ran through many open areas and crossed several bridges. To increase his symptoms, she had him close the windows and turn the heat on full. Crossing the first bridge caused Josh considerable anxiety (SUDS = 7). The therapist had him repeatedly recross it (six times), until his anxiety decreased to a 3. The Sagamore bridge was higher and again provoked a fear reaction, but Josh habituated more quickly this time (after only four crossings). The therapist then had Josh cross it on foot, first with her along and then alone, and this caused a full-blown panic attack. Josh walked the bridge twice more, and was able to hyperventilate and spin while he was on the bridge. Subsequent driving over the bridge did not cause anxiety. Josh went home exhausted, but very pleased.

Josh's Fifth Session

During the second exposure day, Josh drove his therapist to Maine, approximately two hours from Boston. The numerous open spaces, bridges, and high places they encountered en route were used as opportunities for exposure. By the end of the day, Josh was entering situations alone and doing everything he could to maximize scary sensations. He felt triumphant and ready to work on his own. Josh returned to the treatment facility, and his therapist assisted him to develop an exposure plan for the weekend. It included returning to the top of the Prudential Tower, driving to an unfamiliar area in Rhode Island, taking the ferry to Martha's Vineyard, exploring the island (in particular, searching out open spaces and high places), attending church services on Sunday morning and afternoon, and driving to an unfamiliar place in western Massachusetts.

Session 6

Content

The primary goal of this final session is to assist the patient to design a personal program for continuing exposures at home and handling difficult times ahead. The workbook reading begins with a review of the three maintaining mechanisms of panic disorder, and the patient is asked to rate the extent to which each is still operative for him. He is then urged to use these ratings to plan continued practices in the months ahead. The patient is advised that symptoms naturally fluctuate over time (e.g., during periods of stress) and that, although this may be scary, it does not imply he has experienced a "relapse." Instead, periods of exacerbation should be anticipated and should be viewed as calls and opportunities for reapplication of the skills learned during treatment. As homework, the patient is asked to make a list of stressful situations he anticipates in the near future and a plan for responding to them.

Process

The therapist begins the session by reviewing the exposures the patient experienced over the weekend and providing praise and suggestions as appropriate. The reading and homework assignments are then reviewed. The patient is assisted to work on his plans for continued skills practices (based on his ratings of needs) and for dealing with anticipated stressors and symptom increases. In doing this, the therapist may provide suggestions as to general stress management skills (e.g., problem solving, time management, communication, and relaxation) that might be useful.

Josh's Sixth Session

When Josh and his therapist reconvened on Monday for the last session, he reported that he had completed all planned exposures with only mild anxiety. He was ecstatic about his accomplishments and said his wife and family were as well. The therapist reviewed Josh's ratings of skills in need of continued practice and assisted him to develop an exposure plan for the coming week at home. The plan included repeatedly crossing a long and high bridge that leads into his town, going to the top floor of a television tower, driving to his parents' house, and visiting his grandparents who live in a different state. Josh's list of potential stressful events was then reviewed. The main one was worry about the health of his daughter, who was born with a heart defect and had undergone surgery. The therapist assisted Josh to examine how that worry might place him at increased risk of panic attacks and a possible relapse. They briefly discussed some skills, including problem-solving and communication skills, to help him cope with the worry. When Josh left, he was expressing excitement and curiosity about the flight back home.

Quantitative Measures and Posttreatment Follow-up

Figure 4.3 and 4.4 show data from several measures obtained during Josh's treatment and at six-month follow-up. As can be seen, treatment gains were maintained and in some cases

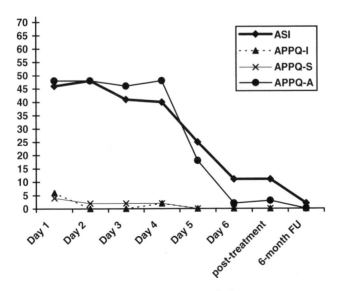

Figure 4.3   Josh's questionnaire data before, during and after treatment. ASI: Anxiety Sensitivity Index (0–64); APPQ-I: Albany Panic and Phobia Questionnaire-Interoceptive Scale (0–64); APPQ-S: Albany Panic and Phobia Questionnaire-Social Phobia Scale (0–64); APPQ-A: Albany Panic and Phobia Questionnaire-Agoraphobia Scale (0–72); 6-month FU: 6-month follow up time point

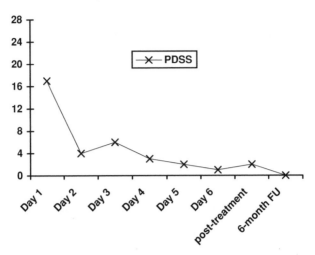

Figure 4.4 Clinician-rated Panic Disorder Severity Scale (PDSS) before, during and after treatment (PDSS scores can range from 0 to 28)

extended during the follow-up period. The structured diagnostic interview was readministered at the six-month follow-up, and Josh no longer met criteria for panic disorder or agoraphobia.

SUMMARY

The present chapter illustrated a brief cognitive-behaviour therapy approach to treat panic disorder with moderate to severe agoraphobia. It was developed in an attempt to combine active ingredients of existing scientific therapies for PDA. The treatment was described, and differences from as well as similarities to traditional CBT were pointed out. A case study demonstrated the clinical application of treatment skills.

The initial results of this treatment format are promising, and short-term follow-up assessments (1–6 months) show maintenance of improvement (Baker et al., 1999; Heinrichs et al., 2000; Spiegel & Barlow, 2000). Further efficacy research is currently underway, particularly in regard to longer-term maintenance of treatment gains.

REFERENCES

American Psychiatric Association (1998). Practice guideline for the treatment of patients with panic disorder. *American Journal of Psychiatry*, **155** *(Suppl. 5)*, 1–34.
American Psychological Association (1993, October). *Task Force on Promotion and Dissemination of Psychological Procedures. A report to the Division 12 Board.* Washington, DC: Author.
Baker, S. L., Spiegel, D. A., & Barlow, D. H. (1999, August). Two-week cognitive behavioral treatment of severe agoraphobia: A case study. Poster presented at the Annual Meeting of the American Psychological Association, Boston, MA.
Barlow, D. H., & Craske, M. G. (2000). *Mastery of your anxiety and panic, Third edition (MAP-3), Client workbook for anxiety and panic.* San Antonio, TX: Graywind Publications Incorporated/The Psychological Corporation.

Clark, D. M., Salkovskis, P. M., Hackmann, A., Wells, A., Ludgate, J., & Gelder, M. (1999). Brief cognitive therapy for panic disorder: A randomized controlled trial. *Journal of Consulting and Clinical Psychology*, **67**, 583–589.

Côté, G., Gauthier, J., Laberge, B., Cormier, H. J., & Plamondon, J. (1994). Reduced therapist contact in the cognitive behavioral treatment of panic disorder. *Behavior Therapy*, **25**, 123–145.

Craske, M. G., & Barlow, D. H. (2000). *Mastery of your anxiety and panic, Third edition (MAP-3), Client workbook for agoraphobia*. San Antonio, TX: Graywind Publications Incorporated/The Psychological Corporation.

Craske, M. G., Rowe, M., Lewin, M., & Noriega-Dimitri, R. (1997). Interoceptive exposure versus breathing retraining within cognitive-behavioural therapy for panic disorder with agoraphobia. *British Journal of Clinical Psychology*, **36**, 85–99.

Di Nardo, P. A., Brown, T. A., & Barlow, D. H. (1994). *The Anxiety Disorders Interview Schedule for DSM-IV: Lifetime Version (ADIS-IV-L)*. Albany, NY: Graywind Publications.

Ehlers, A., Fiegenbaum, W., Florin, I., & Margraf, J. (1995, July). *Efficacy of exposure in vivo in panic disorder with agoraphobia in a clinical setting*. Paper presented at the World Congress of Behavioural and Cognitive Therapies, Copenhagen, Denmark.

Feldman, J. M., Giardino, N. D., & Lehrer, P. M. (2000). Asthma and panic disorder. In D. I. Mostofsky & D. H. Barlow (Eds.), *The management of stress and anxiety in medical disorders (pp. 220–239)*. Boston, MA: Allyn and Bacon.

Fiegenbaum, W. (1988). Long-term efficacy of ungraded versus graded massed exposure in agora-phobics. In I. Hand & H. Wittchen (Eds.), *Panic and phobias: Treatments and variables affecting course and outcome* (pp. 83–88). Berlin: Springer-Verlag.

Fiegenbaum, W., & Tuschen, B. (1996). Reizkonfrontation [Cue exposure]. In J. Margraf (Ed.), *Lehrbuch der Verhaltenstherapie (Kap. 21)* [Handbook of behavior therapy (Ch. 21)]. Berlin: Springer.

Hahlweg, K., Fiegenbaum, W., Frank, H., Schroeder, B., & von Witzleber, 1. (2001). Short-and long-term effectiveness of an empirically supported treatment for agoraphobia. *Journal of Consulting and Clinical Psychology*, **69**, 375–382.

Hecker, J. E., Losee, M. C., Fritzler, B. K., & Fink, C. M. (1996). Self-directed versus therapist-directed cognitive-behavioral treatment for panic disorder. *Journal of Anxiety Disorders*, **10**, 253–265.

Heinrichs, N., Baker, S. L., & Spiegel, D. A (2000, November). *Intensive sensation focused treatment for panic disorder with agoraphobia*. Poster presented at the annual conference of the Association of Advancement of Behavior Therapy, New Orleans.

Hofmann, S. G., & Barlow, D. H. (1999). The costs of anxiety disorders: Implications for psychosocial interventions. In N. E. Miller & K. M. Magruder (Eds.), *Cost-effectiveness of psychotherapy* (pp. 224–234). New York, NY: Oxford University Press.

Hofmann, S. G., Bufka, L. F., & Barlow, D. H. (1999). Panic provocation procedures in the treatment of panic disorder: Early perspectives and case studies. *Behavior Therapy*, **30**, 305–317.

Hofmann, S. G., & Spiegel, D. A. (1999). Panic control treatment and its application. *Journal of Psychotherapy Practice and Research*, **8**, 3–11.

Hofmann, S. G., Spiegel, D. A., Vitali, A., Baker, S. L., & Barlow, D. H. (1996). *Ungraded massed exposure (flooding) for agoraphobia: Treatment manual*. Unpublished manuscript. Boston: Boston University.

Howard, K. I., Kopta, S. M., Krause, M. S., & Orlinski, D. E. (1986). The dose-effect relationship in psychotherapy. *American Psychologist*, **41**, 159–164.

Keller, M. B., Yonkers, K. A., Warshaw, M. G., Pratt, L. A., Golan, J., Mathews, A. O., White, K., Swots, A., Reich, J., & Lavori, P. (1994). Remission and relapse in subjects with panic disorder and panic with agoraphobia: A prospective short-interval naturalistic follow-up. *Journal of Nervous and Mental Disease*, **182**, 290–296.

Kessler, R. C., McGonagle, K. A., & Zhao, S. (1994). Lifetime and 12-month prevalence of DSM-III-R psychiatric disorders in the United States: results from the national comorbidity survey. *Archives of General Psychiatry*, **51**, 8–19.

Klerman, G. L., Weissman, M. M., Ouellette, R., Johnson, J., & Greenwald, S. (1991). Panic attacks in the community: social morbidity and health care utilization, *Journal of the American Medical Association*, **265**, 742–746.

Marks, I. M., Swinson, R. P., Basoglu, M., Kuch, K., Noshirvani, H., O'Sullivan, G., Lelliott, P. T., Kirby, M., McNamee, G., Sengun, S., & Wickwire, K. (1993). Alprazolam and exposure alone and combined in panic disorder with agoraphobia: A controlled study in London and Toronto. *British Journal of Psychiatry*, **162**, 776–787.

Otto, M. W., Pollack, M. H., & Sabatino, S. A. (1996). Maintenance and remission following cognitive behavior therapy for panic disorder: Possible deleterious effects of concurrent medication treatment. *Behavior Therapy*, **27**, 473–482.

Rijken, H., Kraimaat, F., de Ruiter, C., & Garssen, B. (1992). A follow-up study on short-term treatment of agoraphobia. *Behaviour Research and Therapy*, **30**, 63–66.

Robins, L. N., & Regier, D. A. (Eds.) (1991). *Psychiatric disorders in America: the epidemiologic catchment area study*. New York: Free Press.

Sokol, L., Beck, A. T., Greenberg, R. L., Berchik, R., & Wright, F. D. (1989). Cognitive therapy of panic disorder: A nonpharmacological alternative. *Journal of Nervous and Mental Disease*, **177**, 711–716.

Spiegel, D. A. *Sensation-focused treatment for panic disorder with agoraphobia: Patient workbook*. Manuscript submitted for publication.

Spiegel, D. A., & Baker, S. L. *Sensation-focused treatment for panic disorder with agoraphobia: Therapist guide*. Manuscript submitted for publication.

Spiegel, D. A., & Barlow, D. H. (2000). *8-Day treatment of panic disorder with moderate to severe agoraphobia: Preliminary outcome data*. Poster presented at Annual Conference of the Association for Advancement of Behavior Therapy, New Orleans.

Turovsky, J., Carter, M. M., Korotitsch, W. J., & Barlow, D. H. (1994, November). *The role of in vivo exposure in cognitive behavioral couples group treatment of panic disorder*. Paper presented at the meeting of the Association for Advancement of Behavior Therapy, San Diego, CA.

Vitali, A. E., Barlow, D. H., Spiegel, D. A., Detweiler, M. F., Turovsky, J., & Carter, M. (1996, March). *The effect of exposure instructions on the outcome of cognitive behavioral therapy for panic disorder*. Poster presentation at the meeting of the Anxiety Disorders Association of America, Orlando, Florida.

CHAPTER 5

Brief Cognitive Behavioral Intervention for Anger

Raymond W. Novaco and **Kelly L. Jarvis**
University of California, Irvine, CA, USA

The treatment of anger is a challenging clinical enterprise. This turbulent emotion, ubiquitous in everyday life, is a feature of a wide range of clinical disorders. It is commonly observed in various personality, psychosomatic, and conduct disorders; in schizophrenia; in bipolar mood disorders; in organic brain disorders; in impulse control dysfunctions; and in a variety of conditions resulting from trauma. The central problematic characteristic of anger in the context of such clinical conditions is that it is "dysregulated"—that is, its activation, expression, and effects occur without appropriate controls. Because anger can be co-mingled with many other clinical problems, getting leverage for therapeutic change can be an elusive goal. Because anger activation is thought to be a precursor of aggressive behavior, it may easily be viewed as a salient clinical need, while at the same time be unsettling for mental health professionals to engage as a treatment focus.

The involvement of anger in clinical disorders is what elicits our attention here, but we cannot lose sight of the fact that anger is a functional part of everyday life. As a normal human emotion, anger has considerable adaptive value, although there are sociocultural variations in the acceptability of its expression and the form that such expression takes. In the face of adversity, it can mobilize psychological resources, energize behaviors for corrective action, and facilitate perseverance. Anger serves as a guardian to self-esteem, operates as a means of communicating negative sentiment, potentiates the ability to redress grievances, and boosts determination to overcome obstacles to our happiness and aspirations. Like aggressive behavior, anger has functional value for survival. In attempting to provide therapy for anger problems, clinicians must always be mindful of this functionality, as it has paramount significance for treatment engagement.

Mental health professionals who work in hospital or community settings should find value in providing brief psychotherapy for anger, not only because it is a significant activator of violent behavior but also because it is evoked by many stress-related conditions and may represent a significant breakdown in a person's capacity to cope. Recurrent anger is often a product of troubled life histories and easily becomes part of a dysfunctional style of dealing with life's challenges. People who are beset with anger have difficulties in personal relationships, in work performance, and in maintaining optimal physical health. The degree

Handbook of Brief Cognitive Behaviour Therapy. Edited by Frank W. Bond and Windy Dryden.
© 2002 John Wiley & Sons, Ltd. ISBN 0-470-02132-2.

and scope of the impairment to health and psychosocial adjustment associated with anger dysregulation, as well as the presence of comorbid problem conditions, will determine whether or not anger treatment should be conducted in a "brief" format. However, significant gains have been achieved in a number of studies with cognitive behavioral therapy (CBT) for anger implemented in 6–12 sessions, varying with problem severity. In this chapter, we will delineate the conditions for utilizing brief CBT for anger problems and present the key components of the intervention. Case illustrations will be given, and procedures for assessment will be described. Key aspects of gaining leverage for therapeutic change with clients who are reluctant or ambivalent about parting with their anger coping styles will be discussed.

ANGER AS A PROBLEM CONDITION

The adaptive value of anger is unmistakable. It is well known that anger has utility for communicating threat (Ekman & Davidson, 1994), potentiating aggression towards meeting threat (Cannon, 1932; Bandura, 1972), and providing information for identifying priorities and expectations (Schwarz & Clore, 1988). Yet, there are numerous interpersonal and societal problems that result from this emotion and the violence that it subtends (Novaco, 1986). Apart from its connection with aggressive behavior, anger dysregulation has been shown to have significant bearing on medical disorders. Several decades of research have established the link between anger, hypertension, and coronary disease (Chesney & Rosenman, 1985; Diamond, 1982; Dembroski et al., 1985; Friedman, 1992; Johnson, 1990; Siegman & Smith, 1994; Williams & Williams, 1993). Robins & Novaco (2000) have argued that anger control is a health promotional mechanism.

Enthusiasm for the study of anger was very much enhanced by this relatively recent identification with mortality associated with medical disorders. This is ironic, because people have been dying as a result of anger and hostility for a rather long time, mostly, though, from anger-induced uncivilized behavior, as opposed to anger-induced internal disease processes. However, as clientele shifted from the socially less esteemed (e.g., forensic populations) to some very desirable groups (e.g., corporate executives) that could be assessed and treated in medico-laboratory settings, the popularity of anger research grew exponentially.

Interest in anger was expanded by the medical relevance theme, but the women's movement for equal opportunity also provided a boost, which occurred on several fronts. Credence was given to women's anger, both in the legitimization of their discontent with social inequality and in breaking the social stereotype of anger as a male province. In the latter regard, anger became an equal-opportunity product. It was found that women get angry just as often as men, and with as much intensity. Attention was also given to domestic violence and its prevalence. In that domain, anger is a significant activator or correlate of spousal abuse and also bears on what happens to children who witness domestic violence or are victimized by it, a subject that we discuss later. Thus, anger received increased recognition in conjunction with the women's movement, but anger activation has mixed valuation in that societal change context.

The problem designate status of anger is less than straightforward. It would be more than odd to pathologize an emotional state that has important energizing and potentiating functions. Given that anger is a normal human emotion, ascertaining whether a person's anger experiences constitute a psychological problem condition hinges on the defining parameters. Frequency, intensity, duration, and mode of expression comprise a set of such parameters, about which we will elaborate below, as this bears on the applicability of brief CBT.

The judgment of whether someone has an "anger problem" is dependent on the audience and its sociocultural context. Nevertheless, how often someone becomes angry, the degree of anger experienced, how long the arousal lasts, and behavior when angry are dimensions by which a person's anger response patterns can be gauged to constitute a problem condition. Because information about anger reactions is very typically obtained from self-report, we must recognize at least two types of biases, *proximity* and *reactivity,* that bear on how such reports about anger experiences are to be appraised.

Proximity Bias

When people report anger experiences, they most typically give accounts of things that have "happened to them." For the most part, they describe events physically and temporally proximate to the anger arousal. As a rule, they provide accounts of provocations ascribed to events in the immediate situation of the anger experience. The provocation sources are ordinarily identified as the aversive behavior of others, such as insults, unfair treatments, or deliberate thwartings. Anger is prototypically experienced as a justified response to some "wrong" that has been done, portrayed in the telling as being something about which anger is quite fitting. Thus, anger accounts can be seen to have a "proximity bias" (Novaco, 1993).

Psychological investigators and clinicians alike have been seduced to attend to anger incident accounts. Clinicians, of course, are pressed with the situational imperative of needing to listen to a client who wants to talk. Indeed, angry people want to be heard. Researchers, particularly when focused on finding main effects rather than higher-order interactions, obtain anger self-reports based on daily diary data or classifications of open-ended descriptions, whereby respondents confine their account of the anger instigation to proximate situations. Assigning the causes of anger to discrete occurrences is uniformly the case in the community and student studies by Averill (1982), the autobiographical narrative studies by Baumeister et al. (1990), and the college student questionnaire studies of Ben-Zur & Breznitz (1991) and Harris (1993). Recently, Kassinove et al. (1997) applied this same discrete-event, main-effects conception in a cross-cultural study.

The response to the question, "What makes you angry?", hinges on self-monitoring proficiencies and is often based on intuitions. Precisely because getting angry involves a loss in self-monitoring capacity, people are neither good nor objective observers when they are angry; and because anger is very much a blaming reaction, people are inclined to point. Inspecting any particular episode, the immediate "causes" of the anger are readily identified and ascribed to be the responsible factors. For example, a person might report that he became angry *because* "the dog's barking kept me from sleeping," "that stupid driver wouldn't let me pass," or "that louse tried to break in the line." Because the anger is contiguous with particular local stimuli that are aversive, it is viewed as being a product of them. People are inclined to attribute the causes of their anger to personal, stable, and controllable aspects of another person's behavior.

Far less commonly do people disaggregate their anger experiences into multicausal origins, some of which may originate from prior, remote events and ambient circumstances, rather than from acute, proximal events. In so many instances, anger seems to be a highly automatized response to life stressors. Disturbances, which may or may not have involved anger at the outset, leave residues that linger but are not readily recognized. Moreover, people do not give attentional priority to prevailing contextual conditions, such as work pressures or family strains, that operate as a backdrop to identified provocations. Nor do people recognize that their cultivated worldview provides the landscape for their anger. People who are chronically angry are inclined to perceive malevolent intent in the behavior of others. Such cognitive myopia leads to the sense that anger is uncontrollable and inevitable. Neither is true, given people's long-term control over their life circumstances and their cognitive schemas.

Corresponding to these routine accounts of anger, given by both distressed clients and research study participants, the importance of *attributions* in defining anger has been emphasized by theorists, researchers, and clinicians. Inferences about responsibility are viewed by attribution theorists (e.g., Weiner, 1995) as the generators of anger. While attributions about aversive experiences being rooted in the internal, stable, and controllable elements of another person's behavior have considerable bearing on anger reactions, the analysis remains truncated in range. To be sure, anger is cognitively determined; but anger reactions are primed, shaped, and extended as a function of interconnected networks of provoking and inhibitory factors *embedded* or nested within overlapping physical and social environments, such as the work setting, the work organization, the regional economy, and the sociocultural value structure.

Importantly, anger determinants, anger experiences, and anger sequelae are reciprocally influenced. For example, in a coercive family system, parental anger arises during disciplinary confrontations as an effort to control a child's antagonistic behavior. The parent's display of anger not only prompts further antagonistic behavior by the child but also models anger as a response to noncompliance or being thwarted, thus reinforcing the coercive character of the milieu. Severe anger episodes that involve abusive behavior toward the child produce trauma that can lead to anger being triggered as an automatic response to perceived threat. The link between anger and trauma cuts across forms of traumatic exposure and disorders produced by trauma (Novaco & Chemtob, 1998, 2002). Overall, the common inclination to view anger as a reaction to proximate events is substantially misguided.

Reactivity Bias

In many professional practice and research settings, anger assessment is subject to reactivity as a threat to internal validity. This is particularly the case in the forensic context, but it applies to any setting where the person may be sensitive to audience reaction to anger reports. Reactivity pertains to responses obtained in an assessment procedure that are reactions by persons to their inferences about the test situation, rather than to the explicit elements of the testing—i.e., the person is inclined to produce anger reports in anticipation of what those test responses will mean to some audience. People who are in forensic or other custodial settings have a tendency to "mask" their anger, as they are unlikely to perceive gain in disclosing it. This has important implications for assessing anger in conjunction with evaluating the effectiveness of intervention. Because of both reactivity and treatment resistance (see discussion below), people with anger difficulties will often underreport anger at the outset, thereby making it quite difficult to document treatment gain if the outcome assessment design is only pre-post and has limited measures.

There are multiple sources of reactivity bias in anger assessment. People who have long-standing anger difficulties are often characterized by suspiciousness and distrust, such being the products of troubled life histories. Whoever administers an assessment procedure inquiring about anger may be viewed (very likely, in a forensic setting) as the representative of a threatening system and will thus receive guarded responses. Importantly, the psychosocial symbolism associated with anger (particularly its boiling/eruptive and savage/nonrational aspects) deter a person from disclosing anger experiences and the actions to which anger might dispose them. Moreover, anger can be a protected part of the person, centrally involving matters of self-worth, and is thus not readily revealed or surrendered. As a patient on the anger project at the State Hospital in Scotland (cf. Renwick et al., 1997) once commented in reflecting about life in the institution, "All you've got is your anger." Disclosing anger may be perceived by the subject to carry the psychological cost of losing power and what may be for them the last remaining symbol of personal freedom and personal worth.

We have discussed these limitations in people's accounts of anger experiences to provide a backdrop for clinical judgment about anger problem severity based on client self-reports. In ascertaining the appropriateness of brief CBT anger treatment, the parameters of frequency, intensity, duration, and mode of expression are useful dimensions.

ANGER PARAMETERS

Anger Frequency

How often people get angry surely varies culturally, but there are few data in this regard outside North American samples. The study of normative patterns of anger began with the research by G. Stanley Hall (1899) and was most extensively undertaken by Averill (1982). A variety of small sample studies were conducted over the decades between these studies and several thereafter. On average, in this research, people have reported becoming angry two or three times per week. The data reported in the study by Kassinove et al. (1997), which involved Russian (St. Petersburg) and American (New York) participants, show a bimodal distribution across samples, with 25% reporting anger occurring a few days a week and 33% less than once a week (but more than once a month). The Americans were significantly higher in anger frequency than the Russians, as reflected in 11% of the former reporting getting angry once a day or more, whereas this was the case for only 3% for the latter. Kassinove et al. found no gender differences in anger frequency, and this is a common finding.

To look further into the question of anger frequency, we examined data obtained by the US General Social Survey (Davis & Smith, 1996), available as an electronic database. When 634 men and 817 women were asked, "On how many days in the past seven days have you felt angry at someone?", 63.4% of the sample reported that they had become angry in the previous week, with 20.3% stating that they were angry on three or more days. No significant differences were found with regard to gender, as males and females were equally likely to say that they had felt anger in the past week. Similar to what is routinely found in psychological research with regard to aggressive behavior, age was inversely correlated with frequency of anger. If we consider "frequent anger" to be getting angry on three or more days in a week, people under 30 were the most likely to report this (26.7%), whereas those over 64 were least likely (9.5%) to do so. Across age groupings, the chi-square test was statistically significant; $\chi^2(4) = 85.57$, $p < 0.001$. Curiously, higher income was associated with a greater likelihood of reporting more frequent anger.

In would seem reasonable, then, to consider someone who reports becoming angry every day to be high in anger frequency, if these largely US data are a guide. But there are substantial cultural variations to be taken into account. In the personal experience of the authors, daily anger episodes are quite common in Rome and Naples, whereas becoming angry is relatively rare in China. Most generally, it would be safe to say that a client who reports getting angry two or three times a day can be considered high in anger frequency.

Anger Intensity

Ratings of anger intensity are a typical feature of anger psychometrics, such as Spielberger's (1988) State Trait Anger Expression Inventory (STAXI) and the Novaco Provocation Inventory (NPI) (Novaco, 1983). It is assumed that higher intensity ratings are indicative of greater disturbance, because the ratings are summed across items. Indeed, the intensity dimension functions as a qualitative discrimination, because we partly judge that we are *angry*, as opposed to being "upset," "bothered," or "annoyed," by virtue of the affect intensity. Unlike frequency, degree of intensity is much more clearly indicative of dysfunction, because physiological arousal is an intrinsic element. It is well established scientifically that high arousal disrupts performance, especially mental processes involved in complex tasks. In addition to having cognitive interference effects, high intensity anger leads to impulsive behavior, as it overrides inhibitory controls. People often judge their anger intensity from their behavior in an anger episode, although this is more the case for men than for women (Frost & Averill, 1982).

In a study of the US General Social Survey data (Davis & Smith, 1996), those who had indicated that they had become angry in the previous month ($N = 1115$; 477 males and 638 females) were asked, "How intense would you say your anger or irritation was?" and were asked to rate their anger on a scale from 0 to 10. Similar to what was found for frequency, anger intensity was inversely related to age: $\chi^2(4) = 24.94$, $p < .001$. However, there were gender differences in intensity. Women (64.7%) were more likely than men (55.1%) to rate their anger at a level of 6 or above, but this is at variance with the absence of gender differences in many studies. For example, Kassinove et al. (1997) found no gender differences in anger intensity in either the US or Russian samples.

Trauma populations are likely to manifest anger difficulties, and, pertinent to anger intensity and gender, a large study in Britain concerning people involved in a motor vehicle accident was conducted with regard to post-traumatic stress disorder (PTSD) by Ehlers et al. (1998). They assessed 967 patients (521 men and 446 women) shortly after the accident, and then again at three months and at one year. No differences were found between men and women at any of the assessments. Women were as likely as men to give "very angry" or "extremely angry" self-ratings, which, when combined, constituted 22.1% of the men and 25.1% of the women at the initial assessment (A. Ehlers, personal communication, February 11 and 18, 1999). Although it has often been found that women and men experience anger at comparable levels of intensity, men are more inclined to gauge anger intensity from their behavior, while women are more inclined to weigh anger duration in judging their anger intensity (Frost & Averill, 1982).

Duration

For a number of reasons, the intensity of anger can be expected to influence anger duration: (a) greater elevation in physiological arousal is associated with longer time for recovery to baseline; (b) circumstances that produce strong anger can escalate and extend as a product of angry behavior; and (c) high anger results from matters having substantial significance for the person, and these effects are likely to linger and not be resolved promptly—this leads to rumination about the provoking circumstances that prolongs anger and can revivify it.

There is considerable intersubjective variability in the duration of anger episodes, both within and across studies. For example, early research by Gates (1926) and Melzer (1933) found average durations of 15–20 minutes. Several studies in Averill's (1982) monograph found the median duration to be about one hour. In the Kassinove et al. (1997) study, 39% of the US sample and 53% of the Russian sample reported anger duration of 30 minutes or less. Curiously, 31% and 20% of the US and Russian samples, respectively, reported anger duration of a full day or more. Similarly, Averill (1982) had found a 25% rate of endorsement for anger duration of one day or more. When people report anger for such long periods, it cannot be interpreted straightforwardly, because it is doubtful that arousal and affect are present continuously throughout the interval. It is more likely that the basis for this duration estimate is that thoughts about the anger incident have resurfaced throughout the day.

Rumination is a problematic feature of anger reactions. In the US General Social Survey (Davis & Smith, 1996), the duration of the anger episode was not assessed, but the survey did ask about anger being reactivated by thoughts ($N = 943$; 415 males, 528 females). Women (17.2%) were more likely than men (11.8%) to report thinking about the anger situation "very often"—$\chi^2(2) = 6.1$, $p < .05$—but there were no differences between genders in the likelihood of giving thought to revenge. Thoughts of revenge decline significantly with age.

The prolongation of anger arousal has several problematic consequences. First, blood pressure is significantly affected by prolonged anger and its nonexpression, and this is a substantial factor in essential hypertension (Johnson, 1990). Secondly, when anger arousal does not return to baseline, there are likely to be "excitation transfer" effects, whereby the undissipated arousal adds to arousal activation from new sources and raises the probability of aggressive behavior (Zillmann & Bryant, 1974). Third, rumination about anger incidents interferes with optimal functioning and lessens positive inputs that fortify the self.

Mode of Expression

The behavioral manifestation of anger is the feature having greatest societal import. Most problematically, anger impels both verbal and physical aggression. Verbal aggression pertains to threatening, abusive, and derogatory statements, the common denominator of which is to produce distress in the target person. Physical aggression, which is overt behavior intended to produce harm or damage, may be either directed at the provoking person or displaced to a substitute target. Anger can also motivate "passive" aggression, which is harm-doing behavior in a disguised form—pretended congeniality, deliberate interpersonal coldness, or neglect, with the intention of producing distress in the target person. In addition to these forms of harm-intended behavior, anger may be expressed in constructively minded problem-solving behavior or be given safe ventilation.

Aggressive behavior generally has a low base rate, except in the home and in psychiatric and correctional institutions. In the US General Social Survey data, in response to the question "Did you yell or hit something to let out your pent-up feelings?", relatively few of the respondents ($N = 1114$) said yes (7.9%), with males being a bit more so inclined. The relationship with age was curvilinear. Kassinove et al. (1997) found that 11% of the US sample and 8% of the Russian sample either fought or hit the provoking person or hit or destroyed something. Yelling and arguing occurred for 38% of the Americans (New Yorkers) and 22% of the Russians. "Men more often reported that they did fight or hit a person . . . while women were more likely to yell and argue" (p. 314). Unfortunately, Kassinove et al. did not perform cross-tabulations of behavioral expression with status of the target person, but 62% of the US sample and 58% of the Russian sample were reporting an anger episode that involved either someone they knew and liked or someone they loved. Thus, a substantial proportion of the anger events may have been provocations that involved family or intimates.

Domestic violence is a pressing social problem, internationally. The 1996 British Crime Survey estimate for the total number of domestic violence incidents in 1995 was 6.6 million. However, the Home Office definition of domestic violence was broad and included emotional abuse. In the USA, a recent survey jointly sponsored by the National Institute for Justice and the Centers for Disease Control found that 5.9 million physical assaults were perpetrated against women in the 12 months preceding the survey for a representative sample of 8000 women (Tjaden & Thoennes, 1999). The majority of women (64%) who had been victimized by rape, physical assault, or stalking since the age of 18 experienced this at the hands of intimates. Similarly, the Criminal Statistics for England and Wales for 1997 show that 47% of the 224 female homicide victims were killed by partners, whereas only 8% of the 426 male homicide victims were killed by their partners.

Violence victimization has been extensively documented to have a host of adverse short-term and long-term consequences for women (Browne, 1993; Crowell & Burgess, 1996). It is well recognized that severe psychological adjustment difficulties, such as PTSD and major depression, are a common consequence for abused women (e.g., Cascardi et al., 1995; Schlee et al., 1998). It is estimated that at least 3.3 million children in the USA are at risk yearly of exposure to domestic violence (Carlson, 1990; Straus, 1992). The detrimental effects on a child of witnessing violence between parents include traumatization and learning violent behavior as a response to conflict, each of which has long-term consequences for a child's psychological adjustment and well-being. While some have questioned the weight that should be given to anger in understanding the behavior and treatment of batterers (Dobash, 2000), there is sufficient evidence that anger is involved in domestic violence episodes (e.g., Dutton et al., 1994; Dutton et al., 1996).

Insufficient attention, however, has been given to anger sequelea that result from the trauma of domestic violence. We illustrate this with the following two cases in our on-going research with women and their children in domestic violence emergency shelters (refuges):

> Sarah and her only child, 12-year-old Matthew, had recently come to the shelter. Sarah had experienced two abusive relationships—one with her son's father and one with a recent boyfriend. Matthew first witnessed violence during infancy, when his father physically and verbally assaulted his mother. Although he was not directly abused during his childhood and his mother divorced his father before he turned three, Matthew had been physically attacked by his father in his most recent contact with him. Sarah and

Matthew hid from their abuser for years, remaining homeless for over one year, out of fear of being located. Due to this transience, Matthew had been in four different schools in the last year, and his grades were failing. When asked what concerned her the most about her son, Sarah stated that he displayed high levels of anger and thought that the world was out to get him. She felt that he needed to learn how to manage his anger and how to compromise. She feared that he would grow up to be a batterer like his father.

Alison, the mother of six children, was residing in the emergency shelter with her four youngest. Her six-year-old, Joshua, was of particular concern to her. She had been subjected to years of verbal and emotional abuse by her current husband; he would yell at, swear at, insult, fight, and criticize her on a daily basis. The children witnessed these hostile displays and were targets of verbal abuse. Their father would make hurtful comments to all of them. He once told Joshua that he was no longer his father and that the child therefore had no one to protect or to love him. Although Alison and Joshua maintain a good relationship, she is concerned about her son's temper. He gets angry easily, quickly, and frequently, often over trivial things. He yells, throws things, pushes people, and makes mean comments to others. Despite her efforts, Alison has extreme difficulty calming him down once he is agitated.

In the case histories, both Matthew and Joshua are exhibiting anger reactions as products of traumatic violence exposure. The mere exposure of children to domestic violence has a devastating impact on their personal development and social adjustment (Jaffe & Geffner, 1998; Jaffe et al., 1990a; Hurley & Jaffe, 1990; Rosenberg, 1987). Exposure to domestic violence has been found to contribute to children's delinquency (Koski, 1987) and clinical dysfunction (Butterworth & Fulmer, 1991; Jaffe et al., 1990b), to predict child conduct disorders and personality disorders (Fantuzzo et al., 1991; Jouriles et al., 1989), and to lead to symptoms of PTSD (Lehmann, 1997; Silvern & Kaersvang, 1989).

Among the clinical populations for which anger expression is a substantial problem and who tend to have substantial histories of exposure to violent abuse are institutionalized psychiatric patients. For both forensically and civilly committed patients, recurrent anger has been found to be prevalent among 35% of California State Hospital patients, and this has been replicated across years (Novaco, 1994a & 1997) and for a substantial number of male high-security forensic patients in Scotland (Novaco & Renwick, 1998) and male learning-disability forensic patients in Northumberland, England (Novaco & Taylor, 2001). The last two studies did not involve female patients, but the data from Novaco's California State Hospital research, involving staff observational ratings for over 4000 patients in each of six years, show that female patients are significantly more angry and more assaultive in the hospital than are male patients, and patient self-report data are convergent with this generalization. Anyone who has devoted time to the mental health care of long-term institutionalized patients, forensic and nonforensic, knows that those having anger-regulation difficulties typically acquired this problem during a turbulent childhood, lacking supportive attachment relationships and fraught with exposure to toxic socioenvironmental forces that impair healthy development.

Comorbidity Issues

To be sure, the determination of anger problem severity and the clinical needs of patients will hinge on more than their status with regard to this set of anger-response parameters.

Often comorbid with anger problems are conditions such as thought disorder, personality disorder, depression, PTSD, learning disability, head injury, or substance abuse disorder. Cognitive behavioral anger treatment is, principally, an *adjunctive treatment*, not meant to suffice in addressing a client's broader clinical needs. The "brevity" of this adjunctive treatment will then vary as a function of the degree of impairment presented by other clinical conditions within which the anger problem is nested, as well as by the anger frequency, intensity, duration, and mode of expression. We have, however, in the above presentation sought to demarcate the dimensions of anger reactions that provide information about the severity of the anger problem; this has implications for the therapeutic resources needed to remedy the anger dysfunction. To the extent that anger dysregulation—getting angry frequently, being angry at high intensity, staying angry for extended periods, and either expressing anger in aggressive behavior or recurrently suppressing it without acting to resolve conflict situations—constitutes the client's principal problem, CBT anger treatment may very well serve as the prime clinical service provision. Very commonly, though, people having chronic anger problems have multiple clinical needs and characteristically are as opposed to receiving treatment as they are to other overtures to penetrate their personal space.

THE TREATMENT-RESISTANT NATURE OF ANGRY CLIENTS

A pivotal issue in providing therapy for anger is treatment resistance. Angry people have not only adopted a combative style of responding to the shrapnel of everyday existence, but they also use anger to keep others at a distance. The social distancing aspect of anger serves to minimize exposure to threat, defending their vulnerability. This ego-defensive function protects self-worth, but it also reflects high sensitivity to and vigilance against threats, easily triggered by ambiguous cues. High-anger people view others suspiciously and are inclined to be distrustful. Such characteristics do not make for easy development of a therapeutic relationship.

Chronic anger is an obstinate problem by virtue of its instrumentality. Anger has considerable value in dealing with aversive situations, particularly as it imparts a sense of mastery or control. One can overcome constraints and dispatch unwanted others by becoming angry and acting aggressively. Persons who are so disposed are reluctant to relinquish this sense of effectiveness. The propensity to anger reflects a combative orientation in responding to situations of threat and hardship that is not easily surrendered as a learned style of coping. This has important implications for the clinician's presentation of anger treatment (see below).

Angry people are often fiercely resistant to anger treatment. Because anger can mobilize a person's psychological resources, energizing behaviors that take corrective action, the capacity for anger is needed as a survival mechanism. This is especially salient in those whose lives are enshrouded by violence. Yet even for those not immersed in violent subcultures, proposing "anger management" may be viewed disparagingly as an insidious strategy to stifle the individual human personality or to constrain the will to determine one's own destiny. Anger provides personal resilience. It is a guardian of self-esteem, it potentiates the ability to redress grievances, and it can boost determination to overcome obstacles to one's aspirations. In effect, people can remain attached to anger, because it is so very functional.

Dislodging the attachment to anger is a matter of helping the person to see that chronic anger has costs that outweigh the functions that it has been serving.

ANGER COSTS: PROMPTING MOTIVATION FOR TREATMENT

Clients become inclined to engage in treatment when they recognize that the costs of staying the same outweigh the costs of trying to be different. How sensitized clients are to the costs of recurrent anger reactions can be assessed from three lines of inquiry:

1. the degree to which they are aware of personal anger pattern features
2. the degree of investment in anger habits
3. the degree to which clients are troubled by the experiential correlates and social products of their anger reactions.

Awareness of Anger Pattern Features

At the core of anger dysregulation problems is a deficiency in self-monitoring. Those who are recurrently angry have lost regulatory capacity, in part because they have not prioritized attending to their internal states and the consequences of their behavior. Being aware of becoming angry, of the level of anger intensity, of the behavioral routines associated with their anger, and of the instrumentality or gains produced by the routines is fundamental to self-regulation. It is a bit more difficult to see the reciprocity of anger in personal re-lationships and the detrimental effects that anger has on well-being, but some clients will recognize such adverse elements.

Investment in Anger Habits

Reluctance to change follows from strong investment in anger routines. The degree of investment in anger can be detected from the person's inclination to externalize blame, quickness in justification for anger reactions, and belief in the efficacy of anger in responding to interpersonal conflict. Subjects' ability to consider constructive coping alternatives, as well as their inclination to use such alternatives, is also important to consider in assessing investment in anger habits and resistance to change.

Concern About Anger Experiential Correlates

If the person is troubled by states of tension, agitation, and irritability that demarcate anger or the ruminations and preoccupations that accompany anger, the motivation for change is enhanced. More typically, the person might be concerned by the consequences that angry behavior has produced, such as loss of a relationship, judicial system sanctions, or job difficulties. Sensitivity to and regard for disapproval by others is also indicative of the prominence of the need for change. A person's valuation of negative feedback from significant others bears substantially on self-regulation.

PRESENTING THE PROSPECT OF ANGER TREATMENT

If the presentation of "anger control" therapy suggests to clients that their effectance will be jeopardized, as if they would be robbed of their power, then the leverage for treatment is easily undermined. Learning anger control skills must be seen to offer enhancement of effectiveness in handling the stressful and provoking events of daily life and perhaps some particularly adverse, anger-engendering circumstances. It is not uncommon for people to believe that being designated to receive anger-control therapy implies a "badness" in them that needs to be corrected. The self-worth-sustaining function of anger fuels reactance to any treatment overture accompanied by such implication. "Anger management" interventions, too easily and mistakenly, take on a predominately "*corrections*" approach in its outlook on clients (e.g., "they need to take responsibility for their behavior" or "they don't respond well to criticism"), rather than a *therapeutic* one (e.g., "their anger is so intense, it overrides inhibitory control, and they act without pausing to consider the consequences" or "the views they take of others are biased toward confirmation of threat").

Very importantly, "anger control" must be seen to entail a preventive course and an arousal-regulatory core, as well as involve dealing with overt behavioral skills. Clients must learn to ask themselves, not only "What should I do when I get angry?" but "How can I not get angry in the first place; and, if I do get angry, how can I keep the anger at a moderate level of intensity?" They can be helped to see that, whatever they want to accomplish that is lasting and meaningful, uncontrolled anger does not increase its likelihood of attainment. The costs of unregulated anger are the keystone for therapeutic change; but the clinician must recognize that angry clients remain attached to their anger partly because they do not feel safe in examining those costs, and they lack consistent support for being otherwise.

MAINTAINING TREATMENT ENGAGEMENT

Having obtained treatment engagement from a person with anger problems does not secure its unbroken continuance. People with long-standing anger are likely to be short on social supports to bolster self-esteem and to be inclined toward hopelessness. They are also inherently impatient. In addition to being ambivalent about treatment, they may have poorly defined or unrealistic goals for the course of therapy. This leads to frustration when desired treatment effects are not quickly forthcoming. Expecting disappointment, they are inclined to disengage from therapy, the impulse for which may be activated by relatively minor events in their day-to-day lives or in the course of treatment. Because angry people, by their long-standing behavior, increase the probability of exposure to aversive events, the therapist should be prepared for such occasions of client frustration and demoralization.

It is imperative that the clinician be patient and mindful when faced with expressions of frustration or annoyance, viewing this as a manifestation of the clinical problem, and not "taking it personally." Rather than making undue personal attributions about the client's reactions, the therapist can utilize the manifest crisis as an opportunity to teach anger-coping skills. Instead of merely providing reassurance and attempting redirection, the therapist can engage and explore the client's frustration and impatience, thereby teaching how to communicate about anger and how to deal with conflict. Beyond the ordinary inertia impeding change, angry patients may feel hopeless of ever being different, particularly if they have been institutionalized. As a very high-anger patient in one of California's state hospitals once poignantly told the senior author, "I'm poor, and I've got nobody"; similarly, a forensic patient in Scotland, at the start of a group treatment ("anger management," see below), said, "It's taken me a long time to get like this—what is this going to do for me in 12 weeks?" Much of the therapy entails bolstering the client's resolve.

From the standpoint of both anger assessment and anger treatment, the clinician must bear in mind that anger is often part of a personal history of trauma, fear, and sadness associated with abuse, abandonment, and rejection. Revising anger schema, calming hyperarousal, and building a repertoire of constructive behavior for response to provocation takes time and convergent support from other helping service professionals. Given the reactive disposition of clients with anger problems, it is advantageous for a treatment program to be structured and to target anger problem features systematically. The cognitive behavioral intervention for anger that began with Novaco (1975) has such advantages, whether delivered as a group-based "anger management" program (Ramm & Novaco, 2002) or as individual "anger treatment." Importantly, though, one must distinguish differences in the "levels" of such interventions.

THERAPEUTIC INTERVENTIONS FOR ANGER: DIFFERENTIATING LEVELS

There are several levels at which psychotherapeutic interventions for anger can be delivered, as differentiated by Novaco et al. (2000). These are 1) general clinical care for anger, 2) provision of anger management, 3) anger treatment, and 3R) anger treatment protocol research. The intervention levels reflect the degree of systematization, complexity, and depth of therapeutic approach. Increased depth is associated with greater individual tailoring to client needs. Correspondingly, greater specialization in techniques and in clinical supervision is required with more complex levels of intervention. The brief cognitive-behavioral treatment for anger (Novaco, 1975) is a level 3 intervention, except that some treatment-resistant clients require a "preparatory phase" and extended support from the therapist.

In providing level 1 "general clinical care for anger," the clinician identifies anger as a relevant treatment issue and addresses the anger-related difficulties as part of a wider mental healthcare program. This level pertains to the broad provision of counseling, psychodynamic therapies, cognitive and behavioral therapies, and/or psychopharmacology applied across individual, couple, family, or group formats. In seeking explicitly to address anger, such therapeutic efforts actively incorporate new knowledge about anger and aggression and may utilize selected components of a CBT protocol (e.g., training in self-monitoring, modifying cognitive schema, encouraging coping self-statements, and using muscle-relaxation exercises) at opportune points in the treatment provision. General clinical care for anger may indeed serve as a comparison or control condition for anger treatment, as was done in the Chemtob et al. (1997b) study with Vietnam combat veterans, which used the Novaco (1993) outpatient procedures, modified for work with severe PTSD.

It is useful to distinguish "anger management," as a psychoeducational intervention, from more specialized anger treatment, especially as many efforts are now being made to provide services for anger control in a variety of settings. The term "anger management," which was first used by Novaco (1975) to describe an experimental cognitive behavioral treatment, can now better designate a level 2, *psychoeducational* approach that is less treatment intensive and that is structured by a syllabus of some sort. It imparts information about the nature of anger, including its determinants, signs, manifestations, and consequences. It also imparts information about ways of controlling anger, such as changing perceptions or beliefs, using relaxation, and adopting alternative behaviors for dealing with provocation. This type of intervention is often implemented in a group format, providing a forum for sharing anger experiences, peer support, and peer modeling, as well as serving the through-put objectives of a clinical service system.

Compared to what will be categorized below as "anger treatment," the provision of anger management is more time-limited and is more structured. Homogeneous across group members, it is not individually tailored. While there are occasions for participant discussion, it is less interactive than treatment and more unidirectional in information flow. As a psychoeducational approach, it involves less client disclosure and is thus less threatening. Correspondingly, the personal investment for the client is lower. It therefore does not address treatment engagement issues, which are intrinsic to the profiles of treatment-resistant patients. Lastly, while evaluative measures may be used, there tends not to be explicit use of individual client assessment data.

For the level 3 intervention, designated as "anger treatment," anger dyscontrol is approached in terms of the client's core needs. However, as stressed earlier, the intervention should be understood as an adjunctive treatment. It focuses on psychological deficits in self-regulation and explicitly integrates assessment with treatment. Precisely because its point of departure is to expect client resistance to change and its clients are characteristically high in threat-sensing, suspicion, and avoidance, it hinges on the provision of a therapeutic relationship.

Anger treatment targets enduring change in cognitive, arousal, and behavioral systems. It centrally involves cognitive restructuring and the acquisition of arousal reduction and behavioral coping skills, achieved through changing valuations of anger and augmenting self-monitoring capacity. Because it addresses anger as grounded and embedded in aversive and often traumatic life experiences, it entails the evocation of distressed emotions—i.e., fear and sadness, as well as anger. Therapeutic work centrally involves the processes of "transference" (the learning of new modes of responding to cues previously evocative of anger in the context of relating to the therapist) and of "countertransference" (negative sentiment on the part of the therapist to the frustrating, resistive, and unappreciative behavior of the client). The CBT anger treatment, which involves provocation hierarchy exposure, has followed a stress inoculation approach since Novaco (1977), as influenced by the work of Meichenbaum (1985).

Advanced therapeutic skill is required to deliver anger treatment, and supervision is essential in working with treatment-resistant patients. Anger treatment protocol research (level 3R) incorporates all of the attributes of level 3 intervention, but it diligently follows a designated protocol in delivering the treatment, and inclusion/exclusion criteria are specified for client participation. This level of intervention is explicitly evaluative and stipulates time points and procedures for assessment. As part of research design procedure, it incorporates checks on treatment protocol fidelity. In the enterprise of scientific discovery, it seeks knowledge about anger assessment and treatment.

"PREPARATORY PHASE" FOR TREATMENT ENGAGEMENT

In some clinical service contexts, particularly forensic settings, angry patients may be very guarded about self-disclosure and quite ambivalent about earnestly engaging in assessment and treatment. Because of the instrumental value of their anger and aggression, they do not readily recognize the personal costs that their anger routines incur; and because of the embeddedness of anger in long-standing psychological distress, there is inertia to overcome in motivating efforts to change. The first author's observations during his work with Chemtob and colleagues on the Vietnam veteran anger treatment trial and subsequent discussions with Ron Tulloch at Stockton Hall Psychiatry Hospital in Yorkshire, UK, led to the formulation of a "preparatory phase," first implemented by Renwick et al. (1997) as a five-session procedure. This is a protocol-guided block of five to seven sessions, varying with client competence and motivation. It has been successfully implemented as a six-session procedure in work with learning-disability forensic patients (Taylor & Novaco, 1999). The rationale for this preparatory phase is to foster engagement and motivation in patients, while conducting further assessment and developing the core competencies necessary for treatment.

Prospective participants in anger treatment often lack a number of prerequisites for optimal involvement in a self-regulatory, coping skills intervention program. They may have had some training in arousal control, and they may not have much difficulty in identifying emotions and distinguishing degrees of intensity. But they are likely to be unaccustomed to making self-observations about their thoughts, feelings, and behavior, or to rudimentary self-monitoring. Many may not recognize the degree to which thoughts, emotions, and behavior are interconnected. For others, however, the educational aspects of the preparatory phase are of less importance than the engagement issues, and they may get through the material very quickly.

The preparatory phase is thus constructed to "prime" the patient motivationally and to establish basic skills of emotion identification, self-monitoring, communication about anger experiences, and arousal reduction. It serves to build trust in the therapist and the treatment program, providing an atmosphere conducive to personal disclosure and to the collaboration required by this therapeutic approach. The latter includes building a common language about the model of anger that guides the treatment (Novaco, 1994b). While designed to be relatively nonprobing and nonchallenging, it may, for some institutionalized patients (cf. Novaco et al., 2000), elicit considerable distress, as clients may find it to be an intensive experience that raises vulnerability issues for them. Consequently, intersession follow-up meetings with patients on the ward may need to be done to support them in coping with the impact of the sessions. Because the preparatory phase can be pitched to the client as a "trial period," its conclusion leads to a more explicit and informed choice by the client about starting treatment proper.

CBT ANGER TREATMENT—STRESS INOCULATION FOR ANGER CONTROL

The cognitive behavioral approach to anger treatment involves the following key components:

1. client education about anger, stress, and aggression
2. self-monitoring of anger frequency, intensity, and situational triggers
3. construction of a personal anger provocation hierarchy, created from the self-monitoring data and used for the practice and testing of coping skills
4. arousal-reduction techniques of progressive muscle relaxation, breathing-focused relaxation, and guided imagery training
5. cognitive restructuring by altering attentional focus, modifying appraisals, and using self-instruction
6. training in behavioral coping in communication and respectful assertiveness as modeled and rehearsed with the therapist
7. practicing the cognitive, arousal-regulatory, and behavioral-coping skills while visualizing and role-playing progressively more intense anger-arousing scenes from the personal hierarchies.

Provocation is simulated in the therapeutic context by imagination and role-play of anger incidents from the life of the client, as directed by the therapist. This is a graduated exposure to a hierarchy of anger incidents produced by the collaborative work of client and therapist. This graduated, hierarchical exposure, done in conjunction with the teaching of coping skills, is the basis for the "inoculation" metaphor and is most central to the "stress inoculation" approach (cf. Meichenbaum, 1985). The therapist helps the client to arrange a gradation of provoking situations specific to the client, constructing scenes providing sufficient detail to generate a good imaginal image. The scenarios are described in matter-of-fact terms but incorporate wording that captures the client's perceptual sensitivities on provoking elements, such as the antagonist's tone of voice or nuances of facial expression. Each scenario ends with provocative aspects of the situation (i.e., not providing the client's reaction), so that it serves as a stimulus scene. In addition, the therapist should know the moderating variables that will exacerbate or buffer the magnitude of the anger reaction, should the scene need to be intensified or attenuated. Prior to the presentation of hierarchy items, whether in imaginal or role-play mode, anger-control coping is rehearsed and arousal reduction is induced through deep breathing and muscle relaxation.

TREATMENT OUTCOME STUDIES

Since CBT for anger was first implemented and experimentally evaluated by Novaco (1975), research on anger treatment has been modest, compared with that for depression or anxiety. Other CBT approaches have not followed the stress inoculation framework, such as can be found in the studies by Deffenbacher and his colleagues, which have almost exclusively involved college students without demonstrable clinical pathology or history of violence. Quite representatively, Deffenbacher et al. (1995) selected their treatment recipients by upper quartile scores on self-reported trait anger, by the subjects having expressed interest in counseling for anger management, and by their volunteering over the telephone. Such sample inclusion criteria do not reflect the clinical needs of the angry patients seen by mental health service providers in community and institutional settings. Reviews of treatment efficacy for anger therapy can be found in Edmonson & Conger (1996), Tafrate (1995), and Beck & Fernandez (1998). Unfortunately, these meta-analyses are overloaded with college student studies, and all fail to include case studies and multiple baseline studies, which have typically involved real patients with serious problems.

In contrast to college student volunteer studies, a controlled anger treatment trial with a seriously disordered population was conducted by Chemtob et al. (1997b), which was missed in Beck & Fernandez's review (1998). Significant treatment effects were obtained on multiple measures of anger reactions and anger control for the specialized anger treatment, compared to a multimodal, routine care control treatment condition. The anger-control treatment gains with these severe PTSD and severe anger cases were maintained at 18-month follow-up. The participants in that study had serious clinical disorders, validated by multiple assessment and diagnostic procedures, and had intense, recurrent post-war problems with anger and aggressive behavior (see also Chemtob et al., 1997a). Other control group studies involving successful outcomes for the stress inoculation approach to anger treatment with clinical populations are Schlichter & Horan (1981) with adolescent offenders and Stermac (1986) with forensic patients. In addition, Saylor et al. (1985) and Feindler and her colleagues (Feindler & Ecton, 1986; Feindler et al., 1986; Feindler et al. 1984) have done exemplary controlled research with adolescents in psychiatric facilities. Benson et al. (1986) also obtained successful treatment effects with mentally retarded adults in a group treatment grounded in the Novaco CBT approach as have Taylor et al. (2002) using individual treatment.

In addition, a number of case studies and multiple baseline design studies involving a variety of serious clinical disorders have provided further support for the efficacy of cognitive behavioral interventions based on the Novaco approach to anger treatment. Some examples of successful treatment results have been reported by Novaco (1977) with a hospitalized depressed patient, by Nomellini & Katz (1983) with child-abusing parents, by Bistline & Frieden (1984) with a chronically aggressive man, by Spirito et al. (1981) with an emotionally disturbed boy, by Lira et al. (1983) with a brain-damaged patient, by Black & Novaco (1993) with a mentally handicapped man, by Dangel et al. (1989) for adolescents in residential treatment, and by both Bornstein et al. (1985) and Howells (1989) with institutionalized forensic patients. Renwick et al. (1997) achieved significant treatment gains with very angry and assaultive psychiatric patients with serious mental disorder in a maximum-security hospital.

Brief CBT anger management interventions have been successfully utilized in prisons, often delivered in group format, as reported by McDougall et al. (1990), Serin & Kuriychuk (1994), Smith et al. (1994), and Towl & Dexter (1994), with 3–16 sessions across studies. A six-week, brief CBT, anger management program was applied to adolescent offenders in open custody by Valliant et al. (1995), but they failed to obtain treatment effects, apparently due to lack of "participant motivation." While the outcome evaluation assessments in these prison-based studies have been thin, a rather extensive outcome evaluation was conducted by Watt & Howells (1999) in two studies conducted in Western Australia with violent offenders in maximum and minimum security prisons, who received a group anger management program in 10 two-hour sessions delivered over five weeks. Measures of anger knowledge, anger disposition, anger expression, observed aggressive behavior, and prison misconduct showed no treatment gains for the program, compared to nonequivalent waiting-list controls. The nonrandomness of the treatment group assignment may have been a factor in the nonsignificant effects, but the authors were inclined to attribute the absence of effects to "low motivation for participants" and other program administrative factors. We have called attention to the treatment engagement issues in our presentation earlier.

At this juncture, we now turn to what we consider to be an important domain for anger treatment that is receiving our attention in our developing research on domestic violence.

NEW DIRECTIONS: ANGER AND CHILDREN

Programmatic research by Cummings and his colleagues has shown that children can distinguish between different types of emotional exchanges between adults and that children display a heightened sensitivity to angry adult interactions (Cummings et al.,1981; Cummings et al., 1989c; El-Sheikh et al., 1989; Cummings et al., 1991). This research, primarily conducted in a laboratory context, has examined children's emotional, behavioral, and physiological responses as a result of exposure to interadult anger. Substantial evidence has been obtained that preschool children express anger, show distress (e.g., crying, worry, or fear), and behave aggressively toward peers in response to interadult conflict involving anger displays (Cummings et al., 1985 & 1989a). Emotional distress in children is most likely to occur when the anger is physically expressed (Cummings et al., 1989b; Cummings et al., 1981). Infants who had been frequently exposed to interparental anger (as reported by the parent) exhibited greater signs of distress at angry interactions in the home, both naturally occurring and simulated by the investigators (Cummings et al., 1981).

Preschool children can distinguish between an angry and a friendly interaction between adults (Cummings et al.,1989c). Angry interactions between the child's mother and a research assistant were more likely to elicit preoccupation with the interaction, expressed concern, support seeking, and protective responses toward the mother (the latter were called "social responsibility" by the investigators). Children who had been exposed to physical violence in their homes, as reported by both parents, showed significantly more protective responses toward the mother than children who had not witnessed physical violence, and significantly more overall distress with increasing age. Exposure to angry interactions between adults was found by Cummings et al. (1991) to have effects on children aged 9–19 years somewhat similar to those observed with preschool children. Angry interactions elicited negative emotional responses, and those exchanges that involved physical aggression evoked the most severe negative responses.

A study by Hennessy et al. (1994) compared physically abused and not physically abused children, aged 6–11 years, in their response to interadult anger. Both sets of children came from homes having verbal and physical aggression between the parents. When asked to report their emotions in response to videotaped segments of adult interactions involving different forms of anger (nonverbal, verbal, verbal-physical, resolved, and unresolved), physically abused children responded with greater fear than nonabused children across types of anger, showing more sensitivity to whether or not the anger was resolved.

Resolution of anger is important to children's experience of interadult conflict (Cummings et al., 1989b; Cummings et al., 1993; Shifflett-Simpson & Cummings, 1996). According to Cummings et al. (1993), children perceive unresolved anger as being more intense than resolved anger. Even unobserved resolution (where the adults argued in the presence of the child, left the room, and then returned interacting happily with no mention of the previous argument) appeared to affect positively the child's negative emotional reaction to the conflict. Compared to resolved anger, unresolved anger elicited more angry reactions in children, regardless of gender or age, and more sadness in boys than in girls. Similar effects for harmonious endings were found in Davies et al. (1996).

To illustrate the real-life manifestations of the above laboratory-studied phenomena, we present the case of a young boy in our own research program.

Case Illustration: A Six-Year-Old Boy

Kyle was a six-year-old boy, the middle child of five. His four siblings and his mother had moved into the domestic violence emergency shelter one week prior to our research assessments. His father was an avid drug user, and, like all of his siblings, Kyle was aware of his father's drug habits and specifically mentioned his use of crack cocaine and marijuana. Kyle's father would regularly force the boy's mother (and the children) to panhandle for money to support his drug habits; they would approach people in mall parking lots and ask for money, too scared to return home until they had enough to buy what their father needed. His father also forced his mother to perform the drug purchasing transactions for him. When asked what he most worried about, Kyle replied that he worried that his mother would go to jail for handling his father's drugs and that he would have to live with his father. When asked in what way his mother made him feel loved, Kyle responded, "by leaving my dad."

In addition to being exposed to his father's drug use and being made to beg for money from strangers, Kyle had witnessed severe violence in his home since infancy. His father both verbally and physically abused his mother and the children as well, although less frequently. Kyle could recount occasions on which his father physically assaulted his mother and could describe the wounds that resulted from these attacks. When asked about these events, Kyle replied that he often felt sad and scared.

Throughout the interview, Kyle offered descriptions of events that involved several fantasy-like elements. These fantasies tended to include elements of revenge, escape, and heroism. For example, he told stories of protecting his mother from his father's blows by hitting his father back after he had attacked her. However, his mother reported that the child had never intervened during the violence. In another such story, Kyle described jumping off a building to save his mother, while leading the police to arrest his father. The story concluded with his father going to jail and his family being taken away to somewhere safe.

During the administration of a PTSD questionnaire, Kyle created an elaborate story, lasting over 30 minutes, of a car accident involving his entire family. The story included the car's sinking and the family's being met by a group of dolphins and sharks. The dolphins played with and helped his mother and his siblings. Kyle reported saving his family by jumping into the driver's seat of the car and driving his mother and siblings to safety. Sharks devoured his father.

Several of Kyle's other fantasies also involved violence, but the theme of fighting sides, of "good versus bad" was salient. During the car accident story, he developed a plot of good and bad sharks; the "good" sharks swam his mother and his siblings to safety and killed his father. Kyle himself killed the "bad" sharks. When asked how well he slept, Kyle said that each night before he fell asleep he saw "good and bad demons" fighting in his head. When asked about regret for actions done or undone, Kyle responded that he wished he could kill his father.

This tragic case of a young boy struggling to make sense of his family life and to assert a semblance of control over the cruel vector of violence with which his mother, siblings, and he have been beset depicts the circumstances under which anger dysregulation takes hold. It serves to convey the multifactorial nature of the anger problem, its embeddedness in overlapping systems of distress and dysfunction, and its reciprocity with violence. The paramount need at the time of refuge is safety, but one can see that remediation of the trauma and emotional distress experienced by children like this entails far more than a brief psychological therapy. Maternal unemployment, maternal depression, inadequate housing, lack of transportation, instability in schooling, and general healthcare issues, as well as the ever-present fear of being located by the abusive father, complicate anger treatment in such cases and limit its efficacy.

Nevertheless, brief CBT can be expected to have value for children with anger dysfunctions. Indeed, in what was possibly the first published treatment of an angry client, Witmer (1908) reported the case study of an 11-year-old boy who had been subject to "outbursts of uncontrollable and unreasoning anger" and to "mean moods." Witmer, who adopted an educational approach to his treatment of children, described an incident, near the end of the boy's treatment, where the boy protested about having to wash his hands at mealtime and threatened not to return to the table. He did return, demonstrating to the clinician his use of a core CBT anger-control technique, namely, self-instruction: "I nearly got mad, but I just said to myself, 'I will control my temper' " (p. 178). Much more recently, Snyder et al. (1999) found, in a randomized control-group design with adolescents in psychiatric hospitals, that a four-session, anger-management group CBT produced significant effects on both self-report and staff ratings. The intervention provided education about anger, stressed the role of interpretation and perception in activating anger reactions, sought to promote alternative, non-anger-engendering explanations of other's behavior, reviewed the functions of anger, examined forms of appropriate expression, suggested constructive coping strategies, and provided opportunities for practice of coping skills through structured role-plays and for peer feedback about performance.

The cognitive behavioral treatment of anger has been shown to have applicability to a wide range of client populations. We seek to advance its development in the treatment of children exposed to family violence trauma, in an effort to address anger dysregulation in its nascence. A contextual perspective on anger and on intervention for anger problems, however, recognizes that anger reactions are shaped and maintained by environmental, interpersonal, and intrapersonal subsystems and that anger has important adaptive functions. We therefore are mindful of the need to mobilize community resources (e.g., family court, social services, pediatric medicine, special education, transportation, and housing) to buttress psychotherapeutic efforts. Anger is embedded in personal and environmental systems and is grounded in ongoing adaptations to survival demands that emerge in those systems. Its course of development is affected by interdependent and evolving systems that may either inhibit or escalate anger. Exclusively clinical models impose unnecessary boundaries on what are considered to be the relevant factors that determine anger, influence its course, and manifest its effects.

REFERENCES

Averill, J. R. (1982). *Anger and aggression: An essay on emotion.* New York: Springer-Verlag.

Bandura, A. (1972). *Aggression: A social learning analysis.* Englewood Cliffs, NJ: Prentice-Hall.

Baumeister, R. F., Stillwell, A., & Wotman, S. R. (1990). Victim and perpetrator accounts of interpersonal conflict: Autobiographical narratives about anger. *Journal of Personality and Social Psychology,* **59**, 994–1005.

Beck, R., & Fernandez, E. (1998). Cognitive-behavioral therapy in the treatment of anger: A meta-analysis. *Cognitive Therapy and Research,* **22**, 63–74.

Benson, B. A., Rice, C. J., & Miranti, S. V. (1986). Effects of anger management training with mentally retarded adults in group treatment. *Journal of Consulting and Clinical Psychology,* **54**, 728–729.

Ben-Zur, H., & Breznitz, S. (1991). What makes people angry: Dimensions of anger-evoking events. *Journal of Research in Personality,* **25**, 1–22.

Bistline, J. L., & Frieden, F. P. (1984). Anger control: A case study of a stress inoculation treatment for a chronic aggressive patient. *Cognitive Therapy and Research*, **8**, 551–556.

Black, L., & Novaco, R. W. (1993). Treatment of anger with a developmentally handicapped man. In R. A. Wells & V. J. Giannetti (Eds.), *Casebook of the brief psychotherapies*. New York: Plenum Press.

Bornstein, P. H., Weisser, C. E., & Balleweg, B. J. (1985). Anger and violent behavior. In M. Hersen & A. S. Bellack (Eds.), *Handbook of clinical behavior therapy with adults* (pp. 603–629). New York: Plenum Press.

Browne, A. (1993). Violence against women by male partners: Prevalence, outcomes, and policy implications. *American Psychologist*, **48**, 1077–1087.

Bureau of Justice Statistics (1998). Violence by intimates: Analysis of data on crimes by current or former spouses, boyfriends, or girlfriends. US Department of Justice (NCJ-167237).

Butterworth, M. D., & Fulmer, K. A. (1991). The effect of family violence on children: Intervention strategies including bibliotherapy. *Australian Journal of Marriage and the Family*, **12**, 170–182.

Cannon, W. (1932). *The wisdom of the body*. W. W. Norton: New York.

Carlson, B. E. (1990). Adolescent observers of marital violence. *Journal of Family Violence*, **5**, 285–299.

Cascardi, M., O'Leary, K. D., Lawrence, E. E., & Schlee, K. A. (1995). Characteristics of women physically abused by their spouses and who seek treatment regarding marital conflict. *Journal of Consulting and Clinical Psychology*, **63**, 616–623.

Chemtob, C. M., Novaco, R. W., Hamada, R. S., Gross, D. M., & Smith, G. (1997a). Anger regulatory deficits in combat-related post-traumatic stress disorder. *Journal of Traumatic Stress*, **10**, 17–36.

Chemtob, C. M., Novaco, R. W., Hamada, R. S., & Gross, D. M. (1997b). Cognitive-behavioral treatment for severe anger in post-traumatic stress disorder. *Journal of Consulting and Clinical Psychology*, **65**, 184–189.

Chesney, M. A., & Rosenman, R. H. (Eds.) (1985). *Anger and hostility in cardiovascular and behavioral disorders*. Washington, DC: Hemisphere.

Crowell, N. A., & Burgess, A. W. (1996). *Understanding violence against women*. Washington, DC: National Academy Press.

Cummings, E. M., Ballard, M., & El-Sheikh, M. (1991). Responses of children and adolescents to interadult anger as a function of gender, age, and mode of expression. *Merrill-Palmer Quarterly*, **37**, 543–560.

Cummings, E. M., Ianotti, R. J., & Zahn-Waxler, C. (1985). The influence of conflict between adults on the emotions and aggression of young children. *Developmental Psychology*, **21**, 495–507.

Cummings, E. M., Ianotti, R. J., & Zahn-Waxler, C. (1989a). Aggression between peers in early childhood: Individual continuity and developmental change. *Child Development*, **60**, 887–895.

Cummings, E. M., Simpson, K. S., & Wilson, A. (1993). Children's responses to interadult anger as a function of information about resolution. *Developmental Psychology*, **29**, 978–985.

Cummings, E. M., Vogel, D., Cummings, J. S., & El-Sheikh, M. (1989b). Children's responses to different forms of anger between adults. *Child Development*, **60**, 1393–1404.

Cummings, E. M., Zahn-Waxler, C., & Radke-Yarrow, M. (1981). Young children's responses to expressions of anger and affection by others in the family. *Child Development*, **52**, 1274–1282.

Cummings, J. S., Pelligrini, D. S., Notarius, C. I., & Cummings, E. M. (1989c). Children's responses to adult angry behavior as a function of marital distress and history of interparental hostility. *Child Development*, **60**, 1035–1043.

Dangel, R. F., Deschner, J. P., & Rasp, R. R. (1989). Anger control training for adolescents in residential treatment. *Behavior Modification*, **13**, 447–458.

Davies, P. T., Myers, R. L., & Cummings, E. M. (1996). Responses of children and adolescents to marital conflict scenarios as a function of the emotionality of conflict endings. *Merrill-Palmer Quarterly*, **42**, 1–21.

Davis, J. A., & Smith, T. W. General Social Survey [Electronic data file] (1996). Chicago, IL: National Opinion Research Center (Producer); Bellevue, WA: MicroCase Corporation (Distributor).

Deffenbacher, J. L., Oetting, E. R., Huff, M. E., & Thwaites, G. A. (1995). Fifteen-month follow-up of social skills and cognitive-relaxation approaches to general anger reduction. *Journal of Counseling Psychology*, **42**, 400–405.

Dembroski, T. M., MacDougall, J. M., Williams, R. B., Jr., Haney, T. L., & Blumenthal, J. A. (1985). Components of type A, hostility, and anger-in: Relationship to angiographic findings. *Psychosomatic Medicine*, **47**, 219–233.

Diamond, E. L. (1982). The role of anger and hostility in essential hypertension and coronary heart disease. *Psychological Bulletin*, **92**, 410–433.

Dobash, R. E. (2000). Changing violent men. Los Angeles: Sage.

Dutton, D. G., Saunders, K., Starzomski, A., & Bartholomew, K. (1994). Intimacy-anger and insecure attachment as precursors of abuse in intimate relationships. *Journal of Applied Social Psychology*, **24**, 1367–1386.

Dutton, D. G., Starzomski, A., & Ryan, L. (1996). Antecedents of abusive personality and abusive behavior in wife assaulters. *Journal of Family Violence*, **11**, 113–132.

Ehlers, A., Mayou, R. A., & Bryant, B. (1998). Psychological predictors of chronic posttraumatic stress disorder after motor vehicle accidents. *Journal of Abnormal Psychology*, **107**, 508–519.

Edmondson, C. B., & Conger, J. C. (1996). A review of treatment efficacy for individuals with anger problems: Conceptual, assessment, and methodological issues. *Clinical Psychology Review*, **16**, 251–275.

Ekman, P., & Davidson, R. J. (1994). *The nature of emotion.* New York: Oxford University Press.

El-Sheikh, M., Cummings, E. M., & Goetsch, V. (1989). Coping with adults' angry behavior: Behavioral, physiological, and verbal responses in preschoolers. *Developmental Psychology*, **25**, 490–498.

Fantuzzo, J. W., DePaola, L. M., Lambert, L., Martino, T., Anderson, G., & Sutton, S. (1991). Effects of interpersonal violence on the psychological adjustment and competences of young children. *Journal of Consulting and Clinical Psychology*, **59**, 258–265.

Feindler, E. L., & Ecton, R. B. (1986). *Adolescent anger control: Cognitive therapy techniques.* New York: Pergamon Press.

Feindler, E. L., Ecton, R. B., Kingsley, R. B., & Dubey, D. R. (1986). Group anger-control training for institutionalized psychiatric male adolescents. *Behavior Therapy*, **17**, 109–123.

Feindler, E. L., Marriott, A., & Iwata, M. (1984). Group anger control training for junior high school delinquents. *Cognitive Therapy and Research*, **8**, 299–311.

Friedman, H. (1992). *Hostility, coping, and health.* Washington, DC: American Psychological Association.

Frost, W. D., & Averill, J. R. (1982). Differences between men and women in the everyday experience of anger. In J. Averill, *Anger and aggression: An essay on emotion* (pp. 281–316). New York: Springer-Verlag.

Gates, G. S. (1926). An observational study of anger. *Journal of Experimental Psychology*, **9**, 325–331.

Hall, G. S. (1899). A study of anger. *American Journal of Psychology*, **10**, 516–591.

Harris, M. B. (1993). How provoking! What makes men and women angry. *Aggressive Behavior*, **19**, 199–211.

Hennessy, K. D., Rabideau, G. J., Cicchetti, D., & Cummings, E. M. (1994). Responses of physically abused children to different forms of interadult anger. *Child Development*, **65**, 815–828.

Howells, K. (1989). Anger-management methods in relation to the prevention of violent behavior. In J. Archer & K. Browne (Eds.), *Human aggression: Naturalistic accounts* (pp. 153–181). London: Routledge.

Hurley, D. J., & Jaffe, P. G. (1990). Children's observations of violence: II. Clinical implications for children's mental health professionals. *Special Issue: Child psychiatry. Canadian Journal of Psychiatry*, **35**, 471–476.

Jaffe, P., Hurley, D. J., & Wolfe, D. (1990a). Children's observations of violence: I. Critical issues in child development and intervention planning. *Special Issue: Child psychiatry. Canadian Journal of Psychiatry*, **35**, 466–470.

Jaffe, P., & Geffner, R. (1998). Child custody disputes and domestic violence: Critical issues for mental health, social service, and legal professionals. In G.W. Holden & R. Geffner (Eds.), *Children exposed to marital violence: Theory, research, and applied issues* (pp. 371–408). Washington, DC: American Psychological Association.

Jaffe, P., Wolfe, D. A., & Wilson, S. K. (1990b). *Children of battered women.* Newbury Park, CA: Sage.

Jouriles, E. N., Murphy, C. M., & O'Leary, K. D. (1989). Interspousal aggression, marital discord, and child problems. *Journal of Consulting and Clinical Psychology*, **57**(3), 453–455.

Johnson, E. H. (1990). *The deadly emotions: The role of anger, hostility, and aggression in health and emotional well-being.* New York: Praeger.

Kassinove, H., Sukhodolsky, D. G., Tsytsarev, S. V., & Solovyova, S. (1997). *Journal of Social Behavior and Personality*, **12**, 301–324.

Koski, P. R. (1987). Family violence and nonfamily deviance: Taking stock of the literature. *Marriage and Family Review*, **12**(1–2), 23–46.

Lehmann, P. (1997). The development of posttraumatic stress disorder (PTSD) in a sample of child witnesses to mother assault. *Journal of Family Violence*, **12**, 241–257.

Lira, F. T., Carne, W., & Masri, A. M. (1983). Treatment of anger and impulsivity in a brain damaged patient: A case study applying stress inoculation. *Clinical Neuropsychology*, **4**, 159–160.

McDougall, C., Boddis, S., Dawson, K., & Hayes, R. (1990). Developments in anger control training. *Issues in Criminological and Legal Psychology*, **15**, 39–44.

Meichenbaum, D. (1985). *Stress inoculation training*. New York: Pergamon Press.

Melzer, H. (1933). Students' adjustment in anger. *Journal of Social Psychology*, **4**, 285–309.

Nomellini, S., & Katz, R. C. (1983). Effects of anger control training on abusive parents. *Cognitive Therapy and Research*, **7**, 57–68.

Novaco, R. W. (1975). *Anger control: The development and evaluation of an experimental treatment*. Lexington, MA: D. C. Heath.

Novaco, R. W. (1977). Stress inoculation: A cognitive therapy for anger and its application to a case of depression. *Journal of Consulting and Clinical Psychology*, **45**, 600–608.

Novaco, R. W. (1983). Novaco Provocation Inventory. In M. Hersen & A. S. Bellack (Eds.), *Dictionary of behavioral assessment techniques* (pp. 315–317). New York: Pergamon.

Novaco, R. W. (1986). Anger as a clinical and social problem. In R. J. Blanchard & D. C. Blanchard (Eds.), *Advances in the study of aggression*. Vol. 2 (pp. 1–67). New York: Academic Press.

Novaco, R. W. (1993). Clinicians ought to view anger contextually. *Behaviour Change*, **10**, 208–218.

Novaco, R. W. (1994a). Anger as a risk factor for violence among the mentally disordered. In J. Monahan & H. Steadman (Eds.), *Violence and mental disorder: Developments in risk assessment*. (pp.1–59) Chicago: University of Chicago Press.

Novaco, R. W. (1994b). Stress inoculation treatment for anger control: Therapist procedures (1993–1994 revisions). Unpublished manuscript, University of California, Irvine.

Novaco, R. W. (1997). Remediating anger and aggression with violent offenders. *Legal and Criminological Psychology*, **2**, 77–88.

Novaco, R. W., & Chemtob, C. M. (1998). Anger and trauma: Conceptualization, assessment, and treatment. In V. M. Follette, J. I. Rusek, & F. R. Abueg (Eds.), *Cognitive behavioral therapies for trauma* (pp. 162–190). New York: Guilford Press.

Novaco, R. W., & Chemtob, C. M. (2002). Anger and combat-related posttraumatic stress disorder. *Journal of Traumatic Stress*, **15**, 123–132.

Novaco, R. W., Ramm, M., & Black, L. (2000). Anger treatment with offenders. In C. Hollin (ed.), *Handbook of offender assessment and treatment*. London: John Wiley.

Novaco, R. W., & Renwick, S. J. (1998). Anger predictors of the assaultiveness of forensic hospital patients. In E. Sanavio (Ed.), *Behavioural and cognitive therapy today: Essays in honour of Hans J. Eysenck* (pp. 213–222). Amsterdam: Elsevier Science.

Novaco, R. W., & Taylor, J. L. (2001). Assessment of anger and aggression in offenders with developmental disabilities (submitted for publication).

Ramm, M., & Novaco, R. W. (2002). An evaluation of anger management groupwork with continuing-care psychiatric patients at The State Hospital. Unpublished manuscript.

Renwick, S., Black, L., Ramm, M., & Novaco, R. W. (1997). Anger treatment with forensic hospital patients. *Legal and Criminological Psychology*, **2**, 103–116.

Robins, S., & Novaco, R. W. (2000). Anger control as a health promotional mechanism. In D. I. Mostofsky & D. H. Barlow (Eds.), *The management of stress and anxiety in medical disorders* (pp. 361–377). Boston: Allyn and Bacon.

Rosenberg, M. S. (1987). Children of battered women: The effects of witnessing violence on their social problem-solving abilities. *Behavior Therapist*, **10**, 85–89.

Saylor, C. F., Benson, B. A., & Einhaus, L. (1985). Evaluation of an anger management program for aggressive boys in residential treatment. *Journal of Child and Adolescent Psychotherapy*, **2**, 5–15.

Schlee, K. A., Heyman, R. E., & O'Leary, K. D. (1998). Group treatment for spouse abuse: Are women with PTSD appropriate partners? *Journal of Family Violence*, **13**, 1–20.

Schlichter, K. J., & Horan, J. J. (1981). Effects of stress inoculation on the anger and aggression management skills of institutionalized juvenile delinquents. *Cognitive Therapy and Research*, **5**, 359–365.

Schwartz, N., & Clore, G. L. (1988). How do I feel about it? The informative function of mood. In K. Fiedler & J. Forgas (Eds.), *Affect, cognition, and social behavior* (pp. 44–62). Toronto: C. J. Hogrefe.

Serin, R. C., & Kuriychuk, M. (1994). Social and cognitive processing deficits: Implications for treatment. *International Journal for Law and Psychiatry*, **17**, 431–441.

Shifflett-Simpson, K., & Cummings, E. M. (1996). Mixed message resolution and children's responses to interadult conflict. *Child Development*, **67**, 437–448.

Siegman, A. W., & Smith, T. W. (1994). *Anger, hostility, and the heart*. Lawrence Erlbaum Associates: Hillsdale, NJ.

Silvern, L., & Kaersvang, L. (1989). The traumatized children of violent marriages. *Child Welfare*, **68**(4), 421–436.

Smith, L. L., Smith, J. N., & Beckner, B. M. (1994). An anger management workshop for women inmates. *Journal of Contemporary Human Services, March*, 172–175.

Snyder, K. V., Kymissis, P., & Kessler, K. (1999). Anger management for adolescents: Efficacy of brief group therapy. *Journal of the American Academy of Child and Adolescent Psychiatry*, **38**, 1409.

Spirito, A., Finch, A. J., Smith, T. L., & Cooley, W. H. (1981). Stress inoculation for anger and anxiety control: A case study with an emotionally disturbed boy. *Journal of Clinical Child Psychology*, **10**, 67–70.

Spielberger, C. D. (1988). *Manual for the State-Trait Anger Expression Inventory*. Tampa: Psychological Assessment Resources.

Stermac, L. E. (1986). Anger control treatment for forensic patients. *Journal of Interpersonal Violence*, **1**, 446–457.

Straus, M. A. (1992). Children as witnesses to marital violence: A risk factor for lifelong problems among a nationally representative sample of American men and women. *Report of the Twenty-Third Ross Roundtable*. Columbus, OH: Ross Laboratories.

Tafrate, R. C. (1995). Evaluation of treatment strategies for adult anger disorders. In H. Kassonove (Ed.), *Anger disorders* (pp. 109–128). Washington, DC: Taylor & Francis.

Taylor, J. L., & Novaco, R. W. (1999). Anger treatment research project for learning disability offenders: Preparatory phase treatment manual. Unpublished manuscript, Northgate and Prudhoe NHS Trust.

Taylor, J. L., Novaco, R. W., Gillmer, B., & Thorne, I. (2002). Cognitive-behavioural treatment of anger intensity in offenders with intellectual disabilities. *Journal of Applied Research in Intellectual Disabilities*, **15**(2), 151–165.

Tjaden, P., & Thoennes, N. (1999). Prevalence and incidence of violence against women: Findings from the National Violence Against Women Survey. *The Criminologist*, **24**, 1–19.

Towl, G., & Dexter, P. (1994). Anger management group work with prisoners: An empirical evaluation. *Groupwork*, **7**, 256–269.

Valliant, P. M., Jensen, B., & Raven-Brook, L. (1995). Brief cognitive behavioural therapy with male adolescent offenders in open custody or on probation: An evaluation of the management of anger. *Psychological Reports*, **76**, 1056–1058.

Watt, B. D., & Howells, K. (1999). Skills training for aggression control: Evaluation of an anger management programme for violent offenders. *Legal and Criminological Psychology*, **4**, 285–300.

Weiner, B. (1995). *Judgments of responsibility: A foundation for a theory of social conduct*. New York: Guilford Press.

Williams, R., & Williams, V. (1993). *Anger kills*. New York: Harper Perennial.

Witmer, L. (1908). The treatment and cure of a case of mental and moral deficiency. *The Psychological Clinic*, **2**, 153–179.

Zillmann, D., & Bryant, J. (1974). Effect of residual excitation on the emotional response to provocation and delayed aggressive behavior. *Journal of Personality and Social Psychology*, **30**, 782–791.

CHAPTER 6

Cognitive Therapy for Generalised Anxiety Disorder

Adrian Wells

*Academic Division of Clinical Psychology,
University of Manchester, Manchester, UK*

Generalised anxiety disorder (GAD) is characterised by excessive and uncontrollable worry. In order to meet criteria for GAD according to DSM-IV (APA, 1994), an individual must show "excessive anxiety and worry (apprehensive expectation), occurring more days than not for at least six months about a number of events or activities" (p. 435). In addition to worry, there should be three or more out of six other somatic or cognitive symptoms. Somatic symptoms of muscle tension are a particularly common feature. A specification of at least 6 months for the duration of the disorder facilitates a differentiation between transient stress reactions and GAD. GAD is a chronic and fluctuating disorder that can have an early onset. Some patients report that they have been worriers for most of their lives. Yonkers et al. (1996) reported that in their sample, age of onset ranged from 2 to 61 years, with a mean of 21 years. Co-occurrences of GAD with other emotional disorders are common. Sanderson & Barlow (1990) reported that out of a sample of 22 patients with GAD, 59% met criteria for social phobia, 27% for panic disorder, 27% for dysthymia, and 14% for depression. Yonkers et al. (1996) reported that 52% of their GAD sample met criteria for panic disorder, 32% were socially phobic, and 37% met criteria for major depression.

EFFECTIVENESS OF PSYCHOLOGICAL TREATMENT

Treatments for GAD have consisted of behavioural (e.g., biofeedback, relaxation), analytic, cognitive-behavioural, and non-directive therapies. Behavioural approaches consisting of applied relaxation (Borkovec & Costello, 1993), cognitive therapy treatments based on Beck's (1976) generic model of anxiety, and combined cognitive therapy and applied relaxation (e.g., Barlow et al., 1992) lead to the best improvements in GAD. However, both the proportion of treatment responders and degree of treatment response are modest. In a review of treatment outcome studies conducted since 1980, Durham & Allan (1993) reported a percentage of improvement in trait-anxiety ranging from 6% to 50%. Fisher & Durham (1999)

Handbook of Brief Cognitive Behaviour Therapy. Edited by Frank W. Bond and Windy Dryden.
© 2002 John Wiley & Sons, Ltd. ISBN 0-470-02132-2.

used Jacobson's methodology to estimate the proportion of patients who return to normal functioning after treatment. If we use trait-anxiety as the outcome variable across six randomised, controlled trials, approximately 60% of patients improve overall, but, on average, slightly less than 40% can be classified as recovered. However, there appears to be considerable variability in outcome within and across studies, with the majority of studies showing recovery rates of less than or equal to 30%. The most effective treatments appear to be individual cognitive-behavioural therapy, with an overall recovery rate of 51%, and applied relaxation, with a rate of 60%. Individual behavioural therapy (e.g., anxiety management training) and analytic psychotherapy performed very poorly, with overall recovery rates of 11% and 4%, respectively. These statistics represent overall recovery rates at 6-month follow-up. Studies with longer-term follow-up are required.

Clearly, these estimates suggest that GAD is a difficult disorder to treat effectively. Improvements in treatment are likely to emerge from a better understanding of the mechanisms underlying chronic and uncontrollable worry. If these mechanisms can be targeted and modified in treatment, the effectiveness of interventions should be enhanced. Before setting out a theory-based approach of this kind, we will examine in the next section the nature of worry, since this is the cardinal feature of GAD.

THE NATURE OF WORRY

In early work, Borkovec et al. (1983) defined "worry" as follows: "Worry is a chain of thoughts and images, negatively affect-laden and relatively uncontrollable" (p. 10). They viewed worry as a problem-solving activity closely related to fear processes. Worry has been conceptualised as a predominantly verbal process, and it can be distinguished from other types of distressing thoughts, namely, obsessions (Wells & Morrison, 1994) and depressive rumination (Papageorgiou & Wells, 1999). It has been suggested that worry may be a form of coping (Wells, 1994a; 1995), and Wells & Matthews (1994) assert that at least two varieties of worry should be distinguished, an adaptive variety and a maladaptive variety. The adaptive variety is oriented toward problem-solving and leads to problem-focused behaviour. However, the maladaptive variety generates a range of negative outcomes in which the individual attempts to formulate coping solutions until some internal goal state is achieved.

Further distinctions between types of worry, important for understanding pathological worry processes, have also been suggested. Wells (1995) suggested that it is useful to distinguish between two broad types of worry in understanding GAD. The distinction is based on differences in the content and form that worry takes. These two worry types have been termed type 1 and type 2. Type 1 worry refers to worry about external events and internal non-cognitive events such as physical symptoms. Type 2 worry consists of worry about one's own cognitive events and processes. This is essentially worry about worry, also known as meta-worry since it involves metacognitive monitoring and appraisal of one's own thoughts. Examples of meta-worry themes include appraisals of loss of control of thinking and of harm resulting from worrying. A more recent definition of "worry", taking into account conceptual and empirical developments, has been presented: "Worry is a chain of catastrophising thoughts that are predominantly verbal. It consists of the contemplation of potentially dangerous situations and of personal coping strategies. It is intrusive and controllable, although it is often experienced as uncontrollable. Worrying is associated with a motivation to prevent or avoid potential danger. Worry may itself be viewed as a coping strategy but can become the focus of an individual's concern" (Wells, 1999: p. 87).

A COGNITIVE MODEL OF GAD

A cognitive model of GAD (Wells, 1995; 1997) has been advanced to account for the mechanisms responsible for generalised, excessive, and uncontrollable worry. The concept of meta-cognition is central in the model. This is the dimension of information processing that monitors, interprets, and regulates the content and processes of thinking. This area of enquiry provides a potential framework for understanding the regulation of cognitive processes and the mechanisms of dysfunctional thinking styles such as chronic worry (Wells & Matthews, 1994; Wells, 2000).

The meta-cognitive model of GAD is depicted in Figure 6.1. The onset of worry in GAD is often triggered by an intrusive thought which typically occurs in the form of a "what if" question (e.g., "What if my partner is involved in an accident?"). This initial thought activates positive meta-cognitive beliefs about the usefulness of worrying as a coping strategy. Examples of positive beliefs held by GAD patients are as follows: "worrying helps me cope", "worrying keeps me safe", "If I worry I won't be taken by surprise". The person with GAD thus executes worry sequences consisting of a range of "what if" questions and the generation of potential coping strategies. This catastrophising or iterative sequence, is referred to as type 1 worry, since the content of the individual's concerns focuses on external events and non-cognitive internal events (e.g., physical symptoms). Type 1 worry is associated with emotional responses, as depicted by the bi-directional dotted line in Figure 6.1. The contemplation of dangerous scenarios leads to activation of

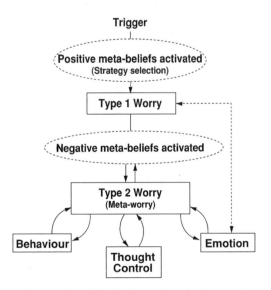

Figure 6.1 A metacognitive model of GAD. Reproduced with permission from Wells, A., 1997, *Cognitive Therapy of Anxiety Disorders: A Practice Manual and Conceptual Guide*, p. 204. Chichester, UK: © John Wiley & Sons Limited

an anxiety programme and the somatic and cognitive symptoms associated with anxiety. Type 1 worrying is practised until it is interrupted by competing goals or activities that lead to a diversion of attentional resources away from worrying. However, in the absence of these disrupting influences, persons with GAD continue to worry until they conclude that they will be able to cope effectively with the anticipated danger. This assessment is based on internal cues, such as a felt sense that they will be able to cope or the feeling that all important outcomes have been considered. When internal goal states that signal it is safe to stop worrying are achieved, emotional responses decrease. The bi-directional dotted arrow between emotion and type 1 worry in Figure 6.1 depicts the effect of emotions on type 1 worry. In some instances, emotional responses prime the need to continue worrying as a coping strategy or a way of avoiding stress symptoms. Moreover, emotional responses may be interpreted as signalling the need to continue the work of worrying.

Most individuals, not only GAD patients, hold positive beliefs about worrying. However, GAD patients are less flexible in their selection of coping strategies, and tend to engage worrying as a predominant strategy, moreover, individuals with GAD also hold negative meta-cognitive beliefs about worrying and the consequences of worrying. Examples of negative beliefs are as follows: "worrying could make be go crazy", "I must control my worry or I'll cease to function", "worry is uncontrollable", and "worrying will damage my body". During worry episodes, negative beliefs become activated, and this leads to negative appraisal of the worry process. Negative appraisals or type 2 worry influences emotional responses. Type 2 worry intensifies anxiety, and if worrying is interpreted as imminently dangerous, rapid escalation of anxiety in the form of panic attacks may result. The relationship between type 2 worry and emotion constitutes a vicious cycle (as depicted in Figure 6.1), in which cognitive and somatic symptoms associated with anxiety can be interpreted as evidence of loss of control and/or the harmful nature of worrying. Anxious responses may also be interpreted as a sign of a likely failure to cope that contributes to a need for continued type 1 worry. Thus, when negative beliefs and type 2 worry develop, the individual with GAD experiences increased difficulty in achieving an internal signal that it is appropriate to stop worrying. This process contributes to the chronicity and generalisation of worrying. Two further mechanisms associated with type 2 worry are also involved in problem maintenance. These are behavioural responses and thought control.

A range of behavioural responses may be used by the person with GAD in order to avert the feared catastrophes associated with worrying. Often these are subtle behaviours, such as reassurance seeking or information search, and avoidance of triggers for worry, such as particular situations. A problem with these behaviours is that the non-occurrence of a catastrophe associated with worry may be attributed to them, and therefore the individual fails to learn that worrying is harmless. Moreover, strategies such as seeking reassurance can lead to conflicting or new information that may serve as additional triggers for worrying.

Another important coping strategy is depicted by the thought control cell in Figure 6.1. Since the person with GAD is in a state of dissonance about worry, in which both positive and negative beliefs co-exist, the individual rarely attempts actively to interrupt the worry process once it is initiated. Interrupting the worry sequence before a subjectively acceptable resolution has been accomplished is equivalent to abandoning coping attempts. Worrying is practised in special ways or alternative external sources of worry resolution are sought so that the dangers of worrying may be minimised. Because affected persons rarely interrupt the worry sequence before the goal of worrying is achieved, they have few experiences of successfully interrupting or controlling worry, and thus negative appraisals and beliefs concerning uncontrollability remain unmodified. One way of resolving the dissonance that exists between positive and negative beliefs is to avoid the need to worry in the first instance. This may be accomplished through behavioural strategies such as avoiding situations as outlined above, but may also be accomplished through thought-control strategies that consist of attempting not to think about worry triggers. For instance, a person currently concerned about competency at work may attempt not to think about work when away from that environment. A problem with *thought suppression* of this kind is that it is rarely entirely effective, and this can be taken as evidence supporting the uncontrollability of thoughts. In summary, the feedback cycles linking type 2 worry to behaviour and thought control depict processes in which behavioural and thought-control responses deprive the individual of the opportunity to discover that worrying is subject to voluntary control and/or does not lead to catastrophe. Moreover, avoidance of situations that might trigger worry removes an opportunity for the individual to develop alternative strategies for appraisal and coping with threat.

In summary, worrying becomes excessive and disabling because negative beliefs about worry and type 2 worry increase anxiety and decrease the ease with which the individual can meet internal states that terminate the worry process. The sense that worrying is uncontrollable is a product of negative beliefs concerning uncontrollability that are strengthened by the paradoxical effects of maladaptive control strategies and the failure to attempt active and more effective control strategies. In particular, patients try not to think about the content of a worry or they may attempt to challenge the content of type 1 worry (an ineffective strategy for modifying maladaptive beliefs about worry). However, they seldom attempt to discontinue the catastrophising process and challenge negative beliefs about worrying.

Negative meta-beliefs concerning worry can emerge from several influences, such as social learning events, the observed effects of worry on arousal, and the possible negative effects of worry on thinking. For instance, worrying under some circumstances appears to increase the frequency of intrusive thoughts. This cognitive effect may be interpreted as evidence of failed mental control and may thus contribute to the development of negative beliefs and type 2 worry.

A BRIEF REVIEW OF RESEARCH

In this section research on GAD is briefly reviewed. Several studies provide data that are consistent with the central predictions of the GAD model. The model predicts that pathological worry should be associated with positive and negative beliefs about worry. Research on non-GAD individuals with elevated worry shows that these individuals give positive reasons for worrying, such as motivation, preparation, and avoidance (Borkovec & Roemer, 1995). More direct support for a relationship between meta-beliefs and worry has been reported by Cartwright-Hatton & Wells (1997), who developed the Meta-Cognitions Questionnaire (MCQ) to assess dimensions of positive and negative beliefs about worry and individual differences in metacognitive processes. This questionnaire has five subscales with good psychometric properties. The subscales are as follows: (a) positive beliefs; (b) beliefs about uncontrollability; (c) cognitive confidence; (d) negative beliefs about thoughts including themes of punishment and responsibility; and (e) cognitive self-consciousness. Both positive and negative beliefs are positively correlated with worry proneness. In a preliminary comparison of DSM-III-R-diagnosed GAD patients, patients with obsessive compulsive disorder, and a mixed diagnosis group, GAD and obsessive-compulsive patients reported significantly greater negative beliefs concerning the uncontrollability and danger associated with thoughts than the other group. The greater endorsement of beliefs about uncontrollability supports the subsequent revision of GAD criteria, appearing in DSM-IV (APA, 1994), to include uncontrollability as a diagnostic criterion. GAD patients also showed significantly higher scores than non-patient controls on negative beliefs about thoughts concerning superstition and punishment. Wells & Carter (2001) compared MCQ scores among groups of individuals with DSM-III-R GAD, social phobia, and panic disorder, and among non-patients. Consistent with predictions based on the GAD model, there were no significant differences in positive beliefs about worry among the groups (positive beliefs are thought to be normal). However, GAD patients showed higher scores than other anxious and non-patient groups in negative beliefs concerning uncontrollability and danger. GAD patients were characterised by high negative metacognition scores, a finding which set them apart from the other anxious patients and non-patients. For instance, GAD patients could be distinguished significantly from the anxious and non-patients groups by higher levels of type 2 worry. Fewer overall distinctions between groups were obtained in type 1 worry, as would be predicted.

In a test of the relative contribution of type 1 worry and type 2 worry to pathological worry, Wells & Carter (1999) demonstrated that among non-patients, type 2 worry was an independent, specific predictor of pathological worry when co-variances with type 1 worry and trait anxiety were controlled. However, type 1 worry did not contribute independently to pathological worry. This relationship held when a measure of the uncontrollability of worry was entered in the equation. These data support the idea that metacognitions are associated with pathological worry and GAD.

Consequences of Worry

The cognitive model assumes that use of worry as a coping strategy has potentially deleterious consequences for emotional regulation, thereby contributing to negative beliefs about worry. Data from several sources support the view that worry may be problematic for mental regulation. In particular, brief periods of worry appear to lead to increments in negative thought intrusions (Borkovec et al., 1983; York et al., 1987). Furthermore, after exposure to a stressful event, brief periods of worry appear to lead to an incubation of intrusive images related to that event over a subsequent 3-day period (Butler et al., 1995; Wells & Papageorgiou, 1995). These data suggest that using worry as a processing strategy may in some circumstances present its own problems and may contribute to problems of intrusive thoughts. It is likely that such effects reinforce appraisals of diminished control and support negative metacognitions.

Ineffective Thought Control

Several studies have explored the effects of thought control by suppression on subsequent thinking processes (e.g., Wegner et al., 1987). These studies have produced mixed findings, but, generally, thought suppression appears rarely to be effective, and there is some evidence that it may produce paradoxical effects (see Purdon [1999] for a review). Studies of individual differences in the use of thought-control strategies support the idea that some strategies may be unhelpful for self-regulation. In particular, the tendency to use worry or punishment as control strategies is positively associated with vulnerability to emotional disorder (Wells & Davies, 1994; Reynolds & Wells, 1999).

TREATING GAD WITH METACOGNITIVE FOCUSED CBT

A specialised type of metacognitive focused cognitive therapy has been devised on the basis of the present model (Wells, 1997). The model suggests that cognitive-behavioural interventions could be improved by focusing treatment on challenging type 2 worry and negative and positive metacognitive beliefs. Existing cognitive behavioural approaches have tended to teach anxiety-management strategies and use cognitive methods aimed at evaluating the validity of an individual's type 1 worry. Such approaches are likely to produce only modest results because they fail to challenge underlying metacognitions concerning the uncontrollability of worrying, the dangers of worrying, and the advantages of worrying. Moreover, previous treatments have tended to be technique driven rather than based on an individual disorder specific case conceptualisation. The availability of a specific model, as described here, provides the basis for generating idiosyncratic case conceptualisations.

Structure of Treatment

A particular treatment sequence is advocated. First, an idiosyncratic case formulation can be derived, based on the model. Second, patients are socialised to the model, and this is followed by initial cognitive-behavioural strategies aimed at challenging beliefs in the uncontrollability of worry. Therapy proceeds by challenging negative beliefs concerning the dangers of worry, and later, in treatment, positive beliefs concerning the advantages of worry are targeted. During the final stages of treatment, relapse-prevention strategies are implemented. These include modifying residual beliefs, exploring alternative strategies for appraising and dealing with threat, and compiling a "therapy blueprint". This specialised form of treatment is typically scheduled for 12 weekly sessions of 45–60 minutes in duration. However, it is often the case that fewer sessions are required, depending on factors such as patient co-morbidity and therapist competency.

Eliciting Metacognitions and Case Conceptualisation

An idiosyncratic case conceptualisation is presented in Figure 6.2. Construction of such a formulation depends on eliciting negative and positive metacognitions. With respect to negative metacognitions, two sub-categories of type 2 worry and negative beliefs are relevant. These are (a) beliefs and appraisals concerning the uncontrollability of worry, and (b) beliefs and appraisals concerning the danger of worry. An initial case formulation is constructed from a detailed review of a recent distressing worry episode. Verbal methods, such as questioning the consequences of not controlling worries and running an

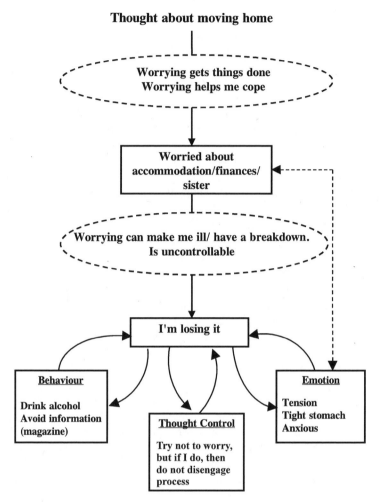

Figure 6.2 An idiosyncratic case conceptualisation of GAD based on the metacognitive model

advantages/disadvantages analysis of worrying, provide efficient tools for eliciting negative and positive metacognitions. Negative metacognitions can also be elicited with self-report measures such as the Anxious Thoughts Inventory (Wells, 1994b), the Meta-Cognitions Questionnaire (Cartwright-Hatton & Wells, 1997), and the GAD scale (Wells, 1997).

When exploring the behavioural components of the model, it is helpful to divide behaviours into thought-control strategies, and other behaviours. In particular, when eliciting thought-control strategies, one should record the use of suppression of triggers and the minimal use of attempts to interrupt the worry process directly once initiated. This information is included in the thought control cell. Other behaviours can be documented in the separate behaviours cell.

The following dialogue illustrates the line of questioning used to generate the components of the case formulation presented in Figure 6.2.

THERAPIST: You've described how recently you have been worrying much of the time. When was the last time you had a particularly distressing episode of worry?

PATIENT: This morning I became very tense and worried about finding a new place to live.

T: Was that a typical worry episode?

P: Yes, only I felt worse than I have for a couple of weeks.

T: OK. I'd like to explore what happened this morning with you in detail. What was it that triggered off your worrying—was it a thought, situation or feeling? (*elicitation of trigger*).

P: It was a thought. I was thinking that I had to find a new place to live.

T: What were the worrying thoughts you had about that? (*elicitation of type 1 worry*).

P: I was thinking, what if I can't find a place, or I can't afford it?

T: So it sounds as if you started worrying about finding a new place to live. Did you have any other worries like that?

P: I was thinking about how I was going to cope with it and I started to think about how I could raise some more money if I needed to. I was also worrying that I wouldn't be able to help my sister because of my own problems.

T: What happened to the way you felt when you were worrying like that? (*exploring emotional response*).

P: I felt tense and stressed out.

T: Did you have any other symptoms?

P: No—mainly feeling very tense in my body and tightness in my stomach.

T: Did you feel anxious?

P: Yes, tense and anxious.

T: When you felt that way and you were worrying intensely, did you have any negative thoughts about what was happening to you? (*elicitation of type 2 worry and negative beliefs*).

P: I'm not sure. Like I couldn't cope, you mean?

T: Could anything bad happen if you continued to worry like that?

P: I'd end up embarrassing myself.

T: How would that happen?

P: I'd just break down and lose my nerve.

T: That sounds like a disadvantage or danger of worrying. Are there any other dangers like that?

P: I could make myself ill with worry and have a nervous breakdown.

T: Were you worried about these things this morning?

P: Yes, I thought I was going to lose it.

T: If worrying is so dangerous, why don't you control it?

P: I can't. I do try but most of the time it's uncontrollable.

T: What do you do to try and control it? (*elicitation of behaviours*).

P: I try to think about something else, and not the thing I'm worried about. Sometimes I'll drink alcohol to stop it. When I'm worrying about my health, I avoid reading the health pages in magazines.

T: Have you ever tried not to engage in the process of worry? I mean if you get a worrying thought you decide to leave it and not do anything with it. Neither try to get rid of it nor try to think it through (*elicitation of thought-control*).

P: No, not really.

T: OK, you've mentioned some disadvantages or dangers of worrying. Do you think there are any advantages to worrying? (*elicitation of positive beliefs*).

P: I definitely think it helps me get things done. It's only because I'm worried about finding a new place to live that I'll have to sort it out.

T: Any other advantages?

P: If I worry about things I'll be prepared. It's like I need to worry in order to cope with bad things in the future.

T: So it sounds as if you believe worrying helps you cope?

P: Yes, it's like I'm right to worry.

T: OK. I've been able to draw together these different strands of the problem so that we may begin to understand the factors contributing to your problem. Let's go through this together.

Socialisation

Socialisation to the model consists of sharing the model in verbal and diagrammatic forms with the patient. A central message to convey is the idea that excessive and problematic worrying is problematic because worry itself has become a source of anxiety and worry, and that the problem is driven by a range of unhelpful beliefs about worrying.

Verbal and behavioural socialisation strategies include delineating the dissonance that exists between negative and positive worry beliefs, and asking whether the patient thinks that there may be problems in holding conflicting beliefs about worry. Hypothetical questions can also be used to illustrate the model. For instance, patients may be asked: "How much of a problem would you have if you no longer believed that worrying was dangerous or uncontrollable?" A further useful question here is this: "If your life depended on worrying, that is, you had to worry in order to survive, how much of a problem would you have?" The principal aim in using these strategies is to illustrate how the problem is not merely worry, but the meaning and beliefs the patient attaches to worry.

Socialisation experiments consisting of thought-suppression attempts can be usefully applied to illustrating the role of unhelpful coping strategies in maintaining negative appraisals of worrying. Patients are asked to avoid thinking a particular target thought (e.g., about a yellow elephant) for a period of two minutes. Typically, patients are unable to deny completely the access of such thoughts to consciousness. Their occurrence is used as evidence that attempts not to think thoughts are often ineffective, and this can strengthen negative beliefs about the loss of control of thinking. This sets the scene for therapy that will explore alternative ways of dealing with worrying thoughts that are capable of modifying negative beliefs about the uncontrollability and dangerousness of such thoughts.

Modifying Type 2 Worry and Negative Beliefs About Uncontrollability

Experience in implementing this treatment suggests that it is particularly effective to commence with modification of negative metacognitions concerning the uncontrollability of worrying. The model assumes that worrying can be subject to control, contrary to the patient's beliefs.

An initial exploration of modulating influences on worry provides the means of weakening beliefs concerning uncontrollability. The therapist examines with the patient occasions in which worry was displaced by competing or distracting activities, and uses these occurrences as examples of the potential controllability of worrying. It is useful for the therapist to ask patients whether they have ever actually tried to give up worrying once it is initiated. Patients report that they attempt to reason with their worry or think that they must work through a worry topic in order to feel better able to cope. It should be highlighted that a patient does not unambiguously know whether worry can be postponed because this has not been attempted, or because ineffective suppression strategies have been used. The effectiveness of reattribution strategies should be gauged by asking patients how much they believe (0–100%) a negative belief before and after use of such strategies.

One of the most significant procedures for challenging uncontrollability appraisals is the worry postponement experiment. Here, patients are asked as a homework assignment to notice the onset of worry and postpone the worry sequence until a specified time period later in the day. Once this time period arrives, the patient can either decide not to worry or to worry for a fixed time period to test further that worry can be controlled. Ratings of belief in the uncontrollability of worrying (0–100%) should be tracked across the use of this experiment. It is important to note that this experiment is not advocating the suppression of thoughts. The idea is that the patient avoids engaging with the worry and running an iterative catastrophising sequence. An initial worry thought (i.e., a trigger) may remain in consciousness, but the patient fails to engage the catastrophising (type 1 worry) process associated with it. This type of experiment can be illustrated with the use of metaphor. For example, not engaging with a worrying thought can be likened to allowing an itch to happen without scratching it. In this metaphor, unhelpful suppression can be likened to trying never to have an itch in the first instance.

Modifying Appraisals and Beliefs Concerning the Danger of Worrying

Negative beliefs that worrying can cause mental or physical catastrophe should be explored and modified through verbal reattribution methods such as examining the evidence and counter-evidence for these ideas. Questioning the evidence that worrying is harmful may achieve initial weakening of the belief. Patients provide various types of information in support of negative beliefs about the dangers of worrying. For instance, worry is often equated with stress, and it is argued that since stress is harmful, worry must also be harmful. A useful strategy here is the decatastrophising of the nature of stress. In particular, the therapist can provide corrective information, emphasising that stress is not synonymous with harm, and that stress reactions can be advantageous for coping and survival. A further strategy is to review the fact that worry and stress are not the same process, and highlight the dissonance that exists between the patient's positive and negative beliefs about worry: (e.g., if worrying is harmful, how can it be that you believe it helps you cope?). Further weakening of negative beliefs about worry can be accomplished by questioning the *mechanism* by which worry causes harm, and reframing distorted beliefs about pathological mechanisms. For instance, some patients believe that worrying increases blood pressure, and because elevated blood pressure is harmful, this means worry must be harmful. Education is useful in these circumstances: elevated blood pressure is typically harmful only under some circumstance (e.g., when chronically elevated), and there is no evidence that worrying produces chronic effects.

Appraisals and beliefs concerning the dangers of worrying are amenable to modification by behavioural experiments. Re-attribution experiments offer one of the most effective and indispensable techniques for challenging beliefs in GAD. In this instance, the person with GAD may be asked to try deliberately to lose control of worry or cause a "mental catastrophe" by worrying excessively. This can be performed during the previously allotted postponed worry period. In the next stage, it is followed by asking individuals to worry more and try to lose control or cause a catastrophe when worrying is naturalistically activated, rather than postponing the activity. An additional strategy for challenging negative beliefs about worrying consists of normalisation of the worry process via the results of mini-surveys. Surveys can be conducted by the patient and therapist to determine the prevalence of worrying among other people. For example, a patient was recently asked to question her husband and two friends to determine how often they had worried over the past month. The patient predicted that other people would have worried little if at all. She was surprised to discover that one of her friends had worried more than she had, and contrary to her predictions everyone disclosed that they had worried.

Modifying Positive Meta-Beliefs

Positive beliefs are challenged by reviewing the evidence and counter-evidence for them and by the use of "mismatch strategies". The mismatch strategy consists of asking a patient to write out a detailed description of the events portrayed in a worry scenario. These events are then compared with the events that actually transpired in a worried-about situation. This strategy can be practised for situations that are avoided and combined with subsequent exposure to avoided situations. The strategy is used to illustrate how the worry narrative does not accurately depict reality, and, as such, the usefulness of worry as a coping strategy can be questioned.

An effective experimental strategy for challenging positive beliefs about worry consists of asking the patient to engage in daily activities while increasing worrying and then to repeat this while decreasing worrying. This procedure can be used to test patients' predictions that worrying enhances coping or increases the probability of positive events. If these beliefs are correct, then abandonment of worrying should lead to evidence of not coping while enhancement of worrying should lead to better outcomes.

Strategy Shifts and Relapse Prevention

Residual beliefs and residual avoidance should be formulated and modified towards the end of treatment. The final stage of treatment usually consists of examining alternative strategies for appraising and dealing with threat and "what if" triggers for worrying. One strategy consists of encouraging patients to use positive endings for "what if" thoughts. Rather than contemplating the worst consequence in response to these triggers, patients are asked to practise generating positive outcomes and consequences, and to use evidence other than a "felt sense" to make predictions about coping. Relapse prevention consists of generating a summary of the patient's understanding of the nature of GAD and a description of effective strategies for dealing with worry. To this end, a therapy blueprint can be constructed that presents a detailed summary account of material learned in therapy. This typically consists of an example of an idiosyncratic case conceptualisation, examples of negative and positive beliefs with counter-evidence, and a summary of useful strategies and results of behavioural experiments.

Summary

The metacognitive model of GAD suggests that excessive and generalised worry results from the repeated use of worrying as a coping strategy and the existence of particular metacognitions. Treatment based on the model shifts emphasis away from teaching anxiety control strategies and challenging the content of type 1 worry to modifying dysfunctional metacognitions and exploring alternative self-regulatory strategies. The results of empirical studies on anxious non-patients and on individuals with GAD support central aspects of the model. Preliminary data from patients treated with metacognitive therapy suggest that this treatment approach may be highly effective and can be delivered well within a 12-session course of treatment. Further controlled evaluations of the treatment are in progress.

CONCLUSION

In this chapter a specific model of GAD was described and the treatment based on the model outlined. For further information on assessment and the implementation of this treatment, the interested reader should consult Wells (1997). The present model aims to advance our understanding of GAD by presenting an account of cognitive-behavioural maintenance mechanisms. A more detailed analysis of maintaining factors facilitates a revision of treatment strategies and provides a basis for more precise theory-driven targeting of specific psychological factors. It is likely that, as we refine our psychological models and treatments, the efficacy of interventions and the ease with which cognitive behavioural modification can be achieved will be enhanced.

REFERENCES

American Psychiatric Association (APA) (1994). *Diagnostic and statistical manual of mental disorders*—Revised, 4th ed. Washington, DC: APA.

Barlow, D.H., Rapee, R.M., & Brown, T.A. (1992). Behavioural treatment of generalised anxiety disorder. *Behavior Therapy*, **23**, 551–570.

Beck, A.T. (1976). *Cognitive therapy and the emotional disorders*. New York: International Universities Press.

Borkovec, T.D., & Costello, E. (1993). The nature, functions, and origins of worry. In: G.C.L. Davey & F. Tallis (Eds.). *Worrying: Perspectives on theory, assessment and treatment* (pp. 5–33). Chichester, UK: Wiley.

Borkovec, T.D., Robinson, E., Pruzinsky, T., & DePree, J.A. (1983). Preliminary exploration of worry: Some characteristics and processes. *Behaviour Research and Therapy*, **21**, 9–16.

Borkovec, T.D., & Roemer, L. (1995). Perceived functions of worry among generalised anxiety subjects: Distraction from more emotionally distressing topics? *Behaviour Therapy and Experimental Psychiatry*, **26**, 25–30.

Butler, G., Wells, A., & Dewick, H. (1995). Differential effects of worry and imagery after exposure to a stressful stimulus: A pilot study. *Behavioural and Cognitive Psychotherapy*, **23**, 45–56.

Cartwright-Hatton, S., & Wells, A. (1997). Beliefs about worry and intrusions: The Meta-Cognition Questionnaire and its correlates. *Journal of Anxiety Disorders*, **11**, 279–296.

Durham, R.C., & Allan, T. (1993). Psychological treatment of generalized anxiety disorder: A review of the clinical significance of results in outcome studies since 1980. *British Journal of Psychiatry*, **163**, 19–26.

Fisher, P.L., & Durham, R.C. (1999). Recovery rates in generalized anxiety disorder following psychological therapy: An analysis of clinically significant change in the STAI-T across outcome studies since 1990. *Psychological Medicine*, **29**, 1425–1434.

Papageorgiou, C., & Wells, A. (1999). Process and meta-cognitive dimensions of depressive and anxious thoughts and relationships with emotional intensity. *Clinical Psychology and Psychotherapy*, **6**, 156–162. Special Issue, *Metacognition and cognitive behaviour therapy:* Chichester, UK: Wiley.

Purdon, C. (1999). Thought suppression and psychopathology. *Behaviour Research and Therapy*, **37**, 1029–1054.

Reynolds, M., & Wells, A. (1999). The Thought Control Questionnaire: Psychometric properties in a clinical sample, and relationships with PTSD and depression. *Psychological Medicine*, **29**, 1089–1099.

Sanderson, W.C., & Barlow, D.M. (1990). A description of patients diagnosed with DSM-III-R generalized anxiety disorder. *Journal of Nervous and Mental Disease*, **178**, 588–591.

Wegner, D.M., Schneider, D.J., Carter, S.R., III, & White, T.L. (1987). Paradoxical effects of thought suppression. *Journal of Personality and Social Psychology*, **53**, 5–13.

Wells, A. (1994a). Attention and the control of worry. In: G.C.L. Davey & F. Tallis (Eds.). *Worrying: Perspectives on theory, assessment and treatment*. Chichester, UK: Wiley.

Wells, A. (1994b). A Multidimensional Measure of Worry: Development and preliminary validation of the Anxious Thoughts Inventory. *Anxiety, Stress, and Coping*, **6**, 289–299.

Wells, A. (1995). Meta-cognition and worry: A cognitive model of generalised anxiety disorder. *Behavioural and Cognitive Psychotherapy*, **23**, 301–320.

Wells, A. (1997). *Cognitive therapy of anxiety disorders: A practice manual and conceptual guide*. Chichester, UK: Wiley.

Wells, A. (1999). A metacognitive model and therapy for generalised anxiety disorder. *Clinical Psychology and Psychotherapy*, **6**, 86–96. Special Issue, *Metacognition and cognitive behaviour therapy*. Chichester, UK: Wiley.

Wells, A. (2000). *Emotional disorders and metacognition: Innovative cognitive therapy*. Chichester, UK: Wiley.

Wells, A., & Carter, K. (1999). Preliminary tests of a cognitive model of generalized anxiety disorder. *Behaviour Research and Therapy*, **37**, 585–594.

Wells, A., & Carter, K. (2001). Further tests of a cognitive model of GAD: Worry and metacognitions in patients with GAD, panic disorder, social phobia, and depression. *Behavior Therapy*, **32**, 85–102.

Wells, A., & Davies, M.I. (1994). The Thought Control Questionnaire: A measure of individual differences in the control of unwanted thoughts. *Behaviour Research and Therapy*, **32**, 871–878.

Wells, A., & Matthews, G. (1994). *Attention and emotion: A clinical perspective*. Hove, UK: Erlbaum.

Wells, A., & Morrison, A.P. (1994). Qualitative dimensions of normal worry and normal intrusive thoughts: A comparative study. *Behaviour Research and Therapy*, **32**, 867–870.

Wells, A., & Papageorgiou, C. (1995). Worry and the incubation of intrusive images following stress. *Behaviour Research and Therapy*, **33**, 579–583.

Yonkers, K.A., Warshaw, M.G., Massion, A.O., & Keller, M.B. (1996). Phenomenology and course of generalized anxiety disorder. *British Journal of Psychiatry*, **168**, 308–313.

York, D., Borkovec, T.D., Vasey, M., & Stern, R. (1987). Effects of worry and somatic anxiety induction on thoughts, emotion and physiological activity. *Behaviour Research and Therapy*, **25**, 523–526.

CHAPTER 7

ACT at Work

Frank W. Bond

*Department of Psychology, Goldsmiths College,
University of London, New Cross, London, UK*

and

Steven C. Hayes

Department of Psychology, University of Nevada, Reno, NV, USA

Redesigning work and management processes in order to reduce workers' exposure to sources of stress has been advocated by occupational health psychologists, in both the UK (e.g., Cox et al., 2000) and USA (e.g., National Institute of Occupational Safety and Health [NIOSH], 1996). Furthermore, outcome research has provided empirical support for work redesign interventions that target such variables as lack of worker control, role ambiguity, poor workplace communication, career concerns, poor organisational climate, heavy workload, or shift work (e.g., Bond & Bunce, 2001; Landsbergis & Vivona-Vaughan, 1995). Despite these successes, it also seems to be important to address the psychological styles or approaches that workers bring to stressful work situations. First, some sources of stress may not be completely avoidable (e.g., underpromotion). Second, workers' efforts to modify stressful situations may themselves be inhibited by poor psychological coping strategies (e.g., use of avoidance strategies). Finally, work-related stress does not occur in a vacuum, and psychological styles that increase stress reactions at home (e.g., being overcontrolling) may also result in feeling stress at work. Consistent with this line of thought, researchers investigating stress at work have found that psychological styles, such as type-A behaviour pattern (TABP) and locus of control, are reliable predictors of occupational stress (e.g., Jex, 1998).

Research by Bond & Bunce (submitted) confirms the significance of these two individual characteristics in predicting stress, but it also highlights the even greater importance of another psychological style that has yet to receive much attention in the work stress literature: acceptance. Psychological acceptance refers to people's willingness to experience difficult private events (e.g., thoughts, emotions, sensations, and memories), without avoiding, struggling, or suppressing them. Bond & Bunce found that poor psychological acceptance predicts, in one year's time, mental ill-health and poor productivity to a significantly greater extent than does TABP, locus of control, and work-related sources of stress. They also found that low levels of acceptance predict these stress outcomes across several types of industries (e.g., nursing, advertising, and central government civil service). Such findings clearly suggest a need to consider this particular individual characteristic when assessing and promoting occupational health.

Acceptance and commitment therapy (ACT, pronounced as a whole word, not by its constituent letters, A-C-T) (Hayes et al., 1999b; see also Zettle & Hayes, Chapter 3 in this volume) is one cognitive-behaviour-based treatment that is particularly focused on the improvement of psychological acceptance. In this chapter, we describe how ACT can be used in a brief, group-based, worksite stress-management intervention (SMI). It is the protocol for this SMI that forms the core of this chapter, but before presenting it, we will briefly discuss ACT theory and outcome studies (although see Zettle & Hayes, Chapter 3 in this volume, for a more thorough discussion of both). Importantly, we also discuss how Bond & Bunce (2000) validated our worksite ACT protocol in a UK media organisation, and how they demonstrated that this intervention worked for the reasons actually specified by ACT theory.

ACT: THEORY AND RESEARCH

ACT is based on a functional contextual approach to psychological dysfunction (e.g., Hayes, 1993) that maintains that, due to a person's previous learning history, certain situations (e.g., being criticised by the supervisor) evoke unwanted thoughts, emotions, and sensations. Nevertheless, these negative, internal events lead to strain (defined here as impairment of psychological or physiological well-being [Bunce, 1997]), only in a certain context: one in which they are (a) taken literally (e.g., If I *feel* fearful, then there is *really* something to fear) and (b) are construed as events that need to be changed or avoided. In such a context, these unwanted, internal events function as the problems that they are construed to be and, thus, result in strain; however, these same negative thoughts, emotions, and sensations will not lead to impaired functioning if they are placed in a different context: one in which they are accepted (Hayes, 1994). (See Hayes et al. [1999a] for a more in-depth discussion of functional contextualism and its relationship to ACT.)

In a context of acceptance, people are mindful that they are engaged in processes called thinking and feeling, but they are, in a sense, "mindfully inactive". They merely observe and describe their internal events without participating in them, that is, without taking them literally, and without needlessly trying to change, avoid, or otherwise control them, no matter how unwanted or unpleasant they may be (Hayes, 1987). Observing and describing unwanted internal events increases the degree to which people can *act* to obtain the goals that they have in a given situation, without first waiting for their own historically produced *reactions* (e.g., fear and sadness) to change (Hayes, 1987). Such action will increase the probability that people can attain more positive reinforcement, and avoid more punishment, than they could by participating in, and thus becoming entangled in, any unwanted internal events (e.g., worry, unhappiness, or fear). Contact with these improved contingencies will, in turn, help prevent or reduce strain. To clarify this diagrammatically, ACT maintains the following:

Unwanted thoughts, emotions, and sensations + (the context of) literality, change or avoidance → strain

—and—

Unwanted thoughts, emotions, and sensations + (the context of) acceptance → unwanted thoughts, emotions, and sensations *that do not result in strain*

It should be emphasised that adopting a context of acceptance may not, at least at first, prevent a given stressor from evoking negative thoughts, emotions, and sensations; however, the more people accept these negative internal events, the more likely it is that the given stressor will cease to trigger them, due to extinction processes (Linehan, 1993). Nevertheless, it is not helpful for ACT clients to think that acceptance is a way to avoid (even eventually) experiencing unwanted internal events. Most people have learning histories that will result in certain situations evoking unwanted internal events; and in these inevitable circumstances, it is in the best interests of clients (or SMI trainees) to react willingly (i.e., with acceptance) to these internal events.

Unlike ACT, many other cognitive behaviour approaches to emotional and behavioural change have traditionally maintained that people with emotional disorders become less distressed, because the "*content*" of their thoughts becomes more functional (e.g., Beck, 1976; Beck et al., 1979); that is, because their thoughts change, for example, from "I am a *failure*" to "I am an *adequate person*". The context in which people hold their "dysfunctional" thoughts (e.g., willingly) has not been emphasised very strongly (with the exception, perhaps, of rational emotive behaviour therapy (REBT) [see Ellis & Robb, 1994]). Recently, however, acceptance strategies have been integrated, to varying degrees, into CBT treatments, and with good reason as well. As Hayes et al. (1996) note, a large literature now documents an association between emotional willingness and positive outcome in psychotherapy. Specifically, acceptance-based psychotherapy methods have been developed for problems such as borderline personality disorder (Linehan, 1993), substance abuse (Marlatt, 1994), relationship problems (Koerner et al., 1994), and generalised anxiety disorder (Wells, 1995; Chapter 6, this volume). Nevertheless, ACT was the first CBT to promote psychological acceptance without also targeting psychological content for change, and it seems to be the one that focuses on acceptance processes to the greatest extent. Other CBTs that employ acceptance techniques (e.g., REBT) still emphasise the content of cognition over the context in which it is held. As a result, the "content CBTs" and ACT advocate different primary goals for dealing with undesirable cognitive content; that is, change vs. acceptance, respectively.

Although the outcome literature on ACT is increasing rapidly (see Hayes et al. [1999a] for a recent review), it is not yet known whether ACT will generally produce better outcomes than will content-oriented CBTs. Research thus far, however, demonstrates (a) fairly equivalent, beneficial effects of these two kinds of treatment, and (b) that each works though different processes. Regarding this second point, ACT quickly reduces the believability, or literality, of people's negative, internal events (e.g., because I am fearful, it does not mean that there is *really* something to fear), but the frequency of these experiences is reduced more slowly (Zettle & Hayes, 1986). Conversely, content-oriented cognitive therapy (CT) (Beck et al., 1979) reduces the frequency of people's negative, private events fairly quickly, but the believability of these events, when they inevitably occur, is reduced more slowly (Zettle & Hayes, 1986).

ACT AS A WORKPLACE STRESS MANAGEMENT INTERVENTION

Given the ability of ACT to improve acceptance and psychological well-being (see Hayes et al., 1999a), Bond & Bunce (2000) hypothesised that ACT might be effective as a worksite SMI, and so tested this hypothesis in a randomised, controlled trial in a large UK media organisation. ACT was compared with a waiting-list control group and a risk management approach designed to increase worker innovation (the latter is not discussed further in this chapter, due to its irrelevance to CBT, but see Bond & Bunce, 2000).

Bond & Bunce (2000) wished to test the efficacy of ACT using a brief, group-based implementation method. To this end, they adapted the "2 + 1" method of psychotherapy delivery (e.g., Barkham & Shapiro, 1990) in which participants receive three, three-hour sessions, two on consecutive weeks, and a third three months later. This particular brief format has the advantage of allowing participants to carry out homework assignments that encourage the application of learned acceptance strategies in their work environments. They then receive feedback on their efforts during the following sessions. Such a delivery strategy, unique in SMI research, may be useful in helping people to learn more effective behaviours in less therapeutic time (e.g., Bond & Dryden, 1996), thereby making an SMI more cost-effective and thus more attractive to organisations.

As Bond & Bunce (2000) predicted, the results of their study indicated that ACT significantly improved people's mental well-being and tendency to innovate, in comparison to the control group. (Mental well-being was measured by the General Health Questionnaire [GHQ] [Goldberg, 1978] and the Beck Depression Inventory [BDI] [Beck et al., 1961].) Furthermore, research using the "four tests for mediation" recommended by Baron & Kenny (1986) (Kenny, 1998) showed that the ACT intervention improved people's mental health (GHQ) and propensity to innovate, because it increased their psychological acceptance (as measured by the Acceptance and Action Questionnaire [AAQ] [Hayes et al., submitted]). Unlike content CBTs, ACT did not lead to these improvements as a result of making participants' cognitive content more functional. Indeed, there was no significant pre-test/post-test change for the ACT group on the measure of cognitive content used in this experiment (i.e., the Dysfunctional Attitude Survey [DAS] [Weissman, 1979]). Thus, it appeared that psychological acceptance, and not cognitive content, was the mechanism, or mediator, by which ACT improved the stress outcomes of participants in the UK media organisation.

These findings support the ACT hypothesis of the mechanism by which this intervention effects change. They are also consistent with several other studies on ACT in such areas as depression (Zettle & Hayes, 1987; Zettle & Rains, 1989), coping with psychotic symptoms (Bach & Hayes, 2002; García & Pérez, 2001), anxiety (Luciano & Gutierrez, 2001; Roemer & Orsillo, 2002), and pain (Geiser, 1992; Hayes et al., 1999a; Luciano et al., 2001; see also McCracken, 1998), among other problems.

It appears, then, that our ACT protocol, presented in this chapter, can decrease strain and improve innovation propensity in a work environment, and it does so because it increases psychological acceptance (Bond & Bunce, 2000). Understanding the mechanism by which ACT works is, of course, helpful for theoretical reasons, but it is also essential for therapeutic ones. For, unless we understand why an intervention works, it is impossible to maximise its effectiveness. To elaborate, by knowing that acceptance mediates the effects that ACT has on stress-related outcomes, psychologists can propose and test techniques that may manipulate this variable more effectively, and thus better help workers to improve their mental health and effectiveness at work.

Other than that of Bond & Bunce (2000), we are not aware of another outcome study that has (a) evaluated rigorously the mechanisms by which an SMI works, or (b) used such a detailed SMI protocol in a successful, randomised controlled trial. For these reasons, we believe that our programme may be helpful to practitioners who wish to implement a brief, group-based SMI, and particularly a brief, group-based, CBT SMI, in a workplace setting.

ACT MANUAL

Training Session I (Week 1)

At the beginning of this session, the participants are told that any personal information that is revealed or discussed in this or any session is confidential and should not be shared or discussed with anyone at all outside the room (including partners and family members). Anyone not prepared to make such a commitment to privacy is asked to leave. In addition, the participants are told that they are free to leave this or any subsequent training session at any time and for any reason, and the fact that they left will not be reported to anyone.

What is Stress?

Firstly, the participants are asked, "What are your symptoms or signs of stress?", and their responses are noted on a whiteboard. After several people provide some examples, an overhead projector slide of various signs of stress is presented. This slide notes many physical (e.g., sleep loss), mood (e.g., irritability), thinking (e.g., poor memory), and action signs (e.g., crying) of stress. After these are read out and questions are dealt with, it is noted that these signs of stress are relevant to the individual and that they centre on mental and physical well-being, but it is also noted that the organisation, as a whole, may also show signs of stress, and that these signs centre on organisational ineffectiveness, employee turnover, and sick absence rates. An overhead projector slide of organisational signs of stress is then displayed, and then there is a brief discussion and question time on these organisational signs of stress.

What Causes Work Stress?

The participants are told that there are two sources of work stress: work/organisational-related factors and individual characteristics. The latter are discussed first, and they are displayed on an overhead projector. They include personality (e.g., optimistic vs. pessimistic), pre-existing psychological well-being (e.g., history of anxiety or depression that pre-dates the current job), social support (e.g., good friends and/or a helpful partner), and home-based factors (e.g., a bad partnership or noisy neighbours). These factors are discussed briefly and then an overhead projector slide of work-related sources of stress (taken from Cooper & Marshall [1976]) is displayed, comprising factors intrinsic to the job (e.g., long hours and work overload), role in the organisation (e.g., conflicting job demands, or lack of clear objectives or duties), relationships at work (e.g., those with superiors, subordinates, and colleagues), career development (e.g., job security, retirement, and stagnation), and organisational structure and climate (e.g., lack of freedom and autonomy).

The participants are told that these workshops will not focus on changing the individual or work-related sources of stress; rather, they will focus on changing how individuals react to these types of stressful events. The participants are told the following:

> Consider for a moment that you are a bathroom or kitchen sink. The sources of stress that we have just discussed are like taps that can pour water (or stress) into a sink, and the more taps that flow, the more water there is that is poured into the sink. Now, under most circumstances, a sink will not overflow with water, if it is unplugged, but if it is plugged, the sink will become overwhelmed with water and overflow, causing damage. The goal of these stress-management sessions is not to stop the water from flowing, but, rather, to help you to unplug your sinks so that the stresses that you encounter will not overwhelm you.

Beginning ACT

Since most people believe that undesirable thoughts and emotions (i.e., negative psychological content) interfere with effective and enjoyable living, the participants have probably spent a great deal of effort trying to eradicate this content, and, first of all, examples of this eradication effort are elicited from the participants. For example, they may have tried to avoid, change, justify, rationalise, deny, ignore, or tolerate their psychological content. In order to elicit these examples, the trainer asks a question, such as, "How have you tried to deal with your (anxiety, unhappiness, worries [i.e., unwanted psychological content])?" It is likely that the participants will respond to this question by listing a number of popular and culturally reinforced methods. These might include alcohol, relaxation training, religion, meditation, avoidance, social reassurance, distraction, positive thinking, "analysing" the situation, and maybe even psychotherapeutic techniques that involve changing one's beliefs.

And How Has That Worked?

ACT facilitates a contest between two main players. On the one hand, there is the mind of the participants. By "mind" it is meant a set of rules and constructions that order the world (e.g., "Men should be hard as nuts"). On the other hand, there is the direct experience of each participant; for, the participants have directly contacted certain contingent relationships in the world; that is, in a given situation, if I do X, then Y will occur. These contingent relationships and one's "mind" are in fundamental conflict. The goal of ACT is to "blow" the trainees' minds, so that their experiences can play a greater role in their lives (i.e., so that they can more often make direct contact with contingencies of reinforcement). To accomplish this goal, the concept of "workability" is stressed; that is, the participants are told, "Ask yourself: have your rules delivered? If you do what your mind tells you (if you follow your verbal constructions), are the consequences you actually experience those that the rules specify?" If the answer is "yes", then it is unlikely that the participants display cognitive, emotional, physiological, and behavioural stress symptoms. Since, for many, the answer to this question is not "yes", it is likely that their "mind" has not been very beneficial in helping them to alter the impact of their unwanted emotions, cognitions, and physiological sensations (i.e., their negative experiences).

To determine how helpful their mind has been, the trainer asks how the participants' favoured, experiential avoidance strategies have assisted them in altering the form of, frequency of, or susceptibility to their negative experiences. For example, consider this situation in which a participant wanted to stop worrying needlessly about work:

TRAINER: What have you tried to do to stop worrying?

PARTICIPANT: I've tried to talk myself out of the worry by "thinking things through", relaxing, doing something not related to work—like watch TV or clean my house.

T: Right. Good. Let me ask you this. Your mind says, "Don't worry: relax, watch TV, think things through, and then you won't worry." Right?

P: Right.

T: OK, and how has that worked? For example, as you've done what your mind has told you to do, have you been able to stop worrying or even worry less, and have you then been able to enjoy or be involved fully in what you need to do?

P: Sometimes, but not always, and even if I can stop worrying, it's only very temporarily.

T: Right, so, overall, would you say that you have been able to stop worrying unnecessarily?

P: No, and it's a continuous battle: I spend so much time trying to stop worrying that I become exhausted. Really, it's not unusual for me to get headaches because of all of the worrying that I do.

T: Isn't that interesting? It seems like a paradox, doesn't it? I mean, you do what your mind says: do something to stop worrying: watch TV, think it through, clean your house, but it doesn't work: you still worry.

P: Yes, but what can I do?

T: What does your mind tell you to do?

P: A lot. Relax! You're crazy. Do less work. It's not the end of the world if things go wrong. Take a break, etc.

T: Have you done these things?

P: Of course—I've certainly tried.

T: And how have they worked? Have they paid off in a fundamental way, so that by doing them you have transformed the situation and you are no longer bothered by worrying? Or are you, unbelievably, sinking in deeper, worrying more, feeling worse?

P: I feel like I'm sinking deeper: I can't relax!

T: Incredible, isn't it? I mean if we had an investment adviser with this track record we would have sacked him long ago, but here your mind keeps leading you into efforts that don't really, fundamentally pay off, but it keeps following you around, nattering on, and it is hard not to give it one more try. I mean what else can you do but go along with what your mind tells you to do? But maybe we are coming to a point in which the question will be "which will you go with? Your mind or your experience?" Up to now the answer has been "your mind", but just notice what your experience tells you about how well that has worked.

Conversations such as these are conducted with several members of the group, and it is always emphasised that listening to one's mind is not always effective in relieving the effects of stress, worry, unhappiness, etc. (and it's not even always effective in helping people to achieve the goals that they wish to accomplish). After three of these conversations, the trainer speaks as follows:

Isn't this interesting? We do what our mind tells us to do about our thoughts and feelings, but it doesn't seem to help. In fact, it can even make us feel worse. Why is this the case? Well, human language has given us a tremendous advantage as a species, because it allows us to break things down into parts, to formulate plans, to construct futures we have never experienced before, and to plan action. And it works pretty well. If we look just at the 95% of our existence that involves what goes on outside the skin, it works terrifically. Look at all the things the rest of creation is dealing with and you'll see we do pretty well. Just look around this room; almost everything we see in here wouldn't be here without human language and human rationality: the plastic chair, the lights, the heaters, our clothes, the television. So, we are warm, it won't rain on us, we have light and TV: with regard to the stuff with which non-humans struggle, we are in good shape, really. You give a dog or a cat all these things: warmth, shelter, food, social stimulation, and they are about as happy as they know how to be.

So, the really important things in our life, important to us as a species competing with other life forms on this planet, have been done with human language. In a very significant way, we human beings realise this, and this realisation is encapsulated in a pervasive rule that most all of us buy into: if you don't like something, figure out how to get rid of it, and get rid of it. Now, this rule works extremely well in 95% of our life. But, not in the world inside the skin: that last 5%. It's a pretty important 5%, as well, because that is where satisfaction, contentment, and happiness lie. I don't want you to take my word for this; look at your own life, and in your own experience, not in your logical mind, is it not the case that, in the world inside the skin, the rule actually is, if you aren't willing to have it, you've got it?

For example, this woman struggles with worry; she's not willing to have it. But, if it is really, really important not to worry or be anxious, and if you then start to worry or be anxious, that is something to worry and become anxious about. Let's put a name to this phenomenon. Let's say: in the world outside our body, conscious, deliberate, purposeful control works great. So, figure out how to get rid of what you want to get rid of and do it. But in the areas of consciousness, your life history, self, emotions, thoughts, feelings, behavioural predispositions, memories, attitudes, bodily sensations, and so on, such control often isn't helpful. In this world under our skin, the solution isn't deliberate control; the problem is control. If you try to avoid your own history, your own worries, your own anxiety, depression, and their triggers, you are in a no-win struggle. See, what I am saying here is that we can't control our thoughts and feelings, or anything that happens under our skin, in our mind, in our body.

Consider this. Suppose I had all of you hooked up to the best polygraph that's ever been built. This is a perfect machine, the most sensitive ever made. When you are all wired up to it there is no way you can be stressed or anxious without the machine knowing it. So, I tell you that you have a very simple task here: all you have to do is stay relaxed. If you get the least bit anxious, however, I will know it. Now, I know you want to try hard and I want to give you an incentive to do so, so I also happen to have a .44 magnum pistol which I'll hold to your head. If you just stay relaxed, I won't blow your brains out, but if you get nervous (and I'll know it because you're wired up to this perfect machine), I'm going to have to kill you. Your brains will be all over the walls. So, just relax!—— What do you think would happen? Guess what you'd get? Bam! How could it be otherwise? The tiniest bit of anxiety would be terrifying. You'd all be thinking, "Oh my God! I'm getting anxious! Here it comes!" Bam! You're dead meat. How could it work otherwise?

You, of course, have the perfect polygraph already hooked up to you: it's called your nervous system. It is better than any machine humans have ever made. You can't really feel something and not have your nervous system in contact with it, almost by definition. And you've got something more powerful and more threatening than any gun—your own self-esteem, self-worth, the workability of your life. So, you actually are in a situation that is very much like this. You're holding the gun to your head and saying, "relax!" or "don't worry", or "snap out of this unhappiness". So what you then get is—bam!: more worry, more anxiety, more unhappiness, and you throw in a little humiliation, self-downing and feelings of inadequacy to boot. So, see if this isn't true for you: people's thoughts and emotions cannot be effectively, nor always, controlled by their own thoughts and other people's instructions. Sadly, even pleasant thoughts and emotions can't be verbally controlled.

Consider this. What if I pointed out a person to each of you and said that if you fall in love with that person within two days, I'll give you £10 million. Could you do it? Could you fall in love on command, in order to earn lots of money? What if you came back in two days and said, "I did it, pay me the money!", and then I said, "Sorry, it was a trick: I don't have that kind of money." What are you going to do? If you really can fall in love that way, it wouldn't matter if I tricked you, but I suspect you would be awfully mad. In other words, it's not just getting rid of emotions that is difficult, but it is equally difficult to create them, even ones you like, in any kind of controllable, highly predictive, deliberate way.

Willingness as an Alternative Strategy

We've seen how trying to control our thoughts, feelings, and other products of our mind is not a reliable, or even helpful, strategy for reducing our problems. But what is the alternative? It's willingness. If one is willing to have an emotion or thought, and not get rid of it or alter it, then one can escape the inevitable consequences of control; that is, if you refuse to have it, you've got it. This consequence is inescapably the case both because the control strategy doesn't work, and because the strategy itself results in an increase in the events it is designed to prevent. That is, the more you don't want to be anxious, the more anxious you will probably become.

One way to conceive of the different outcomes of willingness and control is through clean versus dirty discomfort. Clean discomfort is the discomfort that we all experience in our lives as a function of living. Clean discomfort varies in level; it might be relatively low at times, as when we feel irritated at someone for putting us down, or it may be high, as when we have a major argument with our partner or we lose a job. Life serves up painful events, and our painful reactions to them are natural and entirely acceptable. It is when we are unwilling to accept these natural reactions—the clean discomfort—that we wind up with what we term dirty discomfort. Dirty discomfort is emotional pain created by our efforts to control the normal, natural clean discomfort that we experience. That is, when we are trying to avoid, control, or get rid of the clean discomfort, a whole new set of painful feelings, emotions, and thoughts appear. This dirty discomfort is the unnecessary addition of pain on top of pain: fear of fear, guilt over guilt, shame over guilt, blame over fear, or blame over unhappiness, as in "you've only yourself to blame for being unhappy in this situation". This simple additive process results inevitably in an increased likelihood that people will use control/avoidance strategies and, thus, carry on in a vicious circle of ever increasing control and pain.

Acceptance, or willingness, involves moving in the opposite direction: towards the pain, rather than away from it; towards the emotions, thoughts, and feelings that we dislike. Consider this. Suppose you were caught in quicksand. Naturally, you'd try to get out. But almost everything you've learnt about how to get out will create problems for you: if you try to walk, jump, climb, or run, you just sink in deeper, because you end up trying to push down on the sand. If you struggle, wiggle, push with your hands, or crawl, you sink in deeper. Often, as people sink, they panic and start flailing about, and down they go. In quicksand, the only thing to do is to create as much surface area as possible: to stretch out on the quicksand, getting in full contact with what you've been struggling with, but without more struggle. That will be hard: not hard in the sense of effortful, because to apply effort is to struggle; no, I mean hard as in tricky. It is tricky, because your mind is telling you to struggle in a situation where using this strategy is counterproductive; but let's not be too hard on your mind, as it has been taught that this control strategy works, and it can't see anything else to do. Furthermore, it has learnt this ineffective control strategy so well that you can't just tell it to stop using it and expect that it will.

Now, we are going to practise some acceptance strategies; strategies that encourage you to get into full contact with your bodily sensations, thoughts, and emotions without struggling with them; without trying to control them: that is, without trying to make them go away or avoid them.

Willingness Exercise I: "Just Noticing"

I'd like each of you to sit comfortably and close your eyes while we do an exercise. I am going to ask you to "just notice" various things that happen inside your skin: in your body. Your goal in this exercise is to act as if you were watching a film or TV; that is, your goal is to "just notice" what is occurring in your body; it is not to change it, avoid it, or struggle with it in any way: it is just to notice it. Remember, you are watching a film or TV; you are an audience member; you are not the director who controls what will be on the screen; your role is not that of the editor, who takes away scenes that he or she thinks should not be seen or experienced; and your role is not that of the producer, who finances the film and decides whether or not it will appear at all. Rather, your job, again, is just "to notice" what is actually shown on screen: what your body and mind provide you with.

Now, I'd like you to notice your breathing—see how your breath comes into your body, streams down into your lungs and goes back out of your body again. Remember, do not change how you are breathing, but just notice how you do it. [This breathing observation continues for about two minutes. Meanwhile, the trainer says things like, "if you find your mind drifting away to other things, just gently bring it back to just noticing your breathing."]

Now I would like you to notice a bodily sensation that you may have right now. Maybe it's a cramp, a tingling sensation, or a pleasant "warmth" in a muscle. Perhaps it may be in your legs, your arms, your neck, or your back. What I would like you to do is to focus on that bodily sensation and, without trying to stop it or alter it in any way, see whether the sensation stays the same or changes in any way. If it does change, just notice how it changes; if it doesn't change, notice that as well." [During the next two minutes or so, the trainer says things like, "if you find your mind drifting away to other things, just gently bring it back to just noticing your bodily sensation."]

Now, I'd like you to imagine yourself walking through a quiet, comfortable valley that is green and lush. The sun is just how you like it and so is the temperature. As you are walking through this valley, you see and hear a gentle stream and decide to walk over to it. You find a perfect spot and sit down by the stream. While sitting there, I'd like you to look into the stream and notice how the water flows gently and clearly along. Also, I'd like you to notice how a trail of leaves flows down the stream, gently passing you. On these leaves, I'd like you to place any thoughts that you have and let the leaves carry your thoughts down the stream, away from your sight.

[During the five minutes that this part of the exercise is done, the trainer says things like, If you find this difficult to do, that's all right, just put that thought, "This is difficult", on a leaf and let it float downstream, as well. If your mind wanders from the leaves and the stream, just bring it gently back to the leaves and place another thought on a leaf. If you are wondering whether or not you are doing the exercise "correctly", place that thought on a leaf and watch it go down the stream.]

Now, I would like you to picture this room in your mind, see where in the room you are sitting, and imagine what you will see when you open your eyes; and, when you are ready, open your eyes.

[The trainer then asks, "How did you find this exercise?" and if it has not come up during the discussion, the trainer next asks, "How does this exercise relate to what we have been discussing?" As should be evident, this "just noticing" exercise begins to show the participants how they can view and watch their thoughts and bodily sensations, without having to alter them or stop them. The trainer also notes that this exercise is useful to do when people start to feel stress.]

Identifying "Stress Buttons"

The participants are now asked to list on a piece of paper the various "stress buttons" that they have. They are told that these are situations, thoughts, emotions, or sensations that cause them stress. For example, it may be that office confrontations, thoughts of failure, unhappiness, concern, or shallow breathing may trigger a stress reaction. Before they start writing down these "stress buttons", the participants are asked to share, with the group, examples of their own triggers, in order to model what is expected. After several people have identified some of their own stressors, questions are elicited, and then participants write down their own "stress buttons".

Homework

For homework, participants are asked to do the following:

1. Notice, in the week between sessions, how cognitive avoidance, cognitive struggle, and a lack of awareness of what they are thinking (or cognitive fusion) promotes stress, when their "stress buttons" have been pressed.
2. Spend at least 10 minutes each day doing the "just noticing" exercise.

These two homework assignments are written down on paper and handed out to the participants at this time. Any questions regarding the homework are taken and answered.

Willingness Exercise II: Face-to-Face

This exercise consists of simply looking at another person for about two minutes. It may seem longer when you actually do it, but that's all the time it takes. What the exercise will consist of, if you are willing to do it, is getting a couple of chairs and pulling them close together. Your job is simply to be with the other person. You don't have to say anything, or do anything, or communicate anything, just be with the other person, experience the other person. Now, your mind will tell you all sorts of reasons why you can't do that: it will make you feel strange, or maybe you will have a desire to laugh, or maybe you'll be worrying about how your breath smells, or you'll be bored or distracted. But the purpose of the exercise is simply to notice these things, to experience everything that you think and feel, and to notice how you sort of come-and-go from being not at all present to experiencing the other person. [As the participants do this, the trainer says things like, "See if you can stay with the reality that there's another person over here, looking at you. See if you can let go of the sense of wanting to do this 'right'. If you find yourself thinking about this, or evaluating it, just notice that you're doing that and then come back out into the room and get in touch with the exercise. See if you can connect with the experience of discomfort in simply being present to another person." After the exercise, the participants' reactions are processed, and, if it has not already come up, the participants are asked, "How does this exercise relate to what we have been discussing?]

At the end of the session, the participants are asked not to discuss with any colleagues the content of this or any other session, or the ideas discussed in it, for six months. This request was made in order to help preserve the internal validity of the Bond & Bunce (2000) experiment in which this manual was first used.

Training Session II (Week 2)

At the beginning of this session, the participants are reminded that any personal information that is revealed or discussed in this or any session is confidential. Anyone not prepared to make this commitment to privacy is asked to leave. In addition, the participants are told that they are free to leave this or any subsequent training session at any time and for any reason, and the fact that they left will not be reported to anyone.

The session begins with a discussion about what the participants noticed, during the previous week, concerning the relationship between avoidance, struggle, and stress, particularly in the areas related to their stress buttons. After this discussion, any problems related to the "just noticing" assignment are considered.

Right Versus Wrong

The Participants are addressed as follows:

If a miracle were to happen, and suddenly all of the stuff that you've been struggling with, everything that makes you stressed, would just cease to be a problem, without any change in the circumstances or people or things that are around you, who would be made wrong by that? For example, if your "unreasonable" deadlines and "horrible" colleagues did not change, but now they did not cause you stress, who would be wrong about why you had been stressed? Would it be you, to any extent? That is, you said that you were stressed as a result of your dreadful colleagues, and they are still as bad as ever, yet now you are not stressed. What happened? Were *you wrong* in thinking that your colleagues made you feel so poorly?

I'm not saying that you have to believe me, but consider for a moment the possibility that you yourself, independent of anyone or anything else, have the ability to make your life bigger, richer, less stressful—that, in fact, nothing has to change before that can start. Now, I wish to be clear that I am not saying that you are to *blame* for the stress or painful emotions that you feel, but I am saying that you are responsible; that is, you are *able* to *respond* to stressful situations, such as horrible colleagues, in a manner that can lead you to have a richer, more stress-free life. [The point here is to help the participants see that they can turn away from the justifications that they have been giving for their stress: the deadlines that they have, or their terrible, dictatorial bosses.]

You may think that what I am saying is rubbish, and if you do, there we are, fine: tell me, and we can discuss it. Often, a reason for being unwilling, that is, of wanting control over your thoughts and emotions, is a desire to be right about something (e.g., the reasons why you are stressed: your horrible colleagues). But no one can make you be unwilling (or willing), so you and everyone else have a choice between, on the one hand, being willing and thus enhancing your lives, doing what works for you, and, on the other hand, being right. If you strive to be right, you make decisions, act, and behave in ways that may help you to be right (e.g., I'll prove that my boss makes our lives hell); but, in so doing, you become a puppet to being right, and your ability to live a full, meaningful life loses out to your greater "need" to be right. So, the choice is this: are you going to be right, or are you going to be alive? If you're striving to be right, your life gradually deadens; if you're striving to live your life fully, your desire to be right will only get in the way of living.

What I am talking about can be compared with a traditional psychology experiment that uses a rat in a maze. If an experimenter puts some food at the right side of the maze, the rat will run round and eventually learn to find the food there every time. Now, if the experimenter moves the food to the left side of the maze, at first the rat will run, over and over again, down to the right where the food no longer is; but, eventually, the rat will begin to run in a different direction and will learn to find the food on the left. Now, people are not like rats, because, sometimes, people will keep running to the right *for the rest of their lives*. What they tell themselves may be things like, "It used to be there!" and "It's not fair! It should still be there!" and "It never used to work that way!" Also, people can tell themselves, "Things shouldn't have changed!" and "They never said that I would be expected to do this!" In the interest of being right, these people never learn to do something different, something that would work better for them in their lives. Does anyone have an example of what I mean by how being right can rob people of a more effective and stress-free life?

But

I'd like to talk about the word "but" for a moment. It's a funny little word that can draw us into a struggle with our thoughts and feelings when we use it to explain our behaviour in terms of private events (i.e., thoughts and feelings). In so doing, we end up pitting one set of private events (e.g., a *desire* to succeed) against another (e.g., I feel so *angry* with my boss). "But" literally means that what follows the word contradicts what went before the word. It originally came from the words "be out". When we use it we often say, "This private event be out that private event." That is, "I should be nice to her as she is my boss, but she is a nightmare; so, to hell with her, I'll say what I like!" As you can see, "but" is literally a call to fight, so it is no wonder it pulls us up into the war zone with our own thoughts and feelings, which makes us more stressed, as we saw from last week's assignment.

Let's consider some examples of this "call to arms": "I love my partner, but I get so angry at him." How about this one?: "I want to do a good job at work, but I am anxious or upset right now." Notice that although both say, "One internal event (e.g., love) should be contradicted by another internal event (e.g., anger)", what the person actually experienced in both cases was two things: for example, love *and* anger. The bit of the sentence after the *but*, or "be out", part isn't a *description* of what happened—it is a *proscription* about how private events, thoughts, and feelings should go together. This proscription, however, is exactly what we are trying to back out of. No one *experienced* that two private events have to be resolved; rather, two private events were experienced: love and anger, for example. If the word "but" is replaced by the word "and", the statement is almost always much more reflective of reality. So, in our examples, it is much more accurate to say, "I love my partner *and* I get angry at him", or to say, "I want to do a good job at work, *and* I am anxious or upset right now." Both things are true: the wanting to do a good job at work and the being anxious and upset. So, I'd like everyone to be aware of this when they use the word "but", and then substitute it for the word, "and", because this switch may make you more sensitive to one of the ways that we get pulled into the struggle with ourselves that makes us more stressed. What are people's thoughts on all of this?

The Observer Exercise

If you would, I'd like you all to close your eyes and follow my voice. Just relax. For a moment now, turn your attention to yourself in this room. Picture the room; picture yourself in this room. Now, begin to go inside your skin, and get in touch with your body. Notice any feelings that are there. Notice any emotions that you are having. Notice any thoughts that you are having. Now, get in touch with the observer: the part of you that noticed the bodily sensations, the feelings, the thoughts. As the observer, hear and follow this.

My body is constantly changing. My body may find itself in different conditions of health or sickness. It may be rested or tired; strong or weak. It started out as a baby and grew continuously, and will continue to change and gradually grow old. I may lose part of my body. It may become fat or thin. Yet, through all of this, the part of me that is observing my body has been constant. I have been me my whole life. Thus, I have a body, yet I don't experience that I *am* my body. When my body changes, I am still me. Focus your attention on this central concept. Allow yourself to realise this as an experienced fact, not just as a thought, or belief, or point of view. Think of all the ways that your body has changed, all of the situations it has been in, while *you* have remained constant. [A period of silence follows.]

Now, consider this: I have roles to play, and yet I am not my roles. My roles are many and constantly changing. Sometimes I'm in the role of a worker, a family member, a friend, or a citizen of a country. I play some role all the time. If I were to try not to, then I'd be playing the role of not playing a role. Even now, part of me is playing a role—the role of a trainee in a work-effectiveness class. Yet, all the while, the observer, the part of me I call "I", is watching. I can play my constantly changing roles, yet all the while I can be there, as a constant, steady observer of it all. So, I have roles, and yet I am not my roles. Allow yourself to realise this as a fact that you have experienced. You know that it is true, and you've known it all along, although sometimes you may forget it; nevertheless, it is how you have *experienced* your life roles, and you are simply allowing yourself to realise that you are observing your own roles.

Now, still as the observer, consider this. I have many emotions. My emotions are countless, contradictory, changing. They may swing from love to hatred, from calm to anger, from stressed to relaxed, and yet *I* have been here through all of these changes and contradictions. Even now, *I* am experiencing emotions—interest, boredom, embarrassment, relaxation. And, throughout, I am capable of observing it all. Though a wave of emotion may come over me, it will pass in time. The observer part of me knows that I am having this emotion, and yet I *am not* this emotion. The emotions that I experience are constantly changing, but the observer remains constant through it all, noticing the changes; thus, I have emotions, but I am not my emotions. Focus your mind on this central concept: I have emotions, but I am not my emotions. Allow yourself to believe this, because *you* have experienced it, not because *I* have told you so. So, think of things you have liked, and don't like any longer; of fears that you once had that are now resolved. Yet, despite these emotional changes, you experience yourself as a constant. You are there through it all. [A period of silence follows.]

Finally, let's turn to what may be the most difficult area: your own thoughts. Consider this: I have thoughts, but I am not my thoughts. My thoughts are constantly changing. In my life, I have gained new ideas, new knowledge, and new experience. I can think something falsely and then find out the truth and think something entirely different. Sometimes my thoughts are foolish and make little sense. Sometimes thoughts come up automatically, from out of nowhere. Yet, all the while, the observer part of me is seeing these thoughts. The observer part of me knows that I have thoughts, and yet I am not my thoughts.

Allow yourself to realise this as an experienced fact. This is the way that it is, though often we forget it. And notice, even as you realise this, your stream of thoughts continues to flow. Indeed, you may get caught up with them, yet in the instant that you realise that, you also realise that a part of you is standing back, watching it all. So now, watch your thoughts for a few moments, and see that watching happens, and then observe that as well. [A period of silence follows].

So, you are *not* just your body, your thoughts, your feelings, your roles. These things are the content of your life, while *you* are the arena, the context, the space in which they unfold. As you see that, notice how you can distance yourself from the things you've been struggling with, and putting up with. You've been trying to change your roles, to get rid of your "bad" feelings, to control your mind; and the more you do that, the worse it gets, the more entangled you become: the less *you* are even "there". You've been trying to change the content of your life, but you don't have to change your roles, thoughts, feelings, and memories before your life can work, as these things are not *you* anyway; so, why struggle with them? Instead, why not focus your efforts on doing things, right now, that will help you to achieve the goals and dreams that you have for yourself. [A few minutes of silence follows.]

Now, again, picture yourself in this room, and now picture the room [the room is described]. When you are ready to come back into the room, open your eyes.——What were people's experiences of this exercise?" [Analysis of the experience is avoided; rather, the focus is on the experience itself.] This exercise [the trainer continues] demonstrates, among other things, that you, the observer you, can take a direction in your work, in your life, regardless of what your thoughts and feelings are saying to you. Your observer you, the true you, can see what is there, feel what is there, and still say, "This is what I need to do to get where I want to go!"

The "Milk, Milk, Milk" Exercise

TRAINER: Let's do another exercise. It's an eyes-open one for a change. I'm going to ask you to say a word. Then you tell me what comes to mind. I want you to say the word, "milk". Say it once.

PARTICIPANT: Milk.

T: Good. Now, what came to mind when you said that?

P: I have milk at home in the refrigerator.

T: OK, who else? What happens when we say "milk"?

P: I picture it.

T: Good. What else?

P: I can taste it, sort of.

T: Right, and can you imagine what it might feel like to drink a glass? Cold, creamy, coats your mouth, goes glug, glug when you drink it? Fine, so let's see if this fits: what shot through your mind were things about actual milk, and your experience with it; and all of that happened when we just thought of and said the word, "milk". Incredible, isn't it? We weren't looking at or drinking any milk: none at all. But yet we were experiencing milk psychologically. You and I were seeing it, tasting it, feeling it, yet we were only handling the word, not the real thing. Now, here is the little exercise, if you're willing to try it. It's a little silly, and so you might feel a little embarrassed doing it, but I am going to do it with you so we can all be silly together. What I am going to ask you to do is to say the word "milk" out loud, rapidly, over and over again and then notice what happens. Are you willing to give it a try?——Right, Let's go. Say "milk" over and over again. [As the participants do this, so does the trainer, but he periodically interjects comments like: "As fast as you can until I tell you to stop. Faster! Keep going faster!" The exercise lasts for three minutes.]

T: OK, now stop. Did you notice what happened to the psychological aspects of milk that were here a few minutes ago?

P: They disappeared after a while.

P: All I could hear was the sound: it sounded very strange. In fact, I had a funny feeling that I didn't even know what I was saying for a few minutes. It felt unreal.

P: We all sounded like a flock of birds after a while.

T: Right, the creamy, cold, gluggly stuff just went away. The *first* time you said it, it was as if "milk" were really "meaning-full"; it was almost solid. But, when you said it again and again and again, you began to lose that meaning, and the words began to be just a sound. So, you see, when you say things to yourself, in addition to any meaning behind those words, isn't it *also* true that these words are just words? The words are just smoke: there isn't anything solid to them. For example, consider the words, "I'm feeling so stressed"; milk, milk, milk, milk. What's the difference? When you have a thought or feeling, it looks as though it's more than what you've experienced it to be. It creates an illusion that it is *what it says it is*. Milk, milk, milk, milk, milk. But no matter what the words are, they are just that: words. They are just symbols we experience. Of course, they're related to things; it's not that the words are meaningless or will ever be meaningless, I don't mean that. What I mean is that when the hologram shows up, looking so solid ("I'm feeling so stressed"; "I can't cope"; "turn left in the maze"), you are not actually experiencing the *real thing*; that is, thinking "stress" is not the same thing as experiencing stress; saying "milk" doesn't leave you with milk on your hands. In both cases, you are having a thought, and that's perfectly acceptable, but saying the word "milk" or "stress" doesn't mean that you are going to end up drowning in it either; it doesn't even mean that milk or stress are near you. So, the problem isn't the word "milk"; the problem is that you think the word is real, that it is not just a hologram; and so, like a drunk person, you begin fighting or running from the polka-dotted elephant. But that's because you are losing yourself in the meaning of these scary thoughts, these words in your head; you are believing that what they say is true: that there really is milk right there, that a stressful event must be imminent; but, remember, while words can trigger fearful thoughts and feelings, they are, at the end of the day, just words; just symbols of the fear, and not the fear itself; and, since they are just symbols, just holograms, why must they be resisted and fought? [At this point, questions and comments are invited.]

The Tin Can Monster Exercise

[Each participant is given an audio cassette with this exercise on it.] Over the last two sessions, we've talked about being willing to experience our thoughts and feelings as what they really are, that is, thoughts and feelings, and not what they say they are (e.g., danger and loss). Based upon this concept of willingness, I would like you to consider a very important question: *out of the place from which there is a distinction between you and "that" ("that" meaning the stuff you struggle with, the thoughts, feelings, or evaluations that come forward when you're doing something), are you willing to feel that, think that, experience that as it is, not as it says it is, and do what works for you in the situation?* This question is the core of what we have been doing. It is a question that we can never stop asking ourselves, because willingness is not an outcome; it is a process. Willingness is a choice to do something and, in that context, to have happen whatever it is that is going to happen.

To be willing can often be like facing a giant, 30-foot monster who is made up of tin cans and string. It is almost impossible to face it willingly. However, if we disassemble him into all the cans, string, and wire that he's made of, each of those individual pieces is easier to face up to. The exercise that we are now going to do, if you are willing to do it, is intended to help you give up the struggle with emotional discomfort and disturbing thoughts by disassembling them. It is also designed to give you the experience of the natural ebb and flow of willingness, to realise that it is not something that you will "get" and "have" forever.

Now, if you are willing, get comfortable and relaxed, shut your eyes, and think of a specific feeling or situation. The situation should be something that you are currently struggling with, something that is important to you. I want you to try to get in touch with the feeling or situation that you've chosen. Notice first if there are any bodily sensations that are associated with what you've chosen. As you think about it, just gently notice what your body is feeling, what your body is doing, and if you notice some specific reaction, just pull it up and look at it. Now, I want you to spend some time letting go of the struggle with that specific bodily feeling. The goal here is not that you like the feeling, but that you are willing to have it and not struggle with it. Good. Now I want you to look for another bodily sensation attached to this situation. [The trainer asks the participants to repeat this procedure for bodily sensations three times.]

Right, I want you to notice whether there are any emotions associated with the feeling or situation that you selected. Just gently put yourself in the situation, and notice whether there are any emotions that appear, and, if so, just gently turn your attention to the first emotion that you noticed. I want you to spend some time just trying to let go of the struggle with that emotion. [This formula is repeated three times for emotions, thoughts, and behavioural predispositions (e.g., wanting to run away). After each repetition, the participants are told "good" in response to their efforts to give up the struggle with each reaction.]

Right, now for the last part. I want you to imagine that you have all the memories of your life on little snapshots, like the index cards filed away in a filing cabinet, all the events of your life from your birth until the present. I want you to get back in touch with the situation that you have selected, and now I want you to open the filing cabinet and start gently flipping through your cards of memories. You can either flip back from the present time to your past, or start as far back as the memories go, and start flipping towards the present, but if you find yourself pausing at any picture, stop flipping and spend a few minutes with the memory. It doesn't matter whether or not it seems to make sense as to why you stopped at that picture; if you find yourself stopping at any point, just stay there for a moment. As you stop, just notice who else is in the picture. What were you feeling and thinking at the moment? What were you doing? Now, see if you can let go of the struggle that may be associated with the memory; it might be a pain associated with the picture, or an unwillingness to leave it because of the happiness associated with it; whatever your reactions to the memory, just see if you can gently let go of your struggle with it, if you can let yourself be willing to have that memory exactly as it is, have exactly what happened to you as it happened. That doesn't mean you'll like it, but that you are willing to have it [Three more memories are explored.] Right, when you're ready, I want you to close the filing cabinet, and picture the room as it was when you shut your eyes and began the exercise. When you can picture it, just open your eyes and come back to the present. Does anyone want to share any of their experiences?

During the next week, I should like you to play this tape and do this exercise once daily. When you do it, please use as your material the "stress buttons" that you wrote down last week. After you have done it every day for one week, I would like you to do it one time each week until we next meet in three month's time.

Letting Go of the Struggle, in Order to Achieve your Values and Goals

If you are willing, I would like to go around the room and have each person tell us what they value, what they wish to do and achieve, that has been interfered with by the struggles that they have had with their stress. Then, I would like each person to commit publicly to let go of these needless struggles that are interfering with their values; but I only want you to make such a commitment, if you are really prepared to choose to give up this struggle. If there are values that you have, goals that you wish to achieve, that you feel unprepared to state here, try stating them to your partner, or a close friend or family member; and if you find that you are not willing to do that, at least state them to yourself in the mirror. The goal here is to make as public a commitment as you can to letting go of the struggle that is getting in your way of achieving the values and goals that you have.

After this, the trainer asks for comments and answers any final questions. The participants are also reminded again about the homework.

At the end of the session, the participants are asked not to discuss with any colleagues the content of this or any other session, or the ideas discussed in it, for six months. Again, this request was made in order to help preserve the internal validity of the Bond & Bunce (2000) experiment in which this manual was first used.

Session III: The Three-Month Follow-up (Week 14)

This follow-up session is designed as a "booster session", in that its aim is to practise the willingness techniques that were covered in the first two sessions and address any questions and comments that the participants have.

At the beginning of this session, the participants are reminded that any personal information that is revealed or discussed in this or any session is confidential. Anyone not prepared to make this commitment to privacy is asked to leave. In addition, the participants are told that they are free to leave this training session at any time and for any reason, and the fact that they left will not be reported to anyone.

Firstly, the **"just noticing"** exercise done in session I is repeated. After this, the participants are asked to reveal the biggest hooks, or internal events, that they had a hard time letting go of. The **tin can monster** exercise is then done, using these hooks as the material. After comments and questions are elicited about this exercise, the **face-to-face** exercise is done again. After the trainer deals with comments and questions about it, a **group-sharing** exercise is done. Specifically, all participants, if willing, are asked to stand up in front of the group, one by one, and state which of their values or goals have been interfered with by stress struggles. Then, with a view towards achieving, or living, these values and goals, they are asked to declare what their intentions are in the area of (a) letting go of needless struggle, and (b) letting go of "right and wrong" in work and home.

After this exercise, the **observer** exercise from session II is repeated, and any final questions and comments are addressed. Lastly, the participants are encouraged to continue to employ willingness exercises at least three times a week; and if they choose to do these exercises, hopefully they will do so, not because the trainer is recommending it, but because their experience tells them that acceptance of negative thoughts and feelings is less stressful than avoidance of them. In addition, the participants are reminded that acceptance is a process; it is not an end state: no one will reach it permanently. It is necessary, therefore, constantly to be mindful and aware that thoughts and feelings are just that: thoughts and feelings, and not the events that they represent (i.e., internal events are not to be taken literally).

THE FUTURE AND ROLE OF ACT AT WORK

Due to the initial success of this brief, group-based, ACT protocol, we and our colleagues are currently testing its efficacy in several other (i.e., non-media-related) industries (e.g., education, advertising, and banking). In so doing, we are examining, in particular, ACT's ability to reduce stress-related outcomes that are of vital concern to organisations; these include absenteeism, turnover, and impaired performance. We believe that it is crucial to demonstrate that this intervention can improve such work-related outcomes, *in addition* to mental health ones. Failure to show such work-related improvements is likely to limit severely the number of organisations (and industry sectors) that would use ACT, or any other individual-focused intervention, as a means of improving their employee's mental health.

While we are confident of ACT's ability to reduce work-related stress, we do not believe that organisations can responsibly use this, or any other type of individual-focused intervention, as their sole strategy for dealing with occupational stress. We agree with the UK health and safety legislation (see Cox et al., 2000) that holds organisations responsible for identifying and reducing stress-related risk factors that centre on the design and management of work (e.g., low levels of control, role conflict, and repetitive work). Thus, we consider individual-focused interventions, such as ACT, important adjuncts to a more comprehensive risk management approach to occupational stress. Indeed, we hypothesise that the combination of work redesign and ACT may serve as the most comprehensive and effective strategy for improving mental health and work-related outcomes. We expect that future research will investigate this possibility.

REFERENCES

Bach, P., & Hayes, S.C. (2002). The use of acceptance and commitment therapy to prevent the rehospitalization of psychotic patients: A randomized controlled trial. *Journal of Consulting and Clinical Psychology*, **70**(5), 1129–1139.

Barkham, M., & Shapiro, D.A. (1990). Brief psychotherapeutic interventions for job-related distress: A pilot study of prescriptive and exploratory therapy. *Counselling Psychology Review*, **3**(2), 133–147.

Baron, R.M., & Kenny, D.A. (1986). The moderator-mediator variable distinction in psychological research: Conceptual, strategic, and statistical considerations. *Journal of Personality and Social Psychology*, **51**, 1173–1182.

Beck, A.T. (1976). *Cognitive therapy and the emotional disorders*. New York: Meridian.

Beck, A.T., Rush, J., Shaw, B., & Emery, G. (1979). *Cognitive therapy of depression*. New York: Guilford Press.

Beck, A.T., Ward, C.H., Mendelson, M., Mock, J.E., & Erbaugh, J.K. (1961). An inventory for measuring depression. *Archives of General Psychiatry*, **4**, 561–571.

Bond, F.W., & Bunce, D. (2000). Mediators of change in emotion-focused and problem-focused worksite stress management interventions. *Journal of Occupational Health Psychology*, **5**(1), 156–163.

Bond, F.W., & Bunce, D. (2001). Job control mediates change in a work reorganization intervention for stress reduction. *Journal of Occupational Health Psychology*, **6**.

Bond, F.W., & Bunce, D. (submitted). The role of acceptance in occupational stress: A longitudinal study.

Bond, F.W., & Dryden, W. (1996). The effect of control and certainty beliefs on inference formation: Clinical implications from research. In W. Dryden (Ed.), *Research in counselling and psychotherapy: Practical applications*. London: Sage Publications.

Bunce, D. (1997). What factors are associated with the outcome of individual-focused worksite stress management interventions? *Journal of Occupational and Organizational Psychology*, **70**, 1–17.

Cooper, C.L., & Marshall, J. (1976). Occupational sources of stress:A review of the literature relating to coronary heart disease and mental ill health. *Journal of Occupational Psychology*, **49**, 11–28.

Cox, T., Griffiths, A., Barlowe, C., Randall, R., Thomson, L., & Rial-Gonzalez, E. (2000). *Organisational interventions for work stress: A risk management approach*. Norwich, UK: Health and Safety Executive/Her Majesty's Stationary Office.

Ellis, A., & Robb, H. (1994). Acceptance and rational-emotive therapy. In S.C. Hayes, N.S. Jacobson, V.M. Follette, & M.J. Dougher (Eds.), *Acceptance and change: Content and context in psychotherapy*. Reno, NV: Context Press.

García, J.M., & Pérez, M. (2001). ACT as a treatment for psychotic sysmptoms. The case of auditory hallucinations. *Análisis y Modificación de Conducta*, **27**, 455–472.

Geiser, D.S. (1992). *A comparison of acceptance-focused and control-focused psychological treatments in a chronic pain treatment center*. Unpublished doctoral dissertation available from the University of Nevada, Reno.

Goldberg, D. (1978). *Manual of the general health questionnaire*. Windsor: National Foundation for Educational Research.

Hayes, S.C. (1987). A contextual approach to therapeutic change. In N. Jacobson (Ed.), *Psychotherapists in clinical practice: Cognitive and behavioral perspectives*. New York: Guilford Press.

Hayes, S.C. (1993). Analytic goals and the varieties of scientific contextualism. In S.C. Hayes, L.J. Hayes, H.W. Reese, & T.R. Sarbin (Eds.), Varieties of scientific contextualism (pp. 11–27). Reno, NV: Context Press.

Hayes, S.C. (1994). Content, context, and the types of psychological acceptance. In S.C. Hayes, N.S. Jacobson, V.M. Follette, & M.J. Dougher (Eds.), *Acceptance and change. Content and context in psychotherapy*. Reno, NV: Context Press.

Hayes, S.C, Bissett, R.T, Korn, Z., Zettle, R.D., Rosenfarb, I.S., Cooper, L.D., & Grundt, A.M (1999b). The impact of acceptance versus control rationales on pain tolerance. *Psychological Record*, **49**, 33–47.

Hayes, S.C., Bissett, R.T., et al. (submitted). Psychometric properties of the Acceptance and Action Questionnaire.

Hayes, S.C., Strosahl, K., & Wilson, K.G. (1999a). *Acceptance and commitment therapy: An experiential approach to behavior change*. New York: Guilford Press.

Hayes, S.C., Wilson, K.G., Gifford, E.V., Follette, V.M., & Strosahl, K. (1996). Emotional avoidance and behavioral disorders: A functional dimensional approach to diagnosis and treatment. *Journal of Consulting and Clinical Psychology*, **64**, 1152–1168.

Jex, S.M. (1998). *Stress and job performance*. London: Sage.

Kenny, D.A. (1998). *Mediation*. Retrieved 23 November 2000 from the World Wide Web: http://nw3.nai.net/~dakenny/mediate.htm.

Koerner, K, Jacobson, N.S., & Christensen, A. (1994). Emotional acceptance in integrative behavioral couple therapy. In S.C. Hayes, N.S. Jacobson, V.M. Follettte, & M.J. Dougher (Eds.), *Acceptance and change. Content and context in psychotherapy* (pp. 109–118). Reno, NV: Context Press.

Landsbergis, P.A., & Vivona-Vaughan, E. (1995). Evaluation of an occupational stress intervention in a public agency. *Journal of Organizational Behavior*, **16**, 29–48.

Linehan, M.M. (1993). *Cognitive behavioral treatment of borderline personality disorder*. New York: Guilford Press.

Luciano, C. & Gutierrez, O. (2001). Anxiety and acceptance and commitment therapy (ACT). *Análisis y Modificación de Conducta*, **27**, 373–398.

Luciano, C., Visdómine, J.C., Gutiérrez, O., & Montesinos, F. (2001). ACT (acceptance and commitment therapy) and chronic pain. *Análisis y Modificación de Conducta*, **27**, 473–502.

Marlatt, G.A. (1994). Addiction and acceptance. In S.C. Hayes, N.S. Jacobson, V.M. Follette, & M.J. Dougher (Eds.), *Acceptance and change. Content and context in psychotherapy* (pp. 175–197). Reno, NV: Context Press.

McCracken, L.M. (1998). Learning to live with the pain: acceptance of pain predicts adjustment in persons with chronic pain. *Pain*, **74**, 21–27.

National Institute of Occupational Safety and Health (NIOSH, 1996). *National occupational research agenda*. Cincinnati, OH: NIOSH Publication No. 96–115.

Roemer, E., & Orsillo, S. (2002). Expanding our conceptualization of and treatment for generalized anxiety disorder: Integrating mindfulness/acceptance-based approaches with existing cognitive-behavioral models. *Clinical Psychology: Science and Practice*, **9**, 54–68.

Weissman, A.N. (1979). *The dysfunctional attitude scale: A validation study.* Unpublished doctoral dissertation, University of Pennsylvania.

Wells, A. (1995). Meta-cognition and worry: A cognitive model of generalised anxiety disorder. *Behavioural and Cognitive Psychotherapy*, **23**, 301–320.

Zettle, R.D., & Hayes, S.C. (1986). Dysfunctional control by client verbal behavior: The context of reason giving. *The Analysis of Verbal Behavior*, **4**, 30–38.

Zettle, R.D., & Hayes, S.C. (1987). A component and process analysis of cognitive therapy. *Psychological Reports*, **61**, 939–953.

Zettle, R.D., & Rains, J.C. (1989). Group cognitive and contextual therapies in treatment of depression. *Journal of Clinical Psychology*, **45**(3), 436–445.

CHAPTER 8

Cognitive Therapy for Social Phobia

Adrian Wells
Academic Division of Clinical Psychology,
University of Manchester, Manchester, UK

Social phobia is characterised by anxiety and apprehension in social or evaluative situations in which the individual may be subject to scrutiny by others. Individuals with social phobia are concerned that they will perform in a way that may be humiliating and/or embarrassing. This often consists of a fear of showing anxiety symptoms such as trembling, sweating, blushing, or babbling. However, other types of concerns may also be evident, such as concerns about being boring, or appearing inadequate or stupid. Two sub-types of social phobia are identified in the diagnostic and statistical manual of mental disorders (DSM-IV, APA, 1994). A generalised sub-type is characterised by a fear of most social situations, while more specific manifestations of social phobia can be identified in which the individual fears a particular type of situation. For example, fear of public speaking or using public toilets would constitute a specific social phobia. Exposure to feared social situations almost always provokes anxiety in social phobia, and those with this problem realise that their fear is excessive. The experience of social anxiety is often accompanied by physical symptoms such as sweating, trembling, and, blushing, and, as introduced above, these symptoms may be the predominant focus of the social phobic's concerns.

Cognitive behavioural therapies (CBT) of social phobia have consisted of several approaches that can be broadly classified as anxiety management therapies (e.g., Butler et al., 1984), social skills training (e.g., Marzillier et al., 1976), exposure treatments (e.g., Emmelkamp et al., 1985), and combination treatments consisting of cognitive therapy and exposure. Cognitive therapy interventions have been based on rational emotive therapy (e.g., Emmelkamp et al., 1985) or cognitive therapy based on Beck's cognitive theory (e.g., DiGiuseppe et al., 1990). Treatment has been applied in an individual and in a group format. For instance, Heimberg and colleagues have developed and evaluated a cognitive behavioural group therapy of social phobia (Heimberg & Juster, 1994; Heimberg et al., 1998). Cognitive behavioural treatment involving cognitive restructuring plus exposure appears to be an effective treatment (Taylor, 1996) and exhibit a larger effect size than exposure alone, social skills training, and cognitive restructuring alone. Moreover, evidence suggests that the gains obtained in cognitive behavioural interventions continue at follow-up.

Handbook of Brief Cognitive Behaviour Therapy. Edited by Frank W. Bond and Windy Dryden.
© 2002 John Wiley & Sons, Ltd. ISBN 0-470-02132-2.

Heimberg et al. (1993) reported that patients receiving cognitive behavioural group therapy continue to do well at 4.5–6.25 years after treatment. The effectiveness of CBT does not allow room for complacency, however. Existing treatments appear to produce only modest levels of improvement in negative cognitions (i.e., fear of negative evaluation [FNE]), and a proportion of patients receive little benefit overall.

A COGNITIVE MODEL OF SOCIAL PHOBIA MAINTENANCE

Partially in response to the modest effects of existing CBT on negative thoughts (FNE) in social phobia, Clark & Wells (1995) proposed a cognitive model of problem maintenance, based on cognitive (e.g., Beck, 1976) and information processing theory (Wells & Matthews, 1994). This model is depicted diagrammatically in Figure 8.1.

As a result of past experience, individuals with social phobia acquire assumptions and beliefs about social situations and the self as a social object. These beliefs, when activated, contribute to negative appraisals of social situations and the cyclical processes that maintain social phobia. Three types of assumptions and beliefs are identified in the model:

1. unrealistic rules for social performance (e.g., "I must always convey a favourable impression")
2. conditional assumptions (e.g., "If I show signs of anxiety, people will think I'm incompetent")
3. unconditional beliefs about the self in a social domain (e.g., "I'm boring, I'm weird").

One or more categories of these beliefs may be identified in individual cases. A problem with high standards and rules for social performance is that they are vulnerable to being broken by circumstances. At this point the individual may become self-absorbed and is likely to

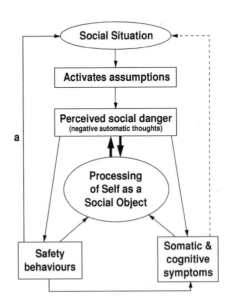

Figure 8.1 A cognitive model of social phobia. Reproduced with permission from Wells, A., 1997, *Cognitive Therapy of Anxiety Disorders: A Practice Manual and Conceptual Guide*, p. 169. Chichester, UK: ©John Wiley & Sons Limited

appraise the self negatively and activate cyclical processes, as depicted in Figure 8.1. Little is known at the present time about the relative strengths of these categories of beliefs in the aetiology of social phobia.

On entering an anxiety-provoking social situation, these negative beliefs are activated and those with social phobia become concerned about their ability to make a favourable impression. This concern is manifest as negative automatic thoughts; for example, "what if I shake", "I am going to blush", "they'll see I'm nervous", and "what if I can't think of anything to say". Negative automatic thoughts of this kind are accompanied by a shift in the direction of attention in which affected individuals become self-conscious and focus attention inward on symptoms and an impression of how they think they appear to others. Much of the information that persons with social anxiety use to infer how they appear to others is internal in origin and occurs in the form of physical feelings (symptoms of anxiety), an image of the self based on this interoceptive data and/or a felt sense. The image of the self typically consists of an "observer perspective", meaning that it entails seeing oneself as if from someone else's vantage point. In images of this type, anxiety symptoms and personal inadequacies are seen as highly conspicuous. For instance, a patient fearful of blushing while talking to her boss had an image of herself in which her entire face from the tip of her chin to the roots of her hair was bright red like a ripe tomato. In reality, her blushing consisted of slight facial coloration around her cheeks and was not of the bright or deep coloration that constituted her observer self-image. Negative observer images of this kind reinforce negative appraisals of performance and negative thoughts about evaluation by others, as depicted by the feedback loop between self-processing and negative automatic thoughts in Figure 8.1. The person with social phobia assumes that the negative observer image accurately reflects what other people can see.

Aside from negative self-processing, a further central component of the social phobia model concerns the coping responses which patients engage in to try to avert social threat and prevent feared catastrophes. These behaviours are labelled safety behaviours in Figure 8.1. Common examples of safety behaviours include avoiding eye contact, saying little, hiding one's face (e.g., to conceal blushing), censoring sentences before speaking (to prevent babbling/incoherence), and wearing extra layers of clothing (e.g., to conceal sweating). Safety behaviours are often intimately linked to prevention of a particular catastrophe or management of a particular aspect of one's presentation. For instance, individuals fearful of blushing may use their hands or hair to conceal their face or use particular types of make-up to conceal the blush response. Individuals fearful of babbling often say little and when they do speak, speak slowly and mentally rehearse sentences before talking. These safety behaviours are problematic in several respects and contribute to the maintenance of social anxiety in the following ways:

1. Safety behaviours are prone to increase or maintain self-consciousness, as depicted by the feedback arrows between safety behaviours and processing of the self in Figure 8.1. This is problematic because the individual pays less attention to external aspects of the social environment that may provide information capable of challenging negative thoughts. When chronic or inflexible, self-consciousness may also interfere with fluent social performance, thereby reinforcing negative self-appraisals. Self-consciousness also intensifies awareness of symptoms.
2. Safety behaviours can support a bias in the interpretation of events in which the non-occurrence of social catastrophes can be attributed to use of the safety behaviour, and not to the fact that social catastrophes are unlikely or not as catastrophic as predicted. For

example, after giving a brief (Five-minute) presentation as a behavioural assessment test in a treatment session, Rachel was asked how she thought she had performed. She replied that it "wasn't too bad, I didn't lose control because I was able to ask questions rather than talk a lot, and I was able to control the shaking in my voice" (safety behaviours). In this case, use of the safety behaviour prevented Rachel from discovering that she would not have "lost control" despite her anxiety.

3. Some safety behaviours intensify the somatic and cognitive symptoms of anxiety. For example, speaking slowly, mentally rehearsing sentences and focusing on one's voice can increase the likelihood of "blanking out" and the experience of subjective difficulty in speaking.

4. Safety behaviours may contaminate the social situation as depicted in the feedback loop labelled "A" in Figure 8.1. Behaviours such as avoiding eye contact, avoiding self-disclosure, and saying little in social situations can lead other people to think that the person with social anxiety is uninterested in them or is aloof and unfriendly.

Anticipatory and Post-event Processing

Emotional distress in social phobia is not restricted to the time spent in social situations. Social phobics experience considerable anxiety and apprehension in the days or weeks leading up to social encounters, and negative emotions and thoughts occur in the hours or days after a social event. These phenomena, not depicted in the situational mainte-nance processes of Figure 8.1, are a component of the social phobia model. In antici-pation of an anxiety-provoking situation, the person with social phobia typically worries about the forthcoming event. This "anticipatory processing" takes the form of negative thoughts about what might happen and may consist of plans of how to cope. Mental plan-ning or preparation that occurs during the anticipatory period can be viewed as a safety behaviour. The problem with anticipatory processing is that it is most often negative and it primes the individual for excessive self-focused attention prior to entering the social situation. Moreover, if social catastrophes do not occur, the individual can attribute the non-occurrence of catastrophe to the anticipatory processing, and thus negative beliefs and predictions concerning the consequences of failed or imperfect performance remain unchallenged.

On leaving a difficult, anxiety-provoking social situation, individuals with social phobia tend to go over aspects of the social situation. This post-event processing is a form of mental "post-mortem". Since attention was dominated by self-processing in the social situation, the post-mortem is based predominantly on how the individual felt and on the distorted impression of the self. There is little information available to the post-mortem capable of disconfirming the individual's social fears and negative self-perceptions. Thus, the post-mortem may contribute to the maintenance of negative beliefs and appraisals and may adversely affect mood after exposure to social situations.

Evidence for the Model

Several key features of the model are supported by research on individuals with social phobia and non-patients high in social anxiety. In particular, the model predicts that social phobia and social anxiety should be associated with heightened self-focused attention, and this relationship is supported by numerous studies (e.g., Fenigstein et al., 1975; Hope & Heimberg, 1988). A central component of the model is the idea that social phobics negatively appraise their own performance and behaviour in social situations, and this is supported by the available research evidence (Rapee & Lim, 1992; Stopa & Clark, 1993). For instance, Stopa & Clark (1993) showed that highly socially anxious individuals reported significantly more negative self-evaluative thoughts than low anxiety individuals. However, these subjects did not differ in frequency of negative thoughts concerning negative evaluation by others. Furthermore, social phobics appear to overestimate how anxious they appear to others (McEwan & Devins, 1983).

Consistent with the observer perspective hypothesis derived from the model, social phobics show an observer perspective in images of recent anxiety-provoking social situations. However, they show a field perspective for non-social situations (Wells et al., 1998; Wells & Papageorgiou, 1999). Moreover, these observer perspective images appear to occur spontaneously (Hackmann et al., 1998).

Rachman et al. (2000) explored the nature of post-event processing in individuals high in social anxiety. They found that post-event processing (the post-mortem) was greater in highly socially anxious than lowly socially anxious individuals. In addition, negative thoughts during post-event processing were rated as intrusive experiences inviting comparison with the concept of failures in emotional processing.

Finally, the model predicts that the commission of safety behaviours in social situations interferes with reductions in negative beliefs and anxiety. Therefore, instructions to abandon safety behaviours during brief exposures should facilitate reductions in negative beliefs and anxiety. In a test of this hypothesis, Wells et al. (1995) used a repeated measures crossover design comparing the effects of brief exposure plus abandonment of safety behaviours with brief exposure alone, when each was presented with a specific rationale. The results of this study showed that brief exposure plus abandonment of safety behaviours was more effective than brief exposure alone in reducing anxiety and negative beliefs. It is important to note that this was not a study intended to compare the relative effectiveness of two types of treatment, but was intended merely to assess the effects of dropping safety behaviours during brief encounters with social situations.

COGNITIVE THERAPY FOR SOCIAL PHOBIA

A specific form of treatment for social phobia has been developed on the basis of the present model (Wells & Clark, 1995; Wells, 1997). This treatment has a particular focus that distinguishes the approach from more eclectic treatments. In particular, the model suggests that it is necessary to modify specific maintenance processes during the course of effective treatment. The treatment aims to correct dysfunctional negative self-appraisals and beliefs, and this may be facilitated by modifying unhelpful safety behaviours and redirecting attention during exposure in order to correct faulty beliefs. A course of treatment is typically implemented over a 12–14-session time-frame in which sessions are held weekly and each session is normally 60 minutes in duration. The theoretical approach adopted here suggests that treatment should follow a particular sequence in maximising the efficiency of cognitive-behavioural change.

Structure of CBT

Sessions 1–3 of treatment usually consist of case formulation, socialisation, and cognitive preparation for restructuring, involving manipulations of safety behaviours and of attention. Treatment sessions 4–6 typically focus on a continuation of behavioural experiments, often involving exposure to test negative appraisals and predictions, and also video feedback methods to correct the distorted self-image. Sessions 7–9 continue with cognitive and behavioural reattribution methods, and introduce bandwidth manoeuvres aimed at further interrogating the environment and discovering that social catastrophes are unlikely, even in the event of failed performance. Finally, the latter part of treatment, sessions 10–12, involves consolidation of material learned, relapse prevention, and a continuation of work on the remaining issues (i.e., residual negative beliefs and avoidance). Clearly, there is flexibility in the number of sessions devoted to these phases of treatment, and this partitioning is somewhat arbitrary, but it serves here to provide a basic conceptual structure for planning specific interventions.

If we turn our attention briefly to the sequencing of treatment strategies, it is a logical derivation from the model to use strategies early in treatment that reconfigure the patient's behaviours and focus of attention in a way that maximises subsequent change in negative thoughts and beliefs. More specifically, if behavioural experiments involving exposure proceed without modifying the use of maladaptive safety behaviours and reducing self-focused attention, the effectiveness of such strategies may be impaired.

Case Formulation

In the first treatment session, therapist and patient work together to construct an idiosyncratic case formulation based on the cognitive model. Formulations can be constructed in the following context:

1. recounting in detail recent situations in which the patient felt socially anxious
2. using the initial therapy interview as a vehicle for exploring cognitive processes and behaviours in social anxiety
3. use of specific behavioural assessment tests involving controlled exposures to feared social situations.

When high levels of behavioural avoidance are present, patients may experience some difficulty in remembering and recounting the details of a recent social phobic encounter. In these circumstances, it is helpful to elicit components of the model as they apply to the current therapeutic encounter. However, this strategy is not particularly helpful when there is little or no anxiety during the initial consulting sessions. For instance, some patients with more specific social phobias (e.g., drinking in public) do not experience social anxiety activation as a consequence of the therapeutic encounter alone. In these instances, it is helpful to run a behavioural assessment test (BAT) in which the patient is exposed to an idiosyncratically feared social situation. This may consist of creating an analogue social situation in the clinic, or it may consist of exposure to real social situations outside the clinic setting.

In recounting a recent situation in which the patient felt socially anxious (irrespective of whether this is a naturally occurring situation or a BAT), the therapist must ask a series of questions designed to elicit cognitive, emotional, and behavioural components of the model, which are necessary for constructing an idiosyncratic case formulation. Information must be elicited on the following components:

1. negative automatic thoughts experienced just prior to or on exposure to the feared social situation
2. nature of anxiety symptoms
3. safety behaviours used to avert feared catastrophes and/or conceal symptoms
4. the contents of self-consciousness (i.e., the nature of the distorted self-image).

A high degree of detail is required in each of these domains since subsequent interventions are based on manipulating specific safety behaviours, testing negative thoughts and the details of the individual's negative self-image. It is useful to note that at this stage, in order to simplify assessment and initial case conceptualisation, it is recommended that the therapist postpone detailed elicitation of beliefs and assumptions. The initial aim is to focus on constructing a cross-sectional (symptomatic) case formulation.

The following therapeutic dialogue illustrates the exploration of relevant domains in the construction of the idiosyncratic case conceptualisation presented in Figure 8.2.

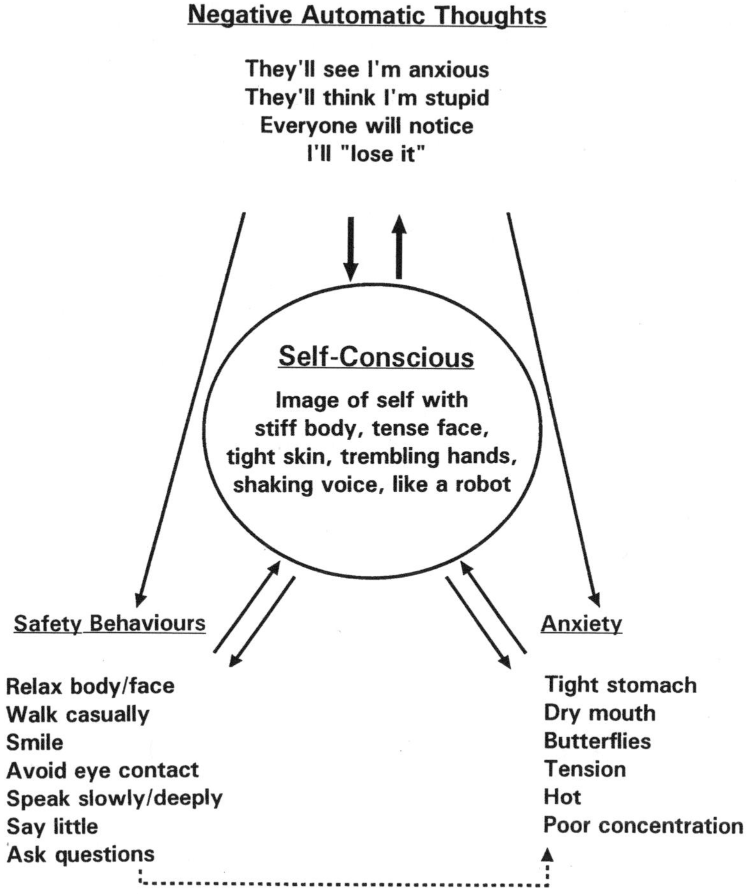

Negative Automatic Thoughts

They'll see I'm anxious
They'll think I'm stupid
Everyone will notice
I'll "lose it"

Self-Conscious

Image of self with stiff body, tense face, tight skin, trembling hands, shaking voice, like a robot

Safety Behaviours

Relax body/face
Walk casually
Smile
Avoid eye contact
Speak slowly/deeply
Say little
Ask questions

Anxiety

Tight stomach
Dry mouth
Butterflies
Tension
Hot
Poor concentration

Figure 8.2 An individual social phobia case conceptualisation

Conceptualisation Dialogue

THERAPIST: I'd like you to think back to the last time that you felt socially anxious. When was that?

PATIENT: I'm anxious most of the time, even walking down the street.

T: When was the last time you felt that way?

P: A couple of days ago I was out to buy a newspaper and I felt anxious walking to the shop.

T: OK, let's focus on that time. When you felt anxious, what symptoms did you notice?

P: My stomach got tight, and my mouth became very dry.

T: So you noticed stomach tightness and your mouth became dry. Did you notice any other symptoms?

P: Yes, butterflies in my stomach and I began to feel tense and hot.

T: Normally when you feel that way do you notice any other symptoms like difficulty concentrating or problems with you memory?

P: If I have to talk to someone I have difficulty concentrating on what they are saying.

T: Did you notice any other symptoms?

P: Sometimes I feel hot, begin to sweat and my body feels rigid.

T: When you were walking along the street and had those symptoms, what thoughts were going through your mind?

P: I thought what if people see I'm anxious—they'll think I'm stupid or something.

T: So the thought was that people will see you are anxious and they might think you are stupid. Did you have any other thoughts like that?

P: What if they notice at the shop—everyone will stare and then I'll really lose it.

T: What do you mean by "losing it"?

P: I'll begin to shake and sweat and everyone will think I'm abnormal.

T: When you have those thoughts and you feel socially anxious, how self-conscious do you feel?

P: Very self-conscious.

T: What are you conscious of? What are you focusing attention on?

P: How I feel and how I look.

T: What do you think you look like when you feel that way?

P: I must look anxious.

T: If I were to see you looking like that, what would I see?

P: A stiffness in my body and tension in my face.

T: What would that look like?

P: My skin would look tight and my hands would be trembling.

T: Where would I see this tightness in your face?

P: There would be a tightness in my cheeks and around my mouth and eyes, and you would hear it in my voice.

T: What would I be able to hear?

P: My voice would be shaking.

T: Would I be able to see anything else?

P: My movements would be stiff and unnatural like a robot.

T: Anything else?

P: No, I can't think of anything.

T: Do you get an image or impression of looking like that?

P: Yes.

T: When you had the negative thought that people might see you are anxious, think you are stupid, and you thought you looked like a robot, did you do anything to prevent people thinking that?

P: I tried to act natural.

T: How did you do that?

P: I tried to relax my body and tried to walk casually.

T: Did you do anything to prevent people from seeing the tension in your face?

P: I tried to relax the muscles in my face or if I am talking to someone I'll put a smile on my face.

T: How does that help?

P: If people see the tension in my face they'll think it's because I'm smiling, not because I'm anxious or weird. Also it means I look interested and so even if they do think I'm weird they'll still like me.

T: Do you do anything else to cope with your symptoms or make sure that people like you?

P: I avoid eye contact because if I see people looking at me I become more anxious.

T: What about your voice?

P: I try to speak slowly and deeply to stop my voice from shaking and I say as little as possible. I try and keep it short.

T: Do you do anything else to cope with your symptoms?

P: I avoid talking about myself and prefer to ask questions.

T: Anything else?

P: No, I don't think so.

T: OK, as you've been answering these questions you can see that I've been drawing out your responses and I have here a diagram summarising what you have said. It shows a number of factors that seem to be involved in maintaining your anxiety. Let's take a look at this and see what you think.

The individual case conceptualisation presented in Figure 8.2 is constructed from this dialogue. Having constructed the formulation, the next step of treatment is selling the model or socialisation. This consists of checking the goodness of fit between the conceptualisation and the patient's experience of social anxiety, and educating the patient about the role of safety behaviours, negative automatic thoughts, and self-processing in the maintenance of the problem. The aim is to establish a mental framework in which to implement subsequent treatment.

Socialisation

Socialisation to the model is achieved by the following:

1. presentation of the model and discussion of relationships between cognition, emotion, and behaviour
2. use of guided discovery to explore the roles of vicious cycles
3. socialisation experiments.

In presenting the model, the therapist should provide a brief account of what happened when the patient encountered a recent social situation. It is useful here to emphasise the occurrence of negative automatic thoughts just prior to the situation that led to the reflexive activation of anxiety and anxiety symptoms. It should be emphasised that the patient has developed a range of coping or safety behaviours that have become counter-productive and lead to a maintenance of the problem. Moreover, a central component of the problem is an excessive self-consciousness that interferes with performance and further prevents individuals from discovering that their fears are exaggerated. This self-consciousness is partly comprised of a distorted impression of how the patients believe they appear to others when anxious, and this distorted impression maintains anxiety.

In conjunction with a more didactic presentation of the formulation, the therapist should use socialisation questions to illustrate key psychological processes. For instance, to illustrate the role of negative self-processing in problem maintenance, the therapist can ask: (a) "Where does your evidence come from to support the idea that you look odd (e.g., weird, like a robot, etc.)"; (b) "Even if a symptom is noticeable, how do you know it looks the way that you think it does—where does your evidence come from?" The aim of this line of questioning is to lead the client to an understanding that much of the information used in negative self-appraisals is internally generated, and comes from an image of the self, or the felt sense of symptoms. In some instances the impression is based on a self-image (which is typically exaggerated) constructed from other people's comments. Further questions illustrating the role of a negative self-image should also be asked. For example,"If you no longer believed that you looked like this [idiosyncratic self-image], how much of a problem would you have?" Similarly, the problematic role of safety behaviours can be illustrated with questions. For example, "Do you think there are any problems that might result from using your safety behaviours"? This can be qualified by further questions such as: "What impact might some of these behaviours have on other people?"; "How do these behaviours affect your symptoms?"; "How do they affect your concentration?"; "Do you think they make you more or less self-conscious?", etc. It should be emphasised that questions of this kind need to be used skilfully to guide the patient to an understanding of the cognitive-behavioural mechanisms involved in the maintenance of social anxiety.

Socialisation through verbal methods is followed by a socialisation experiment. These experiments aim to illustrate the role of behaviours and self-consciousness in maintaining the problem. An experiment that has a dual function of socialisation and cognitive preparation relevant to subsequent disconfirmatory processing is the increased/decreased safety behaviours manipulation. This experiment aims to show the negative effect of self-consciousness and safety behaviours on anxiety, performance, and negative beliefs/predictions.

Attention/Safety Behaviours Experiment

This experiment consists of an increased and decreased safety behaviours manipulation in conjunction with brief exposure (e.g., five minutes) to a real or analogue social situation. First, patients are asked to enter the situation and to use all of their safety behaviours. This can be facilitated by a detailed listing of the safety behaviours that will be implemented during exposure. After this increased safety behaviour phase, therapeutic discussion focuses on the degree of anxiety and self-consciousness, and the patients' appraisals of their performance. The next phase consists of preparing the patients to repeat the brief exposure while abandoning safety behaviours and shifting to external focused attention. Prior to this repeated exposure, it is helpful to guide patients in the practice of dropping safety behaviours. Moreover, specific predictions should be elicited concerning the consequences of decreasing safety behaviours. A useful question to ask in this context is the following: "What do you think will happen if you do nothing to prevent it? (idiosyncratic social catastrophe, e.g., becoming a robot)". The exposure should then be repeated while the patient drops all safety behaviours and focuses attention on other people and the environment. Afterwards the therapist should explore what happened to the degree of anxiety, self-consciousness, and specific predictions after the dropping of these behaviours. Usually, patients find that, contrary to predictions, symptoms and social embarrassment do not worsen as a result of dropping safety behaviours but actually improve. This result is explained in terms of support for the maintenance processes depicted in the case conceptualisation. At this stage in treatment, patients are assigned homework that consists of exposure to specific social situations while practising the abandonment of safety behaviours plus shifting to external focused attention. Dropping of safety behaviours and shifting to external attention in conjunction with exposure experiments should be repeated as subsequent reattribution strategies across treatment.

Video Feedback

Video feedback provides an effective technique for correcting distorted self-images and beliefs concerning the conspicuousness of anxiety symptoms. However, if used inappropriately, feedback methods can increase self-consciousness, increase feelings of embarrassment, and reinforce the negative self-view. It is quite normal for people to be surprised by the nature of their recorded self. The aim of this procedure when used in the context of the present treatment programme is to illustrate how the patient's self-image or beliefs about appearance are distorted in a negative sense. A particular video feedback procedure has been designed for this purpose to overcome the difficulties associated with standard feedback. Normally, we have a videotape recording the patient throughout the first few treatment sessions; thus, exposure to feared analogue social situations used during the increased and decreased safety behaviours manipulations is captured on videotape. Early video recording of this kind ensures that patients are more likely to experience high levels of anxiety and this can be captured on tape. One problem with postponing video recording until later in therapy sessions is that it becomes more difficult to elicit anxiety, and patients can attribute any non-conspicuousness of anxiety depicted on the video to the fact that they were not particularly anxious in the first instance. A problem with patients' viewing themselves on videotape is that it increases self-consciousness, which in turn can negatively contaminate processing of the objective image conveyed. To overcome this, and to emphasise the discrepancy between the self and video images, patients are guided in constructing a detailed "mental video" prior to watching the videotape. The mental video is intended to operationalise in concrete, observable terms the nature of the patient's negative self-image so that the components of this image can be checked against the image captured on the video. This process of operationalisation and detailed analysis can be illustrated in the case of a patient who believed that fear was written on his face when socially anxious. He described this fear as apparent in the form of a furrowed brow, tight lips in which his lips were almost invisible, wide startled eyes, and rigid body. The therapist modelled these responses (e.g., by furrowing his brow), so that each symptom could be defined in observable terms. The presence of each symptom was then checked against the video image. The procedure may be repeated with fine adjustments in order to modify fully the patient's distorted self-image. On completion of the procedure, the accurate video image is used to generate positive self-statements that can be used whenever the negative self-image is activated in social situations. Patients can also be instructed to generate and call to mind a positive replacement self-image that is used in social situations.

Verbal and Behavioural Reattribution

Verbal and behavioural reattribution methods are used throughout therapy to modify specific negative thoughts and predictions. We have already seen how the video feedback experiment and the decreased safety behaviours manipulations provide a means of modifying distorted negative thoughts and predictions. Verbal reattribution methods include questioning the evidence for particular negative automatic thoughts. In many instances, evidence in support of negative thoughts does not arise predominantly from objective events but is located in self-appraisal and feelings. This conclusion should be sought through guided discovery. When tangible evidence of negative thoughts does exist, as for instance, when someone has received negative feedback from others, alternative more positive or benign interpretations of these events should be sought, and, where possible, particular strategies for changing problematic situations or dealing effectively with them without "losing face" can be explored. The nature of thinking errors in negative automatic thoughts can also be identified as a means of gaining distance from negative appraisals and objectively evaluating their validity. Common errors in social phobia include mind-reading (e.g., "She thinks I'm stupid"), catastrophising (e.g., "I won't be able to say anything"), and personalisation (e.g., "No one is talking to me because I am boring").

While verbal reattribution procedures of this kind are useful for weakening beliefs and providing an initial impetus for re-evaluation of thoughts, behavioural experiments provide one of the most powerful means of modifying distorted appraisals and beliefs. These experiments provide a means of testing the reactions of others in social situations and evaluating the consequences of showing signs of anxiety or failed performance. Elsewhere (Wells, 1997), the P-E-T-S protocol has been outlined for the implementation of effective behavioural experiments in cognitive therapy of anxiety. Here, behavioural experiments consist of a phase of *preparation* (P), *exposure* to social situations (E), *testing* of predictions based on negative thoughts and beliefs (T), and a final *summarising* (S) of the results in terms of the cognitive formulation. Preparation consists of identifying key negative thoughts or beliefs to be challenged and the behaviours that prevent disconfirmation of them. In social phobia, negative thoughts often concern the theme of negative evaluation by others. In these circumstances, it is necessary to devise an experimental strategy for assessing thoughts that other people might have. This can be accomplished by making predictions about specific observable behaviours that would be expected when other people make particular appraisals (e.g., if someone thinks you are boring, how will that person behave towards you—what will you be able to see?).

Behavioural experiments may then consist of patients entering social situations and abandoning safety behaviours while observing others for noticeable signs that they might be seen as boring. Another technique consists of the use of probe questions in which the patient is encouraged to ask other people in the social environment, when this is appropriate, what others may have noticed or thought during a social encounter. Once negative thoughts and predictions have been identified and belief ratings made, experiments consist of exposure to feared social situations in which the individual performs a disconfirmatory manoeuvre or test of predictions or thoughts. Examples of tests include deliberately focusing on other people to determine their reactions, dropping safety behaviours, deliberately showing anxiety or instances of failed performance in order to evaluate how others actually react, and intentionally disagreeing with someone to see whether one is rejected. Finally, the results of behavioural experiments are interpreted and summarised in terms of the cognitive formulation, and belief in negative thoughts and predictions is reassessed in light of the experimental results. Experiments should be finely tuned and repeated while tracking belief change so that beliefs can be gradually weakened. Experiments are repeated for homework in order to challenge further negative appraisals and beliefs, and to provide a generalisation of conclusions to more naturalistic settings.

Example of a Behavioural Experiment

J was anxious about a wide range of social situations in which he had to use his hands. He feared that people would notice his hands shaking and think that he was abnormal. A situation was identified that he would normally try to avoid or in which he would use particular safety behaviours. This situation involved counting loose change and using it to pay for goods. He would normally avoid this by making payment with higher denomination notes. Other safety behaviours included tensing his hands and arms and avoiding eye contact with shopkeepers. Part of a treatment session was devoted to executing a behavioural experiment in which, under therapist guidance, the patient bought some goods from a local shop and paid for them with loose change. The first time the experiment was run, the disconfirmatory manoeuvre or test consisted of dropping safety behaviours and focusing attention on the shopkeeper's reaction. The patient predicted that the shopkeeper would look startled and disbelievingly at the patient. The patient discovered that the shopkeeper paid little or no attention to his hands while he was paying for the goods and in fact seemed to be preoccupied with other thoughts. This led to a weakening of the patient's belief. However, the belief in negative evaluation by the shopkeeper was at 44% after this experiment. J attributed his residual belief to the fact that he had not trembled much during the experiment. A second, follow-up experiment was therefore devised in which J would ask to buy some products from different shop while deliberately shaking and dropping his change on the counter. He believed strongly that this would elicit a specific negative reaction from the shopkeeper (Note that this deliberate intensification of symptoms and commission of "failed performance" is a test manoeuvre in the P-E-T-S protocol, just as dropping safety behaviours is.).

Experiments that involve deliberate displays of anxiety or poor social performance (e.g., deliberately spilling a small amount of drink in a bar) can be described as "bandwidth" manoeuvres. Individuals with social phobia often operate within strict and narrow bandwidths of what they believe are "safe" social behaviours. As treatment progresses, experiments are devised that widen bandwidths so that patients can discover that a wide range of behaviours are relatively risk free.

Dealing with Anticipatory Processing and the Post-mortem

Problems associated with anticipatory processing and the post-mortem can he dealt with in treatment by asking patients to ban the post-mortem and reduce the frequency and duration of anticipatory processing. To facilitate compliance with this instruction, an advantages/disadvantages analysis of anticipatory processing and the post-mortem should be undertaken. Here, the therapist reviews with the patient and elicits a full range of the appraised advantages and then disadvantages of engaging in these responses. The aim is to show how the disadvantages outweigh the advantages. Patients are then simply instructed to ban post-mortem processing. Usually, this can be readily accomplished. Anticipatory processing should be curtailed, and alternatives to maladaptive and over-involved anticipatory processing should be reviewed.

Modifying Assumptions and Beliefs

Most of the treatment is devoted to modifying the cyclical in-situation processes that maintain social phobia. However, towards the latter part of treatment, greater attention may be
given to underlying assumptions and beliefs and their modification. It is likely that some, if
not all, conditional assumptions and rules for social performance will have been modified or
at least weakened by earlier tests of negative automatic thoughts and predictions. However,
specific beliefs may remain and require more direct re-evaluation. Unconditional beliefs
about the self as a social object may be of particular importance when the individual reports
long-standing social anxiety and/or low self-esteem.

The techniques used for challenging negative automatic thoughts and predictions can be
used for challenging assumptions and beliefs. Thus, questioning the evidence for assumptions and beliefs, reviewing counter-evidence, and labelling thinking errors offer verbal
reattribution strategies. Conditional assumptions may be treated in a similar manner to predictions and thus be subject to test by behavioural experiments. Unrealistic and rigid rules
for social performance can be modified by questioning the consequences of rule violation,
and decatastrophising the consequences of rule violation through verbal reattribution and
behavioural experiments consisting of deliberately violating the patient's rigid social rules.

Core unconditional negative beliefs about the self are often held as unquestioned and
oversimplified constructs. A preliminary strategy for weakening these beliefs consists of
defining the constructs represented in them and questioning the evidence for the belief. A
particular sequence of strategies for modifying unconditional beliefs has been suggested
(Wells, 1997). Initially, the central dysfunctional concept contained in the belief should be
defined. For example, if a patient believes "I am boring", it is necessary to generate a detailed
definition of being boring. This renders the belief more tangible and facilitates the logical
reanalysis which follows. The next step is to generate a full range of characteristics that
define or constitute the negative attribute represented by the belief (e.g., boringness). The
number of characteristics that the patient has should then be systematically questioned. The
aim here is to show that the patient has few of the defining characteristics. The distorted
nature of the belief should be emphasised and evidence in support of the belief examined.
Any supporting evidence should be reinterpreted and counter-evidence collected and considered. A replacement self-belief should be specified that can be used as a self-statement
whenever the negative belief becomes activated. Finally, patients should be encouraged
to behave in new ways that are capable of sustaining the replacement adaptive belief. A
useful strategy here is the development of a new script for social behaviour that increases
the propensity of positive social feedback from other people. For instance, a patient may
be asked to take a greater interest in work colleagues, offering occasional compliments to
them and greeting them more often when they are encountered in the work environment.

Positive data logs can also provide a means of focusing attention on disconfirmatory
information and of collecting data that are inconsistent with negative self-beliefs. This
strategy consists of asking patients to complete a diary of positive social events each day.

Relapse Prevention

In the final two or three sessions of therapy, an increasing amount of therapeutic time is
given to issues of relapse prevention. This typically consists of asking patients to write

a detailed summary of the information learned during the course of treatment. The summary consists of examples of the idiosyncratic case conceptualisation and an account of the mechanisms responsible for maintaining social anxiety. This therapy blueprint should also include a detailed list of strategies that have been useful in overcoming social anxiety. Before the termination of treatment, it is important to ensure that any remaining avoidance of social situations which may be indicative of underlying unresolved fears is explored and addressed. Residual negative thoughts and avoidance should be conceptualised and targeted with renewed verbal and behavioural reattribution methods. After treatment, booster sessions are normally scheduled at 3 and 6 months' follow-up. These provide an opportunity to consolidate treatment gains and reinforce the implementation of treatment strategies.

Brief Treatment

The original course of treatment, as outlined here, consisted of 12–14 sessions. In an attempt to abbreviate treatment, Wells & Papageorgiou (2001) used clinical experience in delivering this treatment, and theoretical and empirical data to streamline the intervention. Brief cognitive therapy retains many components of the full treatment, but some of these are enhanced or abbreviated. In particular, brief treatment focuses more on modifying excessive self-focused attention and provides a greater emphasis on banning worry in the form of anticipatory processing and post-event processing from the outset of treatment. At least two in vivo behavioural experiments aimed at disconfirming negative beliefs and thoughts are implemented in each treatment session in the brief treatment. These experiments adhere strictly to the P-E-T-S protocol. Consistent with full cognitive therapy, the brief treatment incorporated video feedback methods. In streamlining the intervention, a decision was made to terminate treatment when patients' self-consciousness ratings for a preceding week reached a level of 1 on a 0–8 rating scale and this level could not be attributed to increased avoidance. This criterion was selected as especially relevant since self-focused attention is viewed as a general marker for maladaptive beliefs and processes in emotional disorders (Wells & Matthews, 1994), and it is linked to the maintenance of anxiety in the present social phobia model. In a series of six consecutively referred patients meeting criteria for social phobia, a mean of 5.5 treatment sessions (one hour in duration each) were required to meet termination criteria. The number of sessions ranged from four to eight . The results showed that the brief treatment was highly effective, and patients showed a 57% improvement in dysfunctional cognitions measured by the Fear of Negative Evaluation questionnaire. Gains on all measures were maintained at 3 and 6 months' follow-up.

While these data are encouraging, they should be replicated with larger samples. Moreover, therapy was delivered by experienced therapists, and it is likely that training and constant supervision are necessary to achieve optimum results in brief treatment.

Evidence for Treatment Effects

In a preliminary evaluation of the effectiveness of the standard treatment, Clark and Wells treated 15 patients with social phobia (described by Clark, 1999). Almost all patients had generalised social phobia, and significant improvement was observed in all social anxiety measures and in general measures. In a large-scale randomised trial, Clark and colleagues have demonstrated that the treatment is superior to a pharmacological intervention (fluoxetine plus exposure and placebo plus exposure) at post-treatment (follow-up data are pending) (Clark, 1999).

Evidence for the Effectiveness of Specific Techniques

Several studies have investigated the effect of specific components of the present treatment programme. Wells et al. (1995) demonstrated that during brief exposure to feared social situations, negative beliefs and anxiety decreased more when patients were instructed to abandon their safety behaviours than when they were merely asked to enter the situation for a planned period of time. These results suggest that presenting brief exposure experiments in the context of a cognitive rationale that emphasises disconfirmation of negative beliefs and includes the dropping of safety behaviours is more effective than brief exposure alone.

Wells & Papageorgiou (1998) compared the effects of brief exposure alone with brief exposure plus shifting to external focused attention. Exposure plus external attention was more effective in reducing in-situation anxiety and negative beliefs than the brief exposure alone. Moreover, the attention condition resulted in a greater shift in patients' self-images from an observer to a field perspective after the social exposure.

Finally, a study by Harvey et al. (2000) demonstrated that cognitive preparation involving clear operationalisation of conspicuous symptoms (e.g., running a mental video) in conjunction with video feedback was more effective than video feedback alone in modifying the distorted self-image of individuals with social phobia.

Difficulties in Therapy

Treating social phobia may be a relatively complex undertaking when compared with other disorders which have more basic conceptualisations (e.g., panic disorder). Several vicious cycles operate in social phobia maintenance, and therefore case conceptualisation is more complex. Difficulties also emerge if the true contribution of social phobia to the clients' presenting condition is ambiguous or misidentified. Many patients with various disorders present with social evaluative concerns and anxiety in social situations. Moreover, paranoid thought and conditions such as body dysmorphic disorder may be confused with social phobia. An initial step in the successful formulation and treatment of cases is accurate diagnosis of the patient's presenting problem.

Panic attacks and depression are common presentations in the context of social phobia. Depression may be secondary to the problems associated with social anxiety. If depression does not require treatment in its own right (i.e., is of insufficient severity to interfere with treatment engagement, there is no risk of self-harm). Treatment may proceed by treating social phobia while closely monitoring the impact of this intervention on concurrent depression. Depression may require treatment in its own right if it does not improve as social phobia recedes. Individuals with social phobia may experience panic attacks when exposed to feared social situations. If panic attacks occur outside social situations, or away from anticipation of exposure to social situations, an additional diagnosis of panic disorder may be warranted. In cases of multiple disorder presentations, the therapist's judgement is required to prioritise the focus and sequence of interventions.

Patients with social phobia may be reluctant to engage in specific treatment strategies. For instance, it is useful early in treatment to use exposure to analogue or real social situations in the form of behavioural assessment tests, as initial socialisation and re attribution experiments, however some patients are reluctant to engage in such tasks. To overcome this problem, the therapist should maintain a high degree of forward momentum in therapy. This can be achieved by providing little forewarning of socialisation experiments (e.g., role-playing), by introducing videotaping of sessions from the outset, and by offering a clear and detailed rationale based on the case formulation. Compliance with reattribution experiments, such as those involving the commission of social errors (e.g., shaking and spilling a drink in public), may be facilitated by the therapist practising the experiment in a social situation while being observed by the patient. This provides an intermediate way of weakening negative belief/predictions prior to the patient executing the experiment.

Since treatment consists of exposure to social situations and the deliberate commission of performance failures and displays of symptoms, the treatment process may become contaminated by the therapist's own social anxieties or reticence in social situations. In such cases, it may be helpful for therapists to examine and challenge their own negative automatic thoughts, self-consciousness, and negative predictions.

CONCLUSION

Social phobia is a common and disabling anxiety disorder. CBT is an effective treatment; however, traditional treatments have produced only modest gains in the modification of dysfunctional cognitions. The Clark and Wells model of social phobia was described, and the treatment based on this model (Wells & Clark, 1995; Wells, 1997) was presented. This treatment focuses on modifying a range of cognitive and behavioural processes that are thought to maintain negative self-perceptions in social phobia. Specific models like this one enable therapists to refine the practice of cognitive therapy and to develop new techniques for achieving cognitive emotional change. For a more extensive and detailed description of this form of treatment and of assessment, the interested reader may wish to consult Wells (1997).

REFERENCES

American Psychiatric Association (1994). *Diagnostic and statistical manual of mental disorders* (4th ed.). Washington, DC: APA.

Beck, A.T. (1976). *Cognitive therapy and the emotional disorders*. New York: International Universities Press.

Butler, G., Cullington, A., Munby, M., Amies, P., & Gelder, M. (1984). Exposure and anxiety management in the treatment of social phobia. *Journal of Consulting and Clinical Psychology*, **52**, 642–650.

Clark, D.M. (1999). Anxiety disorders: Why they persist and how to treat them. *Behaviour Research and Therapy*, **37**, 5–27 (Special issue).

Clark, D.M., & Wells, A. (1995). A cognitive model of social phobia. In R. Heimberg, M. Liebowitz, D.A. Hope, & E.R. Scheier (Eds.), *Social phobia: Diagnosis, assessment and treatment* (pp. 69–93). New York: Guilford Press.

DiGiuseppe, R., McGowan, L., Sutton-Simon, K., & Gardner, F. (1990). A comparative outcome study of four cognitive therapies in the treatment of social anxiety. *Journal of Rational-Emotive and Cognitive-Behaviour Therapy*, **8**, 129–146.

Emmelkamp, P.M.G., Mersch, P.P., Vissia, E., & van de Helm, M. (1985). Social phobia: a comparative evaluation of cognitive and behavioural interventions. *Behaviour Research and Therapy*, **23**, 365–369.

Fenigstein, A., Scheier, M.F., & Buss, A.H. (1975). Public and private self-consciousness: Assessment and theory. *Journal of Consulting and Clinical Psychology*, **43**, 522–527.

Hackmann, A., Suraway, C., & Clark, D.M. (1998). Seeing yourself through others' eyes: A study of spontaneously occurring images in social phobia. *Behavioural and Cognitive Psychotherapy*, **26**, 3–12.

Harvey, A.G., Clark, D.M., Ehlers, A., & Rapee, R.M. (2000). Social anxiety and self-impression: Cognitive preparation enhances the beneficial effects of video feedback following a stressful task. *Behaviour Research and Therapy*, **38**, 1183–1142.

Heimberg, R.G., & Juster, H.R. (1994). Treatment of social phobia in cognitive-behavioural groups. *Journal of Clinical Psychiatry*, **55**, 38–46.

Heimberg, R.G., Liebowitz, M., Hope, D.A., Schneier, F.R., Holt, C.S., Welkowitz, L.A., Juster, H.R., Campeas, R., Bruch, M.A., Cloitre, M., Fallon, B., & Klein, D.F. (1998). Cognitive behavioural group therapy vs phenelzine therapy for social phobia. *Archives of General Psychiatry*, **55**, 1133–1141.

Heimberg, R.G., Saltzman, D.G., Holt, C.S., & Blendell, K.A. (1993). Cognitive behavioural group treatments for social phobia: effectiveness at five-year follow-up. *Cognitive Therapy and Research*, **14**, 1–23.

Hope, D.A., & Heimberg, R.G. (1988). Public and private self-consciousness and social anxiety. *Journal of Personality Assessment*, **52**, 629–639.

Marzillier, J.S., Lambert, C., & Kellet, J. (1976). A controlled evaluation of social skills training for socially inadequate psychiatric patients. *Behaviour Research and Therapy*, **14**, 225–238.

McEwan, K.L., & Devins, G.M. (1983). Is increased arousal in social phobia noticed by others? *Journal of Abnormal Psychology*, **92**, 417–421.

Rachman, S., Grüter-Andrew, J., & Shafran, R. (2000). Post-event processing in social anxiety. *Behaviour Research and Therapy*, **38**, 611–617.

Rapee, R.M., & Lim, L. (1992). Discrepancy between self and observer ratings of performance in social phobics. *Journal of Abnormal Psychology*, **181**, 728–731.

Stopa, L., & Clark, D.M. (1993). Cognitive processes in social phobia. *Behaviour Research and Therapy*, **31**, 255–267.

Taylor, S. (1996). Meta-analysis of cognitive-behavioural treatments for social phobia. *Journal of Behavior Therapy and Experimental Psychiatry*, **27**, 1–9.

Wells, A. (1997). *Cognitive therapy of anxiety disorders: A practice manual and conceptual guide.* Chichester, UK: Wiley.

Wells, A., & Clark, D.M. (1995). *Cognitive therapy of social phobia: A treatment manual.* Unpublished manual.

Wells, A., Clark, D.M., & Ahmad, S. (1998) How do I look with my mind's eye: Perspective taking in social phobic imagery. *Behaviour Research and Therapy*, **36**, 631–634.

Wells, A., Clark, D.M., Salkovskis, P., Ludgate, J., Hackmann, A., & Gelder, M. (1995). Social phobia: The role of in-situation safety behaviours in maintaining anxiety and negative beliefs. *Behavior Therapy*, **26**, 153–161.

Wells, A., & Matthews, G. (1994). *Attention and emotion: A clinical perspective. Hove*, UK: Erlbaum.

Wells, A., & Papageorgiou, C. (1998). Social phobia: Effects of external attention on anxiety, negative beliefs, and perspective taking. *Behavior Therapy*, **29**, 357–370.

Wells, A., & Papageorgiou, C. (1999). The observer perspective: biased imagery in social phobia, agoraphobia, and blood/injury phobia. *Behaviour Research and Therapy*, **37**, 653–658.

Wells, A., & Papageorgiou, C. (2001). Brief cognitive therapy of social phobia: A single case series. *Behaviour Research and Therapy*, **6**, 713–720.

CHAPTER 9

Brief Cognitive-Behavioral Interventions for Substance Abuse

F. Michler Bishop

*Alcohol and Substance Abuse Services, Albert Ellis Institute,
New York, NY, USA*

A BRIEF HISTORY OF BRIEF INTERVENTIONS

Over the past quarter-century, many reviews have confirmed the effectiveness of brief interventions for the treatment of substance-abuse disorders (cf. Bien et al., 1993; Heather, 1995a; Institute of Medicine, 1994; Miller et al., 1995; Zweben & Fleming, 1999). Miller et al. (1995) found that brief interventions (with 17 positive studies) had a cumulative evidence score of 239, compared to the next two strongest, social skills training (11 positive studies), with a score of 128, and motivational interviewing (two positive studies) with a score of 87 (p. 18). A more recent review by (McCrady, 2000) found only two treatment modalities—brief interventions and relapse prevention—met the criteria of the American Psychological Association's Division 12 Task Force for empirically validated treatment.

Heather (1995a) points out that three factors have contributed to the growing interest in brief interventions:

1. An increasing awareness that non-seriously dependent drinkers significantly contribute to the social costs of alcohol consumption. In the past, treatment had focused on dependent (and often severely dependent) drinkers. However, drinkers who do not even meet the DSM-IV criteria for abuse are responsible for a great deal of the harmful societal effects of alcohol.
2. Increasing awareness that longer interventions are sometimes no more effective than shorter ones.
3. Increasing pressure to bring down health costs.

In one of the earliest studies, Orford & Edwards (1977) found that subjects who received a combination of inpatient, outpatient, psychiatric, and social work interventions did not do better, on average, than those who received only a single counseling session. Heather (1995b) notes that the men involved all had intact marriages and were socially stable, so any intervention might have been effective. Nevertheless, follow-up at 12 months and at 10 years (Taylor et al., 1985) again found no differences between groups. In a variety of studies over the

Handbook of Brief Cognitive Behaviour Therapy. Edited by Frank W. Bond and Windy Dryden.
© 2002 John Wiley & Sons, Ltd. ISBN 0-470-02132-2.

course of over 20 years, Miller (2000) also reports consistently finding brief interventions to be as effective as longer interventions. Moreover, the large-scale, federally financed, multisite project MATCH (1997, 1998) found that the four-session motivational enhancement therapy (MET) intervention was just as effective for the treatment of alcohol problems as the longer cognitive-behavioral skills training and 12-step facilitation interventions.

Many studies of brief interventions have focused on "opportunistic settings" (Heather, 1995a), such as emergency rooms and internists' offices and have demonstrated that very inexpensive brief interventions can have significant effects (e.g., Fleming et al., 1997; Israel et al, 1996; NIAAA, 1995; Substance Abuse and Mental Health Administration, 1997). One representative study (Israel et al., 1996) of 15 686 patients in 42 primary care doctor's offices is noteworthy for a number of reasons. First, in order to overcome physician resistance to asking about alcohol consumption, in the reception area patients were asked four non-alcohol-related questions about their history of trauma. Later, physicians asked only those patients with previous trauma about alcohol use and related problems. According to specified criteria, problem drinkers were identified and then given either three hours of cognitive-behavioral counseling by a nurse or simply advised to reduce their alcohol intake. One year later, the group given the three hours of counseling had reduced their consumption by 70%, psychosocial problems by 85%, and physician visits by 34%. Those in the advice group had also reduced their consumption by 46%, but not their psychosocial problems or physician visits.

The effectiveness of brief interventions for drug abuse is less clear (Zweben & Fleming, 1999). However, the Sobells have found that their guided self-change program is just as effective with drug abusers as with problem drinkers and alcohol abusers (Sobell & Sobell, 2000). A recent comparison (Stephens et al., 2000) of brief and extended treatments for marijuana use found similar results. The outcomes resulting from two 90-minute individual sessions of a variant of motivational interviewing and from 14 sessions of group cognitive-behavioral and social support sessions were not significantly different. Finally, the Marijuana Treatment Project (Kadden et al., 2000) involved 450 individuals from diverse socioeconomic and ethnic backgrounds who had been using marijuana regularly and heavily for over 10 years. Both the brief intervention (two sessions of motivational interviewing [MI]) and the extended interventions (nine sessions, two of MI, five of CBT, and two more to address lifestyle issues) led to similar, significant decreases in use.

Increasingly, brief interventions are also being used with young people. In an attempt to reduce high-risk, college-age drinking, Marlatt and his associates (e.g., Baer et al., 1992; Breslin et al., 1999; Kivlahan et al., 1990; Marlatt et al., 1998) have successfully used brief interventions to reduce drinking rates, i.e., overall drinking quantity, drinking frequency, and peak consumption per drinking episode. Problems associated with drinking decreased even more rapidly, suggesting that the participants not only reduced their consumption but also learned to drink in a more responsible manner. D'Amico & Fromme (2000) developed a 50-minute risk skills training program that significantly reduced several forms of risky behavior, including heavy drinking, drug use, driving after drinking, and riding with a drunk driver.

Despite the demonstrated effectiveness of brief interventions, Heather (1995b), in a careful analysis of many of the key studies and surveys up to that time, raised a number of concerns. Most surveys treat very diverse kinds of "brief" interventions as equivalent. Hence, five minutes of advice may be lumped together with five sessions of counseling spread over six months. There is also a tendency to act as if all interventions are similar in content when that is not necessarily the case. Chick et al. (1988) describe their advice sessions as "authoritative, concentrated, [and] unequivocal" (p. 159). The "simple advice" session lasting five minutes or less (as opposed to "amplified advice," lasting 30–60 minutes) consisted of the patient's being told: "You have an alcohol problem. The only treatment is to stop drinking." This is in marked contrast to the approach used in Miller's studies (Miller, 2000) and in MET (Project MATCH, 1997) with its stress on empathy and a menu of treatment options.

It is also important to note that some studies find the reverse effect; more treatment leads to better results. For example, Robertson et al. (1986) found nine sessions of "individually tailored cognitive-behavioral therapy aimed at moderation" resulted in better outcomes than three or four sessions of assessment and advice. Chick et al. (1988), who replicated the Orford and Edwards design, but also included women, found that more extended treatment (as opposed to the two forms of brief advice discussed above) resulted in less alcohol-related harm in the two-year follow-up period. And Zweben & Fleming (1999) report on two studies (Baker et al., 1993; Baker et al., 1994) investigating ways to reduce HIV-risk-taking needle use, in which those receiving a more intensive cognitive-behavioral intervention demonstrated lower rates of risk-taking behavior.

Heather (1995b) also expresses the concern that policy makers and purchasers of services may draw the conclusion that brief interventions are just as effective as longer treatment, ignoring the fact that that may be true only for certain populations in certain settings. As a result, funds for longer, more costly services may disappear, despite the fact that there are a number of studies showing that people with more serious problems benefit from more intensive interventions.

From a public health standpoint, the implications seem clear. Briefer, less expensive interventions may have a large effect on drinking and drugging behavior in a community. On the other hand, that may not be true for clients with several overlapping, often interrelated problems like those typically seen by clinicians. As Zweben & Fleming (1999) point out, there are many issues still unresolved, including the most effective length, the effect on different populations, and the variable impact of the distinct components of the intervention.

BRIEF INTERVENTIONS FROM A CLINICIAN'S PERSPECTIVE

People who seek treatment often have multiple problems. They may be drinking heavily and gambling; drinking heavily and using cocaine; or drinking heavily, using cocaine, and having unsafe sex. In addition, they may suffer from other interacting disorders, such as social anxiety, depression, or a bipolar disorder, to name only a few possibilities. However, many studies have excluded people with such problems. For example, the Chick et al. (1988) study exclusions included people who "were mothers in charge of children under 11 years old; had cirrhosis or clinically evident brain damage; had a major medical or psychiatric disorder other than alcoholism; [or] were suicidal" (p. 160).

Clinicians' Beliefs that May Hinder the Use of Brief Interventions

No doubt, many of the people who enter treatment are often complex, difficult clients to work with. However, the underlying irrational beliefs of clinicians may exacerbate the problem. (See Bishop [2001a] and Miller & Brown [1997] for a more in-depth discussion of this issue.)

Addicted Clients Are Too Difficult to Work with; They Relapse Again and Again and They Rarely, if Ever, Really Get Better

In fact, treatment works, contrary to what many people believe (Miller et al., 1995; Project MATCH, 1997; McCrady, 2000). In a follow-up of the National Institute on Drug Abuse's Treatment Outcome Study of over 10 000 clients in over 100 treatment facilities, the researchers (Hubbard et al., 1997) looked at 4000 participants one year after less than three months of outpatient treatment. Compared to one year prior to treatment, cocaine use was down 57.2%; heroin use, down 56.2%; marijuana use, down 76.3%; and alcohol use, down 65.1%. In addition, "predatory illegal acts" were down 70.1% and sexual risk behavior was down 65.2%.

Moreover, addictions may be no more intractable than many other chronic ailments. In a review of over 70 studies relating to three chronic conditions, diabetes, hypertension, and asthma, O'Brien & McLellan (1996) found that less than 30% of diabetics (and asthmatics) make the suggested dietary and/or behavioral changes and less than 50% follow their medication schedules completely. They also report that "30% of insulin-dependent diabetic patients and 50–80% of hypertensive and asthmatic patients have a reoccurrence of their symptoms each year and require at least restabilization of their medication and/or additional medical interventions to re-establish symptom remission" (p. 312). We know that relapses to alcohol and/or drug misuse can result in serious consequences, most commonly accidental injuries. However, complications from relapses in diabetes can result in blindness, impotence, and even amputations, and heart and brain attacks (strokes) may result from relapses in the management of hypertension.

Depression, the mainstay of many traditional therapists who routinely shy away from treating clients with addictive problems, appears to be as difficult to treat. A study by Fortney et al. (1999) found the following health care utilization:

	Hospital days:	Outpatient visits:
Alcohol	79	86
Depression	100	141
Diabetes	54	189

Clients Must Stop—Any Other Outcome Won't Work

In the past—and, unfortunately, in many cases, to this day—abuse and dependence problems labored under a different set of criteria for defining treatment as "effective." Only treatment that led to abstinence was rated as successful or effective. It is a standard that is not applied to any other DSM-IV disorder. Such an all-or-nothing criterion is normally applied to only a limited subset of human afflictions, e.g., measles or a broken leg. In addition, such ailments have unique characteristics. They are usually caused by an agent, such as bacteria or virus. Patients have little to do in order to affect a cure, treatment is not often required over a long time period, and the patient need do very little or nothing to prevent a lapse or relapse. There are major exceptions, such as AIDS and, in some cases, Lyme disease, but, for the most part, the treatment of common agent-caused diseases follows this course. Asthma, diabetes, and hypertension—and addictions—in contrast, often require life-long changes in lifestyle, including taking medication on a daily basis.

Many studies have demonstrated that drinking outcomes vary in many ways and that abstinence is only one possible outcome. Duckert et al. (1992) found that both a brief intervention and short-term therapy led to reduced drinking in terms of less frequent drinking, fewer episodes of heavy drinking, and less drinking per week during periods of moderate drinking. In two large-scale surveys in Canada, Sobell et al. (1996) found that of people who reported having resolved their drinking problem on their own, 38% and 63%, respectively, reported drinking moderately. King & Tucker (2000), in a study of previously alcohol-dependent people who resolved their problems without treatment, found three patterns of problem resolution: immediate and stable abstinence; abstinence followed by moderation; and gradual cutting down, resulting in stable moderation. Those who ultimately became abstinent made an average of 41 attempts at moderation; in contrast, those who ultimately resolved their problems by drinking moderately, made an average of only five attempts. Klingemann (1991) found that 89% of the former heroin addicts in their study and 59% of those who had been abusing or dependent on alcohol were abstinent. However, the two respondents who were not abstaining from heroin altogether continued to use heroin approximately once per month and those who were not abstaining from alcohol drank at most three drinking units per day. One review of 40 studies (Sobell et al., 2000) found that approximately 40% of recovery outcomes were limited drinking and approximately 14% were limited drug use.

Based on a long-term (over 50 years), follow-up study of alcohol abuse and dependence in a group of Harvard undergraduates and a group of nondelinquent, inner-city, Boston youth, Vaillant (1996) concluded: "Rather than progressing, chronic alcohol abuse often appears merely to fluctuate in severity" (p. 248). Many participants from the Harvard group who abused alcohol have spent the last 20 years alternating between moderate drinking and abuse. For the most part, this pattern did not lead to dependence or the need for detoxification. At last contact or at death, 19% of the Harvard group and 37% of the inner-city group were abstinent after treatment; 10% and 14%, respectively, had returned to moderate drinking; 12% and 6% had been reclassified as social drinkers; and 60% and 43% were still abusing alcohol.

Complete abstinence may, in fact, be the best course. Any other choice may inevitably lead to problems, some serious. However, given the research indicating the many ways people resolve their addictive problems, King & Tucker (2000) may be correct in saying, "Taken together, the variable resolution patterns observed here and by others (e.g. Miller et al., 1992; L. C. Sobell et al., 1992) highlight the fact that abstinence-oriented treatments are poorly suited to facilitating the naturally occurring incremental behavior changes that are part of many resolutions" (p. 54).

"Addicts," "Drug Abusers," and "Alcoholics" Lie, Steal and Cheat, and Generally Frighten Me

Why has such a belief taken such a firm hold not only in laypersons' minds—sometimes *including* those who are having problems with addictive behaviors—but in clinicians' minds as well? There are several possible reasons. The side effects of other human maladies such as diabetes and asthma do not appear to harm the sufferer and other people as much as addictions. For example, diabetes does not generally contribute to the sufferer's stealing from his family or injuring people while behind the wheel of an automobile. On the other hand, the side effects of diabetes may include amputations and blindness, both of which have serious consequences for diabetic patients and their families, if not society as a whole.

It has always been difficult for people to decide whether an addictive problem reflects an underlying disease, a disordered state—for example, in the dopamine or seretonin systems—or a moral, character weakness. Governments have also had a similar difficulty in deciding, and over the past 30 years, have treated the problem increasingly as if it were a moral problem, incarcerating more and more users and dealers. Most people think that criminals are virtually impossible to rehabilitate (a belief that has increasingly been reflected in US correctional policies, as monies for rehabilitation have been cut consistently over the past three decades). Hence, if substance abusers are in some sense criminals, they are, *ipso facto*, almost impossible to help. Finally, Hollywood and the news media may have played a role in solidifying these beliefs. However, once economic factors, such as poverty, are factored out, it would often be difficult to determine on the basis of appearance who is in a clinician's office for help with depression or anxiety, and who is there for help with addictions. Moreover, having an addictive problem does not necessarily mean that a client will lie and steal as well.

Client Beliefs that May Hinder the Use of Brief Interventions

Potential clients also carry around irrational beliefs that may affect the effectiveness of brief interventions. However, as is discussed later in this chapter, the wider availability of brief interventions may help bring more people in for some form of help.

Going to a Therapist or Counselor Won't Help

Klingemann (1991) notes that for many of the subjects of his study of natural recovery from alcohol and heroin, "treatment itself was regarded as irrelevant or even as a hindrance to solving the problem" (p. 729). Persons interviewed also reported that "it never occurred to them" to seek professional help and that "they could not find anything in professional aid that corresponded to their ideas of concrete, everyday healing methods" (p. 740).

My Problem Is Not that Serious

King & Tucker (2000) found that 63.5% of their participants—previously alcohol-dependent drinkers who had resolved their problems without treatment—did not think their problems were serious enough to warrant treatment despite the fact that they were assessed as having been alcohol dependent prior to resolving their problems. However, 75% thought they could resolve their problems on their own, and, according to the study, had done so.

Addictions Are Too Difficult To Be Stopped with a "Brief Intervention"

Most clients who actually seek treatment know that resolving their problem is very difficult. They have tried various techniques, at various times, and are in a practitioner's office because of their lack of success. They are often not interested in an approach that might reduce their drinking by half—a typical result of brief interventions. In addition, they believe (not always accurately) that their spouse or boss will not accept anything short of stopping. For years, laypersons understood that for a serious drinking problem, one had to go away for at least 28 days and attend Alcoholics Anonymous, perhaps for a lifetime. Consequently, it is now difficult to convince some clients (and their friends and family) that that might not be true for everyone.

I Cannot Afford the Risk of a Drinking (or Drugging) Diagnosis on My Medical Records Because I Do Not Trust the Confidentiality of My Medical Records

This is not necessarily an irrational belief. A therapist cannot guarantee that the computer records of an insurance company will not be shared with another insurance company, and there is also no assurance that a company's human resource manager will adequately maintain the confidentiality of an alcohol or drug abuse or dependence diagnosis. Concerns about "labeling, privacy and embarrassment about asking for help" (p. 53) were cited by 69.2% of King & Tucker's (2000) participants as a reason for not seeking treatment.

If I Go to a Professional, He Will Just Tell Me I Have to Stop, and I Don't Think I Can Do that Right Now

People with addictive problems, at least in the USA, do not believe that they can find different professionals who will give them alternative treatment approaches to select from. And they are correct in that belief. Almost all treatment facilities offer only programs that require abstinence, and some psychiatrists will not see a patient if they discover that the prospective client has an addiction and is not abstinent.

In contrast, people who develop diabetes or some other ailment may consult a variety of health-care professionals who offer a variety of alternative treatment approaches. The prospective patients may be looking for a cure or for advice that makes sense to them and that they think they can implement. Regardless of the current state of their condition, they know that a doctor will see them, listen to their problem, and give them suggestions for curing or managing their problem. The same is not true for addictions.

Having Someone Preach to Me Won't Help

This is probably not an irrational belief. There is no evidence that psychoeducational programs are very effective (cf. Miller et al., 1995), and there is clear evidence that confrontation often does more harm than good (Miller & Rollnick, 1991; Miller, et al., 1993). However, it is a belief that keeps prospective clients out of practitioners' offices.

BRIEF INTERVENTIONS AND THE STAGES OF CHANGE MODEL

Therapists who work on addictive behaviors see clients who (a) claim that they don't have a problem; (b) think they may have a problem but don't know what to do about it; and (c) know they have a problem and want to prevent future lapses and relapses. These three types of clients are related to the six stages of change in Prochaska & DiClemente's (Bishop, 2001b; Prochaska & DiClemente, 1982; Prochaska et al., 1992) transtheoretical model. That model suggests that everyone changing any behavior, whether using heroin or swinging a golf club, goes through six stages of change: pre-contemplation, contemplation, preparation, action, maintenance, and termination. Pre-contemplators, as the name implies, are not contemplating changing. Perhaps they genuinely do not think they have a problem, or they have tried to change so many times that they are demoralized to the point of denying their problem. People in stages II and III, contemplation and preparation are primarily ambivalent. They think a lot about changing their behavior. They may have read a self-help book or talked to a friend. But they have not brought themselves to the point of actually changing. Or they may have tried several times, and failed almost immediately. The third type of client that therapists see is in either action or maintenance. They know what they want to do and are seeking help to limit lapses and relapses.

Quite commonly, clinicians see clients with several problems and the clients are not in the same stage on each. For example, Sam, a recent client, came into my office reporting that he drank two to five beers a night, smoked marijuana, and was depressed because he had recently been fired. Initially, he did not acknowledge being angry, even though sitting opposite his wife in my office during the last session, he looked angry, and his wife reported that he was always angry and that he had hit her on two occasions during the past year. There was some evidence that he might have been let go simply because of his age, and he definitely had difficulty in finding new work, perhaps an age-related issue, as well. There were also several indications that he drank and smoked marijuana partly to cope with anxiety, but he did not see himself as an anxious person. In brief, he seemed to be ready to change his drinking behavior and motivated to work on his depression. But he did not indicate a willingness to address his marijuana smoking, and did not see anger management or his anxiety as a problem.

The research on the effectiveness of brief interventions tailored to a client's stage of change is practically non-existent. Heather (1995b) and his associates, in a study of male hospital patients, found that among those ready to take action (in terms of the stages of change model), outcomes were comparable for a motivational interviewing intervention, a skills-based counseling intervention, and no intervention at all. However, those "less ready to change" were positively affected by the motivational interviewing intervention. Jamner et al. (1997), using illustrated handouts of role model stories tailored to the users' stage of change, were able to increase the percentage of injecting drug users carrying condoms from 10% to 27% in a targeted area in Long Beach, California.

The techniques discussed below have been culled from research-based treatment approaches, including motivational interviewing, rational emotive behavior therapy (REBT), cognitive-behavioral therapy (CBT), relapse prevention, and harm reduction. All of them can be used in brief interventions with clients, although those brief interventions may lead to longer, more intensive treatment or repeated but infrequent contacts over many years.

Usually, clinicians can quite quickly determine their client's interest or uninterest in changing a variety of problems, both the addictive and nonaddictive ones. However, therapists may also want to use the AUDIT (Alcohol Use Disorders Identification Test) (Saunders et al., 1993), a 10-item screening test that reportedly is especially good at identifying early alcohol problems and risky drinking (Babor & Higgins-Biddle, 2000).

BRIEF INTERVENTIONS FOR STAGE I, PRE-CONTEMPLATIVE CLIENTS

The goal in working with clients who do not recognize or admit to having a problem is to move them from pre-contemplation to contemplation. Motivational interviewing, with its roots in Rogerian psychotherapy, focuses on expressing empathy for the client's situation, developing discrepancy, avoiding argumentation, and rolling with resistance. Many brief interventions have been based on motivational interviewing, involving some variant of FRAMES:

F = After a fairly lengthy assessment, clients are given *feedback* about their drinking behavior.

R = The *responsibility* for change rests within the client.

A = Therapists give clients direct *advice* when that is appropriate.

M= Clients are given a *menu* of treatment options to choose from.

E = *Empathy* is seen as central to change.

S = Therapists work with clients to support *self-efficacy*.

Developing Discrepancy: Uncovering a Client's Conflicting Wants/Goals

One of my clients, Jerry, wants to have a better relationship with his teenage son, but, at the same time, he wants to continue to drink, something he cannot seem to do without drinking heavily. Similarly, it is quite common for college students to want both to hang out in a bar drinking with their friends late into the night *and* to study and do well on an exam. But the two activities are often mutually exclusive. A therapist can empathetically explore and inquire into the discrepancies that seem to exist between what clients say they want and what they are doing (and getting). Even when clients deny that they have a problem with drinking, gambling, or some other addictive behavior, it may be evident that they are experiencing a great deal of misery in their life, their key relationships, their job, etc. Expressing empathy about this fact may help therapists move them to consider other ways of managing their problems.

It is important to air and acknowledge that conflicts regarding goals and values and, in particular, how one uses time are a common aspect of human life. And it is extremely important to express empathy for how difficult it may be to make these choices. No doubt, at times, all humans want to "have their cake and eat it too," and accepting that that is not possible can sometimes be quite difficult. Glasser (1965; 1989), the founder of reality therapy, is well known for asking clients variations of the following three questions: What do you want? What are you doing? How do you like it (what you are getting, the results)?

These questions clearly suggest that people are responsible for their choices and have self-efficacy; they have or can develop the ability to behave differently, and, at least to some extent, fulfill some of their "wants ."

Doing an ABC on Another Problem or Another Person's Problem

Addictive behaviors help people not think (or feel) about the present and the past, and especially about the future. They narrow the "attentional focus," according to one theory (cf Kasell & Unrod, 2000). Therapists may be able to help clients figure out what they are telling themselves to make themselves so resistant to changing. Besides empathizing with the disparity between what clients seem to want over the medium and long run and what they are doing in the short run, therapists can use the ABC technique (Ellis, 1962, 1994; 1996), one of CBT's best-known techniques, to help clients figure out what they want to do and how better to do it.

Ten irrational beliefs seem to be central to addictive behaviors:

1. I can get away with it.
2. It won't matter.
3. I want a drink (to gamble, etc.), and I have to (I should) have what I want when I want it.
4. It's too hard to change.
5. I can't stand it (practicing changing my behavior; the discomfort of not doing what I want to do; the anxiety that I am feeling; my depression, etc.).
6. It's awful (e.g., what is happening; what I have done).
7. I should be different.
8. You should be different
9. The world should be different.
10. If I drink or use drugs, I will get some relief, and I have to have relief.

Clients who are denying are acting as if they do not have a problem and may also be thinking to themselves, "If I admit that I have a problem, they will send me away to rehab." "Speaking honestly to a shrink before never got me anywhere. In fact, many were very disrespectful of me, so why should I be honest with this person?" "I have tried to change before, and every time I've failed. I cannot stand failing again." "I do not want to disappoint my family again."

It is important to help clients uncover what they might be telling themselves and then consider other ways they might think, feel, and act. However, mandated clients and other clients in pre-contemplation present a unique challenge. Because they do not think they have a problem or do not admit to thinking so, they may resist doing an ABC on their non-existent problem. But they may be willing to do an ABC on another person's problems; e.g., the person who sent them to the therapist or convinced them to come. Or they may be willing to do an ABC on another problem; e.g., their inability to get a job.

One does not even have to talk explicitly about the ABC technique to use it as a guide in one's questioning. Recently, I held the following conversation with one of my clients:

THERAPIST: How is your wife making herself so upset? Clearly, she must have been very upset to have said to you, 'Either you go see a therapist or this relationship is over.' What do you think she was thinking?

CLIENT: I don't know. She's nuts.

T: Perhaps she is. Maybe you're right, she really is pretty neurotic. But that doesn't sound like it makes for a happy marriage, and even nutty people *think*. What do you think she is thinking to get so upset?

C: (*After a long pause*) I really don't know.

T: Well, guess. Just take a guess.

C: Maybe she's afraid I'll turn out like her old man. He's a real bastard. Now that's a drunk, if I ever saw one. I'm not a drunk even if she thinks I am, but he sure is.

T: I think maybe you're right, she's upsetting herself by thinking to herself, 'Oh, my God. Sam's going to become just like my dad. Oh, my God, I couldn't stand that.'

C: But I'm not a drunk!

T: I know, I know, but that may be how she is scaring herself and why she is pushing you to see me. What do you think she could say to herself instead?

BRIEF INTERVENTIONS FOR STAGES II AND III, AMBIVALENT CLIENTS

Similar techniques may be used with ambivalent clients, especially developing discrepancies and the ABC technique, but other techniques may also be helpful in motivating a client to take action, that is, in moving a client from stages II and III to stage IV.

Cost/Benefit (Time Effects) Analysis

Considerable research suggests that people who get over their problems on their own do so because they reconsider the pro and cons of their behavior and conclude that their current addictive behavior is not compatible with the other things they want in life. Seventy-eight percent of the respondents recovering from cocaine interviewed by Toneatto et al. (1999) claimed that weighing the pros and cons finally convinced them to quit. In a study of dual recovery from drinking and smoking, Sobell et al. (1995) found that 71.7% of the participants coped with urges to drink by reminding themselves of the negative consequences of drinking; 45.5% used the same technique to cope with urges to smoke; 52.8% and 36.4% used thinking about the positive effects of not drinking or smoking, respectively, to cope with an urge.

Therapists can help ambivalent clients assess the positive and negative effects for them *over time* of drinking (or using) and of not drinking (using). The point is to heighten the client's awareness of the costs and benefits in, for example, two minutes, two hours, 24 hours, two weeks, two years, 20 years, etc. The time periods should be chosen to fit the client. Generally, it is more effective to start with the plusses and minuses *of* drinking (and continuing to drink) and then move to the consequences over time (positive and negative) of *not* drinking or using drugs. It is important to focus on the reasons for continuing the addictive behavior so that the client and the therapist become clearer about what contributes to and supports drinking and using drugs. It is also important to help clients understand that one negative consequence in two minutes of drinking or using drugs is that they have lost the opportunity to practice new coping skills.

Developing an Experimental Plan

Ambivalent clients may not be prepared to develop a permanent plan or policy and commit to one, but they may be interested in trying out an experimental plan for the near future. Therapists can use the same seven questions outlined below (see *Developing a Workable Plan or Policy*), ensuring that the client understands that what is being developed is only an experimental plan. The client is just trying to discover what might work best for him or her.

Urge Coping

Clients, especially ambivalent clients, are not going to try a new behavior if they do not think they will succeed. It is important to provide them with specific skills to use for coping with urges. Toneatto et al. (1999) found that cognitive coping skills were the most common techniques used by people in recovery from cocaine addiction. Deliberate recall of negative consequences was used by 77.5%, learning to stand the urge was used by 65%, recalling the positive consequences of not using cocaine was used by 57.5%, and distraction was used by 47.5%. In the Sobell et al. (1995) study, "toughing it out" was used by 60.4% to cope with an urge to drink and by 48.5% to cope with an urge to smoke; distraction was used by 41.5% and 18.2%, and eating something sweet by 26.4% and 24.2%, respectively. It should be noted that 12% of those having an urge to smoke, drank alcohol to cope. In the Toneatto et al. (1999) study, 56% increased their use of cannabis and alcohol to cope with urges to use cocaine (even though 35% also reported alcohol as a trigger for cocaine use).

Handouts, Bibliotherapy, and Interactive Computer Programs

Several studies have demonstrated the effectiveness of self-help manuals, bibliotherapy, and interactive computer programs (e.g., Heather et al., 1990; Hester & Delaney, 1997; Jamner et al., 1997; Prochaska & Velicer, 1997). Even ambivalent clients may be helped by reading books and using audiotapes (Bishop, 1993; Ellis & Velten, 1992; Kishline, 1994; Miller & Munoz, 1982; Sanchez-Craig, 1993; Sobell & Sobell, 1993; Tate, 1993). Clients who carry cards or handouts with them often tell of using them at difficult moments. For example, in their work to develop better smoking intervention strategies for substance-abusing adolescents, Myers and his associates (Myers et al., 2000) give their participants a handout with the acronym DEADS (Martin, 1994, as cited by Myers et al., 2000), where D = Delay, E = Escape, A = Avoid, D = Distract, and S = Substitute.

Harm Reduction

Many studies indicate that while alcohol and drug users may not be ready to stop, they are motivated to reduce the harm that they are doing to themselves and others (Marlatt, 1998;

Martlatt et al., 1998). For example, in a recent study (Strang et al., 1997) of 32 opiate users who were turned away from treatment, of the 19 participants who were still using the drugs two to three years later, 65% were injecting less often, using less, and using fewer different types of drugs. (Note that 29 stopped using the drugs after obtaining at least some treatment from a general practitioner or a general hospital—more evidence of the "natural recovery" discussed below.)

The most harmful behavior may not be drinking or using drugs. It may be driving home drunk, not using a condom with a prostitute during a cocaine binge, shoplifting, going to a dangerous neighborhood to obtain drugs, or using and exchanging dirty needles. Focusing on such potential long-run, very harmful behaviors may be more beneficial than motivating clients to reduce or stop their addictive behavior.

BRIEF INTERVENTIONS FOR RESTARTING OR MAINTAINING CHANGE: STAGE IV AND V CLIENTS

Restarting Interventions That Have Helped in the Past

As is true of asthmatics and diabetics, many clients who have done fairly well in the past know what has helped. It is just a question of getting them restarted. If yoga and meditation have helped in the past, what have they been telling themselves to convince themselves not to do it? If abstinence worked, how did they convince themselves that they could moderate? What would help get them back on track? Going through the seven questions listed below may help clarify what has derailed them and what might increase the odds that they can get back on track.

Developing a Workable Plan or Policy

Clients in stages IV and V know what they want to do and are looking for help. Perhaps the frequency of lapses and relapses or the severity of a recent relapse has brought them into the therapist's office. The therapist will want to discuss their plan or policy. If they do not have one, developing one will be the primary focus of the session. If they have one but have not been able to stick to it, then the therapist may help them develop a more reasonable one and explore what can be done to increase the odds that they can maintain the plan. I use seven types of questions to help in this process (Bishop, 2001b):

Specifying Questions

What does your client want to do? The therapist may think that it would probably be better if clients stopped altogether. But they may be unwilling or unprepared to do so. If asked, of course, therapists can share their opinion and reasons.

If the client wants to abstain, the therapist can quite quickly move on to the remaining questions. However, if the client wants to do something other than abstain, it is important to help her be as specific as possible in defining her policy or plan. How often in a week is she going to drink or use drugs (or engage in some other form of addictive behavior)? How many drinks is she going to consume in any one sitting? How many drinks is she intending to drink in the first hour? Where is she going to drink? And where is she not going to drink? Does she still want to try to drink while she is alone or only when she is with other people? Perhaps she likes to go out on Sundays for brunch. If so, perhaps her rule should be something like no more than two drinks at any one setting, no more than three drinks per day, and no drinking on three days of the week.

Implementation Questions

Many people make resolutions but few are successful at implementing them. Once the client has identified what she wants to do, it is important to discuss how she intends to carry out her plan (cf. Gollwitzer, 1999). If she frequently stops at a bar on her way home from work, how is she going to get home without stopping? If she wants to abstain but her partner still likes to drink at night, how is she going to cope with that situation?

If she wants to moderate, how is she going to behave at a party? What is she going to say to her host or a waiter? Is she going to act as though she were drinking (for example, sipping on a "gin and tonic" without the gin) or be clear with people that she is not drinking? A lawyer coming up for promotion to partner did not want his firm to know that he had a problem with alcohol (and cocaine). We spent quite a while figuring out what he would feel comfortable in saying. He liked the image that he thought he projected in saying, "I can't drink right now. I'm on antibiotics. I was recently trekking in Nepal (which was true), and I somehow managed to pick up a parasite. I can't drink on the medication."

Likelihood Questions

How likely does the client think it is that she is going to stick to her plan? Even if she gives you a low percentage answer, you may want to ask the next question before discussing why she feels the likelihood is so low.

Commitment Questions

How committed is the client to this plan? If she is only slightly committed to her plan, it is possible that the therapist has persuaded her to accept a plan that is not realistic. The therapist should explore why she is so uncommitted.

Derailing Questions

What does the client think may contribute to her derailing herself? Is there a wedding coming up? Do getting home tired and being alone increase the likelihood that she will call for a delivery from the liquor store (or her heroin dealer)? This is a good time to review the major triggers of her drinking. Negative affect, i.e., anxiety, anger, etc.? Being alone?

Boredom/a desire for some excitement? Physical discomfort? Conflict with others? Pressure from others to drink or use?

Increasing-the-Likelihood Questions

Even if the client feels it is quite likely that she will stick to her plan and she expresses high commitment, the therapist should discuss how she might increase the odds of success. What could she do that would increase the likelihood that she can stick to her plan? Would going to a self-help or support group help? Would entering an outpatient program help? Would getting her spouse involved help? Would a telephone call from the therapist at mid-week help?

Summarizing Questions

Ask the client to summarize what she has decided to do. The therapist could ask her to summarize what she has "agreed" to do, but an agreement is usually between two parties who both have an interest in the outcome. I think it is better to indicate as clearly as possible that the client is making decisions for herself, for her life. While the therapist is there to help, he or she is not personally invested in the outcome. Otherwise, in the future, the client may be afraid to be honest with the therapist.

The Three R's: Review, Revise, and Rehearse

If a client comes back for another session after setting up a plan, the focus of the session is usually on reviewing how well the plan worked, revising it if necessary, and rehearsing for the future. The key to reviewing is maintaining an empathetic, nonjudgmental approach. In rehearsing, role-plays can be especially helpful. The therapist and client can alternate playing the "healthy" and the "craving voice" inside the client's head, and the client can use role-plays to prepare and practice for upcoming potential trigger situations, such as weddings and office parties.

Changing the A's (Activating Events)

Generally, REBT/CBT concentrates on helping clients change the B's, the beliefs that are contributing to their addictive behaviors or other adverse consequences. However, there are times when it may be better for clients to change the A's. That is, it may be more helpful to end a relationship if the client's partner is a chronic drinker or drug user. It may be better to look for a different job if the current one is no longer challenging or if the boss is abusive. Then it is important to back up in time to explore what the client is telling himself that is preventing him from leaving his girlfriend or from finding another job. He may be thinking, "It will be too hard. I couldn't stand being alone. Where would I live? I can't stand the thought of having to look for a new place all by myself." Or, related to a new job, "If I went to an interview, they might find out that I've had a drug problem. Then they wouldn't hire me. I can't stand getting rejected. It's too hard. It's more comfortable to stay where I am."

ABCS FOR ADDICTIVE BEHAVIORS VS. EMOTIONAL UPSETS

It is important for clinicians to remember that working with addictive clients is in some ways different. Most clients who come to therapists *want* to change. They are depressed, suffering from anxiety, or having difficulty in a relationship and they want help. But many addicted clients are not nearly so clear. They are often not sure which is worse: the cure or the disease. Hence, they are not sure they want to change, and even if they think they want to change when they are in the therapist's office, they may change that idea a few hours later.

In addition, addicted clients are interested in changing a behavior. That is, they do not just want to feel better; they want to behave differently. Many cognitive-behavioral therapists may recognize that even their non-addicted clients will have to change their behaviors if they want to feel better, but many clients, especially if they are new to CBT, may not.

PRE-ABS AND POST-BCS

Ellis (1994, 1996) has argued that in helping a client overcome depression, it is critical to address the secondary problem (if it exists): the depression about the depression. Similarly, many clients who have had panic attacks become anxious *about* feeling anxious. As a result, a good REBT/CBT therapist looks at the beliefs and consequences that flow from being depressed, i.e., the post-BCs, the beliefs and consequent feelings (and behaviors) that come after the feeling of depression has set in (or the person has made himself or herself depressed). In contrast, when a client wants to change an addictive behavior, it is important for therapists to move back in time and to focus on the activating events and the beliefs that *precede* an addictive episode. Finding out how the client feels about his behavior is important, but the former is more important.

In training therapists in peer-counseling situations (in which one therapist plays the client and the other the therapist), the beginning of a "session" may sound as follows:

THERAPIST: What would you like to work on today?

CLIENT: Well, I'm still smoking and I'd like to cut down.

T: OK. How do you feel about your smoking?

C: Awful. I want to quit. I say I'm going to quit. And then I just go right on smoking. I just have no willpower at all.

T: Hmm. That sounds pretty upsetting. What makes you so upset?

C: I feel like a complete failure. I have promised my wife that I would stop, and now I am sneaking around smoking while she thinks I have stopped.

T: So it sounds like you're telling yourself something like: "I'm not just a weak-willed person and a failure. I'm a sneak as well."

C: Yes, and I hate that.

T: But how does failing at something make you a failure?

But the client has said that he wants to stop smoking, not feel better about smoking. As noted above, Ellis (1994, 1996) has often argued that it is critical to work on the secondary disturbance—for example, the depression about the depression or the anxiety about the anxiety—before working on the primary disturbance, that is, the depression or anxiety itself. And for such mood disturbances, this may be very correct. However, it is important for therapists working with clients with addictive disorders to work first on the antecedents, the A's (activating events) and B's (beliefs) that precede each addictive episode—smoking a cigarette, in this instance. Otherwise the session may wind up focusing on the B's and C's (consequences) following the episode. Understanding those B's and C's is no doubt important, but an addictive client who is ambivalent about changing may avoid looking at the antecedents and the therapist may be an unwitting accomplice.

To return to the session example above, it is generally preferable to proceed as follows:

THERAPIST: What would you like to work on today?

CLIENT: Well, I'm still smoking and I'd like to cut down?

T: How many cigarettes do you smoke a day?

C: About a pack.

T: What would you like to do?

C: I'd like to stop entirely?

T: When was the last time you had a cigarette.?

C: Right before this session.

T: Did you think about *not* smoking it?

C: No.

T: So there was no debate about it that time.

C: No.

T: When will you smoke the next cigarette?

C: At the break.

T: Suppose you decided not to smoke it, what do you think you would tell yourself to derail your intention?

C: It doesn't matter.

T: What else?

C: I'll feel uncomfortable during the next part of this training if I don't smoke a cigarette.

T: Yes, and I think you may also be telling yourself, "I want a cigarette," which is not irrational or crazy, but you're adding, "and I have to have what I want." It's the second part that is irrational—and like the two-year-old in you. It's great to be able to think like a two-year-old sometimes. I wouldn't want you to kill off that part of you. But two-year-olds have very little or no sense of time. But you *do*. They don't think about tomorrow, but you do. So thinking like a two-year-old may not really be what you want to do. What do you think you could tell yourself if you decided to skip that cigarette?

C: Oh, I don't know.

T: Well, think for a moment. A part of you wants the cigarette and a part is saying, "I want what I want when I want it," but a part of you also wants to quit smoking. What could you say to yourself instead?

C: I don't want it . . . but I think I *would.*

T: Yes, you would in the short run, but you also *want* to stop . . . which means you don't want it in the medium and long run. Would you like to try skipping that one cigarette to figure out what you could say to yourself that might work?

C: Well . . . yeah . . . maybe.

T: It's up to you. I'm not surprised you're conflicted. You're not sure which goal, your short-term or your long-term goal, you *want* to meet.

So the emphasis is on working on the A's and B's that contribute to the behavior as soon as possible during the session. Many skilled therapists naturally combine the two. That is, they start with something that sounds, as in the first session, to be empathetic and to build the relationship before they move to working directly on the behavior itself.

It should be noted that this was an easy client because she knew what she wanted to do and sounded fairly unambivalent about it. She has not been successful in making the change, but she is clear that she wants to stop. Most clients are not nearly as clear. As a result, the therapist has to work in other ways initially to motivate change.

ASSISTED NATURAL RECOVERY

Research into natural recovery reveals that (a) most people recover from addictive problems on their own; (b) many people who recover on their own have specifically avoided seeking help from treatment providers or self-help groups; and (c) many people who claim they have recovered without treatment may have been affected by various "bits and pieces" of information, advice, pressure, and support along the way.

In resolving their difficulties, some people stop completely; that is, they abstain. More frequently, they reduce their behavior in one manner or another (Finney et al., 1999; King & Tucker, 2000; Sobell et al., 1996; Sobell et al., 2000; Tucker & King, 1999, Zinberg & Jacobson, 1976). The term "spontaneous remission" has been used for this kind of recovery, but it is also important to note that many recoveries do not appear to occur "spontaneously." Rather, it appears to involve purposeful behavior and considerable thought and effort on the part of the people recovering. However, Sobell and her associates (Sobell et al., 1993) found that this is not always the case; almost one-third of the reasons given for recovery could be categorized as leading to "immediate" or spontaneous recovery.

The best-known example of natural recovery involved US Army enlistees returning from Vietnam (Robins et al., 1975). Although approximately 20% of the approximately 900 soldiers interviewed reported opiate addiction while in Vietnam, upon return, rates of prior use returned to normal; e.g., about 1% of the group were addicted. An early review of the literature regarding natural recovery from alcohol problems by Smart (1976 as cited in Ludwig, 1985) reported cumulative rates of recovery ranging from 10% to 42% with yearly rates between 1% to 3%. More recently, two-large scale surveys in Canada of 11 634 and

1034 respondents found that 77.5% and 77.7%, respectively, of those reporting a recovery in excess of one year did so on their own without treatment (Sobell et al., 1996). A recent review (Walters, 2000) of spontaneous remission rate research included studies of smokers, problem drinkers, alcohol abusers, and heroin users. Spontaneous remission rates for alcohol ranged from 14.3% to 50.0%. In one study of 406 heroin addicts, the rate was 56.4% (based on a criterion of no daily use in the last three plus years in a 12-year follow-up period).

Regarding alcohol abuse, research indicates that remitters reduce the number of days they drink per week and/or the number of drinks per drinking episode and/or the rapidity with which they drink. In the Sobell et al. (1996) study, the untreated, resolved subjects drank significantly fewer days (from 72.4% of all days prior to resolution to 12.1%) and drank significantly less when they did drink, down from 11.3 drinks, on average, to 2.1 drinks. They also showed a decrease in the intensity of their drink of choice, shifting significantly away from hard liquor to wine.

Brief interventions may have a significant impact on this form of recovery. Heather et al. (1990) have referred to this process as "assisted natural recovery" (p. 1177). Brief interventions might shorten the interval between thinking about cutting down or stopping and actually doing so. As noted previously, King & Tucker (2000) found that people who ultimately abstained, reported trying moderation, on average, 41 times. One study (Hazelden Foundation, 1998) suggests that smokers take an average of 18 years to stop smoking, from the time they first think about stopping to the time that they actually stop for good. On average they relapse 10 times; put another way, they make, on average, 10 attempts before they manage to stop completely. Brief interventions may decrease the number of attempts and the time it takes people to stop.

THE FUTURE OF BRIEF INTERVENTIONS IN CLINICAL PRACTICE

Only a small percentage of the people who might benefit from treatment actually obtain it. Sobell & Sobell (2000) have argued for a stepped-care model, in which the intensity of service would be matched to the intensity of the client's problem. In most cases, brief interventions would be used first. Babor & Higgins-Biddle (2000) note that "alcoholism" seems to be the only term currently well known by the lay public and many health-care professionals. "Abuse," "problem drinking," "hazardous drinking," and "risky drinking" are not well known or in common usage. They argue that the concept of "risky drinking" needs to be introduced and "sold" to both the lay public and to professionals in the same way that early interventions for breast cancer, asthma, and several other human ailments are currently being "marketed" to the public. Currently, other than opportunistic interventions, as in emergency rooms, clinicians provide treatment only when it is sought by an individual with a problem. Prochaska & Velicer (1997), however, found that the abstinence curves both of clients who had been sought out and those who had sought treatment were similar. Hence, they argue that proactive efforts should be made to interest people in brief interventions.

Most clinicians in private practice rarely know how long they will see a client. This may be because they, too, accept the underlying assumption that clients will come until they are "cured." Given that that kind of health-care model may not be appropriate in all cases, a therapist may want to offer a variety of treatment options and discuss them with the client.

In this way, not only will the client know how the therapist may work, but the therapist will also learn valuable information about how the client thinks about treatment, including the anticipated duration of treatment.

Some clients come to my office because they understand that I will not immediately insist on total abstinence and that they can come for as little as one consultation, if they choose to do so. Such a consultation gives me the opportunity to work in a variety of ways according to a client's stage of change, and to suggest other resources, such as books, tapes, on-line recovery meetings, psychiatrists, and yoga groups. Sometimes I never see such clients again and therefore have no idea of how our meeting may have affected them. However, some reappear. They may be worse off than when I first met them, but, on occasion, they have improved various aspects of their lives. They may have eliminated one addictive behavior, e.g., using cocaine, but not another. They may have found employment, or be in a relationship, or have joined a self-help organization. No research that I know of has looked at such situations. When clients reappear after a brief encounter with a treatment professional or some other kind of treatment intervention, what percentage have moved a stage or more or are engaging less often in addictive behaviors (and/or less intensively) or are doing less harm to themselves and others?

Ken, an investment banker, has seen me six times. He is employed, married, and has a good relationship with both his sons, one of whom is working and the other in graduate school. I met his wife during the third session. She shared her concerns, and we discussed Ken's plan to drink moderately—never more than three drinks at any one sitting, never more than four a day, and only five days a week. She was apprehensive and would have preferred that he stopped drinking entirely, but she acknowledged that he generally did what he said he was going to do (to an annoying degree, at times, she reported), and she was willing to be supportive unless he got drunk again. We scheduled his next session in two weeks and will probably schedule the one after that after a three-or four-week interval, as he is doing well at maintaining his goal of moderate drinking. In his opinion, it is better for him to come in right before special events such as office parties, weddings, and national holidays than to meet every week when things are going well.

Peter, a freelance photographer, contacts me by telephone and by e-mail when he gets into trouble with alcohol. I have probably had 10–15 contacts with him over the past two years. In one case, I helped him get himself back to the psychiatrist who had helped him detoxify on an outpatient basis. In another instance, I was successful in getting him to admit himself to a hospital. When he called, he knew he needed to be hospitalized, but he did not want to go because he did not like the hospital in his neighborhood. I helped encourage him to admit himself to another hospital. In a third instance, he was too intoxicated to travel by himself, and, with his permission, I called the police. Fortunately, I was able to communicate to the police that he was delusional (because he was intoxicated) but not dangerous, and that gentle assistance (and transportation) were all that were needed, and they took him to the hospital in a courteous manner. Of course, because his use of alcohol completely disables him and is often dangerous, I would prefer that he abstain completely. But he claims that taking Antabuse®interferes with his ability to work, and he has never stayed for very long as an inpatient or in outpatient treatment groups. So, with brief interventions, he and his psychiatrists and a number of other professionals have attempted to help him struggle with his problem.

Are there any cognitive behavioral techniques that cannot be used in a brief intervention? No. In 5–10 minutes, a practitioner can do a cost-benefit analysis. In 5–10 minutes, one can do an ABC, either on (a) how a person is preventing himself from doing what has helped in the past; (b) how he is preventing himself from reaching his stated goal(s); (c) how he is preventing himself from better managing or overcoming another problem, such as a problem with his boss, parole officer, or girlfriend; or (d) how someone else is upsetting himself or herself about the client's problem (i.e., an ABC on another person's problem). In 5–10 minutes, a therapist and a client can come up with some hypotheses as to the reasons for the addictions that may go back to early childhood—for example, being frequently locked in a closet or being sexually abused. Even if the reasons are partly or totally invented, they may help motivate a client to work on change. Once clients have an understanding of the possible roots of their behavior, they may be more willing to work to regulate it more effectively. In 5–10 minutes, therapists can develop a plan or policy that a client can try to follow in the future. The therapist can also work to increase the client's commitment to such a plan and the likelihood that he or she can follow it. The therapist can also use role-play to practice what a client could say to himself, given an urge or a particular setting, and what he could say to someone else—for example, a waiter who asks him whether he wants a drink.

One impediment to brief interventions may be that clients do not expect or want such rapid-fire "treatment." They may have come with certain expectations about therapy. Given Albert Ellis' reputation and his frequent demonstrations, clients who make an appointment with him probably want a very direct and quick response. However, that is not what most clients seem to expect. A private practitioner may lose clients by moving too quickly. It may give clients the impression that the therapist does not really appreciate the complexity of their problems or the pain that they are suffering. Finally, the fastest way to frighten some clients out of treatment is to suggest that they can be "cured" in a short time. Many have relied on their addictive behaviors—have been dependent on them—for many years. A crippled man may be thrilled to hear that he will soon walk without crutches, but a client with addictive problems may not feel this way. His addictive behavior may have become his "best friend," almost like a lover, and no one contemplates losing his or her best friend or lover without trepidation.

If brief interventions were to become better known and accepted by both professionals and the lay public, some of the barriers to treatment might fall. For example, if clients are going to go for only a few sessions, they might be willing to pay out of pocket, obviating the need for a diagnosis and for insurance reimbursement, and decreasing the fear of an abuse or dependence diagnosis in their medical records. Those who do not think their problems serious enough to warrant treatment might reconsider their decision. And brief interventions may become more popular when people realize that ultimately they are not going to be forced into one and only one treatment modality.

Technology may also begin to play a larger role in brief interventions. Prochaska & Velicer (1997) in their work on smoking cessation found that computer-generated interactive interventions based on expert systems were more effective than self-help manuals. D'Amico & Fromme (2000) used illustrated, computer-generated graphic feedback as the first part of their 50-minute risk skills training program (RSTP), and Marlatt and his associates (Marlatt et al., 1998) used computer-generated, graphic feedback as a part of their brief intervention program focused on college drinking. Hester & Delaney (1997) have been developing an interactive, computer-based program for problem drinkers. And people seeking help on the Web can attend over a dozen Smart Recovery™ online help groups (www.smartrecovery.org).

As I discussed above, beliefs about treatment and, by extension, about brief interventions may have to change significantly before brief interventions become common. Many laypersons (and some professionals) still look to treatment as if an addiction were similar to an acute medical problem, not a chronic illness. Although neither analogy fits addictions perfectly, many clients think an addictive disorder, is more like a broken leg than asthma. Many clients and their significant others continue to look for a once-and-for-all cure. For some, this model may be correct, but others suffer from a more long-term, often chronic problem. As the effectiveness of brief interventions becomes better known, more clinicians may offer them as one of several treatment approaches. Clients may also begin to visit clinicians more frequently on an occasional basis when they experience new difficulties, or as they attempt to make further changes in their lives. The old model of therapy may continue to appeal to some and be appropriate for their problems, but others may prefer periodic, brief interventions for their substance-abuse disorders.

REFERENCES

Babor, T. F., & Higgins-Biddle, J. C. (2000). Alcohol screening and brief intervention: dissemination strategies for medical practice and public health. *Addiction, 95*, 677–686.

Baer, J. S., Marlatt, G. A., Kivlahan, D. R., Fromme, K., Larimer, M., & Williams, E. (1992). An experimental test of three methods of alcohol risk reduction with young adults. *Journal of Consulting and Clinical Psychology, 60*, 974–979.

Baker, A., Heather, N., Wodak, A., Dixon, J., & Holt, P. (1993). Evaluation of a cognitive-behavioral intervention for HIV prevention among injecting drug users. *AIDS, 7*, 247–256.

Baker, A., Kochan, J., Dixon, N., Heather, N., & Wodak, A. (1994). Controlled evaluation of a brief intervention for HIV prevention among injecting drug users not in treatment. *AIDS Care, 6*, 559–570.

Bien, T. H., Miller, W. R., & Tonnigan, J. S. (1993). Brief intervention for alcohol problems: A review. *Addictions, 88*, 315–336.

Bishop, F. M. (1993). *Relapse Prevention with REBT*. Audiotape. New York: Albert Ellis Institute.

Bishop, F. M. (2001a) Hurrah for Research! What Would My Practice Look Like Without the Benefits of Research? *The Addictions Newsletter*, APA, Division 50, XIII, 2.

Bishop, F. M. (2001b). *Managing addictions: Cognitive, emotive and behavioral techniques.* Northvale, NJ: Jason Aronson.

Breslin, C., Sdao-Jarvie, K, Tupker, E., & Pearlman, S. (1999). *First contact: A brief treatment for young substance abusers.* Toronto, Ontario.: Centre for Addiction and Mental Health.

Chick, J., Ritson, B., Connaughton, J., Stewart, A., & Chick, J. (1988). Advice versus extended treatment for alcoholism: A controlled study. *British Journal of Addiction, 83(2)*, 159–170.

D'Amico, E. J., & Fromme, K. (2000). Implementation of the Risk Skills Training Program: A brief intervention targeting adolescent participation in risk behaviors. *Cognitive and Behavioral Practice, 7*, 101–107.

Duckert, F., Amundsen, A., & Johnsen, J. (1992). What happens to drinking after therapeutic intervention? *British Journal of Addiction, 87*, 1457–1467.

Ellis, A. (1962, 1994). *Reason and emotion in psychotherapy.* Secaucus, NJ: Citadel. Rev. ed., Secaucus, NJ: Carol Publishing Group; Revised 1994, New York: Birch Lane Press.

Ellis, A. (1996). *Better, deeper, and more enduring brief therapy: The rational emotive behavior therapy approach.* New York: Brunner/Mazel.

Ellis, A., & Velten, E. (1992). *When AA doesn't work for you: Rational steps to quitting alcohol.* Fort Lee, NJ: Barricade Books.

Finney, J. W., Moos, R. H., & Timko, C. (1999). The course of treated and untreated substance use disorders: Remission and resolution, relapse and mortality. In B. S. McCrady & E. E. Epstein (Eds.), *Addictions: A comprehensive guidebook* (pp. 30–49). New York: Oxford University Press.

Fleming, M. F., Barry, K. L., Manwell, L. B., Johnson, K., & London, R. (1997). A trial of early alcohol treatment (Project TrEAT): A randomized trial of brief physician advice in community-based primary care practices. *Journal of the American Medical Association*, **227**, 1039–1045.

Fortney, J. C., Booth, B. M., & Curran, G. M. (1999). Do patients with alcohol dependence use more services? A comparative analysis with other chronic disorders. *Alcoholism: Clinical and Experimental Research*, **23**, 127–133.

Glasser, W. (1965). *Reality therapy*. New York: Harper & Row.

Glasser, W. (1989). Control theory. In W. Glasser (Ed.), *Control theory in the practice of reality therapy* (pp. 1–15). New York: Harper & Row.

Gollwitzer, P. M. (1999). Implementation intentions: Strong effects of simple plans. *The American Psychologist*, **54** *(7)*, 493–503.

Hazelden Foundation (1998). *National survey of current and former smokers*. Center City, MN: Hazelden Foundation.'

Heather, N. (1995a). Brief intervention strategies. In R. H. Hester & W. R. Miller (Eds.), *Handbook of alcoholism treatment approaches: Effective alternatives* (pp. 105–122). Needham Heights, MA: Allyn & Bacon.

Heather, N. (1995b). Interpreting the evidence on brief interventions: The need for caution. *Alcohol and Alcoholism*, **30**, 287–296.

Heather, N., Kissoon-Singh, J., & Fenton, G. (1990). Assisted natural recovery from alcohol problems: Effects of a self-help manual with and without supplementary telephone contact. *British Journal of Addictions*, **85**, 1177–1185.

Hester, R. K. Delaney, H. D. (1997). Behavioral self-control program for Windows: Results of a controlled clinical trial. *Journal of Consulting and Clinical Psychology*, **56**, 686–693.

Hubbard, R. L., Craddock, S. G., Flynn, P. M., Anderson, J., & Etheridge, R. M. (1997). Overview of 1-year follow-up outcomes in the Drug Abuse Treatment Outcome Study (DATOS). *Psychology of Addictive Behaviors*, **11**, 261–278.

Institute of Medicine (1994). *Reducing risks for mental disorders: Frontiers for preventive intervention research*. Washington, DC: National Academy Press.

Israel, Y., Hollander, O., Sanchez-Craig, M., Booker, S., Miller, V., Gingrich, R., & Rankin, J. G. (1996). Screening for problem drinking and counseling by the primary care physician-nurse team. *Alcoholism: Clinical and Experimental Research*, **20** *(8)*, 1443–1450.

Jamner, M. S., Wolitski, R. J., & Corby, N. H. (1997). Impact of a longitudinal community HIV intervention targeting injecting drug users' stage of change for condom and bleach use. *American Journal of Health Promotion*, **12**, 15–24.

Kadden, R., Christiansen, K., Roffman, R., Kabela, E., & Duresky, D. (2000). Brief Treatments for Marijuana Dependence in Adults: APA Pre-Convention Workshop. Presented at the 108th Annual Convention of the American Psychological Association, Washington, DC.

Kassel, J. D., & Unrod, M. (2000). Smoking, anxiety, and attention: Support for the role of nicotine in attentionally mediated anxiolysis. *Journal of Abnormal Psychology*, **109**, 161–166.

King, M. P., & Tucker, J. A. (2000). Behavior change patterns and strategies distinguishing moderation drinking and abstinence during the natural resolution of alcohol problems without treatment. *Psychology of Addictive Behaviors*, **14**, 48–55.

Kishline, A. (1994). *Moderate drinking: The new option for problem drinkers*. San Francisco, CA: SeeSharp Press.

Kivlahan, D. R., Marlatt, G. A., Fromme, K., Coppel, D. B., & Williams, E. (1990). Secondary prevention with college drinkers: Evaluation of an alcohol skills training program. *Journal of Consulting and Clinical Psychology*, **58**, 805–810.

Klingemann, H. (1991). The motivation for change from problem alcohol and heroin use. *British Journal of Addictions*, **86**, 727–744.

Ludwig, A. M. (1985). Cognitive processes associated with "spontaneous" recovery from alcoholism. *Journal of Studies on Alcoholism*, **46**, 53–58.

Marlatt, G. A. (Ed.) (1998). *Harm reduction: Pragmatic strategies for managing high-risk behaviors*. New York: Guilford Press.

Marlatt, G. A., Baer, J. S., Kivlahan, D. R., Dimeff, L. A., Larimer, M. E., Quigley, L. A., Somers, J. M., & Williams, E. (1998). Screening and brief intervention for high-risk college student drinkers:

Results from a 2-year follow-up assessment. *Journal of Consulting and Clinical Psychology*, **66**, 604–615.

Martin, J. E. (1994). *Project Scrap treatment manual.* San Diego, CA: San Diego State University.

McCrady, B. S. (2000). Alcohol use disorders and the Division 12 Task Force of the American Psychological Association. *Psychology of Addictive Behaviors*, **14**, 267–276.

Miller, W. R. (2000). Rediscovering fire: Small interventions, large effects. *Psychology of Addictive Behaviors*, **14**, 6–18.

Miller, W. R., Benefield, G. S., & Tonigan, J. S. (1993). Enhancing Motivation for change in problem drinking: a controlled comparison of two therapist styles. *Journal of Consulting and Clinical Psychology*, **61**, 455–461.

Miller, W. R., & Brown, S. A. (1997). Why psychologists should treat alcohol and drug problems. *American Psychologist*, **52**, 1269–1279.

Miller, W. R., Brown, J. M., Tracy, L. S., Handmaker, N. S., Bien, T. H., Lorenzo, F. L., Montgomery, H. A., Hester, R. K., & Tonigan, J. S. (1995). What works? A methodological analysis of the alcohol treatment outcome literature. In Hester, R. K., & Miller, W. R. (Eds.) *Handbook of alcoholism treatment approaches: Effective alternatives* (2nd ed., pp. 12–44). Boston: Allyn & Bacon.

Miller, W. R., Leckman, A. L., Delaney, H. D., & Tinkcom, M. (1992). Long-term follow-up of behavioural self-control training. *Journal of Studies on Alcohol*, **53**, 249–261.

Miller, W. R., & Munoz, R. F. (1982). *How to control your drinking.* Albuquerque, NM: University of New Mexico Press.

Miller, W. R., & Rollnick, S. (1991). *Motivational interviewing: Preparing people to change addictive behavior.* New York: Guilford.

Myers, M., Brown, S. A., & Kelly, J. F. (2000). A cigarette smoking intervention for substance-abusing adolescents. *Cognitive and Behavioral Practice*, **7**, 64–82.

National Institute on Alcohol Abuse and Alcoholism (1995). *The physicians' guide to helping patients with alcohol problems.* Rockville, MD: Author.

O'Brien C. P., & McLellan, A. T. (1996). Myths about the treatment of addiction. *Lancet*, **347**, 237–240.

Orford, J., & Edwards, G. (1977). *Alcoholism: A comparison of treatment advice, with a study of the influence of marriage.* Oxford: Oxford University Press.

Prochaska, J. O., & DiClemente, C. C., (1982). Transtheoretical therapy: toward a more integrative model of change. *Psychotherapy*, **20**, 161–173.

Prochaska, J. O., DiClemente, C. C., & Norcross, J. C. (1992). In search of how people change: Applications to addictive behaviors. *American Psychologist*, **47**, 1102–1114.

Prochaska, J. O., & Velicer, W. F. (1997). The transtheoretical model of health behavior change. *American Journal of Health Promotion*, **12**, 38–48.

Project MATCH Research Group (1997). Matching alcoholism treatments to client heterogeneity: Project MATCH post-treatment drinking outcomes. *Journal of Studies on Alcohol*, **58**, 7–29.

Robins, L. N., Helzer, J. E., & Davis, D. H. (1975). Narcotic use in southeast Asia and afterwards. An interview study of 898 Vietnam returnees. *Archives of General Psychiatry*, **32** *(8)*, 955–961.

Robertson, I., Heather, N., Dzialdowski, A., Crawford, J., & Winton, M. (1986). A comparison of minimal versus intensive controlled drinking treatment interventions for problem drinkers. *British Journal of Clinical Psychology*, **18**, 185–194.

Sanchez-Craig, M. (1993). *Saying when: How to quit drinking or cut down.* Tornot: Addictions Research Foundation.

Saunders, J. B., Aasland, O. G., Babor, T. F., De la Fuente, J. R., & Grant, M. (1993). Development of the Alcohol Use Disorders Identification Test (AUDIT): WHO collaborative project on early detection of persons with harmful alcohol consumption. Part II. *Addiction*, **88**, 791–804.

Sobell, L. C., Cunningham, J. A., & Sobell, M. B. (1996). Recovery from alcohol problems with and without treatment: Prevalence in two population surveys. *American Journal of Public Health*, **86**, 966–972.

Sobell, L. C., Ellingstad, T. P., & Sobell, M. B. (2000). Natural recovery from alcohol and drug problems: methodological review of the research with suggestions for future directions. *Addiction*, **95***(5)*, 749–764.

Sobell, L. C., Sobell, M. B., & Toneatto, T. (1992). Recovery from alcohol problems without treatment. In N. Heather, W. R. Miller, & J. Greeley (Eds.), *Self-control and addictive behaviors* (pp. 198–242). New York: Maxwell Macmillan.

Sobell, L. C., Sobell, M. B., Toneatto, T., & Leo, G. I. (1993). What triggers the resolution of alcohol problems without treatment? *Alcoholism: Clinical and Experimental Research*, **17**, 217–234.

Sobell, M. B., & Sobell, L. C. (1993). *Problem drinkers: Guided self-change treatment.* New York: Guilford Press.

Sobell, M. B., & Sobell, L. C. (2000). Stepped care as a heuristic approach to the treatment of alcohol problems. *Journal of Consulting and Clinical Psychology*, **68**, 573–579.

Sobell, M. B., Sobell, L. C., & Kozlowski, L. T. (1995). Dual recoveries from alcohol and smoking problems. In J. B. Festig & J. A. Allen (Eds.), *Alcohol and tobacco: From basic science to clinical practice* (pp. 207–224). Rockville, MD: National Institute on Alcohol Abuse and Alcoholism.

Stephens, R. S., Roffman, R. A., & Curtin, L. (2000). Extended versus brief treatments for marijuana. *Journal of Consulting and Clinical Psychology*, **68**, 898–908.

Strang, J., Bacchus, L., Howes S., & Watson, P. (1997). Turned away from treatment: maintenance-seeking follow-up. *Addictions Research*, **6**, 71–81.

Substance Abuse and Mental Health Administration (1997). *A guide to substance abuse services for primary care clinicians.* Treatment Improvement Protocol Series No. 24. Rockville, MD: US Department of Health and Human Services.

Taylor, C., Brown, D., Duckitt, A., Edwards, G., Oppenheimer, E., & Sheehan, M. (1985). Patterns of outcome: Drinking histories overs ten years among a group of alcoholics. *British Journal of Addiction*, **80**, 45–50.

Tate, P. (1993). *Alcohol: How to give it up and be glad you did.* Altamonte Springs, FL: Rational Self-Help Press.

Toneatto, T., Sobell, L., & Sobell, M. (1999). Natural recovery from cocaine dependence. *Psychology of Addictive Behaviours*, **13**(4), 259–268.

Tucker, J. A., & King, M. P. (1999). Resolving alcohol and drug problems: Influences on addictive behavior change and help-seeking processes. In J. A. Tucker, D. M. Donovan, & G. A. Marlatt (Eds.), *Changing addictive behaviors* (pp. 97–126). New York: Guilford Press.

Vaillant, G. E. (1996). A long-term follow-up of male alcohol abuse. *Archives of General Psychiatry*, **53**, 243–249.

Walters, G. D. (2000). Spontaneous remission from alcohol, tobacco, and other drug abuse: Seeking quantitative answers to qualitative questions. *American Journal of Drug and Alcohol Abuse*, **26**, 443–460.

Zinberg, N. E., & Jacobson, R. C. (1976). The natural history of "chipping." *American Journal of Psychiatry*, **133**, 33–40.

Zweben, A., & Fleming, M. F. (1999). Brief interventions for alcohol and drug problems. In J. A. Tucker, D. M. Donovan, & G. A. Marlatt (Eds.), *Changing addictive behaviors* (pp. 251–282). New York: Guilford Press.

CHAPTER 10

Brief Cognitive-Behavioral Therapy with Couples

Norman B. Epstein
Department of Family Studies, University of Maryland, College Park, MD, USA

Donald H. Baucom
Department of Psychology, University of North Carolina at Chapel Hill, Chapel Hill, NC, USA

Wendy Hunt
Department of Family Studies, University of Maryland, College Park, MD, USA

and

Jaslean J. La Taillade
Department of Family Studies, University of Maryland, College Park, MD, USA

Some couples seek therapy when acute problems have seriously disrupted a relationship that had been stable and sufficiently satisfying. Assessment of the couple may indicate that for the most part they have a history of interacting in ways that have satisfied both partners' needs and have allowed the couple to cope effectively with the demands of daily life, such as work schedules, household chores, and child rearing. However, the couple recently have been unable to adapt to particular circumstances, such as the severe illness of a child or the loss of one partner's job, either because their usual strategies are inappropriate for the present situation or because they have become overwhelmed by a pile-up of demands that they face simultaneously. These couples often have a history of good will toward each other and appear to need assistance primarily with developing more effective means of coping with the demands that have created their crisis state of disorganization and distress.

A second group of couples seek therapy after one or both members have behaved in ways that create a crisis by threatening the well-being of their partners and the relationship. Thus, couples in which there has been physical and/or emotional abuse, infidelity, financial losses due to gambling, and other forms of broken trust enter treatment with acute stressors that are tied to the negative behavior of the partners themselves. Furthermore, once trust has been broken, many of these couples have difficulty in restoring it even when both partners are making concerted efforts to behave more positively. On the one hand, the individual who has been betrayed has commonly had basic assumptions (e.g., that the partner would never

Handbook of Brief Cognitive Behaviour Therapy. Edited by Frank W. Bond and Windy Dryden.
© 2002 John Wiley & Sons, Ltd. ISBN 0-470-02132-2.

intentionally hurt him or her) "shattered" (Janoff-Bulman, 1992), and short-term positive changes in the partner's behavior may have minimal impact on the person's new view that the relationship is unsafe. On the other hand, the perpetrator's acute negative behavior may be part of a more chronic problematic pattern, such as abusiveness, that recently escalated to this crisis point. Couples who have chronic negative patterns may lack good will and a desire to collaborate in solving the problems.

A third group of couples may experience no acute problems but initiate therapy when they become convinced that they can no longer tolerate a chronically unsatisfying relationship. Sometimes an individual reports that a specific event changed his or her perspective, as when a person learns that a friend is getting divorced and then begins to view divorce as a more realistic option. In other cases an individual reports, "I just woke up one day and decided that I'm getting older and don't want to waste my whole life in a relationship that doesn't make me happy." The partners in these couples commonly have long-standing patterns of relating to each other that fail to meet their personal needs. For example, one member of a couple may prefer much more autonomy than the other, and the couple's disagreements over their difference may result in both individuals being frustrated. Similarly, if one member of a couple has a form of chronic psychopathology, such as depression or an anxiety disorder, the couple may interact in ways that maintain or exacerbate the symptoms and cause distress for both partners. Some other couples experience distress because their personal characteristics make it difficult for them to work together effectively to handle issues in daily life. Thus, if both members of a couple are generally disorganized and inattentive to detail, the couple may have a messy house, unpaid bills, etc., which contribute to a persistent stressful atmosphere at home. In all of these cases, certain events may motivate one or both partners to initiate couple therapy to address the chronic difficulties that they perceive in their relationship.

Cognitive-behavioral couple therapy (CBCT) (Baucom & Epstein, 1990; Epstein & Baucom, 1989, 1998 and 2002; Epstein et al., 1997) is a relatively structured approach that can be used to treat all of the above acute and chronic relationship problems. Although CBCT is generally intended to focus on couples' current difficulties and be relatively short-term, it also addresses historical factors within the lives of the two individuals and within the development of the couple's relationship. Thus, each person brings a personal relationship history, consisting of his or her family of origin experiences, plus experiences in any other couple relationships that predated the present one. In those earlier relationships, the individual likely developed patterns of behaving toward significant others, including ways of responding to conflict and dissatisfaction. For example, theory and research on adult attachment styles (e.g., Sperling & Berman, 1994) suggest that some individuals enter couple relationships with insecure attachments developed earlier in life, consisting of negative expectancies and emotional distress that their partners will not be available physically or emotionally. In addition, some individuals have had traumatic experiences such as physical abuse or abandonment in prior relationships. The traumatic experiences may have produced conditioned negative emotional responses, such as anxiety; negative cognitions, such as a generalized expectancy that significant others will eventually behave in hurtful ways; and problematic behavior, such as excessive withdrawal from a partner. Cognitive-behavioral interventions can be used to reduce these dysfunctional responses; for example, by challenging the negative expectancies, teaching the individual methods for regulating his or her anxiety and anger, and coaching the individual to express his or her needs in more assertive ways.

Beyond the two partners' personal histories, a couple is likely to have developed patterns of interacting to each other in particular ways as their relationship developed over time, such as one person seeking greater intimacy and the other maintaining some distance. Commonly, these patterns become increasingly automatic over time, such that the partners respond quickly to each other with little or no conscious thought. Furthermore, traumatic past events in the couple's relationship commonly have lasting negative impacts on the relationship. For example, when one person had discovered the other's infidelity, he or she may continue to be hypervigilant, anxious, angry, and vindictive no matter what the unfaithful partner has done subsequently to try to save and improve their relationship (Glass & Wright, 1997; Spring, 1996). CBCT procedures (e.g., challenging unrealistic standards concerning love, teaching individuals methods for managing anxiety symptoms and anger, and training couples in communication skills) are designed to help couples counteract the chronic effects of negative past individual and couple experiences, and to modify unsatisfying ingrained patterns of interaction.

Thus, cognitive-behavioral interventions commonly are applied to both acute and chronic relationship problems that involve demands from outside the couple's relationship or factors involving the partners' own characteristics and behavior. In general, CBCT tends to be time-limited, based on its focus on identifying specific targets for treatment and on teaching couples skills for modifying the cognitions, behavior, and emotional responses that are contributing to their relationship problems (Baucom & Epstein, 1990; Epstein & Baucom, 1998, 2002). Nevertheless, there is still a meaningful distinction to be made between *brief* CBCT (several sessions up to perhaps three months) and standard open-ended CBCT. This chapter delineates the situations and issues for which brief CBCT may be recommended in lieu of open-ended therapy, versus situations in which longer-term therapy seems more appropriate. We will describe how the choice to use brief therapy may be based somewhat on the degree of chronicity of the couple's problems, but that it tends to be based more on the particular goals that are set for changes in the couple's relationship. First, in order to distinguish brief CBCT from standard open-ended CBCT, we present an overview of standard cognitive-behavioral couples treatment procedures. Then, the goals and procedures of brief CBCT are described in order to explicate the differences between the two modalities. Differences in the uses of particular types of interventions in brief versus open-ended therapy are noted. Next, the assessments that are used to make clinical decisions between brief and longer-term treatment are described. Specific case examples are used to illustrate the use of brief CBCT.

THEORY AND TECHNIQUES OF STANDARD COGNITIVE-BEHAVIORAL COUPLE THERAPY (CBCT)

The theoretical model underlying CBCT has developed over the past three decades, with an associated broadening in the types of interventions used. In its earliest form, the approach focused on the ratio of negative to positive behavior that members of distressed couples exhibited toward each other. This model was based on social exchange theory (Thibaut & Kelley, 1959), which described an intimate relationship in terms of "economic" exchanges in which the members' satisfaction was a function of the ratio of benefits received to costs incurred. Behavioral couple therapists such as Jacobson and Margolin (1979) and Stuart (1980) used communication training, problem-solving training, and behavioral contracts to increase couples' positive behavior and decrease aversive acts. The use of effective communication and problem-solving skills also contributes to benefits that the partners receive in their relationship because they allow the couple to solve life problems that they face, such as work pressures, conflicts with in-laws, child behavior problems, etc. The following are brief descriptions of these standard behavioral interventions. Detailed descriptions of how these techniques are taught are provided elsewhere (e.g., Baucom & Epstein, 1990; Bornstein & Bornstein, 1986; Epstein & Baucom, 2002; Guerney, 1977; Jacobson & Christensen, 1996; Jacobson & Margolin, 1979).

Communication skill training involves teaching the couple or reminding them how to share thoughts and feelings with each other constructively and effectively. The primary goal is to help each partner understand the other person and to be understood in a respectful manner, whether or not they agree with each other. Couples are taught to use two roles in communicating with each other: speaker and listener. The speaker learns to express his or her thoughts and feelings by using "I" statements, being brief and specific, stating thoughts and feelings as subjective personal experiences rather than as "the truth," and moderating the impact of expressing negative emotions by including any positive feelings involved in the situation. The listener learns to use appropriate nonverbal behavior while the speaker is talking (e.g., nodding the head, making eye contact), to avoid interrupting the speaker or evaluating his/her ideas, and to reflect and summarize what the speaker has said.

Problem-solving skill training involves teaching the couple four steps: (a) specifically stating what the problem is, in terms of observable behavior; (b) identifying a variety of possible solutions without evaluating them; (c) deciding on a specific solution that is feasible and acceptable to both partners; and (d) deciding on a trial period to implement and evaluate the effectiveness of the solution. As with communication training, the goal is to help the couple develop skills that they can use whenever needed, and therapists do not assume that couples will consistently talk in these ways at home.

Behavioral contracts can vary in their degree of formality and in the extent to which the behaviors that one individual agrees to enact are contingent on those that the other enacts. *Quid pro quo* contracts involve each person agreeing to behave in particular ways that are desired by the partner, in return for the partner behaving in particular ways that the person desires. The details of the contingencies in the contract generally are written down and signed by the two partners. The contingencies may create a stalemate for some couples who refuse to change their behavior unless their partner makes desired changes. In contrast, in a *good faith* contract, in return for performing some behaviors that he or she chooses from a written list of actions that the partner has requested, the individual receives particular rewards that he or she desires. For example, one of Marie's requests was for Carl to spend an evening caring for their children so she could have a dinner out with friends. After Carl did so, he was able to reward himself by purchasing a new computer game that he had wanted. An even less structured format is used in a *holistic contract* (Stuart, 1980), in which the two individuals informally agree to try to increase positive behaviors that their partners have listed, without specifying which changes he or she plans to enact, when they might occur, or what rewards, if any, they will receive in return.

Therapy outcome studies have indicated that these behavioral interventions are successful in increasing global relationship satisfaction for some couples, but not others (see reviews by Baucom & Epstein, 1990; Baucom et al., 1998; Jacobson & Addis, 1993). The limited effectiveness of behavioral interventions has led to expanded cognitive-behavioral conceptual models and interventions. A primary area of development has been the assessment and modification of types of cognitions that can contribute to relationship problems either directly or by influencing partners' negative behavior toward each other (Baucom & Lester, 1986; Eidelson & Epstein, 1982; Ellis et al., 1989; Epstein, 1982; Epstein & Eidelson, 1981). Baucom et al. (1989) identified five types of cognition that may contribute to positive versus negative relationship functioning: assumptions, standards, selective perception, attributions, and expectancies.

Assumptions are the basic beliefs that each person holds about the characteristics of intimate relationships and the partners who comprise them. For example, individuals vary in the degree to which they believe that there are innate differences in needs and personality between women and men, that open disagreement is destructive to a relationship, and that partners cannot change their established relationship patterns (Eidelson & Epstein, 1982; Epstein & Eidelson, 1981). Individuals' assumptions are derived from a variety of life experiences in observing or participating in other relationships. Individuals who hold unrealistic assumptions about couple relationships tend to experience more relationship distress.

Standards are the beliefs that partners hold regarding the way close relationships and intimate partners "should" be. Although it is normal for individuals to hold personal standards (e.g., that partners should not abuse each other), certain standards can be associated with relationship distress if they are unrealistic or extreme (Eidelson & Epstein, 1982). Baucom et al. (1996) found that individuals who are not satisfied with the manner in which their standards are being met in their relationships are more distressed about the relationship and engage in more negative communication.

Selective perception refers to the process of focusing on only a certain subset of information available in a situation while ignoring or not attending to other data. During an interaction between members of a couple, many events transpire quickly, and there is great potential for each person to perceive selectively only particular aspects of them. This can be problematic for a couple when the perception is biased. For example, research studies have indicated that distressed partners selectively notice each other's negative behavior and overlook positive acts (Baucom & Epstein, 1990; Epstein & Baucom, 1993).

Attributions are inferences that partners make to explain the other's behavior as well as other events that occur. Attributions can vary in their accuracy, and individuals commonly assume that their inferences are valid, without seeking additional information. When individuals attribute relationship problems to global and stable characteristics of their partners, they communicate in more negative ways and are more dissatisfied with their relationship (Bradbury & Fincham, 1990; 1992).

Expectancies are inferences that individuals make about future relationship events and partner behaviors. Although expectancies can serve a useful function for a couple by helping them anticipate and mesh their behaviors over time, if the expectancies are based on inaccurate information or assumptions, they can become problematic. For example, an individual who inaccurately predicts that a partner will reject his or her ideas may choose not to express important thoughts and emotions. Pretzer et al. (1991) found that individuals who had lower levels of expectancies that they could solve their relationship problems were more distressed in their relationships.

Recognition of the importance of cognition in couple relationships has led to the use of a variety of cognitive restructuring interventions (Baucom & Epstein, 1990; Dattilio & Padesky, 1990; Epstein & Baucom, 1998, 2002; Epstein et al., 1997; Rathus & Sanderson, 1999). Some interventions are cognitive, such as guiding an individual in considering alternative attributions for a negative partner behavior and coaching an individual in identifying and weighing the advantages and disadvantages of applying a particular standard to his or her couple relationship. Other interventions use behavioral techniques to present partners with new information concerning the validity or appropriateness of their cognitions. For example, partners who practice expressive and listening skills not only may develop more constructive communication behavior but also are likely to exchange important information about each other's values, preferences, and intentions. The new information may counteract partners' negative attributions about each other's motives. Similarly, asking partners to engage in a "role-reversal," in which each person plays the role of the other as they discuss their thoughts and emotions, can increase mutual understanding. Furthermore, training a couple in decision-making or problem-solving skills may increase their expectancies that they can work together collaboratively to resolve relationship issues. In general, cognitive-behavioral couple therapists set up behavioral experiments in which members of a couple try behaving in new ways and observing the effects, in order to change the individuals' views of each other and what is possible in their relationship.

A major goal of interventions for cognitions is to develop the couple's own skills for identifying and modifying their own thoughts. As is more broadly true in cognitive-behavioral therapies, couple therapists assume that some kinds of cognition may be more difficult to challenge or modify than others. For example, it may be easier to increase the degree to which members of a couple notice each other's attempts to behave positively than it is to modify their extremely divergent standards about what types of actions constitute adequate caring behavior. Often, assumptions and standards that constitute an individual's long-standing schemas or belief system about intimate relationships require more extensive, repeated interventions than biases in perceptions and in inferences such as attributions and expectancies. However, there are important exceptions; for example, an individual who has been traumatized by a partner's abusive behavior may have persistent negative expectancies about the partner's potential abusiveness in future situations, because the memories of the past abuse are vivid and upsetting. Therefore, as we discuss the criteria for using brief versus open-ended CBCT, it is important to consider the nature of the cognitions in need of modification and the extent of the interventions that may be required.

A second important development in cognitive-behavioral couple therapy has involved increased attention to emotional factors in couples' relationships. Emotions are viewed not only as end products of partners' cognitions and behaviors, but also as subjective experiences that influence thoughts and actions. Cognitive-behavioral therapists have traditionally believed that partners' mutual understanding of each other's positive and negative feelings is an important contributor to intimacy and relationship satisfaction, so they have emphasized training couples in expressive and empathic listening skills (Baucom & Epstein, 1990; Jacobson & Margolin, 1979). In addition to increasing partners' communication about emotions, cognitive-behavioral therapists have focused on interventions for modifying persistent or extreme negative emotions that interfere with couple functioning. Weiss (1980) described a process of "sentiment override" in which an individual's general feelings toward a partner determine his or her reactions to the partner's current behavior more than the degree to which the partner is behaving in a positive or negative manner. Thus, an individual who has pervasive anger toward a partner may react with anger even when the partner is attempting to behave in a caring or supportive way. Consequently, cognitive-behavioral therapists focus the individual on the global quality of his or her emotional response, address its origins (e.g., to experience anger is to feel less vulnerable to being hurt again), and guide him or her in considering the disadvantages of discounting and even punishing positive responses from one's partner.

Cognitive-behavioral therapists use a variety of other interventions to reduce individuals' global negative emotions toward their partners. For example, Neidig & Friedman (1984) use cognitive and behavioral techniques (e.g., relaxation training and use of other forms of self-soothing, practice of self-statements for anger control, assertiveness training, and use of "time-out" procedures for the purpose of distancing temporarily from one's partner) to reduce couples' destructive anger responses. In our most recent work, we have incorporated a variety of interventions for increasing emotional awareness and expression among individuals who experience inhibition of emotion within their couple relationship, as well as interventions for moderating the experience and expression of negative affect among individuals who have difficulty regulating their emotions (Epstein & Baucom, 2002). For example, when working with an inhibited individual, a therapist may probe for details about the person's experiences, use empathic listening to validate his or her feelings, and repeat emotion-laden terms mentioned by the client (e.g., "It was like hitting my head against a wall") to enhance the individual's emotions. In contrast, an individual who experiences rapid and intense anger during discussions with a partner may be coached in self-instruction and relaxation techniques to reduce affect whenever he or she begins to notice physical cues of anger arousal, such as muscle tension in particular areas of the body.

As is the case with partners' behavioral and cognitive responses, the decision regarding the utility of brief CBCT must take into account how ingrained the partners' inhibited or unregulated emotional responses tend to be. On the one hand, some individuals have relatively compartmentalized emotional responses to specific conditions within their relationship, and interventions that change those conditions can lead to changes in the emotions. For example, Jill became frustrated and angry when Douglas made unilateral decisions about their financial investments. However, when Douglas was willing to listen to Jill's ideas during therapy sessions and to engage in decision-making discussions with her to find a mutually acceptable approach to investing their money, Jill's anger decreased. On the other hand, some individuals have general difficulty in regulating their emotions and may need more extensive assistance to develop the ability to cope with *any* kind of conflict with their partners. In such cases modifying particular situations that trigger an individual's strong emotional responses to a partner may be like trying to put out many small fires when there is a more extensive problem. The individual may need more extensive, open-ended intervention to increase his or her ability to regulate strong emotional responses.

The therapist's choice to use a brief course of therapy may depend on information that the members of a couple are motivated to control their experience and expression of negative affect *and* that they have demonstrated the ability to moderate their emotional responses in some situations. Concerning motivation, some individuals have a strong belief in retaliation (e.g., "Anyone who hurts me is going to pay a big price for it") and a desire to punish their partners. It may be unrealistic to believe that brief couple therapy will be sufficient to demonstrate the drawbacks of such beliefs to the vindictive individual and develop more collaborative cognitions. Concerning the partners' abilities to moderate their emotions in some situations, evidence of prior success with people other than the partner, or with the partner at other times, suggests that brief interventions may be sufficient to improve emotional regulation skills. In contrast, if the individual and couple assessments reveal that a person has strong, indiscriminant, diffuse emotional responses across relationships, situations, and time, it seems unlikely that brief therapy will be effective. In fact, if the mere presence of a person's partner automatically triggers his or her strong emotions, couple therapy itself may be impractical, and that person may need individual therapy to develop the ability to function effectively in joint treatment.

Similarly, if an individual has become emotionally disengaged from a partner, such that he or she has pervasive neutral feelings, no matter how the partner behaves, brief therapy is likely to have limited effectiveness in counteracting the conditions that have contributed to the disengagement. For example, some individuals gradually disengage emotionally as a means of protecting themselves after experiencing many disappointments and hurts over time. Such self-protective responses may be resistant to brief interventions designed to create new experiences with the partner that disconfirm the person's global expectancy that it is dangerous to allow oneself to be vulnerable.

In summary, standard CBCT focuses on the behavior, cognitions, and emotions that the individual members of a relationship exhibit, as well as the couple's dyadic interaction patterns. It is assumed that there is an interplay among behavior, cognition, and emotion in determining how well a couple's relationship meets the needs of the two partners and allows the couple to adapt effectively to the demands they face from outside as well as within their relationship. All of these behavioral, cognitive, and affective factors are relevant to understanding and treating acute or chronic relationship problems. Cognitive-behavioral couple therapists intervene actively to modify patterns of behavioral, cognitive, and affective responses that contribute to a couple's acute or chronic distress. Nevertheless, there are important differences in the ways that these interventions may be used in brief CBCT versus in open-ended therapy. These treatment differences can be understood in the context of differentiating between what we identify as two levels of difficulties that clinical couples typically experience: "primary distress" and "secondary distress."

PRIMARY AND SECONDARY DISTRESS IN COUPLE RELATIONSHIPS

As noted earlier, any couple is faced with adapting to a variety of demands in their life together. By a demand we mean any characteristic or event that places pressure on the couple to respond. Demands may involve characteristics of the individual partners (e.g., an individual's depression), their characteristics as a dyad (e.g., conflicting needs for intimacy), or environmental factors outside their relationship (e.g., children, jobs) (Epstein & Baucom, 2002). Although many demands involve negative characteristics and events that most people would describe as stressors, other demands are based on positive characteristics and needs. Thus, Michael and Denise both had strong desires for intimacy in their relationship, as well as high levels of motivation to achieve in their careers. Both individuals considered their own and their partner's desires for intimacy and achievement to be positive qualities. Nevertheless, finding adequate time and energy to fulfill these positive strivings placed major demands on the couple.

We define *primary distress* as the subjective negative thoughts and emotions that the members of a couple experience when their ways of interacting fail to resolve the demands in their relationship. For example, Michael and Denise periodically discussed how they missed the closeness they used to feel when they had fewer work responsibilities, and they pledged to schedule more "couple time," but this approach did not produce any appreciable change. Over time, both partners felt increasingly lonely and frustrated.

Secondary distress occurs when the members of a couple develop negative ways of trying to cope with sources of primary distress. Thus, Michael and Denise increasingly criticized each other as being selfish and uncaring for not making more career sacrifices in order to invest more time and energy into their relationship. Their arguments took on the quality of a contest concerning which person was more committed to the relationship. At a cognitive level, they each blamed the other for their relationship problems, and their emotional responses increasingly were dominated by anger. Unfortunately, the more the couple argued, the more they also withdrew from each other, and the amount of positive time together actually decreased. Their adversarial arguments and decreased intimacy became destructive patterns in their interactions, and a source of secondary distress. Gottman (1994) has conducted observational studies of specific behaviors that members of couples exhibit when they are asked to discuss issues in their relationship. Consistent with our concept of negative responses that produce secondary distress, he identified four types of behavior in couple interactions that predict marital distress, separation, and divorce: criticism, contempt, defensiveness, and "stonewalling" or withdrawal. Thus, not only are these types of responses ineffective in resolving issues in a couple's relationship; they also become major sources of distress in themselves, and threats to the survival of the relationship.

IMPLICATIONS OF PRIMARY AND SECONDARY DISTRESS FOR BRIEF COUPLE THERAPY

It has been our observation that a large percentage of the complaints that couples bring to therapy involve interactions that produce secondary distress, and that cognitive-behavioral interventions have been focused to a large extent on reducing those negative interactions and the negative cognitions associated with them in a relatively brief period. In fact, most published outcome studies on CBCT have demonstrated the positive effects of interventions that were administered for an average of 11 weekly sessions (Hahlweg & Markman, 1988). These brief interventions varied in their use of communication and problem-solving skill training, behavioral contracting, and teaching couples to be aware of their potentially unrealistic relationship beliefs and biased attributions about each other (Baucom & Epstein, 1990; Baucom et al., 1998). The outcome studies suggest that these types of interventions may be effective in reducing negative interactions involved in secondary distress, and creating a more positive atmosphere in couples' relationships.

For example, Michael and Denise entered therapy feeling distressed about their pattern of arguments and mutual withdrawal. A traditional cognitive-behavioral therapist probably would note that the topic or content of most of their arguments was "selfishness about personal careers." However, the therapist would focus primarily on modifying the negative interaction *process* that Michael and Denise had developed in response to the issue of their personal needs. The therapist would intervene to decrease the couple's aversive arguments and to increase their positive shared time. During sessions the therapist might set ground rules concerning negative behaviors to be avoided and might interrupt the partners whenever they began to criticize each other or withdraw. The therapist probably would also coach the couple in using constructive communication and problem-solving skills, to produce more positive interactions. Although the couple might be assisted in using these skills to devise plans for increasing their available time for intimacy, the major focus would be the skill development rather than the resolution of the core issue of the partners' conflicting intimacy and achievement needs.

The cognitive interventions used most often in brief CBCT focus on developing individuals' skills for monitoring their negative cognitions about their partners and examining information bearing on the validity and appropriateness of those cognitions. In particular, individuals are coached in identifying the attributions that they make concerning the determinants of their partners' behavior, especially the partners' displeasing acts. Research has indicated that members of distressed couples are more likely than happy couples to attribute their partners' negative behavior to global, stable traits that are unlikely to change. These negative attributions tend to be associated with hopelessness about improvement in the relationship, as well as less constructive problem-solving behavior (Bradbury & Fincham, 1992; Pretzer et al., 1991). Therapists stress to couples that the inferences involved in their attributions at times may be inaccurate, so it is crucial to examine whether one's upset with a partner is based on valid attributions. During sessions, therapists coach members of couples to think about other possible explanations for their partners' actions, and to provide each other with corrective feedback about their motives (Baucom & Epstein, 1990; Epstein & Baucom, 1998, 2002; Epstein et al., 1997).

Therapists also may attempt to modify partners' unrealistic or extreme assumptions and standards during brief therapy. In the few existing outcome studies that have added cognitive interventions to behavioral interventions, Baucom and Lester (1986), Baucom et al. (1990), and Halford et al. (1993) gave couples brief didactic descriptions of unrealistic assumptions and standards, and coached them in thinking about the degrees to which they held such beliefs. The attention to these cognitions did not enhance the outcome of therapy, compared to couples who received only behavioral interventions. On the other hand, Huber and Milstein (1985) found that brief (only six weeks) cognitive therapy focused on unrealistic assumptions and standards improved couples' marital adjustment, compared to couples on a waiting list. The lack of consistent evidence that interventions for assumptions and standards actually modify such schemas and improve relationship satisfaction may be due to the brief nature of the interventions in the studies, or their limited scope. In other words, brief CBCT may not allow therapists to explore and challenge partners' assumptions and standards in sufficient depth. In contrast, in open-ended CBCT, therapists are able to use a variety of techniques, such as the "downward arrow" method of asking about the implications of cognitions (e.g., "And if your partner doesn't want to spend as much time together as you do, what would that mean to you?") to identify individuals' basic beliefs. Similarly, open-ended CBCT is more likely to allow sufficient opportunities to challenge an individual's long-standing beliefs, as in coaching the person to consider the advantages and disadvantages of trying to conduct his or her couple relationship according to a particular stringent standard. Thus, brief CBCT requires a relatively superficial treatment of partners' cognitions, which may be effective in some cases, but cannot be assumed to be sufficient in general.

In spite of the encouraging results of outcome studies on brief CBCT interventions, there also have been clear indications of limitations in the effectiveness of the treatment (Baucom et al., 1998). The percentage of couples who score in the non-distressed range on self-report measures of relationship satisfaction at the end of therapy has varied from one-third to two-thirds across studies. In addition, the majority of couples maintain their improvement for up to a year, but relapse rates increase beyond that period. Although the treated couples still are functioning better on the average than those who do not receive therapy, the outcome results suggest that relationship problems often are complex and severe enough to require more extensive intervention than has typically been provided through brief CBCT.

Brief CBCT seems well suited to reduce partners' negative interactions associated with secondary distress and to increase positive ones, in order to create a favorable atmosphere in which the partners can work together to address core relationship issues involving primary distress. For many couples, patterns such as mutual attack, demand-withdrawal, or mutual avoidance may initially place their relationships more at risk than the underlying issues concerning their needs, personality styles, personal standards, etc. The positive outcomes demonstrated for brief CBCT, which typically does not target sources of primary distress, suggest that in some cases the focus on secondary distress can constitute the major therapeutic work. Once the couple is interacting in a positive, collaborative manner, they may require little or no guidance in identifying their core issues and devising new ways of resolving them. In fact, Epstein & Schlesinger (2000) have described application of CBCT for crisis intervention, in which a couple's current ways of interacting have failed to allow them to cope with life stressors and a brief structured approach helps them to devise more effective coping strategies.

In contrast, other couples have core relationship issues that require more extensive treatment, beyond the interventions intended to reduce secondary distress. Examples of core issues mentioned previously that are likely to need additional therapy are past trauma in the individuals' prior relationships or the couple's own relationship, partners' long-standing needs and personality characteristics that involve ingrained responses, extreme and rigid personal standards, and individual psychopathology. We hypothesize that brief CBCT that emphasizes communication training, problem-solving training, forms of behavioral contracting, and other interventions for decreasing negative behavior and increasing positive behavior often will have limited impact on couples who have more extensive primary distress issues. Brief CBCT may be an essential prerequisite but not a sufficient treatment for working on core relationship issues. It seems reasonable to expect that primary distress issues will require additional interventions, the extent of which will depend on the types and severity of individual and couple characteristics that are causing the primary distress. We are not suggesting that primary distress issues are virtually untreatable with brief CBCT, but rather that the value of brief CBCT is much more likely to be its impact on the negative interactions typical of secondary distress. The next section describes developments in CBCT that seem appropriate for helping couples resolve or adapt to core relationship issues. Although effective treatment for such issues may require more lengthy therapy, therapists should consider options for targeting them in brief CBCT. The degree to which brief couple therapy can include interventions for primary as well as secondary distress presently is unknown and awaits empirical investigation.

DEVELOPMENTS IN CBCT THAT ADDRESS PRIMARY DISTRESS ISSUES

Increasingly, cognitive-behavioral therapists have focused on the *content* of issues in couples' relationships, in addition to the *process* by which they attempt to cope with those issues. In general, attending to the process of interactions has been a hallmark of couple and family therapy, and we believe it will continue to be a strength of the cognitive-behavioral approach. However, throughout this chapter we are emphasizing that appropriate individualized assessment and treatment of each couple involves identifying themes associated with particular individual and couple characteristics. For example, our own research has focused on assessment and interventions for partners' standards concerning the boundaries, investment, and power distribution that they believe should exist in their relationships

(Baucom et al., 1996). Boundary standards involve beliefs about the degree of independence versus togetherness that should exist between partners. Investment standards are concerned with the amount of time and energy that individuals should put into instrumental acts that benefit their relationship (e.g., doing household chores) and expressive acts that contribute to their partner's happiness (e.g., affectionate behavior). Power or control standards involve beliefs about the degree to which partners should share decision-making, as well as the degree to which each person should be able to exert pressure on the other to comply with his or her preferences.

Issues in a couple's relationship may be based on differences between partners' standards, or the individuals' dissatisfaction with the ways that their standards are met in their relationship (Baucom et al., 1996). As noted earlier, couples also may need to reconcile differences in their basic needs, such as intimacy and achievement. Other couples may experience difficulty based on the partners being similar in a characteristic, such as Karen and Phil's chronic conflicts that arose from both individuals having strong motivation to be the "leader" in their relationship. Because difficulties in adapting to these types of characteristics are the basis for primary distress, it is important that therapists help couples identify their unresolved core issues and develop new ways of addressing them.

Some interventions focus on instituting specific changes in the couple's interactions that create a better match between the partners' personal needs, personality styles, or other characteristics. For example, a couple might use communication and decision-making skills to devise a better way to manage their daily schedules, so they will have a better chance of meeting both their desires for intimacy and for achievement. The key difference between using these behavioral interventions for primary distress versus for reducing secondary distress is that in this case the behavioral skills are used as tools for helping the couple adapt better to their personal characteristics. The "bottom line" is how well these two individuals with their particular needs, personality styles, etc., can relate to each other.

Thus, communicating in more positive, respectful ways may reduce secondary distress, creating a more positive atmosphere, but it will not resolve core relationship issues unless it also helps the couple plan and carry out changes in their opportunities to express their personal characteristics in satisfying ways. For example, Karen and Phil used expressive and empathic listening skills to gain a better understanding of how each person developed a strong desire to take the lead in close relationships, based on the way that he or she was socialized to be competitive within his or her family of origin. Their discussions reduced their tendencies to attribute each other's competitive behavior to an underlying desire to subjugate the other person. When they made more benign attributions about each other's motives, they responded in a less competitive way when the other person seemed to be pushing for control. With guidance from their therapist they practiced telling each other when they perceived the other person as trying to exercise control, and suggesting that they could discuss ways of cooperating. The therapist warned the couple that each person had long-standing patterns of responding competitively, and that they might continue to respond automatically in that manner from time to time in the future.

The therapist and couple agreed that reasonable goals for adapting to each person's characteristic might include (a) pointing out to each other when it appears that either person is responding competitively, (b) challenging one's own attribution that the partner's intent is to dominate in the relationship, (c) inhibiting one's own desire to retaliate and compete with the partner, and (d) initiating discussions with the partner concerning specific ways to resolve differences in preferences. The therapist also guided Karen and Phil in thinking about the competitive "culture" in each person's family of origin (e.g., how their parents modeled competitiveness, encouraged it among their children, and even ridiculed those who failed to take advantage of opportunities to excel and win). Over the course of several sessions, Karen and Phil were encouraged to examine the impact that the values concerning competitiveness and achievement had on their own lives, the lives of their family members, and on other people who appeared to have similar types of motivation. Karen and Phil identified some positive consequences to living according to their families' values, such as the successes they had achieved in school and their careers. However, they also noted negative impacts on family members' personal lives, such as marital conflict and divorces, chronic anxiety, and psychosomatic symptoms. These discussions increased the couple's motivation to modify the ways in which they carried out the values that they had learned within their families. Although they and their therapist considered it unrealistic and undesirable for them to try to abandon the achievement motivation that had produced many benefits in their lives, they agreed that it was highly desirable to devise ways to balance achievement with cooperation and mutual support. During subsequent sessions the therapist drew the couple's attention to instances in which achievement and cooperation might be in conflict, and they had opportunities to identify and try new ways of relating.

Other interventions involve increasing partners' acceptance that certain characteristics can be changed only to a limited degree, but that they can be satisfied by living with that limited change (Epstein & Baucom, 2002; Jacobson & Christensen, 1996). For example, the therapist may coach an individual in evaluating the advantages and disadvantages of clinging to a standard that the partners should spend all of their free time together. The individual may identify advantages such as few opportunities for feeling jealous of the time one's partner spends with other people, as well as never needing to keep oneself entertained. However, there may be significant disadvantages, such as the impact on the relationship when the partner resents being restricted from most autonomous activities that he or she enjoys.

CRITERIA AND ASSESSMENT METHODS FOR DECIDING BETWEEN BRIEF AND OPEN-ENDED COUPLE THERAPY

This section describes criteria that can help a therapist decide how appropriate brief CBCT may be for intervening with the types of difficulties that a couple has been experiencing. Attempting to dichotomize couples into those for whom brief therapy is appropriate and those for whom it is not would be arbitrary and artificial, because the relevant characteristics exist on continua, and there are no research data indicating particular degrees of characteristics that would result in brief therapy's being ineffective. Nevertheless, therapists can make clinical decisions about brief versus open-ended therapy by considering the extent to which members of a couple present with particular individual histories, certain types of past experiences in their relationship, personality styles, and other personal characteristics.

The major criterion for determining the appropriateness of brief CBCT is the degree to which the couple's difficulties are limited to ineffective interactions that elicit secondary distress, versus the existence of core relationship issues that are producing primary distress. To what extent does a couple's major problem consist of negative behavioral, cognitive, and affective responses to issues in their relationship, rather than long-standing or ingrained core relationship issues concerning the partners' personal needs, personality characteristics, prior life trauma, or psychopathology? In order to identify factors involved in primary and secondary distress, it is important to conduct interviews about the partners' personal and couple histories (Baucom & Epstein, 1990; Epstein & Baucom, 2002). A common procedure for gathering historical information is to conduct one or more joint assessment interviews with the couple, plus an individual interview with each partner. The joint interviews can cover the developmental history of the relationship, including the manner in which the partners met, what characteristics attracted them to each other, how they decided to become more committed to each other, how they coped with various demands and issues that arose within and from outside their relationship, and any traumatic events that have had lasting effects on them. In addition, the couple can be interviewed about their current ways of relating to each other, including behavioral, cognitive, and affective responses to issues between them.

Self-reports of negative patterns associated with secondary distress may be supplemented with the therapist's first-hand observations of the couple's interactions during the session. Behavioral observation can be facilitated by asking the couple to discuss an issue that they have identified as a source of conflict in their relationship, with the goal of trying to make progress toward resolving it while the therapist sits back and watches. Videotaping these interactions allows the therapist to examine the sequences of the couple's interactions more closely. The therapist then can ask the couple how typical their responses during this discussion are of those that they have when they discuss important issues in their relationship at home. In addition, although two partners' memories of past events may be different, the therapist can ask the couple to compare their current interaction patterns with those that occurred earlier in their relationship. Sometimes a couple reports that current negative interactions are merely a continuation of patterns that have always existed in their relationship, rather than a more recent response to particular unresolved issues. The therapist's goal is to determine the conditions in which the couple exhibits negative responses toward each other. Situation-specific responses may be more amenable to brief therapy than global, chronic responses, because interventions for the former can target changes in the eliciting conditions as well as in each person's typical negative responses. For example, a couple may report that they withdraw from each other more whenever they try to address issues at times when they are feeling stressed and exhausted from competing demands from their jobs and children. Brief therapy interventions can help the couple devise new strategies for managing the other demands in their lives, choosing to discuss relationship issues when the conditions are more favorable, and using constructive expressive and listening skills during their discussions.

Thus, brief therapy may be appropriate for helping couples adapt and work together more constructively in response to various environmental demands. Brief CBCT may be especially useful when a couple's history suggests that they functioned well together in earlier times, before their adaptation skills became inadequate or overwhelmed by the current demands. For example, Janet and Bob reported that they had a mutually supportive relationship until their older daughter reached adolescence and pressured her parents for increasing degrees of independence. Janet and Bob had difficulty parenting as a team because they had different beliefs about the types of personal freedom that a 13-year-old should be permitted, and they tended to escalate debates about child rearing into exchanges of criticism. Brief therapy with the couple included didactic presentations by the therapist, concerning normal adolescent development and common shifts that couples need to make as they move from being parents of children to being parents of adolescents who increasingly want to think and behave independently. It also included ground rules for constructive discussions of parenting issues between Janet and Bob, as well as practice of decision-making skills to devise new strategies for coping with changes in their daughter. Brief therapy also may be appropriate for helping couples adapt better to characteristics of the individual partners, such as personality styles, as long as neither person feels threatened by the other's characteristics or refuses to accept them as normal individual differences. For example, George initially was attracted by Brenda's extraverted personality, because he tended to be introverted and liked "the way she brought me out of my shell and got me involved socially." In turn, Brenda was attracted by George's quiet style, because she viewed him as "a steady influence on me, reminding me to focus on the serious side of life as well as the social good times." However, over time the two individuals developed ambivalent feelings about each other's characteristics. George often was frustrated that Brenda was "so busy talking to friends on the phone and keeping up a busy social schedule that we rarely have any time for just the two of us." Likewise, Brenda developed mixed feelings about George's introversion, complaining that "he interferes with some of my fun in life, by pressuring me to cut back on social plans and by getting moody sometimes when we are at parties and out with other couples." The couple entered therapy when their arguments over this issue had escalated in frequency and intensity, to the point of yelling at each other. Because George and Brenda had a history of appreciating aspects of each other's personality style, and appeared to have a positive emotional bond, their therapist judged that a brief course of CBCT might be appropriate.

The major goals of therapy were to (a) reduce the couple's negative interactions concerning the difference in their styles, and (b) help them resolve their difference in a more mutually acceptable way. After discussing these goals with the couple and gaining their approval, the therapist spent the next few sessions guiding George and Brenda in following ground rules for reducing negative interactions (e.g., using temporary "time outs" when their anger began to escalate) and in using constructive expressive and empathic listening skills. The therapist asked the couple to begin practicing communication skills with benign topics rather than focusing on the core issue of their difference in sociability. However, given the couple's overall good will and history of positive interactions, the therapist moved them into discussions of the personality issue during the third session of communication work. George and Brenda had become judgmental about each other's level of sociability, with each person thinking and saying that the other's characteristic is "extreme." Consequently, the therapist encouraged each person to describe past as well as present experiences in socializing with other people, and noted to the couple that both individuals appeared to be functioning within the normal range of human social relationships. The therapist stressed that George and Brenda both had enjoyed aspects of the other's personal style, and that they were facing a challenge of "making some adjustments to make the difference work more smoothly." The couple then was guided in decision-making discussions, in which they brainstormed alternative ways to integrate their personality styles. The therapist then coached the couple in setting up behavioral experiments to try their new approaches at home. As George and Brenda focused more on accepting each other's style as different but normal, controlling negative interactions concerning their differences, and collaborating on ways to balance their needs for socializing versus spending time alone together, the partners' satisfaction with their relationship increased. After 10 sessions of this form of therapy, they were ready to terminate therapy and try to maintain their progress on their own.

In contrast to cases in which couples' negative interactions primarily reflect their difficulty in adapting to particular demands that they face, the assessment interviews may reveal that one or both members of a couple have long-standing personal characteristics that contribute to the problematic pattern. In fact, there may be evidence that an individual often exhibits a negative behavioral response with a variety of other people, not only with the partner. For example, the interviews may indicate that an individual withdraws from conflicts with people and that he or she seems to have developed this pattern within a family of origin in which other members frequently argued in an aggressive manner. Because people's withdrawal responses often are maintained by negative reinforcement (i.e., they terminate aversive conditions, so the individual is likely to use them again in the future), they may become strongly conditioned and resistant to change. Brief therapy may offer opportunities for the therapist to encourage a withdrawing individual to experiment with staying engaged in interactions with a partner. However, it is our experience that the individual gradually decreases withdrawal over time, as he or she perceives a pattern in which continuing to interact with the partner leads to positive rather than aversive results. Consequently, open-ended therapy may be needed to provide the repeated experiences that accumulate to reduce the individual's "over-learned" response.

Similarly, brief interventions often are inadequate to reduce an individual's self-protective responses that persist long after he or she was treated in a traumatic or highly disconcerting manner by the present partner. Rebuilding trust is likely to require an accumulation of positive experiences with the partner, especially in situations in which the individual is able to see that the partner had the option to behave negatively and chose to behave supportively instead. For example, Sheila had been very upset when she initially learned that Colin had told his family members what she considered to be personal and private information about the couple's relationship, including their sexual difficulties. Even though Colin apologized and agreed that he had shared too much personal information with his relatives, Sheila was embarrassed to be in her in-laws' company and continued to be concerned that Colin would divulge more to them. The couple's therapist helped them think about ways in which Colin could demonstrate to Sheila that their relationship was his top priority and that he was committed to maintaining their privacy. However, the therapist also stressed that there was no way to predict when and how Sheila's trust in Colin would increase, so it was important for the partners to be patient and challenge their negative expectancies that any present lack of trust meant that she would never trust him again. Although brief CBCT may be able to help couples cope better with the aftermath of traumatic events, it is likely that the therapist will need to intervene consistently over a longer period in order to help individuals adapt to major disruptions to their core views of their partners.

SUMMARY

CBCT tends to be a relatively brief approach to treatment in general, based on its emphasis on identifying deficits in couples' behavioral skills and in their skills for identifying, testing the validity of, and modifying their own cognitions as needed. Nevertheless, whereas some couples enter therapy with relatively circumscribed difficulties that may be ameliorated by brief interventions, other couples have more complex or ingrained problematic patterns that likely require more in-depth and sustained treatment. In this chapter we have emphasized the difference between primary distress, associated with core relationship issues that typically are long-standing, and secondary distress, which exists when a couple has developed negative interactions in response to unresolved core issues in their relationship. The negative interactions often take on a life of their own, becoming distressing problems in themselves. Not only do these patterns interfere with the resolution of the couple's basic issues such as different personal needs; they may become so upsetting or demoralizing that they threaten the stability of the couple's relationship, and they are the major complaints that many couples bring to therapy.

Brief CBCT often has good potential for decreasing negative couple interactions associated with secondary distress and increasing positive interactions. This level of intervention may be useful for modifying negative interactions associated with either acute or chronic relationship issues. In either case, if the couple has basic good will and is free of debilitating chronic individual characteristics (e.g., psychopathology or residual effects of past traumas in the current or past significant relationships), brief therapy may be sufficient to remove impediments to the partners working constructively and effectively together to resolve basic issues. However, the presence of more extensive personal and couple issues contributing to primary distress may require open-ended treatment that begins with the same interventions for secondary distress used in brief therapy, but that are followed by longer-term interventions that address issues such as divergent and rigid personal standards, rigid personality styles, effects of past traumas, psychopathology, etc. Initial therapy sessions may begin to focus a couple's attention on sources of primary distress in their relationship, but the emphasis is on modifying problematic responses to those core issues. At the point when brief CBCT would be "winding down," open-ended therapy would be focusing more on long-standing patterns.

REFERENCES

Baucom, D.H., & Epstein, N. (1990). *Cognitive-behavioral marital therapy*. New York: Brunner/Mazel.

Baucom, D.H., Epstein, N., Rankin, L.A., & Burnett, C.K. (1996). Assessing relationship standards: The Inventory of Specific Relationship Standards. *Journal of Family Psychology*, **10**, 72–88.

Baucom, D.H., Epstein, N., Sayers, S., & Sher, T.G. (1989). The role of cognitions in marital relationships: Definitional, methodological, and conceptual issues. *Journal of Consulting and Clinical Psychology*, **57**, 31–38.

Baucom, D.H., & Lester, G.W. (1986). The usefulness of cognitive restructuring as an adjunct to behavioral marital therapy. *Behavior Therapy*, **17**, 385–403.

Baucom, D.H., Sayers, S.L., & Sher, T.G. (1990). Supplementing behavioral marital therapy with cognitive restructuring and emotional expressiveness training: An outcome investigation. *Journal of Consulting and Clinical Psychology*, **58**, 636–645.

Baucom, D.H., Shoham, V., Mueser, K.T., Daiuto, A.D., & Stickle, T.R. (1998). Empirically supported couple and family interventions for marital distress and adult mental health problems. *Journal of Consulting and Clinical Psychology*, **66**, 53–88.

Bornstein, P.H., & Bornstein, M.T. (1986). *Marital therapy: A behavioral-communications approach*. New York: Pergamon Press.

Bradbury, T.N., & Fincham, F.D. (1990). Attributions in marriage: Review and critique. *Psychological Bulletin*, **107**, 3–33.

Bradbury, T.N., & Fincham, F.D. (1992). Attributions and behavior in marital interaction. *Journal of Personality and Social Psychology*, **63**, 613–628.

Dattilio, F.M., & Padesky, C.A. (1990). *Cognitive therapy with couples*. Sarasota, FL: Professional Resource Exchange.

Eidelson, R.J., & Epstein, N. (1982). Cognition and relationship maladjustment: Development of a measure of dysfunctional relationship beliefs. *Journal of Consulting and Clinical Psychology*, **50**, 715–720.

Ellis, A., Sichel, J.L., Yeager, R.J., DiMattia, D.J., & DiGiuseppe, R. (1989). *Rational-emotive couples therapy*. New York: Pergamon Press.

Epstein, N. (1982). Cognitive therapy with couples. *American Journal of Family Therapy*, **10** *(1)*, 5–16.

Epstein, N., & Baucom, D.H. (1989). Cognitive-behavioral marital therapy. In A. Freeman, K.M. Simon, L.E. Beutler, & H. Arkowitz (Eds.), *Comprehensive handbook of cognitive therapy* (pp. 491–513). New York: Plenum Press.

Epstein, N., & Baucom, D.H. (1993). Cognitive factors in marital disturbance. In K.S. Dobson & P.C. Kendall (Eds.), *Psychopathology and cognition* (pp. 351–385). San Diego, CA: Academic Press.

Epstein, N., & Baucom, D.H. (1998). Cognitive-behavioral couple therapy. In F.M. Dattilio (Ed.), *Case studies in couple and family therapy: Systemic and cognitive perspectives* (pp. 37–61). New York: Guilford Press.

Epstein, N.B., & Baucom, D.H. (2002). *Enhanced cognitive-behavioral therapy for couples: A contextual approach*. Washington, DC: American Psychological Association.

Epstein, N., Baucom, D.H., & Daiuto, A. (1997). Cognitive-behavioral couples therapy. In W.K. Halford & H.J. Markman (Eds.), *Clinical handbook of marriage and couples interventions* (pp. 415–449). Chichester, England: Wiley.

Epstein, N., & Eidelson, R.J. (1981). Unrealistic beliefs of clinical couples: Their relationship to expectations, goals and satisfaction. *American Journal of Family Therapy*, **9***(4)*, 13–22.

Epstein, N.B., & Schlesinger, S.E. (2000). Couples in crisis. In F.M. Dattilio & A. Freeman (Eds.), *Cognitive-behavioral strategies in crisis intervention* (2nd ed.) (pp. 291–315). New York: Guilford Press.

Glass, S.P., & Wright, T.L. (1997). Reconstructing marriages after the trauma of infidelity. In W.K. Halford & H.J. Markman (Eds.), *Clinical handbook of marriage and couples intervention* (pp. 471–507). Chichester, England: Wiley.

Gottman, J.M. (1994). *What predicts divorce? The relationship between marital processes and marital outcomes*. Hillsdale, NJ: Lawrence Erlbaum.

Guerney, B.G., Jr. (1977). *Relationship enhancement*. San Francisco, CA: Jossey-Bass.

Hahlweg, K., & Markman, H.J. (1988). Effectiveness of behavioral marital therapy: Empirical status of behavioral techniques in preventing and alleviating marital distress. *Journal of Consulting and Clinical Psychology*, **56**, 440–447.

Halford, W.K., Sanders, M.R., & Behrens, B.C. (1993). A comparison of the generalization of behavioral marital therapy and enhanced behavioral marital therapy. *Journal of Consulting and Clinical Psychology*, **61**, 51–60.

Huber, C.H., & Milstein, B. (1985). Cognitive restructuring and a collaborative set in couples' work. *American Journal of Family Therapy*, **13** *(2)*, 17–27.

Jacobson, N.S., & Addis, M.E. (1993). Research on couples and couple therapy: What do we know? *Journal of Consulting and Clinical Psychology*, **61**, 85–93.

Jacobson, N.S., & Christensen, A. (1996). *Integrative couple therapy: Promoting acceptance and change*. New York: W.W. Norton.

Jacobson, N.S., & Margolin, G. (1979). Marital therapy: Strategies based on social learning and behavior exchange principles. New York: Brunner/Mazel.

Janoff-Bulman, R. (1992). *Shattered assumptions: Towards a new psychology of trauma*. New York: The Free Press.

Neidig, P.H., & Friedman, D.H. (1984). *Spouse abuse: A treatment program for couples*. Champaign, IL: Research Press.

Pretzer, J., Epstein, N., & Fleming, B. (1991). The Marital Attitude Survey: A measure of dysfunctional attributions and expectancies. *Journal of Cognitive Psychotherapy: An International Quarterly*, **5**, 131–148.

Rathus, J.H., & Sanderson, W.C. (1999). *Marital distress: Cognitive behavioral interventions for couples*. Northvale, NJ: Jason Aronson.

Sperling, M.B., & Berman, W.H. (Eds.) (1994). *Attachment in adults: Clinical and developmental perspectives*. New York: Guilford Press.

Spring, J.A. (1996). *After the affair*. New York: HarperCollins.

Stuart, R.B. (1980). Helping couples change: A social learning approach to marital therapy. New York: Guilford Press.

Thibaut, J.W., & Kelley, H.H. (1959). *The social psychology of groups*. New York: Wiley.

Weiss, R.L. (1980). Strategic behavioral marital therapy: Toward a model for assessment and intervention. In J.P. Vincent (Ed.), *Advances in family intervention, assessment and theory* (Vol. 1, pp. 229–271). Greenwich, CT: JAI Press.

CHAPTER 11

Child and Adolescence Problems

Alan Carr

Department of Psychology, University College Dublin, Dublin, Ireland

INTRODUCTION

The framework set out in Figure 11.1 outlines the stages of brief cognitive behaviour therapy (CBT) with children and adolescents from the initial receiving of a referral letter to the point where the case is closed. In the first stage a plan for conducting the intake interview is made. The second stage is concerned with the processes of engagement, alliance building, assessment, and formulation. In the third stage, the therapeutic contract, the completion of a therapy plan, and the management of resistance are the primary issues addressed. In the final stage, disengagement or recontracting for a further episode of intervention occurs.

Within the context of this stage-based model of consultation, brief CBT is usefully conceptualized as a developmental and recursive process. At each developmental stage, key tasks must be completed before progression to the next stage. Failure to complete the tasks of a given stage before progressing to the next stage may jeopardize the consultation process and lengthen treatment unnecessarily. For example, attempting to conduct an assessment without first contracting for assessment may lead to co-operation difficulties if the child or parents find the assessment procedures arduous. Brief CBT is an episodic and recursive process insofar as it is possible to move from the final stage of one episode of brief CBT to the first stage of the next.

Episodes of brief CBT with children and adolescents are time-limited to between 6 and 10 sessions.

STAGE 1. PLANNING

In the first stage of brief CBT, the main tasks are to plan whom to invite to the initial assessment session and what to ask them.

Network Analysis

There is often confusion about whom to invite to an intake interview in cases where children or adolescents have multiple problems, are from multiproblem families, or are involved

Handbook of Brief Cognitive Behaviour Therapy. Edited by Frank W. Bond and Windy Dryden.
© 2002 John Wiley & Sons, Ltd. ISBN 0-470-02132-2.

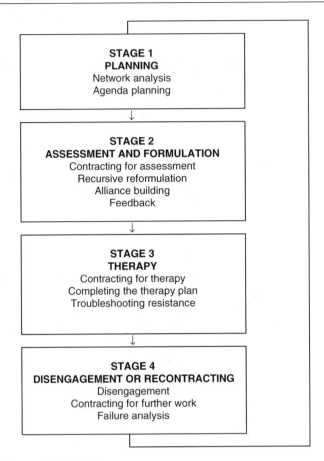

Figure 11.1   Stages of brief CBT

with multiple agencies. In these cases a network analysis may be conducted. For network analysis, it is essential to find out from the referral letter, or through telephone contact with the referrer, who is involved with the problem, and tentatively establish what roles they play with respect to it. With some cases this will be straightforward. For example, where parents are concerned about a child's enuresis, it may be sufficient to invite the child and the parents. In other cases, where schoolteachers, hospital staff, or social services personnel are most concerned about the case, the decision about whom to invite to the first interview is less straightforward. In these complex cases it is particularly important to analyse network roles accurately before deciding whom to invite to the first session. Most network members fall into one or more of the following categories.

- the *referrer* to whom correspondence about the case should be sent
- the *customer* who is most concerned that the referral be made
- the *child* or *children* with the problem
- the legally responsible *guardians*, who are usually the parents but may be a social worker or other representative of the state
- the primary *caregivers*, who are usually the parents but may be foster parents, residential child-care staff, or nursing staff

- the child's main *teacher*
- the *social control agents* such as social workers or probation officers
- *other involved professionals* including the family doctor, the paediatrician, the school nurse, the parent's psychiatrist, etc.

Certain key network members constitute the minimum sufficient network necessary for effective case management (Carr, 1995). These include the customer, the legal guardians, the caregivers, and the referred child. Ideally, all members of the minimum sufficient network should be invited to an intake meeting. If this is not possible, then individual meetings or telephone calls may be used to connect with these key members of the network. Where cognitive behaviour therapists are working as part of multidisciplinary teams, often the main customer for CBT is another team member. In such instances it is often useful to meet with the parents of the child and the referring team member briefly to clarify the reason for the referral and the implications of engaging in brief CBT or declining to do so. Failure to convene such meetings often results in confusion or co-operation difficulties.

From this discussion of network analysis, it is clear that brief CBT is a highly contextual approach to clinical practice. Sensitivity to the problem-maintaining and problem-resolving potential of the child or adolescent's social context contributes to the brevity of therapy. The approach to brief CBT described in this chapter is family-oriented rather than individually focused.

Agenda Planning

In planning an agenda for an intake meeting, a routine intake interview and a core test battery may be supplemented by questions and tests which take account of the specific features of the case. The routine interview should cover the history of the presenting problems. This typically involves questions about the nature, frequency, and intensity of the problems; previous successful and unsuccessful solutions to these problems; and different family members' views on the causes of these problems and possible solutions that they have tried or suspect may be fruitful to explore in future. In addition the intake interview should inquire about the child's individual physical, cognitive, and psychosocial developmental history, and seek an assessment of the family's development and functioning with particular reference to parent–child relationships; inquiry should also be made about inter-parental relationships and the wider social network within which the family is embedded. Assessment of unique features of the case should be based on a preliminary formulation which contains hypotheses about possible antecedents, beliefs, and consequences associated with the presenting problems. These hypotheses may be based on information given in the referral letter or phone call and the literature on the particular problem in question. For example, if a youngster presents with conduct problems, then important hypotheses to consider are that the parent and child are engaged in a coercive cycle of interaction (Patterson, 1982) and the child has a hostile attributional bias (Crick & Dodge, 1994). If a child, on the other hand, presents with school refusal, hypotheses deserving consideration are that the child is experiencing separation anxiety, is being inadvertently reinforced for school non-attendance and has a cognitive bias for interpreting ambiguous situations as threatening, or is being bullied at school (Blagg, 1987).

To develop a thorough understanding of the presenting problems and related issues, a number of different types of assessment meetings may be conducted. These may include some or all the following depending upon the case: child-centred assessment interviews and testing sessions, parental interviews, nuclear family interviews, school interviews, extended family interviews, and interviews with other involved professionals. It is usually more fruitful and more time-efficient to conduct a child-centred assessment, once the views of significant adults in the child's network are known, since it is then possible to ask children how they respond to their parents' and teachers' views of the problem.

A core battery of psychosocial measures that I have found to be particularly useful in clinical practice include the Child Behaviour Checklist (Achenbach, 1991) or the Strengths and Difficulties Questionnaire (Goodman, 1994), the Battle Culture-Free Self-Esteem Inventory (Battle, 1992), the Nowicki-Strickland (1973) Locus of Control Scale, and the Family Assessment Device (Kabacoff et al., 1990). These measures give baseline information on specific behaviour problems, self-esteem, self-regulatory beliefs, and perceived family functioning. Assessment instruments for use with specific childhood problems and disorders are catalogued by Carr (1999) and Graham (1998).

STAGE 2. ASSESSMENT AND FORMULATION

Establishing a contract for assessment, working through the assessment agenda and recursively refining the preliminary formulation in the light of the information obtained, dealing with engagement problems, building a therapeutic alliance, and giving feedback are the more important features of the assessment and formulation stage, which may span one or two sessions.

Contracting for Assessment

At a cognitive level, contracting for assessment involves the therapist, the child or adolescent, and significant network members clarifying expectations and reaching an agreement to work together. The first task is to explain what assessment involves and to offer the parents, the child, and each relevant member of the network a chance to accept or reject the opportunity to complete the assessment. With children and teenagers, misconceptions need to be dispelled. For example, some children believe that when referred for brief CBT they may be involuntarily admitted to hospital or placed in a detention centre. In some instances, children may not wish to complete the assessment, but their parents may insist. In others, parents may not wish to complete the assessment but a referring physician or social worker may forcefully recommend attendance. In such situations, the therapist may facilitate the negotiation of some compromise between parties. The contracting for assessment is complete when family members have been adequately informed about the process and have agreed to complete the assessment.

Recursive Reformulation

The assessment phase of the overall consultation process involves conducting interviews or administering tests to check the accuracy of the formulations and hypotheses made during the planning phase and modifying the formulations or hypotheses in the light of the information gained in the interview or testing sessions. In practice, the first round of interviewing and testing may not only lead to a modification of the preliminary formulation, but may also raise further hypotheses that need to be checked with further interviews or tests. The process comes to an end when a formulation has been constructed that fits with significant aspects of the child's problems, with network members' experiences of the child's problems, and with available knowledge about similar problems described in the literature. This formulation should inform the construction of a treatment plan. Building blocks for treatment plans are described below. A CBT formulation is a mini-theory that explains the way in which particular situational antecedents; beliefs about these, the problem, and related issues; and the consequences of problematic behaviours maintain the presenting problem. A formulation may also highlight factors which predispose the child or adolescent to developing a particular presenting problem.

Here is an example of a formulation for a child who presents with oppositional defiant disorder. John is a 5-year-old boy with a difficult temperament, and this predisposes him to have difficulty in following rules. When he is tired, hungry, or excited, he has great difficulty following instructions from parents and teachers. He believes that such instructions are personal criticisms rather than requests for co-operative behaviour. At home and at school, his parents and teachers typically respond to his unco-operative behaviour either by offering explanations and attention, a response which positively reinforces his lack of co-operation, or by withdrawing, a response which negatively reinforces his lack of co-operation by removing what he perceives to be an aversive stimulus, i.e., instructions and directions for rule following.

The following is an example of a formulation for a case of separation anxiety. Paula is a 9-year-old girl who has had difficulty attending school for 3 months. On those mornings when her father has left early for work and her mother has taken her to school, she notices her mother's intense concern for her well-being when she complains of mild headaches or stomach-aches. In response to this, she has thoughts about possible dangers that may befall her mother, while she (Paula) is at school. These thoughts lead to strong feelings of anxiety, headaches, and abdominal pains. When she insists that she cannot attend school because of these feelings and symptoms, her mother comforts her and returns her to bed, thereby reinforcing the separation anxiety. This pattern does not occur when her father takes Paula to school, because he does not display intense concern for Paula's well-being or reinforce school avoidance. Paula may have been predisposed to developing separation anxiety because of a genetic vulnerability to anxiety (suggested by a family history of anxiety disorders) and a family culture, particularly within the mother's family of origin, in which there is a high sensitivity to illness.

Alliance Building

In addition to providing information, the process of assessment also serves as a way for the therapist, the child, the parents, and other members of the network to build a working alliance. Building a strong working alliance with the child and key members of the child's family and network is essential for valid assessment and effective therapy. *All other features of the consultation process should be subordinate to the working alliance,* since, without it, clients drop out of assessment and therapy or fail to make progress. The only exception to this rule is where the safety of child or family member is at risk; in such cases, protection takes priority over alliance building. Research on common factors that contribute to a positive therapeutic outcome and ethical principles of good practice point to a number of guidelines which therapists should employ in developing a working alliance (Bergin & Garfield, 1994):

- When communicating with the child, parents, and other network members, warmth, empathy, and genuineness should characterize the therapist's communication style (Rogers, 1957).
- The therapist should form a collaborative partnership with the child, the parents, and other members of the child's network (Beck, 1976).
- An invitational approach should be adopted in which children and family members are invited to participate in assessment and therapy procedures (Kelly, 1955).
- The inevitability of ambivalence about change becoming an issue within the therapeutic relationship should be acknowledged (Anderson & Stewart, 1983).

Warmth, empathy, and genuineness allow clients to have the experience of being accepted and understood rather than blamed. While parents may create a context within which children's problems develop, usually this occurs inadvertently. Where it occurs intentionally, typically, wider social or historical factors have created a context within which the parents' intention to harm a child has evolved. Blaming is a concept useful in the judicial system, where seeking justice is the primary goal, but not within a therapeutic system, where understanding and negotiation of behavioural change are the main goals.

The therapist should form a collaborative partnership with the child, the parents, and other members of the child's network so that responsibility for the tasks of assessment and case management may be shared. Therapists and the families with whom they work are both experts, but in different areas. Family members are experts on the specific features of their own family and details of their unique problems. Therapists are experts on general scientific and clinical information relevant to child and family development and the broad class of problems of which the client's is a specific instance.

The invitational approach allows family members to have the experience of choosing to participate in activities which constitute the consultation process and to avoid the experience of being neglected through excessive non-directiveness or coerced through excessive directiveness. This experience of choice associated with an invitational approach increases the probability that family members will co-operate with arduous assessment and treatment tasks.

Often children, parents, or other network members do not follow through on tasks that they have agreed to complete, fail to turn up to appointments, or insist on prolonging the consultation process apparently unnecessarily. This occurs despite their avowed wish to solve the presenting problems. The possibility that co-operation difficulties and resistance may occur and that this will require careful analysis deserves recognition from the outset.

The assessment is complete when the presenting problem and related difficulties are clarified; related antecedent situational factors, beliefs, and consequences have been identified; a formulation has been constructed; possible goals have been identified; options for case management or treatment have been identified; and these options have been discussed with the family.

Feedback

Giving feedback is a psychoeducational process. Children and their parents and siblings are given both general information about the type of problem they face (such as attention deficit and hyperactivity disorder [ADHD] or encopresis) and specific information about the way this relates to the formulation of their own presenting problems. Simplicity and realistic optimism are central to good psychoeducation. It is important not to overwhelm parents and children with information, so a good rule of thumb is to think about a case in complex terms but explain it to clients in as simple terms as possible. Put succinctly:

Think complex—talk simple.

Good clinical practice involves matching the amount of information given about the formulation and treatment plan to the client's readiness to understand and accept it. A second important rule of thumb is to engender a realistic level of hope when giving feedback by focusing on strengths and protective factors first, and referring to aetiological factors later. Put succinctly:

Create hope—name strengths.

In providing psychoeducation about the general type of problem the family face, information on clinical features and predisposing, precipitating, maintaining, and protective factors may be given along with the probable impact of the problem in the short and long term on cognition, emotions, behaviour, family adjustment, school adjustment, and health.

The formulation is fed back to the family as a basis for a therapeutic contract. The process of constructing a formulation is the process of linking academic knowledge of theory and research to clinical practice. If the working alliance is the engine that drives the therapeutic process, the formulation is the map that provides guidance on what direction to take and what building blocks should be included in the brief CBT plan.

In some cases, the process of assessment and formulation releases family members' natural problem-solving skills, and they resolve the problem themselves. For example, some parents, once they discuss their anxiety about handling their child in a productive way during a family assessment interview, feel released to do so.

STAGE 3. THERAPY

When parents and their children have completed the assessment stage, have accepted the formulation, and are aware of the broad therapeutic possibilities, it is appropriate to progress to the therapy stage. The central tasks of this stage are contracting for therapy to achieve specific goals, participating in the completion of the agreed therapy plan, and troubleshooting resistance. If, at this stage, it is apparent that other family problems such as parental depression or marital discord require attention, referrals for this work may be made, and it may be conducted concurrently with the brief CBT programme which focuses explicitly on the child's problems. Alternatively, addressing these problems may be postponed until after the child-focused difficulties have been resolved.

Contracting for Therapy

The contracting process involves inviting children or adolescents and their parents to make a commitment to pursue a specific therapeutic plan to reach specific goals. This plan may be constructed from one or more of the building blocks outlined below. Clear, realistic, visualized goals that are fully accepted by all family members and that are perceived to be moderately challenging are crucial for effective therapy (Carr, 1997; Snyder et al., 1999). Goal setting takes time and patience. Different family members may have different priorities when it comes to goal setting, and negotiation about this is essential. This negotiation must take account of the costs and benefits of each goal for each family member. It is usually a more efficient use of time to agree on goals first, before discussing the details of how they might be achieved.

In this context it is important to give parents and children clear information about research on the costs and benefits of psychological interventions and the overall results of outcome studies (Carr, 2000). Broadly speaking, most CBT interventions developed for children and adolescents are effective in only 66–75% of cases, and about 10% of cases deteriorate as a result of such interventions. The more protective factors that are present in a given case, the more likely it is that therapy will be effective. If therapy is going to be effective, most of the gains are made in the first 6–10 sessions. Relapses are inevitable for many types of problems, and periodic booster sessions may be necessary to help children and families handle relapse situations. A statement of the sacrifices that the child and family will have to make to participate in the brief CBT plan also deserves mention. Common sacrifices include attending a series of consultation sessions, discussing difficult issues openly, completing homework assignments, being prepared for progress to be hampered by setbacks, learning to live with ongoing residual difficulties, accepting that episodes of therapy are time-limited, and accepting that, at best, the chances are only two out of three that therapy will be helpful.

The contracting session is complete when all involved members of the child's network necessary for implementing the therapeutic plan agree to be involved in an episode of consultation to achieve specific goals.

At this point, or indeed earlier in the consultation process, children or parents may point out that they have been through unsuccessful treatment programmes in the past, and that it appears that the psychological assessment or treatment programme being offered is similar to that which failed before. The history of previous treatment will have been reviewed during assessment so the therapist will be familiar with the material the family wish to discuss, if it is raised at this point in the consultation process. However, it may be useful for concerned family members to be invited to give their views on previous unsuccessful treatment programmes. It may also be appropriate to invite family members to ventilate the feelings of fear, anger, or demoralization that have led them to question the value of embarking on yet another treatment programme. Against this backdrop, the similarities and differences between those unsuccessful programmes and the services that are now being offered may be outlined. In many instances there will be many similarities, since most psychosocial interventions involve meeting regularly and talking about problems and their solution with some type of psychosocial or biomedical model as a problem-solving framework.

However, there are some important differences between contextually based brief CBT and other therapeutic approaches. This approach assumes that children's problems are complex

and deserve thorough assessment. This assessment takes account of the clinician's observations of the child but also those of the parents, teachers, and other involved professionals.
All of the information is integrated into a formulation, which is a map of how the problem
evolved and is maintained. Treatment plans are based on this map and on evidence about
the types of treatments that have been shown to work in scientific studies of similar sorts
of problems. Where therapeutic interventions that have failed in the past are recommended
as part of a brief CBT programme, it may be that in the past they were tried for too short a
time, at too low an intensity, or at an inappropriate time in the child's development, or were
used alone rather than as part of a brief CBT therapeutic package. For example, the use of a
reward system in isolation for a week to treat encopresis in a 5-year-old may be ineffective.
However, a reward system used over a period of months may be one component of an overall
effective treatment programme for encopresis in a 7-year-old. Children and their families
may find it useful to explore these comparisons between previously ineffective treatment
experiences and those being offered before committing themselves to a treatment plan.

Therapy Plans

Brief CBT plans are constructed from the following building blocks (Carr, 1999; Graham,
1998) in a family-based approach:

- redefinition
- monitoring problems
- communication training
- problem-solving training
- supportive play
- reward systems
- behavioural control systems
- tension reduction
- cognitive restructuring
- self-instructional training
- home–school liaison.

The practices entailed by these building blocks will be detailed below with reference to
examples.

Family-Based Approach

In brief CBT with children and adolescents, unless there is good reason for doing otherwise,
a family-based approach is typically taken because of the many therapeutic advantages this
approach offers. A family-based approach to children's psychological problems helps family
members communicate clearly and openly about problems and related issues, decreases the
emotional intensity of negative family interactions related to the problem, encourages joint
problem-solving with respect to the child's difficulties, optimizes family support for the
child, and optimizes the family's use of health-care resources and support groups. If fathers
are unavailable during office hours, it is worthwhile making special arrangements to schedule

at least a couple of family sessions which are convenient for the father, since the participation of fathers in their children's therapy programmes is associated with a positive outcome (Carr, 2000). Where parents are separated or divorced, it is particularly important to arrange some sessions with the non-custodial parent, since it is important that both parents adopt the same approach in understanding and managing the child or adolescent's difficulties.

Redefinition

Commonly, the definitions that children and their families hold of the problems and related issues that prompt them to seek professional help are of limited value in helping them to resolve their difficulties. Redefinition of presenting problems and related issues is therefore central to all brief CBT plans. Separating the problem from the person, reframing, and relabelling are three specific redefinition techniques that are used throughout brief CBT with children, adolescents, and families.

Separating the Problem from the Person

Here the child's difficulties are defined as distinct from the child's identity, and the child is described as being aligned with the parents and other network members in requiring a solution to the problem. Thus, the child and parents may be described as a team who are working together to find a way to deal with a fiery temper, a difficult temperament, ADHD, anxiety, depression, encopresis, diabetes, addiction, or whatever the problem happens to be. With young children, the problem may be externalized and personified, and the child and family's task defined as defeating the personification of the problem. For example, obsessive compulsive disorder may be personified as *Mr Too-tid*, enuresis may be personified as *Mr Wet-bed*. The parent's role becomes supporting the child in running Mr Wet-bed or Mr Too-Tidy out of the child's life. This strategy has been pioneered by the narrative therapists White & Epston (1990) and incorporated into the brief CBT of obsessive compulsive disorder in children by March & Mulle (1996). The process of separating the problem from the person and then externalizing the problem counters the destructive tendency to label the child as the problem.

Reframing

Here children and their families are offered a new framework within which to conceptualize a sequence of events, and this new way of conceptualizing the sequence of events makes it more likely that the problem will be resolved rather than maintained. For example, where a mother and child become involved in heated arguments about the child's reluctance to apologize for hitting his sister, the mother may frame this as evidence that the child is intrinsically delinquent, and say that this is the reason that she usually leaves these situations in frustration while her child is still screaming at her. This situation may be reframed by pointing out that the child looks to the parent to learn self-control, and it is difficult to learn self-control if uncontrolled behaviour such as screaming may be used to obtain relief, that is, the relief provided by the mother's withdrawing from the situation before the child has stopped screaming and apologized to his sister. From this example, it may be seen that, here, reframing provides a rationale for the mother to use a reward system for increasing positive behaviour (such as apologizing) or a behavioural control system for decreasing negative behaviour (such as screaming). With reframing, the problem is redefined as part of an interactional process rather than as an intrinsic characteristic of the child.

Relabelling

This is way of altering parents' and children's negative or pessimistic attributions and cognitive biases. With relabelling, the therapist routinely offers positive or optimistic labels for ambiguous behaviour as a substitute for negative or pessimistic labels. So where a parent says, "*He was standing there lazy and stupid, doing nothing, so I told him to get on with it,*" the therapist may relabel this by saying, "*When he was there thinking through what to do next, you encouraged him to start his homework.*" Where a parent says, "*She needs to be at home when she is this ill,*" the sentiment may be reframed as "*while she is recovering, she needs to spend some time at home*". With relabelling, children and families are offered optimistic ways of construing events which open up possibilities for collaboration and problem solving as an alternative to pessimistic constructions of the problem which engender polarization and problem maintenance.

Monitoring Problems

For most difficulties, it is useful to train children and parents regularly to record information about the main presenting problems; their antecedents, consequences, and related beliefs; and the impact of particular brief CBT interventions. A monitoring chart for positive and negative target behaviours is given in Figure 11.2. This may be used where the central difficulty is a child or adolescent's behaviour. For example, it may be useful for youngsters with conduct problems or sleep problems.

In assessment of a problem with this monitoring chart, events that typically precede and follow target behaviours are recorded in the second and fourth columns, respectively. This information may suggest ways in which the frequency or intensity of negative target behaviours may be altered by inviting children and their parents to change the antecedent events that trigger problems or the consequences that reinforce them. The impact of these therapeutic interventions may be monitored with the same chart.

Where the chart in Figure 11.2 is used to monitor positive target behaviours, it may throw light on the antecedent events that trigger these positive behaviours and the consequences that reinforce them, and so suggest ways that the frequency of positive target behaviours might be increased.

A monitoring chart for use when the main problem is altering negative mood states is given in Figure 11.3. This chart may be used where children present with anxiety, depression, pain, and other negative mood states. The first five columns of this chart may be used during the assessment phase when identifying antecedent situations and related beliefs that underpin negative mood changes. During treatment, coping strategies learned during brief CBT (and detailed below) may be recorded in the sixth column and their impact on mood states noted in the seventh column.

TARGET BEHAVIOUR TRACKING FORM

Fill out one line of this form when you have finished dealing with a situation in which any of the following target behaviours occur

1. _____

2. _____

3. _____

This will help you to keep track of
*   the types of situations which trigger these behaviours
*   the consequences of these target behaviours
*   the impact of these consequences on the intensity of target behaviours
*   the frequency of these target behaviours

Day and time	What happened before the target?	What was the target behaviour and its intensity 1 = low 10 = high	What happened after the target behaviour?	What was the intensity of target behaviour after this consequence? 1 = low 10 = high

Figure 11.2 Chart for monitoring antecedents and consequences of positive and negative target behaviours

Communication Skills

Where parents and children have difficulties in communicating clearly with each other about how best to manage the presenting problems, communication training may be appropriate (Falloon et al., 1993). A common problem is that parents have difficulty in listening to their

---

MOOD TRACKING FORM

When you have finished dealing with a situation that changed your mood fill out one line of this form. This will help you to keep track of
* the types of situations in which your mood changes
* what you think about in those situations
* how these affect your mood
* how you cope with these thoughts and situations
* how your coping strategies improve your mood

Day & Time	What happened before your mood changed?	Give a rating for your mood before it changed 1=low 10=high	What negative things were you thinking as your mood changed?	Give a rating for your mood after it changed 1=low 10=high	What positive coping responses did you use? CTR Relaxation Leave situation Get support Other	Give a rating for your mood after you coped 1=low 10=high

Figure 11.3 Mood tracking form for tracking depression, anxiety, pain and other negative mood states

children and children have difficulties in clearly articulating their views to their parents. A second common communication problem is the difficulty parents have in listening to each other's views about how best to manage the child's difficulties in a non-judgmental way. In some instances parents and children have never learned communication skills. In others, good communication skills have been acquired but intoxication or intense emotions such as anger, anxiety, or depression prevent parents and children from using these skills.

SPECIFIC GUIDELINES	GENERAL GUIDELINES
LISTENING SKILLS * Listen without interruption * Summarize key points * Check that you have understood accurately * Reply	* Make a time and place for clear communication * Remove distractions and turn off the TV * Discuss one problem at a time * Try to listen with the intention of accurately remembering what was said
COMMUNICATION SKILLS * Decide on specific key points * Organize them logically * Say them clearly * Check you have been understood * Allow space for a reply	* Try to listen without judging what is being said * Avoid negative mind-reading * State your points without attacking the other person * Avoid blaming, sulking or abusing * Avoid interruptions * Take turns fairly * Be brief * Make congruent *statements*

Figure 11.4   Guidelines for listening and communications skills

Training in using communication skills is appropriate in the former situation, but in the latter the key problem to be solved is how to arrange episodes of communication which will be uninfluenced by intoxication or negative mood states. Communication skills may be artificially subdivided into those used for listening and those used for telling somebody something. These skills are listed in Figure 11.4. Parents and children need, first, to be given an intellectual understanding of these skills. Then the therapist should model the skills for the clients. Clients should at this point be invited to try using the skills to discuss a neutral topic in the session. The therapist should let the episode of communication run for five or ten minutes, and take notes of the various difficulties that occur. Then feedback should be given and, in the light of this, clients shoiuld be asked to complete the episode again. Typical mistakes include interrupting before the other person has finished, failing to summarize what the other person said accurately, attributing negative malicious intentions to other persons when they have not communicated that they hold such intentions, failing to check that the message was accurately sent, failing to check that the message has been accurately received, blaming, and sulking. Once clients can use the skills to exchange views on a neutral topic, they may then use to them exchange views on emotionally loaded issues in the session first and later at home. Communication homework assignments should be highly specific to prevent clients from lapsing into poor communication habits. Thus, specific members of a family should be invited to find out the other person's views on a specific topic. A time and place free of distractions should be agreed and a time limit of no more than 20 minutes set for initial communication assignments.

Problem-Solving Skills

When it is apparent that parents or children need to take a more systematic approach to resolving problems, training in problem-solving skills is appropriate (Falloon et al., 1993). Joint problem-solving training for parents is useful where parents have difficulty co-operatively developing plans for solving children's difficulties. Joint problem-solving

SPECIFIC GUIDELINES	GENERAL GUIDELINES
* Define the problem * Brainstorm options * Explore pros and cons * Agree on a joint action plan * Implement the plan * Review progress * Revise the original plan	* Make a time and place for clear communication * Remove distractions and turn off the TV * Discuss one problem at a time * Divide one big problem into a few small problems * Tackle problems one at a time * Avoid vague problem definitions * Define problems briefly * Show that the problem (not the person) makes you feel bad * Acknowledge your share of the responsibility in causing the problem * Do not explore pros and cons until you have finished brainstorming * Celebrate success

Figure 11.5   Guidelines for problem-solving skills

training for adolescents and parents may be useful where parents and teenagers are having difficulty negotiating about the youngster's increasing autonomy. Individual problem-solving training for youngsters may be helpful when children have specific peer group or academic problems that they repeatedly fail to solve, such as joining in peer activities without aggression or managing homework assignments set by their teachers. As with communication difficulties, clients may have difficulties solving problems because they lack the skills or because intoxication, negative mood states, or other factors interfere with the use of well-developed skills. Where such factors are present, therapy should focus on removing these obstacles to effective problem solving. In problem-solving training, the sequence of stages described for communication training should be followed with a progression from explanation of the skills listed in Figure 11.5, to modelling, to rehearsal in the session with the focus on a neutral topic. Feedback should be given during rehearsal until the skills are well developed. Then clients may be invited to use the skills to solve emotionally laden problems. When families are observed trying to solve emotionally laden problems, often the first pitfall they slide into is that of problem definition. Many clients need to be coached in how to translate a big vague problem into a few small, specific problems. A second pitfall involves trying to solve more than one problem at a time. A third area of difficulty is helping clients to hold off on evaluating the pros and cons of any one solution until as many solutions as possible have been listed. This is important, since premature evaluating can stifle the production of creative solutions. Often families need to be coached out of bad communication habits in problem-solving training, such as negative mind-reading in which they attribute negative thoughts or feelings to others, blaming, sulking, and abusing others. Where families with chronic problems successfully resolve a difficulty, a vital part of the coaching process is to help them celebrate this victory.

Supportive Play

For children, particularly those with conduct problems, who have become embroiled in coercive, problem-maintaining interaction patterns with their parents, an important intervention

SPECIFIC GUIDELINES	GENERAL GUIDELINES
* Set a specific time for 20 minutes supportive play per day * Ask child to decide what he or she wants to do * Agree on an activity * Participate wholeheartedly * Run a commentary on what the child is doing or saying, to show your child that you are paying attention to what they find interesting * Make congruent *I like it when you . . .* statements, to show your child you feel good about being there * Praise your child repeatedly * Laugh and make physical contact through hugs or rough and tumble * Finish the episode by summarizing what you did together and how much you enjoyed it	* Set out to use the episode to build a positive relationship with your child * Try to use the episode to give your child the message that they are in control of what happens and that you like being with them * Try to foresee rule-breaking and prevent it from happening or ignore it * Avoid using commands, instructions or teaching * Notice how much you enjoy being with your child

Figure 11.6   Guidelines for supportive play

is to train parents to provide their children with support. Parents may be coached in joint sessions with their children in how to do this. The guidelines for supportive play set out in Figure 11.6 are first explained. Next, the therapist models inviting the child to select a play activity and engaging in child-led play, while positively commenting on the child's activity, praising the child regularly, and avoiding commands and teaching. Then the parent is invited to copy the therapist's activity, and feedback is given to parents on what they are doing well and what they need to do more of. Finally, the parent and child are invited to complete a 20-minute daily episode of child-led play to increase the amount of support the child experiences form the parent.

Reward Systems

Where the goal of treatment is to help children learn new habits such as complying with parental instructions, going to bed on time, taking medication, playing co-operatively with a sibling, or coping with anxiety-provoking situations, reward systems may be used (Herbert, 1987). Guidelines for using rewards systems are presented in Figure 11.7. It is critical that the target behaviour is clearly defined, is monitored regularly, and is rewarded promptly, using a symbolic system of points, tokens, stars, or smiling faces that is age appropriate and acceptable to the child. Examples of smiling face and points charts are given in Figures 11.8 and 11.9. The symbolic reward system must be backed by tangible rewards or prizes which are highly valued, so that the child may buy these with points or tokens after they have accumulated a sufficient number. When points systems are ineffective, it may be that some adult in the child's environment, such as a non-custodial parent in the case of children

SPECIFIC GUIDELINES	GENERAL GUIDELINES
* Define the target behaviour clearly * Decide when and where the monitoring will occur * Make up a smiling-face chart or points chart * Explain to the child that they can win points or smiling faces by carrying out the target behaviour * Ask the child to list a set of prizes that they would like to be able to buy with their points or smiling faces * Agree on how many points or faces are necessary to buy each prize * Follow through on the plan and review it for effectiveness	* Present the reward system to your child as a way of helping him or her learn grown-up habits * All parental figures in the child's network should understand and agree to using the system * Use a chart that is age-appropriate. Smiling faces or stars are good for children and points may be used for adolescents * The sooner points are given after completing the target behaviour, the quicker the child will learn * Highly valued prizes lead to faster learning * Try to fine tune the system so that successes are maximized * If prizes are not being won, make the target behaviour smaller and clearer or the cost of prizes lower and make sure that all parent figures understand and are committed to using the system * If the system is not working, do not criticize the child * Always keep the number of target behaviours below 5

Figure 11.7 Guidelines for reward systems

from separated families, is not committed to implementing the system. In other instances, the target behaviours may be ambiguous or the number of points required to win a prize too high. Troubleshooting these difficulties is a routine part of coaching families in using reward systems.

Behavioural Control Systems

Where parents have difficulties in helping children to avoid engaging in aggressive and destructive behaviour, training in behaviour control skills is appropriate (Herbert, 1987). Guidelines for a behavioural control programme are set out in Figure 11.10. The programme should be framed as a way for helping the child to develop self-control skills. Specific negative or aggressive behaviours are defined as targets for which time-out from reinforcement is given. When these behaviours occur, the parent gives a command to the child to stop, and this may be followed up by two warnings. If children comply they are praised. If not, they are brought to time-out without any display of anger or any reasoned explanation being given at that time. The time for reasoned explanation is at the outset of the programme or when it is being reviewed, not after misbehaviour. During time-out, the child sits on a chair in the corner of the kitchen, the hall, or his or her bedroom away from family activities and interesting or reinforcing events or toys. After a period of two to five minutes (depending

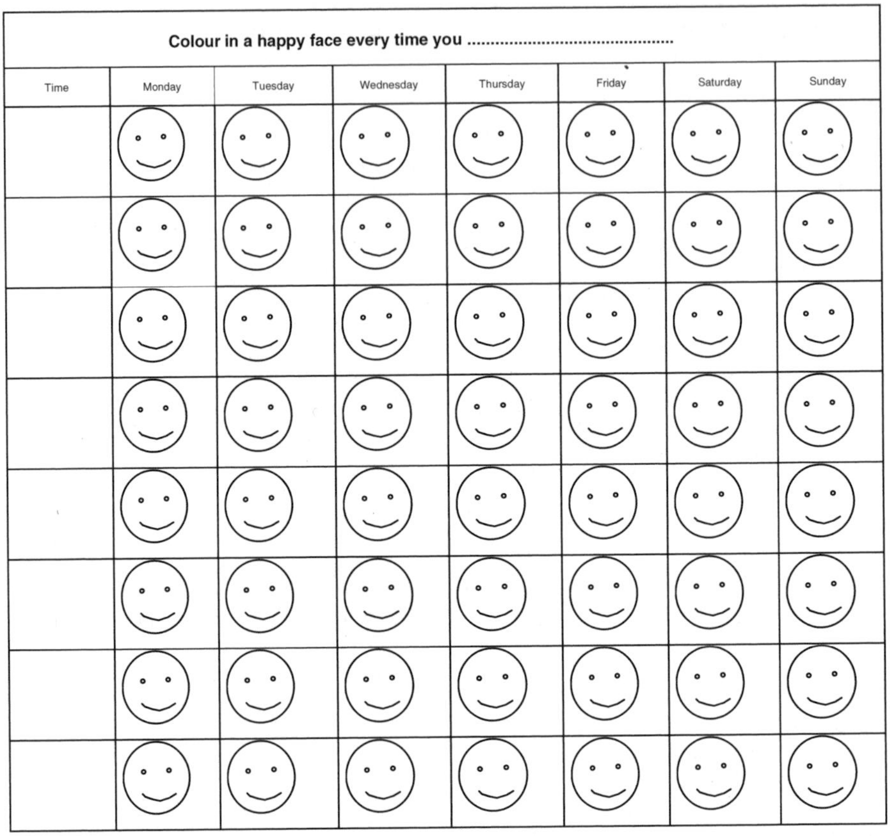

Colour in a happy face every time you							
Time	Monday	Tuesday	Wednesday	Thursday	Friday	Saturday	Sunday
	☺	☺	☺	☺	☺	☺	☺
	☺	☺	☺	☺	☺	☺	☺
	☺	☺	☺	☺	☺	☺	☺
	☺	☺	☺	☺	☺	☺	☺
	☺	☺	☺	☺	☺	☺	☺
	☺	☺	☺	☺	☺	☺	☺
	☺	☺	☺	☺	☺	☺	☺
	☺	☺	☺	☺	☺	☺	☺

Figure 11.8   Child's star chart for child reward systems

upon the child's age), the child is invited to rejoin family activities and is engaged in a stimulating and rewarding exchange with the parent. If children misbehave or protest aggressively while in time-out, they remain there until they have been compliant and quiet for 30 seconds before rejoining family activities and engaging in a stimulating interaction with the parent.

Running a behavioural control programme for the first two weeks is very stressful for most families. The normal pattern is for the time-out period to increase in length gradually and then eventually to begin to diminish. This pattern may be tracked with the time-out monitoring chart in Figure 11.11. During this escalation period when the child is testing the parents' resolve and having a last binge of self-indulgence before learning self-control, it is important to help families maintain the unconditionally supportive aspect of family life. There are two important interventions that may be useful here. First, spouses may be invited to set aside special time where the focus is on mutual marital support. Second, parents may plan episodes of supportive play with the children. The important feature of spouse support is that the couple set aside time to spend together without the children to talk to each other about issues unrelated to the children. In single parent families, parents may be helped to explore ways for obtaining support from their network of friends and members of the extended family.

For these target behaviours you can earn points	Points that can be earned
Up by 7.30 am	1
Washed, dressed and finished breakfast by 8.15	1
Made bed and standing at door with school bag ready to go by 8.30	1
Attend each class and have teacher sign school card	1 per class (max 8)
Good report for each class	1 per class (max 8)
Finish homework	1
Daily jobs (e.g. taking out dustbins or washing dishes)	1 per job (max 4)
Bed on time (9.30)	1
Responding to requests to help or criticism without moodiness or pushing limits	2
Offering to help with a job that a parent thinks deserves points	2
Going to time-out instead of becoming aggressive	2
Apologizing after rule-breaking	2
Showing consideration for parents (as judged by parents)	2
Showing consideration for siblings (as judged by parents)	2
Cash in points for privileges and accept fines without arguing	2

Figure 11.9   Points chart adolescent reward system

With adolescents, a points system, such as that given in Figure 11.9, coupled with a privileges and fines system, such as that given in Figure 11.12, may be used as the cornerstone of a behavioural control programme.

Tension Reduction

Training in tension-reduction skills, such as progressive muscle relaxation exercises, breathing exercises, and visualization, may be included in treatment programmes where physiological arousal associated with anxiety, anger, or other emotions is a central problem (Davis et al., 1988). Children are coached in these skills until they are well developed. In a carefully planned way which maximizes the chances of success, they are then encouraged to use them to reduce arousal in situations which evoke anxiety, anger, pain, or other negative mood states.

SPECIFIC GUIDELINES	GENERAL GUIDELINES
BEHAVIOUR CONTROL PROGRAMME	* Set out with the expectation that you can teach your child one good habit at a time
* Agree on a few clear rules	
* Set clear consequences	* Build in episodes of unconditional special time into behavioural control programme
* Follow through	
* Reward good behaviour	* Frame the programme as learning self-control
* Use timeout or loss of privileges for rule breaking	
* Monitor change visibly	* Involve the child in filling in, designing and using the monitoring chart or system
TIMEOUT	* Monitor increases in positive behaviour as well as decreases in negative behaviour
* Give two warnings	
* Bring the child to timeout without negative emotion	* Do not hold grudges after episodes of negative behaviour
* After five minutes engage the child in a positive activity and praise him for temper control	* Avoid negative mind-reading
	* Avoid blaming, sulking or abusing
* If rule-breaking continues, return child to timeout until thirty seconds of quietness occurs	* Ask for spouse support when you feel bad about the programme Celebrate success
* Engage in positive activity with child and praise for temper control	

Figure 11.10 Guidelines for behaviour-control programmes

With adolescents, it may be appropriate to offer training in these tension reduction skills directly to the youngster alone. With children, parents may be coached, in the consulting room, in helping youngsters to work through these tension-reduction routines, and the parent and child may then practise the exercises at home.

A set of relaxation exercises is given in Figure 11.13. With adolescents, customized relaxation tapes are a useful adjunct to direct instruction, but relaxation tapes without instruction are of little clinical value. Customized relaxation tapes may be made by recording sessions in which adolescents are instructed in relaxation exercises.

When coaching parents in relaxation instruction, the therapist models the process first by going through the exercises with the child while the parents observe. A slow, calming tone of voice and repetition of instructions are used as required to help the child achieve a relaxed state. Before and after the exercises, the therapist, checks with the child how relaxed he or she feels on a 10-point scale where 1 reflects complete relaxation and 10 reflects extreme anxiety. Most children, even on their first trial, will report that they achieve some tension reduction. This should be praised and interpreted to the child and the parents as an indication that the child has the aptitude for developing and refining relaxation skills. The parents may then be invited to instruct the child in completing the exercises daily and to praise the child for completing the exercises.

For a minority of adolescents and children, relaxation exercises lead to increased tension. This may occur because the child is made aware, through completing the exercises, of body tension that is normally ignored. Alternatively, it may occur because focusing attention on somatic processes during the exercises induces anxiety. With youngsters who have had panic attacks, this is particularly common because they are sensitized to construing fluctuations in physiological functioning as signalling the onset of a panic attack. In such instances, the therapist should work on only one or two muscle groups at a time and keep the

Date	Time going in	Number of minutes in time-out	Situation that led to time-out	Pleasant activity that happened afterwards

Figure 11.11 Time-out monitoring chart

training periods very short. Moreover, regular anxiety ratings (on a 10-point scale) should be requested from the child, and when increases in anxiety occur, the therapist should distract the child by asking him or her to engage in the visualization exercise described in Figure 11.13. With such children, it may be necessary to abandon the muscle-relaxation exercises completely and concentrate on training them in visualization or focusing on an external, repetitive, calming visual or auditory stimulus as a means of attaining a relaxed state. (For some of my clients, I have used such stimuli as music, children's hanging mobiles, candlelight, and a bowl of goldfish!) The important thing is to find a routine that children can reliably use to reduce the subjective sense of anxiety as indicated by their status on a 10-point anxiety rating scale. Some children find that, the scene described for the visualization exercise given in Figure 11.13 is not relaxing. In such instances, the child should be asked to describe an alternative relaxing scene, such as being in a wood or on top of a mountain, and this should be used as an alternative.

You can buy these privileges with points	Points	You must pay a fine for breaking these rules	Points
Can watch TV for 1 hour	10	Not up by 7.30 am	1
Can listen to music in bedroom for an hour	5	Not washed, dressed and finished breakfast by 8.15	1
Can use computer for 1 hour	5	Not made bed and standing at door with school bag ready to go by 8.30	1
Can stay up an extra 30 minutes in bedroom with light on	5	Not attend each class and not have teacher sign school card	1 per class
Can stay up an extra 30 minutes in living room	10	Bad report for each class	1 per class
Can have a snack treat after supper	20	Not finish homework within specified time	1
Can make a phone call for 5 minutes	10	Not do daily jobs (e.g. taking out dustbins or washing dishes)	1 per job
Can have a friend over for 2 hours	25	Not in bed on time (9.30)	10
Can visit a friend for 2 hours	30	Respond to requests to help or criticism with moodiness, sulking, pushing limits or arguments	5
Can go out with friend to specified destination for 1 afternoon until 6.00pm	35	Swearing, rudeness, ignoring parental requests	10 per event
Can go out with friend to specified destination for 1 evening until 11.00	40	Physical aggression to objects (banging doors, throwing things)	20 per event
Can stay over at friend's house for night	60	Physical aggression to people	30-100
		Using others' things without permission	30-100
		Lying or suspicion of lying (as judged by parent)	30-100
		Stealing or suspicion of stealing at home, school or community (as judged by parent)	30-100
		Missing class or not arriving home on time or being out unsupervised without permission	30-100

Figure 11.12 Adolescent behaviour control privileges and fines chart

Cognitive Restructuring

Cognitive restructuring involves learning to reinterpret ambiguous situations in less pessimistic, depressing, or threatening ways (Reinecke et al., 1995). In brief CBT with children and adolescents who have problems with anxiety, depression, or other negative mood states,

RELAXATION EXERCISES

After a couple of weeks' daily practice under your supervision, your child will have developed enough skill to use these exercises to get rid of unwanted body tension.

* Set aside 20 minutes a day to do these relaxation exercises with your child.
* Try to arrange to be on good terms with your child when you do these exercises so your child looks forward to them.
* Do them at the same time and in the same place every day.
* Before you begin, remove all distractions (by turning off bright lights, the radio etc.) and ask your child to loosen any tight clothes (like belts, ties or shoes).
* Ask your child to lie on a bed or recline in a comfortable chair with the eyes lightly closed.
* Before and after each exercise ask your child to breathe in deeply and exhale slowly three times while saying the word *relax* to him or herself.
* At the end of each exercise praise your child by saying *Well done* or *You did that exercise well* or some other form of praise.
* Repeat each exercise twice.
* Throughout the exercises speak in a calm relaxed quiet voice.

Area	Exercise
Hands	Close your hands into fists. Then allow them to open slowly. Notice the change from tension to relaxation in your hands and allow this change to continue further and further still so the muscles of your hands become more and more relaxed.
Arms	Bend your arms at the elbow and touch your shoulders with your hands. Then allow them to return to the resting position. Notice the change from tension to relaxation in your arms and allow this change to continue further and further still so the muscles of your arms become more and more relaxed.
Shoulders	Hunch your shoulders up to your ears. Then allow them to return to the resting position. Notice the change from tension to relaxation in your shoulders and allow this change to continue further and further still so the muscles of your shoulders become more and more relaxed.
Legs	Point your toes downwards. Then allow them to return to the resting position. Notice the change from tension to relaxation in the fronts of your legs and allow this change to continue further and further still so the muscles in the fronts of your legs become more and more relaxed. Point your toes upwards. Then allow them to return to the resting position. Notice the change from tension to relaxation in the backs of your legs and allow this change to continue further and further still so the muscles in the backs of your legs become more and more relaxed.
Stomach	Take a deep breath and hold it for three seconds, tensing the muscles in your stomach as you do so. Then breathe out slowly. Notice the change from tension to relaxation in your stomach muscles and allow this change to continue further and further still so your stomach muscles become more and more relaxed.
Face	Clench your teeth tightly together. Then relax. Notice the change from tension to relaxation in your jaw and allow this change to continue further and further still so the muscles in your jaw become more and more relaxed. Wrinkle your nose up. Then relax. Notice the change from tension to relaxation in the muscles around the front of your face and allow this change to continue further and further still so the muscles of your face become more and more relaxed. Shut your eyes tightly. Then relax. Notice the change from tension to relaxation in the muscles around your eyes and allow this change to continue further and further still so the muscles around your eyes become more and more relaxed.
All over	Now that you've done all your muscle exercises, check that all areas of your body are as relaxed as can be. Think of your hands and allow them to relax a little more. Think of your arms and allow them to relax a little more. Think of your shoulders and allow them to relax a little more. Think of your legs and allow them to relax a little more. Think of your stomach and allow it to relax a little more. Think of your face and allow it to relax a little more.
Breathing	Breathe in ...one...two..three....and out slowly..one..two..three..four...five...six ...and again Breathe in ...one...two..three....and out slowly..one..two..three..four...five...six ...and again Breathe in ...one...two..three....and out slowly..one..two..three..four...five...six
Visualizing	Imagine you are lying on a beautiful sandy beach and you feel the sun warm your body. Make a picture in your mind of the golden sand and the warm sun. As the sun warms your body you feel more and more relaxed. As the sun warms your body you feel more and more relaxed. As the sun warms your body you feel more and more relaxed. The sky is a clear, clear blue. Above you, you can see a small white cloud drifting away into the distance. As it drifts away you feel more and more relaxed. It is drifting away and you feel more and more relaxed. It is drifting away and you feel more and more relaxed. As the sun warms your body you feel more and more relaxed. AS the cloud drifts away you feel more and more relaxed. (Wait for 30 seconds) When you are ready open your eyes ready to face the rest of the day relaxed and calm.

Figure 11.13   Relaxation exercises

CTR (challenge-test-reward) training and reattribution training are two techniques that may be used to facilitate cognitive restructuring.

CTR

In challenge-test-reward (CTR) training, youngsters learn the skills required to challenge negative thoughts by asking themselves what the other possible interpretations of the situation are; to test what evidence there is for the negative outcome entailed by the negative thought and the other less threatening outcomes; and to reward themselves for testing the less negative interpretation of the situation. For example, a child with dog phobia who has been coached in CTR may carry out this internal dialogue:

Negative thought: *He's dangerous and will bite me.*
Challenge: *No, an alternative view is he wants to be my friend.*
Test: *I will not run away. There, I didn't run and he didn't bite me. He did want to be friendly.*
Reward: *Well done.*

CTR cognitive restructuring is derived from Beck's cognitive therapy for depression and anxiety (Beck, 1976; Beck et al., 1985). Where CTR skills are taught within a family session, parents may be trained to prompt the child to use these coping skills in depressing or frightening situations, and to offer support and reinforcement for using them effectively. Where family members, particularly parents, have depression or anxiety problems, they can be coached in avoidance of passing on their habits of *thinking pessimistically or dangerously* to their children by using CTR skills themselves.

Reattribution Training

Challenging depressive attributions is a second strategy for reducing the impact of negative thoughts. In particular failure situation that have led to negative thoughts, the youngster and parents are asked to rate the degree to which the negative thought reflects an internal, global, stable attribution. For example, the negative thought, "*I couldn't do the problem because I've always been completely stupid,*" might receive the following ratings:

Internal Due to me	**(1)** 2 3 4 5 6 7 8 9 10	External Due to circumstances
Global To do with many situations	1 **(2)** 3 4 5 6 7 8 9 10	Specific To do with this situation
Stable Is permanent	**(1)** 2 3 4 5 6 7 8 9 10	Unstable Is temporary

An alternative thought—"I couldn't do the problem because it's very hard and I'm having a bad day"—might receive the following ratings, which characterize an optimistic rather than a pessimistic cognitive style:

Internal Due to me	1 2 3 4 5 6 7 8 9 **(10)**	External Due to circumstances
Global To do with many situations	1 23 4 5 6 7 8 **(9)** 10	Specific To do with this situation
Stable Is permanent	1 2 3 4 5 6 7 8 9 **(10)**	Unstable Is temporary

Youngsters and their parents may be trained to ask of each internal, global, stable explanation of failure whether alternative external, specific, or unstable alternative explanations may be offered which fit the available evidence. Reattribution training is based on the reformulated model of learned helplessness (Abramson et al., 1978).

Self-Instructional Training

This may be used, particularly with children who have ADHD, to improve academic skills. Initially, the therapist models the use of self-instructions by completing a task while saying self-instructions aloud. Next, children are guided by therapist instructions in the completion of academic and social tasks, and later by self-instruction which is faded to a whisper and then to internal speech (Meichenbaum, 1977). Tasks chosen for self-instructional training should initially be well within the child's competence; once self-instructional skills have been developed, increasingly challenging tasks may be used. Self-instructions should include self-statements to clarify the task demands (*What do I have to do?*); to develop a plan (*I have to draw a picture*); to guide the child through the plan (*I'll hold the pencil and work slowly*); to cope with distraction (*I'll ignore that noise and stick to the job*); and to self-reinforce on-task behaviour (*Well done*).

Home–School Liaison

Where children show school-based problems, liaison with the school is a vital element of brief CBT. Failure to address significant school-related issues may unnecessarily protract therapy. The most effective way to conduct school liaison is to communicate with the child's schoolteacher by letter, phone, or in person during the assessment phase and then, if appropriate, meet with the child's teacher and parents together during the treatment phase if school-based intervention is required. Two of the most common situations where home–school liaison is vital are 1) conduct problems with comorbid learning problems and 2) school refusal.

Home–School Liaison in Cases of Conduct and Comorbid Learning Problems

Children with ADHD, oppositional defiant disorder, and conduct disorder commonly have home-and school-based conduct problems with comorbid learning difficulties. The

school-based conduct and learning problems may be addressed in a home–school reporting system which is consistent with and runs concurrently with a home-based behavioural
control programme (DuPaul et al., 1991). Specific target behaviours and academic goals
are set jointly by the teacher, child, parent, and therapist and a points system (similar to
that given in Figures 11.9 and 11.12) is agreed. Points from this system may be used to
buy items from a reinforcement menu at home or to achieve specific agreed privileges in
school.

When academic targets are set, the materials should be pitched at the child's attainment
level and broken into small units, with reinforcement given for completion of specific
academic tasks (such as completion of a worksheet) rather than process behaviours (such
as sitting still). Repetitive tasks should be avoided where possible. Behavioural targets
for which the child can earn reinforcers should be highly specific and typically centre on
following instructions to behave in a positive way rather than cease behaving in a negative
way. Fines (such as those given in Figure 11.12) should be used for rule violations, so that
the child loses the number of points he or she would have gained for complying with the
instruction.

Reinforcers (in the form of tokens for children under eight years of age and ticks on
a report card for older children) should be delivered immediately and frequently after the
execution of target behaviours. When reinforcers are being given or response costs are being
implemented, it may be more effective if this is conducted quietly and without drawing the
attention of the class to the process, since the class's response may make both receiving and
losing points equally reinforcing. There should be set times when the child can exchange
tokens for items off the home or school reinforcement menu.

Once children show that they can respond to a continuous reward system such as this,
written contingency contracts may be used where the child agrees to carry out certain listed
target behaviours, and in return the teacher and parents agree to certain rewards if the targets
are met and certain response costs if they are not met.

With older children and teenagers, a daily report card system such as that presented in
Figure 11.14 may be used. After each class, the teacher rates the child's performance on the
four or five listed behaviours and initials the card. The points obtained may be used either
at home or in school to purchase items from a reinforcement menu.

Where the demands of implementing this type of system are beyond the resources of
the school, the therapist may make representations to educational authorities through the
appropriate channels to help the school obtain resources to implement such programmes.

Home–School Liaison in Cases of School Refusal

Where a child refuses to go to school, factors related to the child, the family, and the
school deserve careful assessment and an eventual return to school plan based on a clear
formulation of the problem may involve home-school liaison (Blagg, 1987).

Child-related factors in cases of school refusal include separation anxiety, depression,
other psychological adjustment problems, and physical illness, notably viral infections.
Children may also refuse to go to school because of fear of specific events at school. Children
with learning difficulties and attainment problems may develop a fear of academic failure,
and this may underpin their school refusal. Children with physical disabilities or physical

| Name_____Date_____ |
| For his or her performance today, please rate this child in each of the areas listed below using this 5 point scale |

| 1 | 2 | 3 | 4 | 5 |
| Very poor | Poor | Fair | Good | Excellent |

Target behaviour	Class 1	Class 2	Class 3	Class 4	Class 5	Class 6	Class 7	Class 8
Paying attention								
Completing classwork								
Following rules								
Other								
Teacher's initials								

Figure 11.14 Daily school report card

co-ordination problems which lead to poor performance in athletics may refuse to go to school because of their fear of athletic failure. Children with physical characteristics about which they are embarrassed, such as delayed physical maturity or obesity, may refuse to go to school for fear of being taunted by peers during athletics because of their physical characteristics. Family factors that may contribute to school refusal include parental confusion, anxiety, or anger over the meaning of the child's school refusal and related somatic complaints, and parental conflict about the management of the situation. Parents may inadvertently reinforce school refusal by insisting on school attendance but relenting when the child escalates his or her protests to a dramatic level. Parents may mismanage school refusal because they derive secondary gains from the child's staying at home. For example, the child may provide the homemaker (usually the mother) with companionship. Parents may also mismanage school refusal because parental psychological adjustment problems may compromise their capacity to manage the child's difficulties. Such parental problems may include anxiety, depression, substance abuse, or learning difficulties. Wider family stresses, such as bereavement, unemployment, separation, birth of a child, or moving house, may place such demands on parents that they have few personal resources remaining to help their child develop a pattern of regular school attendance. Children from families in which siblings have a history of school refusal may develop school refusal themselves by imitating their older sibling's behaviour. School-based factors which may contribute to the development of school refusal include bullying by peers, victimization by teachers, threatening events occurring while travelling to or from school, poor academic performance, and poor athletic performance. Important factors in the wider professional system which may contribute to school refusal include poor co-ordination among members of the professional network in the management of the child's school refusal and poor communication between these professionals and the family. The assessment of these factors should involve interviews with the child, the parents, the child's teachers, and involved professionals.

From this information, factors that predisposed the child to develop school refusal may be identified. Those factors that precipitated the occurrence of the episode of school refusal may be pinpointed. Finally, factors that are currently maintaining the condition may be clarified.

Where separation anxiety is present, the next step involves explaining to the child, the parents, and the teacher that the somatic symptoms (headaches and stomach-aches) and the associated worries that cause them can only be resolved by the children proving to themselves that they are brave enough to attend school and tolerate the anxiety and discomfort that it causes. It should be pointed out that a month or two of regular school attendance will resolve most of these symptoms. However, attempts to resolve the anxiety and somatic complaints first before returning to school will actually make the condition worse, since the child will not overcome the fear that causes these symptoms without facing the feared situation, i.e. going to school.

Where factors at school such as bullying, victimization, or academic failure are contributing to the school refusal, these issues must be altered before return to school can be arranged. With bullying or teacher victimization, the bullies or teachers must be confronted and subsequently monitored so that there is no recurrence. With academic failure, remedial tuition may be provided. Where wider family factors, such as parental psychological adjustment problems, are a concern, referral to an appropriate agency for concurrent treatment may be arranged.

With this groundwork laid, the precise details of a return-to-school programme may be planned. This should specify the date and time at which the child will return, whether the child will have an immediate or gradual return building up from a few hours a day to a full day over a period of a week or two, who will escort the child to school, who will meet the child at school, which peers will be appointed as buddies to make the child feel welcome, and which teacher will act as a secure base for the child if he or she experiences anxiety while in school. The child will require some opportunity to rehearse precisely how the return to school will be managed and to plan how he or she will cope with all major difficulties that may occur.

In addition to this return-to-school programme, a reward system should be set, using the principles given in Figure 11.7, to give the child an incentive to tolerate the anxiety that will inevitably be experienced during the first few days at school. The reward system should allow the child to earn a concrete daily reward that is received immediately after school each day and a point system that allows the child to accumulate points that may be used to obtain a more substantial reinforcer each week.

The mornings following holidays, illnesses, and weekends are times when relapses are most likely, and specific plans for arranging an escort to school and a contingency management programme on those occasions need to be made to prevent relapses occurring. Ideally, the child should be accompanied to school and received by peers or a class teacher on arrival, and rewards should be given for managing any separation anxiety experienced on such occasions.

Troubleshooting Resistance

It is one of the extraordinary paradoxes of psychotherapy that clients go to considerable lengths to seek professional advice on how to manage their difficulties yet often do not follow through on such advice or other responsibilities entailed by the treatment contract. This type of behaviour has traditionally been referred to as non-compliance or resistance. Accepting the inevitability of resistance and developing skills for managing it are central to the effective practice of brief CBT (Anderson & Stewart, 1983).

Clients show resistance in a wide variety of ways. Resistance may take the form of not completing tasks between sessions, not attending sessions, or refusing to terminate the therapy process. It may also involve not co-operating during therapy sessions. For clients to make progress with the resolution of their difficulties, the therapist must have some systematic way of dealing with resistance (Carr, 1995). The first step is to describe the discrepancy between what clients agreed to do and what they actually did. The second is to ask about the difference between situations where they managed to follow through on an agreed course of action and those where they did not. The third is to ask what they believed blocked them from making progress. The fourth is to ask whether these blocks can be overcome. The fifth is to ask about strategies for getting around the blocks. The sixth is to ask about the pros and cons of these courses of action. The seventh is to frame a therapeutic dilemma which outlines the costs of maintaining the status quo and the costs of circumventing the blocks.

When resistance is questioned, the factors that underpin it are uncovered. In some instances, unforeseen events—acts of God—hinder progress. In others, the problem is that the clients lack the skills and abilities that underpin resistance. Where a poor therapy contract has been formed, resistance is usually due to a lack of commitment to the therapeutic process. Specific convictions which form part of clients' individual, family, or culturally based belief systems may also contribute to resistance when the clients' values prevent them from following through on therapeutic tasks. The wish to avoid emotional pain is a further factor that commonly underpins resistance.

Questioning resistance is only helpful if a good therapeutic alliance has been built. If clients feel that they are being blamed for not making progress, they will usually respond by pleading helplessness, blaming the therapist or someone else for the resistance, or distracting the focus of therapy away from the problem of resistance to less painful areas.

STAGE 4. DISENGAGING OR RECONTRACTING

The process of disengagement begins once improvement is noticed. The interval between sessions is increased at this point. The degree to which goals have been met is reviewed when the session contract is complete, or before this if improvement is obvious. If goals have been achieved, the family's beliefs about the permanence of this change is established. Then the therapist helps the family construct an understanding of the change process by reviewing with them the problem, the formulation, their progress through the treatment programme, and the concurrent improvement in the problem. Relapse management is also discussed

(Marlatt & Gordon, 1985). Family members are helped to forecast the types of stressful situations in which relapses may occur, their probable negative reactions to relapses, and the ways in which they can use the lessons learned in therapy to cope with these relapses in a productive way. In brief CBT, disengagement is constructed as an episodic event rather than as the end of a relationship. It is recognized that further episodes of brief CBT may be required in the future to address other specific problems.

If goals are not reached, it is in the clients' best interests to avoid doing *more of the same* (Segal, 1991). Rather, therapeutic failures should be analysed in a systematic way. The understanding that emerges from this is useful both for the clients and for the therapist. From the clients' perspective, they avoid becoming trapped in a consultation process that maintains rather than resolves the problem. From the therapist's viewpoint, it provides a mechanism for coping with burnout that occurs when multiple therapeutic failures occur.

Failure Analysis

Failures may occur for a number of reasons (Carr, 1995). First, they may occur because of the engagement difficulties. The correct members of the child's network may not have been engaged. For example, where fathers are not engaged in the therapy process, dropout is more likely. The construction of a formulation of the presenting problem which does not open up possibilities for change or which does not fit with the family's belief systems is a second possible reason for failure. A third reason why failure occurs may be that the therapy plan was not appropriately designed, the therapeutic alliance was poorly built, or the therapist had difficulties in offering the family invitations to complete the therapeutic tasks. Problems with handling families' reservations about change, and the resistance that this may give rise to, are a fourth and further source of failure. Disengaging without empowering the family to handle relapses is a fifth possible factor contributing to therapeutic failure. Finally, failure may occur because the goals set did not take account of the constraints within which family members were operating. These constraints include biological factors such as illness, psychological factors such as intellectual disability, economic factors such as poverty, social factors such as general life stress, and broader socio-cultural factors such as minority-group membership. The analysis of treatment failure is an important way to develop therapeutic skill.

SUMMARY

In brief CBT, the consultation process may be conceptualized as a developmental and recursive process involving the stages of planning, assessment and formulation, therapy, and disengagement or recontracting. In the planning stage, network analysis provides guidance on whom to invite to the intake interview. The minimum sufficient network necessary for an assessment to be completed includes the customer, the legal guardians, the caregivers, and the referred child. In planning an agenda, a routine intake interview and a core test battery may be supplemented by questions and tests which take account of the specific features of the case.

Establishing a contract for assessment, working through the assessment agenda and recursively refining the preliminary formulation in the light of the information obtained, building a therapeutic alliance, and giving feedback are the more important features of the assessment and formulation stage, which may span one or two sessions. At the end of the assessment phase, a formulation is constructed. A formulation is a mini-theory that explains why the presenting problems developed and persist. The formulation is fed back to the family as a basis for a therapeutic contract. A therapeutic contract based on the formulation begins with goal setting. The costs and benefits of goals to involved members of the network must be considered as part of the contacting process. Brief CBT plans are constructed from the following set of building blocks: a family-based approach, redefinition of problems, monitoring problems, communication training, problem-solving training, supportive play, reward systems, behavioural control systems, tension reduction, cognitive restructuring, self-instructional training, and home–school liaison. A systematic method for analysing resistance and resolving it is required to complete brief CBT plans. Disengagement is considered when the end of the therapeutic contract is reached. If goals have not been achieved, this should be acknowledged and referral to another agency considered. Where goals have been reached, relapse management and the options for future booster sessions should be considered.

FURTHER READING

Carr, A. (1999). *Handbook of clinical child psychology: A contextual approach.* London: Routledge.
Graham, P. (1998). *Cognitive-behaviour therapy for children and families.* Cambridge, UK: Cambridge University Press.

REFERENCES

Abramson, L., Seligman, M., & Teasdale, J. (1978). Learned helplessness in humans: Critique and reformulation. *Journal of Abnormal Psychology, 87,* 49–74.
Achenbach, T. (1991). *Integrative guide for the 1991 CBCL/4-18, YSR and TRF profiles.* Burlington, VT: University of Vermont Department of Psychiatry.
Anderson, C., & Stewart, S. (1983). *Mastering resistance.* New York: Guilford Press.
Battle, J. (1992). *Culture-free self-esteem inventories. Examiner's manual* (2nd ed.). Austin, TX: Pro-ed.
Beck, A. (1976). *Cognitive therapy and the emotional disorders.* New York: International Universities Press.
Beck, A., Emery, G., & Greenberg, R. (1985). *Anxiety disorders and phobias.* New York: Guilford Press.
Bergin, A., & Garfield, S. (1994). *Handbook of psychotherapy and behaviour change* (4th ed.). Chichester: Wiley.
Blagg, N. (1987). *School phobia and its treatment.* London: Croom Helm.
Carr, A. (1995). *Positive practice: A step-by-step approach to family therapy.* Reading: Harwood.
Carr, A. (1997). *Family therapy and systemic practice.* Lanham, MD: University Press of America.
Carr, A. (1999). *Handbook of clinical child psychology: A contextual approach.* London: Routledge.
Carr, A. (2000). *What works with children and adolescents? A critical review of research on psychological interventions with children, adolescents and their families.* London: Routledge.
Crick, N., & Dodge, K. (1994). A review and reformulation of social information processing mechanisms in children's social adjustment. *Psychological Bulletin, 115,* 74–101.
Davis, M., Robbins-Eshelman, E., & McKay, M. (1988). *The relaxation and stress reduction workbook* (3rd ed.). Oakland, CA: New Harbinger Publications.
DuPaul, G., Guevremont, D., & Barkley, R. (1991). Attention deficit hyperactivity disorder. In T. Kratochwill & R. Morris (Eds.), *The practice of child therapy* (2nd ed., pp. 115–144). New York: Pergamon.

Falloon, I., Laporta, M., Fadden, G., & Graham-Hole, V. (1993). *Managing stress in families*. London: Routledge.

Goodman, R. (1994). A modified version of the Rutter Parent Questionnaire including extra item on children's strengths: A research note. *Journal of Child Psychology and Psychiatry, 35*, 1483–1494.

Graham, P. (1998). *Cognitive-behaviour therapy for children and families*. Cambridge, UK: Cambridge University Press.

Herbert, M. (1987). *Behaviour treatment of children with problems* (2nd ed.). London: Academic Press.

Kabacoff, R., Miller, I., Bishop, D., Epstein, N., & Keitner, G. (1990). A psychometric study of the McMaster Family Assessment Device. *Journal of Family Psychology, 3*, 431–439.

Kelly, G. (1955). *The psychology of personal constructs. Volumes 1 and 2*. New York: Norton.

March, J., & Mulle, K. (1996). Banishing OCD: Cognitive-behavioural psychotherapy for obsessive-compulsive disorders. In E. Hibbs & P. Jensen (Eds.), *Psychosocial treatments for child and adolescent disorders. Empirically based strategies for clinical practice* (pp. 83-102). Washington, DC: APA.

Marlatt, G., & Gordon, J. (1985). *Relapse prevention*. New York: Guilford Press.

Meichenbaum, D. (1977). *Cognitive-behaviour modification: An integrative approach*. New York: Plenum Press.

Nowicki, S., & Strickland, B. (1973). A locus of control scale for children. *Journal of Consulting and Clinical Psychology, 40*, 148–155.

Patterson, G. (1982). *Coercive family process*. Eugene, OR: Castalia.

Rogers, C. (1957). The necessary and sufficient conditions of therapeutic personality change. *Journal of Consulting Psychology, 21*, 95–103.

Reinecke, M., Dattilio, F., & Freeman, A. (1995). *Cognitive therapy with children and adolescents*. New York: Guilford Press.

Segal, L. (1991). Brief therapy: The MRI approach. In A. Gurman & D. Kniskern (Eds.), *Handbook of family therapy* (vol. 2, pp. 17–199). New York: Brunner/Mazel.

Snyder, C., Michael, S., & Cheavens, J. (1999). Hope as a therapeutic foundation of common factors, placebos and expectancies. In M. Hubble, B. Duncan, & S. Miller (Eds.), *The heart and soul of change: What works in therapy* (pp. 179–200). Washington, DC: APA.

White, M., & Epston, D. (1990). *Narrative means to therapeutic ends*. New York: Norton.

CHAPTER 12

Preventing and Treating Evaluation Strain: A Brief CBT Approach

Paul. E. Flaxman and **Frank W. Bond**

*Department of Psychology, Goldsmiths College,
University of London, New Cross, London, UK*

and

Edmund Keogh

Department of Psychology, University of Bath, Bath, UK

For most people, being "evaluated" is an inherent part of their educational, vocational, and social experience. Such evaluation can take the form of tests, exams, coursework, appraisals, interviews, and peer judgements, to name but a few. For those individuals who respond unhelpfully to evaluative situations (e.g., anxiously or with avoidance), such events may appear overwhelming and discouraging. It is not surprising, then, that evaluation *strain* can seriously restrict people's quality of life and/or goal achievement. Following Jex (1998), we define "strain" as the myriad of unhelpful cognitive, emotional, behavioural, and physiological responses that people can have to "stressors", or life events that require them to adapt or react.

By far the most researched manifestation of evaluative strain is that which occurs in the context of test taking. Almost half a century of research into test anxiety (TA) has detailed the debilitating effects that this evaluative context can have on people's well-being, academic performance, and even social interactions. The present chapter seeks to contribute to the TA literature (discussed below) by detailing a training protocol by Bond et al. (in preparation) that has been used to reduce strain and improve academic performance in 15-and 16-year-old students who are facing important national assessments (Keogh et al., in preparation). We believe, however, that this programme can help people of all ages to overcome problems that centre on evaluative strain.

Our cognitive-behavioural therapy (CBT)-based treatment protocol (described below) is comprehensive, yet brief, and, as we will show, it derives from both the TA and CBT literatures. Thus, we first consider the development of the TA construct, and how its growth has influenced TA treatment research over the last 40 years. As will be seen, TA treatment and conceptual developments have closely followed, if not directly stemmed from, the changing emphases and practices of CBT. Even now, CBT theory and practice are developing, and the goal of our treatment protocol is to integrate some of these advances into the CBT

Handbook of Brief Cognitive Behaviour Therapy. Edited by Frank W. Bond and Windy Dryden.
© 2002 John Wiley & Sons, Ltd. ISBN 0-470-02132-2.

treatment of evaluative strain. In particular, we wish to show how recent conceptualisations of *meta-cognition* and generalised anxiety disorder (GAD) (Wells, 1995; Chapter 6, this volume) can be applied to the treatment of TA and evaluation strain. First, however, we need to define what we mean by these two latter conditions.

TEST ANXIETY(TA): DEFINITION

During the 1960s, and 1970s, two major conceptual developments transformed the TA construct. The first involved the conceptualisation of TA within the "state-trait" theory of anxiety (e.g., Spielberger, 1972). To elaborate, state anxiety refers to a transitory emotional state, characterised by unpleasant feelings of tension and apprehension, and by activation of the autonomic nervous system (e.g., muscle tension and palpitations). Trait anxiety, however, is viewed as a relatively stable personality trait, involving a proneness to perceive a wide range of situations as more or less threatening or dangerous (Spielberger & Vagg, 1995a). TA is viewed as a special case, or "situation-specific" form, of trait anxiety that predisposes people to perceive evaluative situations as threatening (Spielberger, 1972). As a result of this appraisal, they are then likely to experience frequent and intense levels of state anxiety, which are in turn accompanied by worry and other test-irrelevant thoughts (Spielberger et al., 1978; Spielberger & Vagg, 1995a).

A second concurrent development that shaped the TA construct was the hypothesis that TA consists of two distinct response sets: worry and emotionality (Liebert & Morris, 1967). The former is a cognitive response, describing the focusing of *attention* on concerns about one's performance, ability, or adequacy (Deffenbacher, 1980), while the latter refers to an affective response that involves an overawareness of bodily arousal and tension in the face of evaluative situations (Sarason, 1984). The emotionality component of TA has been equated with intense state-anxiety reactions (Spielberger & Vagg, 1995a).

Subsequently, researchers have speculated that the TA construct can be collapsed into four distinguishable components: worry, test-irrelevant thinking, tension, and bodily symptoms (McIlroy et al., 2000; Sarason, 1984). The worry and test-irrelevant thinking components are hypothesised to be facets of an overall concept of cognition in TA. The worry component is distinguished from test-irrelevant thinking in that worry encapsulates thoughts related to performance evaluation, whereas test-irrelevant thinking refers to distracting, but *non-evaluative* cognitions in evaluative situations (McIlroy et al., 2000). The tension and bodily symptoms components, however, are both deemed to be facets of emotionality. The tension component has been equated with the original, overall concept of emotionality, outlined above (e.g., Zimmer et al., 1992), while the bodily symptoms component encapsulates the unpleasant bodily reactions (e.g., headache and upset stomach) frequently reported by test-anxious individuals. Support for this four-factor structure of TA has come from factor-analytic studies of TA measures, such as the Revised Test Anxiety scale (RTA) (Benson & El-Zahhar, 1994; McIlroy et al., 2000).

Both the state-trait and worry-emotionality distinctions helped to identify TA as a multidimensional construct that consists of both cognitive and affective components. A major source of support for viewing evaluation anxiety in this way comes from research showing that each of these components has differential impacts upon performance in evaluative situations (Zeidner, 1998). We now briefly review this literature and then show how it has been used to inform TA treatment interventions.

TA AND PERFORMANCE

Research indicates that high test-anxious individuals frequently experience performance decrements in evaluative situations, and it appears to be the cognitive component of this problem that contributes most to these deficiencies (Hembree, 1988; Sarason, 1984; Wine, 1971; Zeidner, 1998; see also Eysenck & Calvo, 1992). Specifically, most studies find that when the common variance between worry and emotionality is controlled, only worry is negatively associated with academic performance (Deffenbacher, 1980). Despite this relatively greater association between worry and performance, research suggests that the cognitive and emotionality components of TA interact to affect performance. For example, Deffenbacher (1977) found that at low levels of worry, emotionality was unrelated to performance on a graduate admissions test, but such a (debilitative) relationship existed when worry levels were high (see also Keogh & French, 2001).

In the TA literature, the nature of this interaction between the cognitive and emotionality components has been used to explain the facilitating and debilitating aspects of emotional arousal in test situations. Facilitating anxiety refers to emotional arousal that is associated with enhanced performance, whereas debilitating anxiety is used to explain arousal that is related to impeded performance (e.g., Alpert & Haber, 1960; Zeidner, 1998). Referring to this distinction, Alpert & Haber (1960) note that "persons may possess a large amount of both anxieties, or of one but not the other, or none of either" (p. 213). A number of authors have proposed that it is the (cognitive) interpretation and labelling of emotional arousal (i.e., emotionality) that determines the extent to which TA facilitates or debilitates performance (e.g., Deffenbacher, 1980; Hollandsworth et al., 1979; Sarason, 1984; Wine, 1980). For example, Hollandsworth et al. (1979) found that, during a mental abilities task, high and low test-anxious students handled their arousal differently: for the high test-anxious individuals, arousal seemed to act as a cue for distracting, task-irrelevant thinking (i.e., worry); the low test-anxious individuals, however, spoke of getting "psyched up" or of getting "in stride" (i.e., task-relevant thinking) in response to emotional arousal while working on the task. The importance of cognitive appraisal in this context is further supported by research showing that in evaluative situations high and low test-anxious individuals cannot be distinguished on objective measures of physiological arousal (e.g., Hollandsworth et al., 1979; Holroyd & Appel, 1980; Morris & Liebert, 1970).

Research has focused primarily on the debilitating effects of TA on performance, and two explanatory models have traditionally been proposed to account for these effects: the interference and skills-deficit models. The former hypothesises that anxiety-related cognitions (worry and test-irrelevant thoughts) interfere with prior learning in the testing situation itself, and thus inhibit performance (e.g., Sarason, 1984; Wine, 1971, 1980). The skills-deficit model, in contrast, assumes that test-anxious students' reduced performance is due to deficient study or test-taking skills, rather than to interference in the testing situation (e.g., Culler & Holahan, 1980; Kirkland & Hollandsworth, 1979). The interference explanation incorporates the common stereotype of the test-anxious student who "freezes up" in testing situations, rendered unable to retrieve previously learned information, while the deficit explanation suggests that TA stems from an individual's realisation of a skills deficit that is presumed to give them "good reason to be anxious" (Benjamin et al., 1981).

The majority of TA researchers have interpreted its detrimental effects within an interference model (e.g., Hembree, 1988; Musch & Bröder, 1999). A number of authors have, however, moved away from viewing the interference and skills-deficit models as mutually exclusive explanations of TA (e.g., Benjamin et al., 1981; Naveh-Benjamin et al., 1987; Tobias, 1985). For example, Naveh-Benjamin et al. (1987) advocate an "information processing" model which is able to accommodate two types of test-anxious students: those with a skills deficit, who have problems encoding and organising study material; and those who experience problems retrieving material as a result of evaluative strain. This comprehensive model also postulates a causal sequence for test-anxious students whose performance suffers because of deficits at both the encoding and retrieval stages of information processing. To elaborate, an individual may be aware of inadequate skills, leading to anxiety about achievement, which, in turn, results in the adoption of less effective study habits, such as rote memorisation. The resulting poor performance may then be compounded by worry that interferes with memory retrieval and problem solving, in the testing situation itself (Benjamin et al., 1981). Integrative theories such as this one have further encouraged contemporary researchers to view the TA construct as multifaceted and multidetermined. In so doing, they have accommodated for the identification of a variety of different types of test-anxious student. This has, in turn, helped to dispel what Zeidner (1998) calls the "uniformity myth" (p. 30), which refers to a tendency for TA authors to allocate all test-anxious individuals to one homogeneous category.

As we now discuss, the conceptual development of TA from a unitary to a multifactorial construct has served as the impetus for a similar advancement in cognitive behavioural interventions for this problem. Such developments in theory and treatment have mirrored similar theoretical and treatment advances in CBT. Indeed, the TA treatment manual that we describe below is but the latest in such protocols that take into account advances in the theory and practice of CBT.

BRIEF HISTORY AND REVIEW OF TA TREATMENT RESEARCH

Behavioural and cognitive behavioural therapies form the bulk of TA interventions that have been evaluated in outcome research. In fact, some authors have noted how the evolution of these behavioural therapies have mirrored, if not directly informed, the development of TA treatments (e.g., Denney, 1980; Vagg & Spielberger, 1995; Zeidner, 1998). To elaborate, beginning in the mid-1960s, in line with the behavioural Zeitgeist, TA research was mainly focused on Wolpe's (1958) systematic desensitisation (SD) approach. This intervention strategy attempted to treat anxiety-related disorders through a counterconditioning process, whereby people were taught to use relaxation to combat anxiety symptoms (Vagg & Papsdorf, 1995). The predominance of SD during this era of TA treatment is highlighted by Wine (1971), who noted that "all of the published accounts of treatment of test anxious subjects have involved variations of systematic desensitization techniques" (p. 101). Although SD has been shown generally to be effective in reducing TA, there is little evidence that this reduction translates to test performance improvements, among test-anxious individuals (e.g., Fletcher & Spielberger, 1995; Tyron, 1980).

During the 1970s, there was growing dissatisfaction with both empirical and theoretical aspects of a strictly behavioural approach to psychotherapy and experimental psychopathology (Meichenbaum, 1993). This was reflected in a growing literature that focused on the causal role of cognition in emotion and behaviour: a role that behaviour therapists had traditionally eschewed (Goldfried, 1980; although see Zettle & Hayes, Chapter 3 in this volume). During this period, influential works by Bandura (1977), Beck (1970, 1976),

Ellis (1962), Goldfried & Davison (1976), Mahoney (1974), and Meichenbaum (1977) served to transform behaviour therapy into *cognitive*-behaviour therapy. This "cognitive revolution" (Meichenbaum, 1993) taking place in behaviour therapy generally was also mirrored in the TA treatment literature.

Wine (1971) was at the forefront of the cognitive revolution in the treatment of TA. Specifically, she promoted an attentional or "interference" interpretation of the adverse effects of TA on performance (described above). This cognitive conceptualisation was out of step at the time when the dominant assumption was that emotional arousal (i.e., emotionality) was the proper focus of TA theory and treatment. During the 1970s, however, it was becoming increasingly clear that behavioural therapies, with their focus on physiological arousal, were not markedly improving the academic performance of test-anxious individuals (Zeidner, 1998). At the same time, research was beginning to show that cognitive techniques, either alone or in combination with SD, were effective both in reducing TA and improving performance (e.g., Holroyd, 1976; Meichenbaum, 1972). With this combination of findings, TA theory, research, and treatment began fully to embrace the cognitive revolution.

Another development taking place in CBT during the 1970s also strongly influenced TA treatment approaches. Behaviourists had long advocated viewing psychological functioning in terms of adaptive and maladaptive responses, as opposed to unconscious, internal forces (Mischel, 1968). During this time, however, cognitive behaviour therapists were beginning to divide people's responses into three, interrelated types: (physical) actions, cognitive/affective, and physiological (e.g., Lang, 1971). Positing a tripartite response system (Turkat, 1979) encouraged therapists to refine their analyses and identify any dominant system that may have a causal impact on the other two. Such identification is seen as therapeutically beneficial, as it can provide guidance for the design of a targeted treatment programme for people's presenting problems (see Bond, 1998; Bruch, 1998).

TA researchers have also found it useful to adopt this tripartite response system analysis. In so doing, they have viewed TA as consisting of *cognitive* responses (e.g., worry, task-irrelevant thoughts, and self-preoccupation), *affective* responses (e.g., tension and perceived arousal), and *action* responses (e.g., study skills and avoidance). Each of these response types represents a "distinct response channel" through which TA may be expressed (Zeidner, 1998). For the test-anxious individual, the responses from all three systems are hypothesised to interact in a dynamic fashion over the course of the testing process, resulting in what Meichenbaum & Butler (1980) call a "self-perpetuating cycle" of anxiety. TA is not now thought to be manifested or defined by just one type of response, but by the complex interplay between all three types of response (Zeidner, 1998).

Viewing TA as a series of interrelated reactions has had direct implications for treating this problem. Previously, many TA interventions had not distinguished between, and therefore had not differentially targeted, the three response systems. This led to treatments that employed only a limited repertoire of techniques that may or may not have directly affected the response system with which a person's most prominent TA problem was associated. For example, SD (which targets affective responses most directly) may have been used to treat a person whose TA was mostly manifested through worry (a cognitive response). As a result of the tripartite response analysis, however, common consensus now suggests that therapists should treat TA by targeting responses from each, not just one, of the three different response systems (e.g., Algaze, 1995; Meichenbaum & Butler, 1980; Vagg & Spielberger, 1995); although it is acknowledged that a response from one system (e.g., worry) may be more prominent than those from the others (e.g., hyperventilating and avoidance) and, thus, may require the majority of therapeutic attention. Nevertheless, this multiresponse system targeting is now highly recommended and is seen as particularly useful for group psychoeducational and prevention programmes (Deffenbacher, 1988; Meichenbaum, 1985; Zeidner, 1998), which constitute the target of our treatment protocol.

By using such a protocol to this end, group interventions can more adequately compensate for the fact that there is typically far less assessment time to identify the exact topography of each participant's individual response pattern (Deffenbacher, 1988). This compensation can be ensured in group prevention programmes by providing an adequate range of effective techniques targeting all three response modalities. This provision of effective techniques can, in turn, be guided by adopting a *technically eclectic* intervention approach.

TECHNICAL ECLECTICISM IN CBT

Proponents of technical eclecticism subscribe to one particular theory yet use, when needed, techniques from different therapeutic approaches to address best a client's problem (Prochaska & Norcross, 1994). For example, a cognitive behaviour therapist may use the Gestalt technique of the "empty chair" in order to help an "emotionally unaware" person; however, the rationale for using this technique would be couched in (no pun intended) CBT terms. Lazarus (1967) laid the foundations for technical eclecticism in CBT by encouraging behaviour therapists to use any techniques that had been proven to be effective, including cognitive ones (Kwee & Lazarus, 1987). Approaches within the CBT movement such as multimodal therapy (MMT) (Lazarus, 1989), cognitive behaviour modification (CBM) (Meichenbaum, 1977), and stress inoculation training (SIT) (Meichenbaum, 1985) are characterised by technical eclecticism: they are multifaceted and designed to influence all the three response systems that constitute a psychological problem, such as TA (Denney, 1980). To this end, a number of techniques may be adopted, including deep breathing, muscle relaxation, biofeedback, self-instructional training, cognitive restructuring, imagery rehearsal, insight training, and problem solving.

The CBM and SIT approaches have been rather extensively evaluated in TA intervention outcome research (for reviews, see Spielberger & Vagg, 1995b; Zeidner, 1998). For example, a meta-analytic study by Hembree (1988) found that CBM procedures are equally effective in reducing the cognitive and emotionality components of TA. Furthermore, they were shown to be helpful in raising test performance by approximately one-half of a standard deviation in school-aged pupils, and three-quarters of one standard deviation in tertiary (undergraduate) students. Likewise, the SIT approach has been shown to be effective in treating TA (e.g., Meichenbaum, 1972) and other "performance anxieties" (e.g., Altmaier et al., 1982; Sweeney & Horan, 1982). Recent research has also documented the utility of a technically eclectic psychoeducational approach in a public health context. For example, Brown et al. (2000) offered stress management workshops, involving a combination of CBT techniques, to the general public. A group who received one day of training showed significant reductions in anxiety and stress at a three-month follow-up, compared to a waiting-list control group.

An interesting comparison can be made between TA intervention studies and research evaluating stress management interventions (SMIs) in the workplace. Specifically, both have tended to utilise technically eclectic, cognitive behavioural approaches for dealing with strain, and both are often offered as a preventive, as opposed to a curative, measure (Murphy, 1988). Consistent with a tripartite response system and technically eclectic approach to treatment, two reviews of the worksite SMI literature conclude that a combination of CBT intervention techniques is best for reducing stress-related outcomes (e.g., mental ill-health) (Murphy, 1984, 1996).

A number of authors have drawn attention to conceptual and design issues in the implementation of such SMIs (e.g., Bunce, 1997; Reynolds & Shapiro, 1991; Reynolds et al., 1993a & b; Sallis et al., 1987). A key issue in this respect concerns findings which suggest that SMIs differing in technical content can lead to a broadly similar change in outcome (Bunce, 1997), a phenomenon known as the "equivalence paradox" (Stiles et al., 1986). In view of this, Bunce (1997) encourages researchers to isolate mechanisms of change (mediators) in SMIs, a practice aimed at identifying process variables through which differing interventions have their effects. In line with this recommendation for SMIs, we have identified mediators of change in the evaluation anxiety context, based on the manual outlined later in this chapter (Keogh et al., in preparation).

In summary, treatments for TA have developed hand-in-hand with theoretical and technical developments in the general CBT literature. Thus, during the 1960s, behavioural techniques were the treatment of choice; during the 1970s, the "cognitive revolution" took hold and TA treatment protocols incorporated cognitive techniques. Finally, conceptual developments in TA, and anxiety in general, produced a synthesis of cognitive, behavioural, and physiological oriented interventions. In particular, adopting a tripartite response system analysis led to the development of multifaceted treatment interventions, such as MMT, CBM, and SIT, which are characterised by technical eclecticism. In keeping with this symbiotic, developmental history linking CBT and TA, contemporary TA treatment approaches would do well to incorporate current developments from the CBT literature. Indeed, as noted by Lazarus (1992), technically eclectic approaches to CBT encourage continual scanning of the intervention field for better assessment and treatment methods. Scanning the contemporary CBT literature now reveals a recent development that has particular relevance for the alleviation of evaluation strain: *metacognition*.

METACOGNITION: POSITIVE AND NEGATIVE BELIEFS ABOUT WORRY

Metacognition involves the appraisal of cognition itself (e.g., I can't control my thoughts) as opposed to the appraisal of external events (e.g., what if I fail this exam?) and bodily sensations (e.g., my heart is beating too fast). Traditional CBT accounts of emotional disorders have tended to promote the importance of the last two appraisals in the development of psychopathology (Wells, 1995). However, theoretical and empirical research by Wells (see Wells, Chapter 6, this volume) now suggests that metacognition plays an important role in the development and maintenance of problematic worry, which is an important characteristic of various anxiety disorders, including TA (e.g., Wells & Matthews, 1994). Wells (1995) hypothesises that the role metacognition takes in the maintenance of problematic worry is in the form of positive and negative metabeliefs about worry.

Positive metabeliefs about the usefulness of worrying as a coping strategy seem to operate around a theme of "threat avoidance" (Borkovec, 1994; Borkovec et al., 1999; Wells, Chapter 6, this volume). These beliefs may be superstitious in nature ("worrying makes it less likely that a feared event will occur"), or they may involve coping preparation ("worrying about a predicted negative event helps me to prepare for its occurrence"), or they may involve viewing worry as a motivational force ("worrying helps to motivate me to accomplish the work that needs to be done"). According to Wells (1995), such beliefs about the advantages of worrying, or the costs of not worrying, are likely to contribute to longer periods of worry. Furthermore, people may, unhelpfully, credit worry with the non-occurrence of a negative event, reinforcing the belief that worry functions as an effective coping mechanism (Borkovec et al., 1999; Wells, 1995). Such positive beliefs about worry are thought to be common, not only in clinically anxious people, but in the general population as well (e.g., Cartwright-Hatton & Wells, 1997).

In addition to these positive beliefs concerning worry, some individuals also develop negative beliefs about worry. These tend, particularly, to centre on the perceived uncontrollable and/or harmful nature of worry. Wells suggests that such negative, metacognitive beliefs can lead to "Type 2" worry (or metaworry), which is, essentially, worry about worry (Wells, 1997). According to Wells (1995), it is people's development of type 2 worry that accounts for their transition from normal to pathological worry. People with GAD are thought to be worriers who are in a state of dissonance that is created by the co-occurrence of positive and negative beliefs about worry (see Wells, Chapter 6, this volume).

The fact that worry is a defining characteristic of both GAD and TA suggests that Wells' (1995) metacognitive model holds particular relevance for the conceptualisation and treatment of evaluation strain. In this regard, Flett & Blankstein (1994) note that, "the treatment of GAD is relevant to TA treatment and vice versa" (p. 172). Moreover, Wells (2000) views GAD as the most "normal" of the anxiety disorders (p. 155). He suggests that an understanding of the cognitive processes involved in the disorder can contribute to an understanding of anxiety vulnerability more generally.

This hypothesised common ground between metacognition in GAD and TA has been directly tested in a study by Matthews et al. (1999). These authors used the Metacognitions Questionnaire (MCQ) (Cartwright-Hatton & Wells, 1997) to demonstrate the importance of positive and negative metacognitive beliefs about worry in TA. The MCQ includes five subscales designed to measure positive and negative beliefs about worry, metacognitive monitoring, and judgements of cognitive efficiency. Matthews et al. (1999) found significant correlations between these metacognitive dimensions and the four dimensions of TA (tension, worry, test-irrelevant thinking, and bodily symptoms) as measured by Sarason's (1984) reactions to tests (RTT) questionnaire. In particular, negative beliefs about the uncontrollable and harmful nature of worry were positively related to all four of the TA dimensions, while positive beliefs about worry were positively correlated with tension and bodily symptoms. Matthews et al. (1999) also demonstrated a link between metacognitive beliefs, worry, and coping in an evaluation context. Specifically, factor analysis of the measures used in their study produced a general metacognitive factor, which included all of the MCQ scales, a measure of worry, and "emotion-focused" coping. This factor was significantly and positively correlated with all four of the RTT scales. These findings suggest that TA relates to various aspects of cognition, spanning metacognition, worry, and maladaptive coping strategies.

This recent demonstration of an overlap between TA, metacognition, and coping holds implications for the prevention and treatment of evaluation strain. Indeed, Matthews et al. (1999) highlight the importance of considering both metacognition and maladaptive coping in the treatment of TA. For the modification of metacognitive beliefs, they suggest that

CBT techniques, used for disorders such as GAD, may be applied "straightforwardly" to TA (p. 123). Thus, techniques developed by Wells (1997) for modifying metacognitive beliefs in GAD patients may offer an effective method for reducing the impact of worry in evaluation anxiety. These techniques include verbal reattribution methods, which challenge the validity of an individual's beliefs about worry (e.g., by reviewing situations when worry was displaced by alternative activities), behavioural exercises such as encouraging worriers to "postpone" their worry, and "mismatch" strategies involving a comparison of the content of worry with the actual outcome from the worried about event (see Wells [1997] for a full description of these techniques).

It is also important to consider the treatment implications that stem from the finding that maladaptive coping strategies (i.e., emotion-focus and avoidance) relate to both metacognitive beliefs and TA. As Matthews et al. (1999) note, TA stemming from inadequate coping skills may require training in the use of task-focus coping. This treatment requirement can be met by techniques that direct attention away from interfering worry and bodily sensations and back toward the task. In this regard, Borkovec et al. (1999) discuss the incorporation of "attention-directing" instructions into traditional relaxation methods. To elaborate, these authors encourage individuals with GAD (which is associated with high levels of muscle tension) to practice shifting their attention to "present-moment" experience as soon as they achieve relaxation. Such attention-directing instructions have previously been shown to reduce cognitive interference and to improve the performance of test-anxious students (e.g., Sarason, 1984).

In sum, metacognitive beliefs about worry appear to be related to TA. It would appear, therefore, that treatments for TA and evaluation strain are likely to be enhanced by the inclusion of metacognitive techniques. Furthermore, the finding that metacognitive beliefs relate to maladaptive coping strategies calls for the inclusion of task-focus training in performance-related settings. Both types of technique hold considerable promise for alleviating the impact of worry in evaluative situations.

For these reasons, the treatment protocol we detail in the remainder of the chapter incorporates both metacognitive techniques and task-focus instruction within a technically eclectic, brief CBT framework. In so doing, it builds upon the history of TA treatment by taking heed of the latest developments in the CBT literature. In our opinion, these developments constitute a new and exciting era in the treatment and prevention of evaluation strain.

THE MANUAL

Context

The manual presented in the final part of this chapter was developed for use with Year 11 pupils (aged 15 and 16 years) at a secondary school in the UK. This is the academic year in which pupils complete the General Certificate of Secondary Education (GCSE) assessments, in the form of nationally standardised coursework and examinations. GCSEs serve as a critical step for students wishing to secure a place at university and, thus, perhaps unsurprisingly, media accounts of high student stress levels abound just before people take these exams each summer. Consistent with these anecdotal reports, a study that we carried out at the school, identified TA as a significant predictor of performance, above and beyond intelligence (Keogh et al., in preparation). As a result of these findings, the head teacher (principal) at the school we examined wished to collaborate in an intervention study, designed to improve performance. It is the manual that we used in this intervention study that we present here.

Intervention Study Participants

The total Year 11 cohort consisted of 209 pupils (113 boys, 96 girls), with a mean age of 15.6 years. From this pool, 80 individuals (40 boys, 40 girls) were randomly selected to take part in "stress management workshops". It was hoped that such random selection would allow the results of the experiment to be generalised to the "typical" British classroom.

Participants attended 10 weekly, one-hour workshops during school hours, missing one of their timetabled lessons each week. None of the workshop sessions had more than 10 students. The days and times of the weekly sessions were alternated to ensure that participants would not be absent from the same curriculum subject each week. Members of staff were made aware of the timetable for the workshops, and measures were put in place to allow participants to catch up on any missed material.

Delivery Format

Although the manual consists of 10, one-hour sessions, we believe that this treatment format could be altered. For example, the sessions could be collapsed such that they are presented in a "2 + 1" delivery model (e.g., Barkham, 1989; Barkham & Shapiro, 1990). Such a model involves two sessions being offered on consecutive weeks, followed by a third sometime later, with each session lasting approximately three hours. Although this type of design has not been evaluated in the TA treatment literature, Bond & Bunce (2000) have adopted it successfully in two (adult) worksite SMIs.

Manual Content

The manual involves both didactic teaching components and numerous active learning exercises and homework assignments. We have attempted to make these as relevant as possible to the 15–16-year-old students who participated. To this end, we encouraged participants to offer specific examples that could be used to illustrate the nature of evaluation strain. The importance of student collaboration in shaping the manual content became evident during the initial stages of the school intervention. Specifically, we began by discussing how the workshops could provide useful skills for coping with examination stress. However, because of the temporal distance between the examinations and the beginning of the SMI (June and January, respectively), the participants were not primarily concerned about exams at that time. They were, in fact, much more concerned with the ongoing coursework assignments that are included in the overall GSCE assessment. As a result, we changed tack and, in the beginning sessions, used the coursework requirements, not the exams, as a useful example of a "stressor" that could illustrate a source of evaluative strain.

Although the examples contained in the manual are relevant to the school cohort that participated in this experiment, we are keen to promote this protocol as a useful tool in the alleviation and prevention of many types of evaluation strain. Thus, we hope that minor adjustments to the level of information and the examples used will allow its adaptation to other contexts.

The manual incorporates the following 10 sessions:

1. Education phase I—A definition of "stress"
2. Education phase II—When stress becomes a problem
3. Thoughts, emotion, and behaviour
4. Relaxation I—Progressive muscular relaxation (PMR)
5. Relaxation II—Shortened relaxation techniques
6. Worry I—The nature and function of worry
7. Worry II—Modifying metabeliefs
8. Problem solving
9. Imagery
10. Review.

Up to a point, our manual is similar to existing technically eclectic CBT approaches such as SIT (Meichenbaum, 1985) and CBM (Meichenbaum, 1977). Thus, the first two sessions involve a conceptualisation of evaluation strain within a cognitive behavioural model, and, as in SIT, we have included a combination of relaxation training and cognitive strategies. Our training protocol differs from these previous approaches, however, by incorporating a major focus on worry (sessions 6 and 7), which has been guided by recent developments in the cognitive behavioural literature.

An important issue with regard to the technical content concerns the omission of a study skills training (SST) component. SST usually provides information on structuring study time, and effective methods of encoding, organising, processing, and storing information (Zeidner, 1998). Some TA authors have recommended the inclusion of SST in intervention studies (e.g., Dendato & Diener, 1986; Naveh-Benjamin, 1991). There is, however, a danger of overloading the participants with too much information (e.g., Gonzalez, 1995), and this was a concern in the school context. Moreover, Vagg & Spielberger (1995) note that other cognitive training components in such interventions already aid students in organising and structuring their activities in evaluative situations.

Evaluation

The school prevention programme, reflected in the manual detailed below, produced several benefits for pupils who attended the stress management workshops (Keogh et al., in preparation). Specifically, our intervention resulted in significantly lower levels of stress, depression, and dysfunctional attitudes, as compared to our control group. The programme also led to higher levels of motivation and, most importantly perhaps, GCSE performance. In fact, GCSE scores were significantly higher in the intervention group (mean = 59.53) than they were in the control group (mean = 50.32), based on the following grade points system: $A^* = 8, A = 7$, down to $F = 2$. Furthermore, we identified motivation and dysfunctional attitudes as mechanisms, or mediators, by which our intervention led to these improvements.

SESSION 1: EDUCATION PHASE I—A DEFINITION OF "STRESS"

Overview

The first two sessions, termed "Education phases I and II", define stress and anxiety. We place particular emphasis on explaining the bodily, emotional, cognitive, and behavioural manifestations of stress, and we attempt to socialise the students into the cognitive behavioural model (Wells, 1997). A description is thus provided of the reciprocal links between the various response modalities (i.e., bodily, emotional, cognitive, and behavioural). This serves as an explanatory model for understanding the nature and treatment of stress and anxiety. Every effort is made at this early stage to highlight the collaborative nature of this training, which we promote by eliciting examples of strain from, and therefore relevant to, the group.

Introduction

The concept of "evaluation stress" is discussed. Participants are told that, over the coming weeks, they will learn practical coping skills that will help them cope with such stress.

> These coping skills involve a number of exercises that require a fair amount of practice. To encourage you to practise, some homework assignments will be set, but they will not be too demanding, requiring work only a few times each week. Although the main focus of the weekly sessions is on exam and evaluation stress, you can apply the coping skills you learn in other areas of your lives.

What Is Stress?

The above question is posed to the group. They are encouraged to offer symptoms or any other words used to describe stress. The trainer facilitates a brief discussion of what stress means to them, and how it affects their lives. It is explained that a crucial first step in overcoming stress is recognising it whenever and wherever it occurs—"The first step to managing it is to become aware of it."

Origins of the Stress Response—"Fight or Flight"

Students are introduced to the idea that the stress response, in certain situations, is extremely beneficial, and are provided with the evolutionary backdrop to this benefit.

> Although we often talk about stress as a negative thing, it is in fact a normal reaction that has evolved in humans and animals to ensure their survival. Stress and anxiety in primitive humans constituted the in-built responses that helped them to fight or flee in the face of danger, and so survive. In the primitive environment many dangers were physical and life-threatening (e.g., being attacked by a predator), and so the stress response made both the mind and body alert to threats. Even in the modern world we sometimes face physical

threats such as being attacked by a dog, or being threatened by someone. The way we react to such physical threats is perfectly normal and helpful. As soon as we become aware of danger, certain things happen to our bodies, to our minds and to our behaviour, all of which are designed to make us react to physical threat in a suitable way. Let us look at each of these response systems in turn.

Bodily Response (or Physiology)

When humans perceive danger, a message is sent to the nervous system. Certain parts of the nervous system then get the body ready for action (fight or flight). Two chemicals, *adrenaline* and *noradrenaline*, are released from the adrenal glands on the top of the kidneys.

These bodily reactions make our hearts beat faster and stronger, speeding up blood flow around the body, blood pressure increases, and our bodies become tense, preparing us for action. Blood is redirected away from our skin, fingers, and toes to our major muscles where it is likely to be needed. This redirection of blood is a useful evolutionary characteristic—if we are being attacked and our bodies are cut, less blood will be lost. This is also why people who are highly stressed or anxious sometimes look pale.

All of these bodily changes are also accompanied by an increased breathing rate which gets more oxygen through our bodies, further preparing us for action. We also experience an increase in perspiration (sweating). This no doubt evolved to keep the body from overheating during dangerous encounters. Finally, there is a decrease in the activity of our digestive systems (we don't need to be digesting food while we tackle a predator).

Thinking Response

The main thing that happens to our mind when we are threatened is that it becomes much more focused on the source of the perceived threat. This increase in attention on the source of danger (e.g., a predator) ensures that we obtain all the necessary information to allow us to make the appropriate response (e.g., escape!).

Behavioural Response

The behavioural response to physical threat is normally in the form of fight or flight (i.e., an aggressive urge to stand and fight, or to escape from the situation). This is again the ideal reaction when we are faced with an immediate physical threat.

Emotional Response (Feelings)

Humans experience a wide range of emotions. When faced with physical threats, we experience feelings of fear or possibly aggressive feelings in line with our fight or flight tendencies. Although most people are familiar with these emotions, they are quite difficult to explain in words. Emotions are essentially the product of an interaction between our minds (e.g., perceiving a threat) and our physiological reactions (e.g., butterflies in the tummy).

The majority of the threats we face today are far more discrete and far less (if at all) threatening to our existence; e.g., exams, coursework deadlines, family problems, delays, and social situations. However, if we *perceive* these things as threatening, then our bodily, thinking, and behavioural responses are the same as when we are faced with an immediate physical threat.

How Our Bodily Sensations, Feelings, Thoughts, and Behaviour Interact

Although the bodily, thinking, and behaving responses to stress have been mentioned separately, they do have effects on each other. In particular, as we just discussed, the bodily response and the thinking response can interact to produce feelings (emotions) such as fear and anxiety. These feelings can then have an influence on how we will behave. The following example illustrates how the different responses influence each other. [Adapted from Holdsworth & Paxton, 1999.] Imagine that a friend of yours walks past you on the street and doesn't say anything or even acknowledge you. You *think* your friend has ignored you. Because you think this, you *feel* angry (your heart pounds, and your body becomes tense). Now that you feel angry, you walk after him and tell him that he is rude (*behaviour*). Your friend is surprised. He tells you that he was thinking about something and didn't see you! When he tells you this, you no longer think your friend was ignoring you, you no longer feel angry, and your behaviour towards him will change. This diagram [Figure 12.1] shows all the ways in which the different responses are related.

Note that in the example of your friend "ignoring" you, it is the *thought or belief* about the situation that results in the other reactions (i.e., anger and confrontation). This is an important link to understand. Situations and events do not *directly* result in stress; rather, it is our interpretation of the situation or event that is crucial. We will talk more about the importance of our thoughts and beliefs in the future sessions.

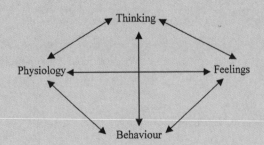

Figure 12.1 Interacting response systems

Homework

Participants are given a sheet to record any bodily, thinking, behavioural, or feeling responses they have in challenging or threatening situations.

While describing the importance of the homework assignments, the trainer assures participants that they do not have to share personal information in the group if they do not want to.

SESSION 2: EDUCATION PHASE II—WHEN STRESS BECOMES A PROBLEM

Overview

The second "education" session continues by describing the different response modalities through which strain can be manifested. This is achieved by detailing how the responses described in the first session can become maladaptive. This is followed by a discussion of how the modalities interact to produce "vicious cycles" that may maintain maladaptive responding.

Recap

The session begins by recapping the different human response systems described in the previous session.

Unhelpful Stress Response

So, we have seen that the stress response is useful in situations where there is an immediate threat or danger. The stress response was, however, designed to switch off once the threat had passed. The non-physical "threats" we face in the modern world such as coursework deadlines or relationship problems often take a while to resolve. As a result, our bodies and minds may be responding to such situations for long periods of time, or the response may be too extreme for the situation. As a result, the stress response, which was helpful in the face of an immediate physical threat, may become *unhelpful* and thus a problem.

Now look at this stress-performance curve [Figure 12.2]. This graph applies to challenging situations in which we have to perform, such as exams or social situations. When a certain stress level is reached, performance starts to drop. This is because we can become distracted by the stress response so that we are less able to concentrate on what we are doing. The point at which stress becomes a problem is different for everyone, as are the situations that bring about stress. The important thing is for us to become aware of how we are reacting to challenging situations so that we know when the stress response is becoming unhelpful.

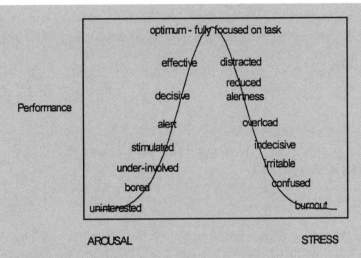

Figure 12.2   The stress-performance curve

In the same way as we did in the last session, let's look at the different systems of the stress response, and the forms they can take as they become unhelpful and problematic.

Unhelpful Bodily Response (Physiology)

If we are stressed for a long period, the muscle tension in the body can lead to unpleasant feelings of tension. We may experience this as a stiff neck or shoulders. The muscle tension may also bring about trembling and shaking in the body. The mouth can go dry when we are stressed, and this is sometimes experienced as a difficulty in swallowing. The slowdown in the digestive system can produce feelings of nausea. The change in our breathing pattern can make us feel light-headed, and we may experience blurred vision and a ringing in the ears. These bodily changes are not necessarily dangerous, but we can start to notice them and to focus on them more than is necessary.

Notice the "unhelpful" nature of these bodily changes. See how this contrasts with what we discussed in the last session, where we saw that the bodily reaction to physical threat is extremely helpful.

Unhelpful Thinking Response

We saw in the last session that when we are faced with a physical threat, our minds focus on the source of the threat or danger. When we face non-physical threats, such as deadlines or relationship problems, we may spend a lot of time thinking about possible sources of threat. This can be unhelpful in such situations because it again means that we are less able to concentrate on what is actually going on (e.g., coursework preparation). Being constantly on the lookout for threat and danger results in our worrying and feeling pretty miserable.

Stress-related thinking often becomes biased toward a negative interpretation of events. This means that we start to develop an exaggeratedly negative thinking style that involves predicting the most extreme negative outcomes to situations. This type of thinking is sometimes called "catastrophising". Here are some examples of this type of negative thinking:

A person makes one mistake on coursework and thinks, "I never do anything right."

"My friends haven't called me today: they must not like me—they think I'm worthless."

It is also common for stressed people to ignore positive things that happen and focus only on the negative. For example, students may focus on one poor grade, even though they also received a range of good grades. Stress is also sometimes connected to a "perfectionist" thinking style; e.g., "If my work isn't perfect it isn't acceptable"; "If I don't get an 'A' I'm a failure." [The trainer elicits examples of a negative thinking bias from the group.]

This kind of extreme "catastrophic" thinking can make us feel anxious and unhappy. Always being on the lookout for negative things diverts our attention from actually solving the problems we face. Also, such extreme styles of thinking rarely offer an accurate reflection of reality.

Unhelpful Behavioural Response

One of the most common behavioural reactions to stress is to try to escape from or *avoid* the source of the stress. If the source of the stress is an annoyed and hungry tiger, avoidance seems like a sensible thing to do. If, however, the source of stress is a coursework deadline, an exam, or a relationship concern, then avoidance is one of the worst things we can do. There are many ways we avoid doing things like our coursework; for example, we might watch TV or spend a lot of time organising notes without actually doing any work. In fact, avoidance is an unhelpful response in most situations, as we typically need to face up to, and deal with, challenging events. If we don't, our self-confidence can suffer, and the stress can get worse. Also, the more situations we avoid, the less likely it is that we will be able to achieve our goals and live a happy and fulfilled life.

Another common unhelpful behavioural response is to indulge in unhealthy behaviours such as eating and drinking the wrong kinds of food and drinks (e.g., sweets, chips, and sugary or caffeine drinks), or smoking. When we are faced with life's challenges, we need to be as healthy as possible. Doing unhealthy things affects our immune systems and makes us more likely to become ill, resulting in more stress.

Unhelpful Emotional Response

Experiencing emotions is part of the human condition. The emotional response can become unhelpful if the emotion we experience is too excessive or inappropriate for a particular situation. For example, feeling "concerned" about coursework deadlines or social situations is fine, but if that concern becomes extreme anxiety, it may interfere with our performing well.

Vicious Cycles of Stress

As we discussed in the last session, these response systems (bodily, thinking, behavioural, and emotional), although mentioned separately, interact in important ways. Also, the systems often interact in such a way as to produce a "vicious cycle" of stress, keeping us stressed and anxious for longer than is necessary.

For example, people who experience panic attacks become fearful of the bodily response to stress, such as a rapidly beating heart or dizziness. They may think that these symptoms indicate a serious health problem such as a heart attack. Because people become anxious about their own bodily response, these bodily reactions increase in intensity, and so the people become even more anxious, until they are in such a state of distress that they panic. This type of vicious cycle is sometimes referred to as a "fear of fear", because it is the reaction to fear itself that keeps fear and stress going. Likewise, those who have to give a speech or a talk to the class may be fearful that the audience will notice their shaking or sweating. They may be frightened of being embarrassed, increasing the intensity of the bodily response, and so the cycle goes on.

Another vicious cycle can start up when people *worry* excessively. As we will see in some of the future sessions, worry involves a constant stream of negative interpretations and predictions. Some people who worry become concerned that they may be going "mad" because of their constant worrying. Thus, they become worried about worry.

Avoiding situations (unhelpful behavioural response) can also set us on a vicious cycle of stress. When we avoid situations we are worried about, we never learn to cope in those situations. For example, a pupil who is very afraid of school may never go in and may even end up being taught at home. This is not very helpful because such pupils will not learn that school can in fact be a safe place, and so they will always remain fearful of school.

Homework

The participants are asked to fill in a record sheet similar to the one used in the previous homework assignment. This time they are asked to note down any problematic aspects of the stress response modalities. They are also asked to plot these "unhelpful" aspects on a vicious cycle. The participants are told that the purpose of this exercise is to increase awareness of how they respond to life's demands. The trainer goes through an example in the session to aid understanding.

SESSION 3: THOUGHTS, EMOTION, AND BEHAVIOUR

Overview

The first two "education" sessions were designed to introduce the general idea that stress involves the interplay between a set of response systems (bodily, thinking, behavioural, and emotional). Session 3 follows on from this by focusing more on the nature of this interplay. Specifically, in this session, the importance of thoughts, beliefs, and interpretations (the cognitive response modality) is emphasised. Also, the ways in which different types of belief impact upon the affective and behavioural response systems are illustrated. Finally, participants are taught methods for challenging problematic modes of thinking and are given the opportunity to practise these methods in session.

The structure and the exercises in the first half of this session are adapted from Free's (1999) cognitive therapy manual.

Recap

While reviewing the homework assignment, the trainer reiterates the ways in which the response modalities (bodily, thinking, feeling, and behavioural) can interact to produce vicious cycles of stress.

The purpose of session 3 is as follows:

— explaining how our feelings and our behaviours are linked to our thoughts
— teaching you how to become aware of and analyse your thoughts
— teaching you how to challenge unrealistic negative thinking patterns.

How Our Feelings and Behaviours Are Linked to Our Thoughts

In the section below, Ellis' (1977) A-B-C model is used to demonstrate the mediational role cognitions play in eliciting different kinds of emotional response. Relevant examples are inserted into the A-B-C sequence to show how different beliefs about the same situation can result in contrasting emotional consequences (e.g., anxiety vs. excitement). Free (1999) recommends introducing the A-B-C process by eliciting examples of how *other* people would react. This should then lead to participants being able to identify their own response sequences, but avoids any defenciveness involved in self-disclosure.

To help you understand the important influence our thoughts have on how we feel and behave, imagine you are playing or watching a football match, and the referee blows his whistle for a penalty. We will experience different emotions when the referee blows his whistle, depending on whether we think the penalty is fair or not (e.g., is the penalty given for or against our team?) That is, it is our *interpretation* or *belief* about the situation that dictates how we will subsequently feel and behave.

This sequence of events in which our thoughts come between things that happen in our lives and the feelings we experience is sometimes called the *A-B-C sequence.*

A stands for an *activating event* (the referee blowing his whistle).

B is for *belief* or thought (whether we think the penalty is fair or not).

C is for emotional and behavioural *consequences*—the emotion you feel (e.g., excitement, joy, anger, disappointment, fear, etc.), and the way you behave (e.g., jumping up and down with joy, or shouting at the referee!).

There are lots of different A's, B's, and C's. In these sessions we are mainly discussing the negative or unhelpful B's and C's that can get in the way of our living a happy and fulfilled life.

A's can be any event such as seeing a vicious-looking dog, coursework deadlines, having exams, or experiencing a relationship break-up. A can also be an "internal" event such as shakiness, butterflies in the tummy, or a heart pounding.

B's can be unhelpful beliefs or attitudes like "I *must* always get A grades", or "If I fail I'm useless". They can be brief, automatic thoughts or worries like, "I'll be no good at this", "I won't be able to do that", or more general beliefs such as "I'm no good".

There are also different kinds of C's (emotional and behavioural consequences). In these sessions we are particularly concerned with feelings of anxiety or fear. These emotions are also linked to how we will behave in the face of a particular situation; e.g., we may *avoid* going to a party if we are nervous.

It is easier to see the relationship between the A, B, and C components by putting them in a three-column format like this:

A (*Activating event*)	**B** (*Belief or interpretation*)	**C** (*Consequence*)
Noise during the night	• *someone breaking in* • *neighbour's cat*	• *fear* • *annoyance*

So, imagine that the A (activating) event is a noise you hear during the night. Imagine that the thought is, "someone is breaking in and will cause me harm". What would the emotional and behavioural consequences be? What if the B thought was, "Oh, it's the neighbour's cat again",—what would the emotion and behaviour be?

Exercise: The A-B-C model

The participants are given the opportunity to try some pre-set examples. Some "A" event examples are a coursework deadline, going to a party, and giving a speech to an audience. The participants are asked to come up with different thoughts and beliefs (B) that people may have about these events, and the likely emotional and behavioural consequences (C) of those thoughts.

So, you can see that the way we think about an activating event determines our subsequent emotions and behaviours; thus, if we can challenge the way we think (B) about an event (A), we can then change the emotional and behavioural consequences (C) that we experience. Such a change can be extremely beneficial if we are prone to unhelpful or unrealistically negative thoughts about challenging situations.

Now I am going to show you how to become more aware of the thoughts and beliefs you have (B), particularly in stressful situations (A). Gaining such awareness is crucial, as you can't do anything about unhelpful beliefs, emotions, and behaviours until you can identify them and what triggers them.

Becoming Aware of Thoughts and Beliefs

Becoming aware of negative thoughts and beliefs is important because they often occur automatically without our being aware of them. When we do notice them, we often view them as if they were a true reflection of reality. For example, if someone is nervous about going to a party, they become convinced there really is something to be nervous about, even though, in reality, there may not be.

To help you to become aware of the thoughts and beliefs you have in stressful situations, I am going to tell you about a "thought-catching" exercise. This exercise draws a comparison between "catching" thoughts and catching a shy animal.

The Thought-Catching Exercise [Adapted from Free, 1999: P. 61]

Catching your negative thoughts is like hunting a very shy animal, capturing it alive, and taking it back to a zoo to be tamed. First of all you need to know what the animal looks like. We have some knowledge of the characteristics of negative thoughts from the last session. We can look for their tracks or droppings. We can tell where they've been by the emotion they leave behind—a stab of anxiety, a brief sinking feeling, a flash of anger. Be on the lookout for those signs, and see if you can catch a glimpse of the negative thoughts that precede the emotion. As you get used to it, you will be able to see more of the negative thought, until you are able to write it down in a complete sentence.

Another thing you can do is to study the habits of the negative thoughts. See what time of day they come out, and in what circumstances. You can then be waiting the next day, or the next time you are in a similar situation.

Or you can set traps for the negative thought. You can set up a situation in which you think they are likely to occur. If parties make you anxious, go to one, and see what negative thoughts you have. Once you know your negative thoughts and worries, you can put them in the A-B-C framework to become really aware of the effect they have.

So, in summary, thought catching involves:

1. knowing the characteristics of negative thoughts
2. looking for their tracks, i.e., the emotion they leave behind
3. knowing their habits and being on the lookout for them
4. setting traps.

Are Your Thoughts and Beliefs Realistic?

The next section in session 3 involves encouraging participants to question the validity of their cognitions that may emerge from the self-awareness process. Thus, the series of questions below (adapted from Meichenbaum, 1985) set up cognitions as "hypotheses worthy of testing". This questioning style can help individuals view their cognitions as "possibilities" as opposed to "certainties".

Worrisome and negative thoughts often contain certain types of thinking errors. We saw some of these thinking errors in the last session. People who are stressed tend to ignore positive aspects of situations or themselves, to "catastrophise" and jump to (often negative) conclusions.

There are a number of probing questions you can ask yourselves to test your thoughts against reality, helping you to avoid falling into these negative and distorted thinking styles:

— What is at stake?
— Does the situation reflect a *threat* signalling potential harm, or a *challenge*, signalling an opportunity?
— Do I have the resources to handle this situation?
— Am I concentrating on the negative things and ignoring the positives?
— How do I know that the feared event will happen?
— Are there other ways of looking at the situation?
— Have I only had failures in these situations in the past, or were there times I did OK?
— What am I saying to myself right now?
— What is the evidence for my conclusion?
— Is there evidence that contradicts this conclusion?

Such questions are designed to help you test the "reality" of your negative thoughts and worries (i.e., do they really represent the facts of the situation?). The more you practise asking yourselves such questions in stressful situations, the more effectively you will be able to notice your own thinking errors whenever they occur. It is useful for us to see how extreme negative thoughts don't necessarily reflect reality, and can be challenged. Once we realise this, we can stop focusing on them so much and focus on the actual situation instead.

Exercise: Challenging "unrealistic" negative thinking

The participants are put into pairs for this exercise. Each pair is given two or three "irrational" cognitions (e.g., If I'm not liked by everyone, I'm worthless; if I fail my exam/coursework, it means I'm a complete idiot). One member of each pair (the "unrealistic thinker") is asked to read out the thought to the other (the "challenger"); the challenger is asked to go through the list of reality-testing questions (e.g., what is the evidence for that conclusion?). The challenger is then asked to come up with a more balanced, "realistic" thought for the situation or topic. Individuals take turns at being the challenger and being the unrealistic thinker.

After this exercise, the unrealistic thinker's thought and the challenger's thought are entered into the A-B-C framework, and the different emotional and behavioural consequences of each are discussed.

The trainer emphasises that although, in this exercise, someone else is challenging the irrational thoughts, the goal is for the participants to practise challenging their own negative thinking patterns.

So, the aim is to be aware that, when we face challenging situations, we often accept these negative conclusions and interpretations as "certainties" or "truths". They often involve absolutist thinking, using words like *always, never, must, can't*, etc. By asking ourselves the questions just outlined, we can learn to turn the certainties of negative outcomes into possibilities (e.g., by asking how likely is it that the feared outcome will occur). In this way, we can learn to develop a more balanced interpretation of events and situations that will reduce unpleasant feelings like anxiety and depression, and will stop us behaving in unhelpful ways (e.g., by avoiding situations).

This process of challenging extreme negative thinking patterns is a skill that can be learnt. It's just like learning to play a sport or a musical instrument—it takes practise. I will be encouraging you to practise this over the coming weeks. The more you practise, the more likely the skill will become a part of your everyday life.

[Homework]

It is important for you to become aware of the interactive nature of the different ways you personally respond to situations. Over the next week, use the shy animal exercise and the A-B-C framework to see how you personally react. In particular, make note of (a) the situations that make you stressed, (b) what thoughts you have, and (c) what kinds of emotions and behaviours are linked to those thoughts.

Once you are aware of your own thinking styles, use the probing questions (outlined above) to assess how useful or realistic they are. To do this, take one particular worry or negative belief you have about a situation and jot down an answer to each of the questions for that thought. Is the thought realistic? Are there other ways to look at the situation? See if you can come up with a more balanced realistic thought or belief about the situation.

SESSION 4: RELAXATION I—PROGRESSIVE MUSCULAR RELAXATION (PMR)

Overview

By this stage, the participants are hopefully developing an understanding of the reciprocal nature of the different response modalities in stressful evaluative situations. In line with this aim, the previous session, which primarily focused on the cognitive modality, involved instruction on how cognitions impact upon the other response modalities.

The relaxation exercises introduced in session 4 are offered *primarily* as a means of reducing the unhelpful aspects of the *bodily response*, such as excessive tension, light-headedness, and trembling. The interactive response system theme continues, however, with instruction on how reducing bodily arousal can help reduce maladaptive responding in the other response systems. An important issue in this respect is that the participants' attention can be drawn to such bodily manifestations of stress at the expense of focusing on the task at hand. Thus, the relaxation exercises are discussed alongside instruction on diverting attention back toward dealing with evaluative situations.

A full discussion of the relaxation techniques used in these sessions can be found else-where (e.g., Bernstein & Borkovec, 1973; Öst, 1987). The exercises themselves are designed so that individuals can progress from the relatively time-consuming tense-relax exercises, taught in session 4, to exercises which take up little time, and that are convenient enough to use in everyday situations (in session 5).

From the outset of session 4, relaxation is introduced as an active coping skill that requires a fair amount of practice. Drawing comparisons to athletic and artistic endeavours is useful here, equating the learning of relaxation skills with the learning of other skills, such as swimming or playing a musical instrument.

Session 4 is structured in such a way as to allow for a first practice of the full progressive muscle relaxation (PMR) technique. The participants are also instructed in the awareness and adoption of "efficient" breathing patterns; this offers the opportunity for group members to experience the effect different breathing patterns can have in lowering heart rate, arousal, and tension. The second half of this session involves playing a relaxation tape containing instructions for full PMR.

Recap

The "reality testing of thoughts" homework assignment from the previous session is dis-cussed. The participants are asked whether they were able to come up with more realistic "rational" beliefs. Any problems (such as not believing rational belief alternatives) are dealt with. The trainer reiterates the importance of the continued practice of the "challenging thoughts" exercise.

Relaxation and the Bodily Symptoms of Stress

Over the next two sessions, you will be introduced to different relaxation exercises. As you will remember from the previous sessions, the symptoms of stress were divided into bodily, thinking, behavioural, and emotional components. These relaxation exercises help you to cope effectively with the bodily symptoms of stress such as tense muscles, stiff neck, tight chest, difficulty in breathing, trembling, stomach churning, difficulty in swallowing, faintness, and blurred vision. It is important to remember (from session 2) that such symptoms themselves can increase and maintain stress. If we experience these bodily symptoms when we are faced with challenging situations like exams, we can become overly focused on them. This is a problem because we need to concentrate as much as possible on the situation so that we can perform effectively. Relaxation techniques can help to reduce the impact of these negative symptoms, allowing us to focus our attention back on to what we need to be doing.

The exercises we will do need practice. Just knowing about them is not enough for them to be of use. It is important that you practise the exercises both in the weekly sessions and at home. I will tell you roughly how many times and for how long you need to practise each of the exercises, and I will give you homework tasks to encourage you!

These relaxation techniques are extremely useful for when you feel stressed. Although we are mainly interested in anxiety related to coursework and exams, these techniques, once learnt, can be used in every stress-provoking situation you face. They will allow you to reduce physical tension whenever you want to. When your body is free from tension, your mind tends to be calm as well, and you are better able to focus on what you are doing, be it coursework, exams, a social situation, a sporting event, or whatever.

The first relaxation exercise you will learn takes some time to complete (about 20–25 minutes), but once you have practised it for a while, you will learn ones that you can use quickly (i.e., in about 30 seconds) whenever you feel stressed. It is important that you persevere in these early stages and practise the exercises, so that you can experience the positive benefits.

Relaxed Breathing

Before starting on the relaxation exercises, the trainer discusses "efficient" breathing rhythms.

Exercise: Abdominal breathing

When doing relaxation exercises, you should try to adopt the correct breathing technique. Optimal breathing involves the use of the abdomen rather than the chest. You should avoid holding your breath or breathing rapidly. Taking a lot of quick deep breaths can make you feel dizzy and faint and make anxiety worse. Slow, regular, and deep breaths are best. One way to develop the skill of correct breathing is to spread your hands over the abdomen and feel the tummy muscles stretch each time you inhale, ensuring that the chest area moves only slightly. As you do this, imagine that your lungs are filling up from the bottom to the top. Breathe through your nose, filling your lungs so that the stomach muscles stretch.

The breathing out or exhalation phase is the relaxation phase. When we breathe out, we let go of the tension that develops in the body. Breathing out is a built-in mechanism for relaxation that we all have. This exhalation phase is the foundation for the relaxation exercises you will learn about.

Now I want you to take some deep breaths. Concentrate on the breathing-out part. As you breathe out, note any sensations. An important aim of the breathing exercise is to help you to notice the difference between feeling tense and feeling relaxed.

The participants are encouraged to practise abdominal breathing as often as possible (especially when they feel tense) so that it becomes a habit. They are also instructed on using the breathing exercise as a stepping-stone to bringing their attention back to the "present moment" situation.

The Relaxation Exercises

There are four types of relaxation exercise you will learn about in this session and the next. These are called:

1. Progressive muscle relaxation, (PMR)
2. Shortened progressive muscle relaxation

3. Cue controlled relaxation
4. Differential relaxation.

This week you will hear about progressive muscle relaxation. In the last 25 minutes of this session, I will play a tape and we will all have a practice. I will then give you each a tape to take away to practise with at home. You will also be given some rating sheets to fill in. *Remember, practice is important*!

Progressive Muscle Relaxation (PMR)

PMR involves a number of tense-relax exercises for different parts of the body. It's a very useful approach because it helps us learn to make the distinction between tense and relaxed muscles. We can then recognise when we are tense and so relax in response to this. This is sometimes referred to as "muscle sense".

Throughout the exercise, it is important that you breathe slowly and regularly, as you were shown earlier. For each part of PMR, the aim is to tense different muscles and really feel the tension before relaxing. In this way we can develop a keen awareness of the difference between tension and relaxation.

The students are then played a tape containing full PMR instructions. They are asked to close their eyes and not to try too hard to relax, but just to "go with it". After the tape is finished, the students are asked how they feel, and about any difficulties they encountered while attempting to relax.

A full description of the exercise is not provided here, but it is adapted from Bernstein & Borkovec (1973).

Homework

Needless to say, the homework assignment following session 4 is to practise PMR as frequently as possible; e.g., at least once a day for the next week. Ideally, copies of a PMR relaxation tape should be given to participants (as we did at the school). Failing that, relaxation scripts can be prepared, and participants can either memorise the exercise sequence, or make their own tapes from the scripts.

SESSION 5: RELAXATION II—SHORTENED RELAXATION TECHNIQUES

Overview

Session 5 introduces additional relaxation techniques for coping with problematic bodily arousal. The techniques introduced here constitute shortened versions of the full PMR method introduced in the previous session. The aim is that participants can progress to using these shortened techniques in everyday situations, and particularly in evaluation contexts (e.g., exams, social encounters). The techniques themselves continue to be discussed alongside a task-focus rationale.

Recap

The students' experiences with the PMR technique are discussed. They are asked to comment on any problems they experienced. The trainer discusses a few common problems, including:

— cramp
— movement/"twitching"
— falling asleep
— intruding thoughts
— becoming overly focused on bodily reactions
— not feeling relaxed
— takes a long time.

Reducing the Time It Takes

"Once you have practised and learnt the full PMR routine, the muscles involved in the tensing and relaxing stages can be combined to make the exercise quicker. Thus, we can now reduce the number of muscle groups to four":

1. hands, arms, and biceps
2. face and neck
3. chest, shoulders, back, and abdomen
4. legs, calves, and feet.

Exercise: Four muscle group relaxation

The muscles in these four groups can be tensed by using combinations of the tensing exercises that you learnt last week.

So, first of all, the hands, arms, and biceps can be tensed by holding your arms out in front of you and bending your elbow at 45 degrees. Make a fist and tense your forearms and upper arms. Hold it for a moment and notice the tension before you let it go and relax.

For the facial muscles, you can tense all the different parts at the same time. Frown, squint your eyes, wrinkle up your nose, and pull the corners of your mouth back. At the same time, push your chin towards your chest, but do not allow the chin to touch; try to get a feeling of pushing and pulling your chin at the same time so that your neck is tense. [This exercise may produce much hilarity in the group!]

For the chest, shoulders, back, and abdomen, take a deep breath and hold it; pull your shoulder blades back and together while at the same time making the stomach hard, either by pulling it in or pushing it out.

The tensing of the legs and calves involves lifting your legs off the floor so they are stiff straight out in front of you, with your toes pointing towards your face.

Shortened PMR/ "Recall" Relaxation

As you develop the relaxation skill and recognise the different sensations of tension and relaxation, even shorter exercises can be used. As the exercise become shorter and more convenient, it becomes more useful for our everyday lives.

Shortened PMR is different from the previous exercise insofar as the tensing stage is omitted. The purpose of this version is to reduce the time it takes you to become relaxed.

Exercise: Shortened PMR

Focus all your attention on each of the four muscle groups in succession, and very carefully identify any feelings of tightness or tension. Thus, for each muscle group:

- Recall what it was like when you relaxed these muscles, just letting them go and allowing them to become more and more deeply relaxed.
- *Relax:* let go of all the tension in each muscle group. Use the breathing-out phase to deepen the relaxing sensation.
- Focus on the relaxation sensation for a few seconds.
- If relaxation is achieved, go on to the next muscle group. If there is still some tension, repeat the procedure for that group.

At the end of this exercise, it is useful to employ a counting technique, which can deepen the relaxation once it has started. So, count to yourself slowly from one to ten, and feel yourself becoming more and more relaxed as you progress through the numbers.

You should also try out this exercise in different situations. For example, practise it while sitting or lying down, and even in environments where there is a lot going on. In this way, you can see how distractions in the world affect your ability to relax. The essential aim is to be able to relax anywhere, in any circumstance, so you can effectively cope with stress whenever and wherever it occurs.

Cue-Controlled Relaxation

The purpose of cue-controlled relaxation is to link a word, thought, or number to the sensation of relaxation. A common example is thinking the word "relax" or "calm" as you exhale during relaxation exercises. If we practise saying this to ourselves as we relax, the word becomes associated with our feelings of relaxation. Eventually, the word itself can help us to achieve relaxation.

The participants are also encouraged to identify a "cue" to remind them to relax throughout the day. At the school a building was chosen as the reminder. Pupils were asked to notice their breathing rhythm and relax their muscles every time they passed by the building (which they did several times each day). As an alternative reminder, participants can be given stickers to place on watches or mobile phones.

Differential Relaxation

If we are stressed and anxious, our bodies can become very tense when we are performing daily activities such as talking to others, eating, or doing our coursework. As a result of this, the muscles needed for performing that activity may become more tense than they need to be, and muscles that we don't need may become unnecessarily tense. In both of these cases, we may start to think too much about our bodily reactions and not enough about the situation or task we face.

It is helpful for us to learn to use only those muscles that are crucial for any particular task. The rest of our muscles can therefore remain relaxed, reducing stress and tension.

Whatever you are doing, if you notice that you feel very tense, you can quickly relax yourself by remembering to carry out the following sequence [adapted from Kennerley, 1997]:

— drop your shoulders
— untense the muscles throughout the body
— check your breathing rhythm (slow abdominal breaths are best)
— and then refocus on the task or situation.

Just running through this simple sequence can make us feel immediately more relaxed. It can be helpful when we are faced with challenging situations like exams because it can give us a sense of control over an unhelpful bodily response to stress. This in turn can help to ensure that we don't focus too much on our bodily feelings at the expense of the task or situation at hand. Remember that a relaxed body can lead to a relaxed and calm mind.

Homework

The homework is continued practice of all relaxation techniques. The participants are encouraged to continue using the full PMR tape at home, but to adopt the shorter versions of the exercises to practise in everyday situations.

SESSION 6: WORRY I—THE NATURE AND FUNCTION OF WORRY

Overview

Session 6 returns to a discussion of the cognitive modality, dealing specifically with worry, a central feature of evaluation anxiety.

This first worry session describes the nature and functions of worry. The first section below involves making a distinction between successful problem solving and worry. This stems from investigations that have suggested that inappropriate or poor problem solving may play a central role in the maintenance of worry (e.g., Davey, 1994; Tallis et al. 1991). The distinction between problem solving and worry is dealt with again in session 8.

Recap

Any issues regarding the continued practice of the relaxation exercises are discussed. The trainer reiterates that the relaxation techniques are most effective for an unhelpful bodily response to stress. The importance of continued practice is emphasised. The participants are told that the next two sessions will again focus on the thinking response to stress, specifically worry.

Worry vs. Problem Solving

It is important to know the difference between *problem solving* and *worry*. When we are faced with challenges like coursework and exams, problem solving is the most useful thinking strategy to use. To solve problems, we need to find out all the information necessary for us to perform well. For example, asking ourselves how long we have to revise, what kind of books and notes we need for our coursework assignment, or where we can get help. Each of these questions would be useful ways of approaching study challenges. Basically, problem solving involves everything that we need to do to ensure that a situation (e.g., coursework or exam revision) has a successful outcome. Thus, problem-solving strategies can lead to successful outcomes to whatever situation we are in. You will learn how to use problem solving in session 8. Today we are concerned with worry.

We saw in the first session that when we are faced with an immediate physical threat (e.g., being attacked by an animal), our thinking becomes focused on the threat. This ensures that we respond in the best way possible to reduce the possibility of being harmed. When we are faced with lingering threats, such as many non-physical ones (e.g., exams, coursework, relationship problems, or family problems), this stress response continues for some time, because the problems that cause it may not immediately go away. For example, a coursework deadline may be a few weeks away, and relationship problems may take time to resolve. If we perceive such situations as threatening, we may try to cope by focusing our minds on lots of possible negative scenarios. When we experience a seemingly uncontrollable stream of concerns about situations turning out badly, we are worrying. Worry is problem solving "gone wrong".

Definition of Worry

- thoughts concerning the consequences of failure (e.g., "What will happen if I fail?")
- a seemingly uncontrollable stream of negative thinking (e.g., "What if it all goes wrong?", "I'm no good at this", "I'll never get enough work done", "I don't think he/she likes me", etc.).
- self-preoccupation with one's performance, ability, or adequacy (e.g., "Am I good enough/strong enough to cope with this situation?").
- generally focusing attention on concerns about performance, consequences of failure, negative self-evaluation, or evaluation of one's ability relative to others.

Notice how these examples of worry concern situations where a person is trying to figure something out that cannot be resolved, because no one could ever have enough information to resolve it completely. For example, how can anyone predict the future? How can we ever know whether or not we are currently "good enough" for something?

The second section below involves a discussion of what is essentially the interference model of TA, as outlined previously. Within this model, the worry component of anxiety is hypothesised to interfere with task processing by diverting attentional resources from the task at hand (Wine, 1971). Individuals high in evaluation anxiety are conceptualised as being in a "struggle for attention" situation in which attention is split between processing task-relevant information and worry (Wells, 1994).

What Effect Does Worry Have?

The trainer introduces the idea of "attentional resources", which speaks to our limited ability to process information, such as thoughts, worries, and task demands.

> In an exam, social situation, or coursework, a person with low levels of stress will most likely concentrate on the task at hand, while a highly stressed person will "plunge inward", focusing on distracting negative thoughts and possible negative outcomes. Thus, high levels of stress often result in our focusing in on ourselves, i.e., worrying. When we do this, our performance suffers because a smaller amount of our limited attentional resources is devoted to the task. Worry, therefore, distracts attention from learning, remembering, and organising task-relevant information.
>
> "Blanking out" in an exam or a social situation may be due to our focusing too intently on our worries, such that we do not have the attentional resources to understand or respond to a question or a social interaction. Not surprisingly, such "freezing-up" can lead us into a vicious cycle of panic and more worry. The relaxation exercises you learnt last week will help you in such a situation, as will some of the techniques you will learn about next week.

The section below introduces a *metacognitive* perspective to the maintenance of worry. The emphasis here is upon *positive* beliefs about worry. These "metabeliefs" tend to concern possible motivational or avoidance benefits of worrying (e.g., "If I didn't worry, I wouldn't do the things I need to do"; "As long as I worry, I can prevent bad things from happening to me"). Wells (1995) suggests that such beliefs about the advantages of worrying or the costs of not worrying are likely to contribute to longer periods of worry.

Why Do We Worry?

> Worriers are frequently afraid that bad events are going to occur in the future. Their constant worry is triggered by internal "cues" (bodily sensations) and external "reminders" (e.g., a teacher talking about the coursework or exams) of an upcoming event (the exams!). These reminders can start off a series of "What if . . ." type worries (e.g., what if I fail?).
>
> People often believe that worry is helpful to them in such situations. Do you think worry can be helpful?

Exercise: Advantages of worry

The participants are asked to think of any advantages they may gain by worrying. This is designed to elicit any *positive* metabeliefs they have regarding the usefulness of worry as a coping strategy.

Positive Beliefs About Worry

So, worriers may believe that worrying is helpful to them. For example, some may think that it helps to *prevent* a feared situation from happening. Others may think that worrying is necessary, in order to *motivate* them to take action in a situation (e.g., prepare for exams or begin an essay).

The following list shows several positive beliefs about worry, some of which you mentioned in the "advantages of worry" exercise. [These examples are adapted from Borkovec, 1994.]

1. "Worrying makes it less likely that the feared event will occur." Quite often the feared event is unlikely to happen anyway (e.g., failing all your exams).
2. "Worrying helps me to work out ways to avoid or prevent something bad from happening." That is, worrying helps the worriers to control things in a way which helps them to avoid fearful outcomes.
3. "Worrying about a bad thing happening helps me to prepare for it if it does happen."
4. "If I don't worry, I wouldn't do the things I need to do" (e.g., If I didn't worry about the exams I wouldn't do enough preparation).

So, many worriers believe that worry actually serves a useful purpose, and they may even worry about not worrying! The problem is that worrying can in fact be very unhelpful. You have already learnt that it can use up a large part of our limited attentional resource. We will discuss the unhelpful nature of worry in more detail in the next session. To help with that discussion, I now want you to do another exercise to find out what disadvantages you experience through worrying.

Exercise: Disadvantages of worry

The participants are asked to think of any disadvantages they experience by worrying. This is designed to elicit any *negative* metabeliefs they have regarding the uncontrollable or harmful nature of worry.

Negative Beliefs About Worry

So, some people also have negative beliefs about worry. One of the most common beliefs in this respect is that worry is *uncontrollable*. The problem is that if people have this belief about worry, it is unlikely that they will bother trying to manage their worry, and may feel overwhelmed by it. Another negative belief about worry is that it is harmful in terms of our health or even our sanity (e.g.," If I don't stop worrying, I might go mad").

In fact, worry, although it may start up almost "automatically", *is* controllable. Furthermore, worry is a very common phenomenon and there is no evidence that it drives you "mad". Often, the beliefs that we have about our worry are the problem, even more so than the actual worry itself.

In the next session we are going to talk more about these beliefs about worry. These beliefs may keep you worrying for long periods of time, and can also increase stress. I will show you that these beliefs are not necessarily correct, and can in fact be challenged, so that worry becomes less of a problem in your lives.

In the meantime, I am setting you a homework assignment that involves your becoming more aware of the kinds of beliefs you have about worrying over coursework deadlines.

Homework

By next week I want you to identify and list as many of your "worry thoughts" as you can about the approaching coursework deadline. I particularly want you to note down any thoughts you have about the worry. For example, why are you worrying? Is it because you believe that you have to worry to prevent failure? Is it because you can't help it? Is your worry uncontrollable? Do you worry about the worry?

You are not required to discuss the content of your worries with the group. Rather, we will discuss the homework assignment in general terms next week.

SESSION 7: WORRY II—MODIFYING META-BELIEFS

Overview

The purpose of session 7 is to modify negative and positive metabeliefs about worry. The techniques are adapted from Wells (1997) and include offering counter-evidence, showing that worries offer inaccurate representations of situations, highlighting the disadvantageous nature of worry as a coping strategy, and showing that situations can turn out positively when worry is not used.

Recap

The participants are reminded of the advantages and disadvantages of worry exercises. The homework assignment, which was designed to encourage an awareness of metabeliefs about worry, is used to guide this session.

The aim of this week's session is to show you that worry is something that you have a certain amount of control over. We will also discuss why worry is not a very useful strategy for coping with life's challenges (e.g., coursework, exams, and relationships). So, the outline of today's session is as follows:

- demonstrating that worry is controllable
- challenging beliefs that worry is helpful
- using coping "self-statements" to divert our attention back to the task or situation at hand.

The Controllable Nature of Worry

Many of you mentioned that worry can seem *uncontrollable*, and that once it starts there is nothing you can do about it. But what happens when your attention is diverted to something else? What happens to the worry then? (e.g., reading a good book, watching TV, becoming absorbed in a task, or talking to a friend about something else). [The participants are encouraged to think of a time recently when they were worrying and something happened to distract them from their worry.]

When we are using our minds to concentrate on something else, we "let go" of our worry in that we are no longer attending to it. This does *not* mean that we should try hard to think about something else instead of the worrisome thoughts. Trying to "suppress" or avoid thoughts in this way rarely works. In fact trying hard not to think about something can make us think about it all the more. [The trainer can use a thought-suppression exercise to demonstrate this. For example, participants can be asked *not* to think about David Beckham or a pink elephant for a period of 60 seconds. The participants usually report a difficulty in not thinking about the specified object.]

Letting go of worry involves a refocusing on the "present moment", or on the task at hand (e.g., coursework assignment or a social situation). If we concentrate on the situation, and on what needs to be done, our attention moves away from any worries we have. Also, by concentrating on the task, it is more likely that we will cope with life's challenges (e.g., exams) successfully. This is important because, as we will discuss shortly, constant worry can affect our ability to perform in many situations.

As we discussed in the last session, another negative belief that people have about worry is that it is dangerous or harmful. Such beliefs often involve thinking that worry will affect our health or drive us mad. In fact, worry is a very common phenomenon. Just about every person in the stress-management groups said that they worry about certain things in their lives. Although it seems unpleasant, and can make us feel down, worry does not drive us mad. If it did, just about everyone would be mad and that is clearly not the case. Shortly, I will tell you about certain things you can try so that you can discover for yourselves the control you can have over worry. Before that I want to discuss how worry is an unhelpful strategy for dealing with life's challenges.

The Unhelpful Nature of Worry

In the last session, many of you expressed the belief that worry has a useful role to play in helping you to get things done (motivation) and in preventing bad things from happening (avoidance of threat). Beliefs about worry being a good strategy can be linked to an almost "superstitious" belief; e.g., "I don't want to tempt fate by positive thinking". Also, there can be a belief that by repeatedly focusing on negative outcomes, the likelihood of being unable to cope with that outcome, if it does occur, is reduced; e.g., "If I think the worst, and then the worst happens, I won't be that disappointed", "worrying about a bad thing happening helps me to prepare for it if it does happen". One of the most common beliefs held about worry over the coursework deadline is that worry spurs us into action; e.g., "If I didn't worry, I wouldn't do the things I need to do".

These kinds of beliefs have very important implications. People who hold these beliefs will continue to worry when faced with stressful situations because they think that worry helps them to cope with problems in a successful way.

The reason people think this is because of something called *reinforcement* (the basics of positive and negative reinforcement are explained). "I have said that worry usually involves predicting the worst outcome from some event, and concern about the consequences of that outcome (e.g., I'm going to fail my exam, and everyone will think I'm stupid). The problem is that because worry usually involves extremely negative outcomes, those outcomes rarely occur. Because the bad things that people worry about don't happen, they think that worry is useful because it prevents the feared thing happening. Likewise, if good things happen (e.g., grades turn out OK), then the worriers again associate this with their worrying. But, what use is worrying if it doesn't reflect reality?

In fact, in certain situations, worry makes it more likely that the bad thing will happen. This is because worry diverts our attention from whatever we need to be doing (e.g., revising, working on coursework, preparing for a social situation, or using problem-solving strategies), leaving less attention available for performing successfully. So, worrying in exams will reduce the amount of attention we can give to the exam tasks; worrying in a social situation will mean we concentrate less on what's being said, or what's going on. This means that we have to work twice as hard to make sure that the situation turns out OK.

As we discussed in session 3, worry will also result in negative emotions such as fear or anxiety. These emotions also get in the way of our performing well in any situation, and they make us feel distressed, bad, miserable, irritable, etc. Also, if we use worry as a problem-solving strategy, it sets up our minds to pay attention only to the range of negative outcomes that are consistent with the content of the worry. [A simple experiment is described to illustrate this, showing that worried and anxious people are more likely to notice and remember words such as "fear", "threat", and "danger" than words like "fun", "joy", and "happy"]. This makes it less likely that the worrier will notice and remember positive things. [The group are shown how this relates to a negative thinking bias such as "ignoring the positive", discussed in session 2.]

So, worriers often believe that worry helps them to solve problems and deal with situations. Sometimes it appears that "worry works" because problems are solved, and we cope with the stressful situation (reinforcement). The problem is that worry comes at a severe cost. Worrying has been compared to running a race with a weight strapped across your back. You may well get to the finish line, but it will take you a lot longer, and will be much harder than someone who doesn't have the weight of worry strapped to them.

Developing Useful "Self-Talk": Diverting Attention Back to the Task

To encourage ourselves not to use worry to solve our problems and to exert control over worry, we can start to "talk to ourselves" in a different way.

Saying things to ourselves like, "It's the exams in two weeks, I'd better start worrying", or "I can't stop worrying, I must be going mad", will naturally lead to more worry and all the negative consequences of worry outlined previously. [The participants are encouraged to see the relevance of this within the A-B-C sequence discussed in session 3, using worry as the activating event (A) and beliefs about worry at B.]

If you face a situation and you do find yourself worrying, there are a number of self-statements you can use to refocus your thoughts on the task and toward useful ways of dealing with the situation. Here are some examples [adapted from Meichenbaum, 1985; Meichenbaum & Deffenbacher, 1988]:

Worrying upsets you; it's not useful.

Focusing on worry won't help you make the grade; focus on the task instead.

Don't dwell on your worry; just think what you will do step-by-step.

What are some of the helpful things you can do instead of worrying?

You can't stop worry starting, but you can use it as a reminder to focus on the present.

Does my worry reflect reality?

You can adapt statements like these to suit your own situation; make them personal and meaningful to you.

If we get used to using such self-statements, we can learn to direct our attention back to the task, and toward useful problem-solving strategies (which you will hear about in the next session). If we try these statements out when we are faced with a problem or stressful situation, we can learn that we don't have to worry to ensure that bad things don't happen. Likewise, they can help us realise that we can "postpone" worry by diverting our attention back to the situation at hand. The reinforcement process will be at work again here. This time we will be reinforced and quickly develop habits of focusing on the task or situation rather than on worry.

Homework (Two Parts)

1. During the week, pick a situation you will be going into that you think will make you worry. At some point before the situation, write down, in as much detail as possible, the content of your worries. This includes what it is about the situation you are worried about, and any pictures or images you have in your mind about how you think the situation will turn out. Once the situation or event has passed, note down in as much detail as possible, what happened: did the situation turn out positively, or not? The important thing for you to do is to compare the content of your worries about the situation with what actually happened. Do your worries reflect reality?
2. When you have completed the first assignment, try this: think of another situation you will face during the course of the week that may involve some worry on your part. It is better at this stage to choose a situation that is not too stressful, i.e., one that doesn't have really major consequences. What I want you to do is to try out *not* worrying. If you like, postpone your worry until later in the day. Let your worry go, and focus on what you need to do about the situation or event. I want you to note down whether you were successful at not worrying, what you "did" instead of worry, and what happened in the situation.

We won't be sharing the specific content of your worries or the situation with the group. Rather, next week, we will discuss in general terms what happened.

SESSION 8: PROBLEM SOLVING

Overview

The problem-solving training is introduced primarily as an effective method for dealing with an unhelpful behavioural response to challenging situations. Participants are reminded that avoidance and procrastination are rarely useful strategies for coping. As we have omitted a study-skills training component, particular attention is paid to applying the problem-solving process to the participants' coursework situation. This is done by getting the group to work through the problem-solving stages, with a coursework deadline as a problem, or "stressor".

An important theme in this session is to offer problem solving as a useful alternative to worry (i.e., as a strategy to reduce the impact of maladaptive cognitions). Focusing on solving problems step-by-step can help participants realise that they do not have to use worry to ensure successful outcomes. This process also serves to direct attention away from worry and back to the task at hand, further illustrating the controllable nature of worry.

The problem-solving training component is adapted from Meichenbaum (1985) and Tallis (1990).

Recap

The homework assignment of reality testing and postponing worry is discussed in relation to both positive and negative beliefs about worry.

Worry vs. Problem Solving Revisited

When we covered the nature of worry in session 6, I asked you to define problem solving. Remember that worry is essentially "problem solving gone wrong". It is unlikely that worry will lead us to a successful solution to our problems, because it does not involve a useful search for the information needed to ensure the problem is solved. Rather, worry involves a negative interpretation or prediction of a negative outcome; e.g., I will fail this exam; I'll never be able to do that; what if it all goes wrong?

Problem-solving strategies are more likely to lead to a successful outcome. They encourage us to focus on and try out possible solutions to our problems. Notice how this contrasts with worry, which involves an exaggerated focus on negative outcomes.

The problem-solving approach which I will tell you about today can help you to organise and focus your thinking so that you devise solutions to your problems.

Outline of Problem Solving

1. defining the problem
2. brainstorming solutions
3. weighing up the pros and cons

4. choosing a solution and planning for action
5. doing it!
6. reviewing the outcome.

The students are given hypothetical examples of problems to work with in pairs (course-work deadline, relationship break-up). As each stage of the problem-solving process is covered, they are asked to "try out" the techniques with the given problem examples.

Defining the Problem

Defining the problem is not always easy. Worry will tell you where there is a problem but it won't necessarily tell you the exact nature of the problem. The problems that we face are often quite complex, such as family or relationship difficulties.

It is always worth thinking carefully about what is bothering you. It is helpful to distinguish different aspects of the problem and separate it into a collection of more manageable tasks. For example, someone who is very fearful of exams may experience the following worry: "It's only one week to the exams, I'm going to have to face it all again".

This imminent situation might reflect several problems to be dealt with:

- I'll have to do lots of work between now and then.
- I'm going to have to cope with the horrible feelings of anxiety; I might panic.
- I'm going to have to talk to friends outside the exam hall, before we go in.
- I'm going to have to cope with feeling sick and faint on the morning of the exam.

Notice how the above problem involves many different aspects for this individual. It is good practice to break down a problem like this, so that you can know *exactly* what it is that is making you worried. The very act of writing down the problem like this can be helpful.

It is not a good idea to attempt solving all the different problems at once. The best thing to do is take them one at a time. Having to put some problems on hold while you deal with others may mean you continue to worry. However, if we successfully deal with one of our problems, we will be much less stressed when we come to deal with the others.

When first trying out problem-solving methods, it is worth starting with the easiest problems; i.e., ones you are sure you can do something about.

[The students are encouraged to try to break down their problem examples into different components.]

Brainstorming Solutions

Once the problem has been clearly defined, we can come up with a number of possible solutions. In other words, ask yourself, "What can I do about it?"

This process involves "Brainstorming"—thinking up as many examples as you can. It is important at this stage not to judge the solutions you come up with. Write down any you can think of, no matter how positive or negative they seem. We can sort out the good ideas from the bad ones later. So, if you think that robbing a bank is a solution to a financial problem, write it down! The idea is that the more choice you have, the higher the chance that you will select a solution which is right for you. Also, some solutions can look good "on paper", but may not work when you try to implement them; if we have several solutions, we can try another one.

When coming up with possible solutions, it is sometimes helpful to put yourself in someone else's position and consider how that person would respond if asked to deal with your problem. Brainstorming like this can help you to get out of the habit of saying "yes—but" in response to any possible solutions.

[The students are now given the opportunity to practise brainstorming in their groups to come up with solutions to the given problems.]

Weighing up the Pros and Cons

The next stage in problem solving is to list the pros and cons associated with each possible solution.

Pros are the good things associated with a particular decision, and cons are the bad things or drawbacks. By doing this, you can decide which of your solutions can be kept and which can be rejected. It is now that we judge the different solutions.

It may be that there are more pros associated with one solution than another. However, just counting the pros and cons is not a good way to decide. Some of the pros or cons may be far more important to you than others in the same group.

A way of getting around this is by placing a rating next to each pro and con. The rating can then represent how important each statement is. So, for example you could use a range from 1 to 10, with 1 representing not very important, and 10 representing the most important. When this has been done for both the pros and cons groups, you can add up the ratings to get a total for each.

[The students are now given the opportunity to practice weighing up the pros and cons for their group examples.]

Choosing a Solution and Planning for Action

This is the all important "decision-making" stage.

It is necessary to make a fairly quick decision about which solution(s) will be chosen. People who worry often have difficulty in making decisions.

One way to get used to making quick decisions is by taking "sensible risks", i.e., making quick decisions about things where the consequences are not too serious either way. For example, you might be in a book or record store with a small amount of money, having noticed two items you really like. You could do a quick pros and cons analysis of each in your head, and then just go ahead and buy one. Don't stand there for ages trying to decide which to buy. It is impossible for you to know which one you will enjoy the most. Don't worry about making the "wrong" decision. Does it really matter that much if it is wrong?

After you have practised making quick decisions in situations such as this, try some harder, more important ones. It is good to set yourself a deadline by which time you will make the decision. If you are used to being very cautious, making quick decisions can feel unpleasant at first. However, learning to make quick decisions about problems means you will have less to worry about. As you learn that faster decision making isn't always followed by a major catastrophe, you will find it easier and easier to do.

You can now take your first choice solution and start to plan how to put it into action. Planning for action can be assisted by asking yourselves the following questions:

- What will be done?
- How will it be done?
- When will it be done?
- Who is involved?
- Where will it take place?
- What is my back-up plan?

When answering these questions, it is important to be as specific and concrete as possible. Write out the answers and your plan of action. It is extremely helpful to be able to "rehearse" your plan of action in your imagination.

It is important to turn your decision into action as soon as possible. The whole point of using problem solving is to work out a successful way of dealing with whatever it is that is causing you worry.

[The students are now asked to make their solution decisions with their group examples.]

Doing It!

Try out your solution. Make sure you have a back-up plan in place. Ensure you are prepared, physically and mentally.

Reviewing the Outcome

In this last stage it is important to evaluate your problem-solving attempt to see whether it was successful.

If turning your chosen solution into action worked, and the problem is solved, congratulate yourself! It is a very good idea to reward yourself if your strategy is successful. Treat yourself by going to the cinema, or buying something for yourself. Rewards work by reinforcing behaviours. If your successes are rewarded, you will be more likely to repeat whatever you did to achieve those successes. So, if you reward your successful problem solving, you will be more likely to engage in successful problem solving the next time you have a problem.

If your solution does not work, try to understand why it didn't. It is important to remember that you did not fail. You can expect disappointments, particularly when you first start using problem-solving techniques. You should congratulate yourself for having tried. Learn as much as you can from the experience and go back to your solution list and try another one. Or you could go back and redefine the problem, so that you are sure you know exactly what it is.

Problem solving is a skill much like all the other techniques you have learnt. Just knowing about it isn't enough. You must practise. Don't fall into the trap of thinking that one setback means you will always fail.

Summary

A useful way to summarise the problem-solving process is to see it as involving the following questions [from Tallis, 1990]:

- What am I worried about?
- What do I want to happen?
- What can I do to make it happen?
- What is actually likely to happen?
- What is my decision?
- Did it work?

Homework

The participants are encouraged to try out the problem solving in real life. To this end, they are asked to think of a problem they are having and to try to solve it using the step-by-step problem-solving guide.

SESSION 9: IMAGERY

Overview

Mental imagery techniques have played a major role in cognitive and behavioural therapies ever since Wolpe (1958) introduced systematic desensitization. In the TA literature, guided imagery techniques have been shown to be effective in reducing both the worry and emotionality components of the problem (e.g., Sapp, 1994).

The imagery techniques introduced in this session have various aims. Relaxation images can aid the relaxation process and thus be effective for reducing bodily arousal; the coping images can provide an alternative (less catastrophic) view of a situation, thereby challenging irrational thinking patterns; and the mental practice techniques can help students prepare for challenging situations through the mental rehearsal of appropriate behavioural response patterns. In sum, these imagery techniques provide a useful adjunct to other methods of combating maladaptive responding in all response modalities.

Recap

The homework assignment on problem solving is discussed. The students are asked whether they managed to replace worry with the problem-solving strategies. Any problems with the process are elicited and discussed.

We have seen that the way we think can be related to how we feel. Images, or pictures we see with our "mind's eye", work in very much the same way as our "self-talk". Thus, if we are fearful of a situation, it is likely that we will see a "snapshot" of the feared situation. When we are stressed and anxious, these images often involve negative events and outcomes (e.g., someone who is anxious about giving a presentation may imagine it going wrong; someone who is anxious about exams may imagine experiencing panic in the exam).

In the same way as we did with our beliefs in session 3, we can become aware of, monitor, and adapt the images we develop. If our images are negative, irrational, or only involve unsuccessful outcomes to a stressful situation, we can learn to replace them with more helpful images.

For many years, psychologists have helped people to use imagery to overcome problems such as stress and anxiety, and also to improve performance in many different situations. These sub-headings represent an overview of the imagery techniques which have proved helpful:

- coping imagery
- motivation imagery
- mental rehearsal
- relaxation imagery.

I will shortly tell you about each of these in turn. First, we are going to practise using our imaginations.

The students are asked to close their eyes and relax by the shortened method introduced in session 5. The following imagery scene is read aloud by the trainer:

Exercise: Controlling mental images

Imagine a big, bright yellow lemon. Notice the skin of the lemon. The skin could be rough or smooth. Feel the skin. Sniff the lemon. Cut the lemon in half and notice how the colour is much lighter on the inside than the outside. Notice the organisation of the segments inside. There are several segments with tiny pouches of succulent bitter juice. Sniff the lemon again and then squeeze it. Taste the sour juice!

The students' experiences with the imagery exercise are discussed. They are asked whether they puckered and salivated when they "tasted" the juice. The example is used to illustrate the power of the imagination to create sensations, and our ability to control our images.

If you had difficulty developing or controlling the previous lemon image, or if the image wasn't very clear, do not worry. Different people have different thinking styles, and some will use images more often than others will. Developing images is a skill very much like the other techniques you have learnt.

Coping Imagery

In coping imagery, the individual can picture him or herself coping in a feared or difficult situation. This helps the person cope better in that situation in the future.

You do not have to imagine yourself performing perfectly in any particular situation, only coping with any problems that you expect to arise. It is better to imagine yourself coping with any experienced anxiety rather than imagining yourself experiencing no anxiety at all. We cannot get rid of anxiety completely. For example, you can imagine yourself coping with feelings of stress in an exam by focusing fully on the task at hand.

The students are given a handout detailing a case study of a girl who suffers from exam stress, and details of coping imagery techniques used to alleviate her stress.

Case study

Emma was 18 years old when she came for counselling at her teacher's suggestion. She was going to sit her exams in two months and was afraid that she would have to leave the exam hall and throw up as she had done on previous occasions because she was so nervous. This set of exams was extremely important, as she needed to pass them if she was to go to university. Within the first 15 minutes of being in an examination hall, she would have a panic attack. At this point she would leave the hall and run to the toilet. This would take up valuable time and often she would not be able to return to finish the exam. The counsellor obtained details from her about what she would normally do the night before and on the day of the exam. The disadvantages of undertaking specific behaviours that contributed to her state of anxiety, such as speaking to unconfident friends, were discussed. Then she was asked to close her eyes and to picture the following coping imagery.

Imagine yourself coming home from school the evening before your exam. See yourself sitting down at the kitchen table as usual drinking tea with your mum. Then picture yourself going upstairs to your bedroom, sitting at your desk and preparing for the next day's exam. Later, you can hear your dad calling you for dinner. See yourself sitting with the family and enjoying the food. Afterwards you return to your bedroom and continue studying. About 9.30 pm you collect your papers together and tidy your desk. You prepare your pens and papers ready for the morning. You put on your favourite music and relax in your armchair. See if you can hear the music now. About 10 pm, picture yourself getting ready for bed and, after thinking about the next day you finally drop off to sleep. Next morning your alarm clock goes off and you wake up feeling refreshed. You get yourself ready for school and have your usual breakfast with your sister. Picture your mum giving you a lift in the car to school. On arrival, you avoid friends who are usually pessimistic and have a quiet chat with your more confident friends. However, one of your less confident friends sees you and comes over for a chat. She tells you that she has been unable to prepare properly because she has felt so anxious about failing. You feel your own anxiety rising and that familiar churning in your stomach has returned. You tell your friend that you need to go to the toilet and you leave her with your other friends. In the toilet you use the breathing exercise you have learnt and manage to calm yourself down. Now picture yourself going into the exam hall, leaving your bags at the rear, and then finding your desk. You sit down and place your pens and pencils on the desk. You familiarise yourself with the room and any instructions on the front of the examination paper. Notice the feeling of excitement and possible tension. You notice your breathing. Now picture the teacher instructing everybody to start. As your anxiety starts to return, you focus on your breathing exercise again. Although this takes up a few moments of your time you begin to feel better again and you start the exam. Notice how you are breathing calmly and slowly, and gradually progressing through the questions. Notice that you are so absorbed with them that you have not got time to notice what anybody else is doing. See yourself putting up your hand and asking for an additional answer book. Later, you hear the examiner give everybody a 10-minute warning that the exam is about to finish. You then read over your answers and correct any obvious mistakes. When time is called, see yourself checking that the answer books have your name and exam number on. Then picture yourself leaving the hall and chatting to your fiends outside.

The session was recorded so that Emma was able to listen to it daily as a sort of homework assignment. The outcome was a great improvement. She did not feel anxious nor did she need to leave the hall and throw up. (Adapted from Palmer & Dryden, 1995).

There are several steps involved in coping imagery [from Palmer & Strickland, 1996]:

Step 1: Think of a future event that you are anxious about.
Step 2: Identify the aspects of the event you are most anxious about.
Step 3: Think of ways you can overcome those problems.
Step 4: Imagine yourself in the feared situation, coping with the problems you are anxious about.
Step 5: Practise this coping imagery regularly, especially every time you begin to feel anxious about the event.

Repeated practice of the coping image can increase our confidence in our ability to cope with the stressful situation. It also helps us to "see" different ways of dealing with the problem. Imagining a negative scenario leads us to believe there is only one possible (negative) outcome to the situation. "Seeing" with our mind's eye that there are different ways of coping with problems and stressful situations can help to "de-awfulise" the problem.

People who are very stressed about situations may even avoid imagining the feared situation because it gives them unpleasant feelings. This is not a good strategy for dealing with stress; avoidance rarely is. Coping imagery can give people confidence because it allows them to see that there are ways of coping in difficult situations.

Motivation Imagery

A huge amount of research has been conducted on the use of imagery by sportsmen and-women. One way imagery has been used in this context is to encourage high levels of motivation. Take a look at this example:

At 14 years of age, Duncan Goodhew, a future swimming champion, determined he was going to the Olympics. It was his target, his goal throughout the years of hard training. He imagined how it would be, the race, and what it would feel like afterwards, and this image drove him on and sustained him over the years [From Acres, 1994].

This technique of visualising where you want to go and what you want to achieve can be extremely useful in all walks of life. If you are lacking motivation for the exams or your coursework assignments, develop images of where you want to get to in the future. In this way, you can become more willing to work hard to achieve your goal.

[The trainer discusses the use of this type of motivational imagery in the context of setting and achieving short-and long-term goals.]

Mental Rehearsal

Sportsmen and -women don't use imagery only to focus on their dreams and goals. They also use it to practise the skills required for their sports. Psychologists have found that mentally rehearsing a task or skill leads to performance improvement. Mental practice can help us perform better in many of the things we have to do. The technique essentially involves practising successful completion of the task in our minds.

The list of tasks this technique can be used with is very long indeed. It can be used in all areas of our lives; e.g., performing in the orchestra, acting in the school play, or playing for the football team. Before we go into a challenging situation, we can imagine ourselves in that situation performing to the best of our ability. This kind of rehearsal can lead to outcomes consistent with the content of our images.

This effect was recently demonstrated by sport psychologists who were carrying out research with golfers. They found that golfers who imagined a ball going in the hole improved their putting performance. They also found that golfers who imagined the ball missing the hole experienced a marked decrease in performance. [Any possible reasons for this effect are elicited from and discussed with the students.]

Relaxation Images

Imagery is also used as part of the relaxation process. Imagining pleasant scenes, or imagining our bodies sinking or floating, can help deepen our feelings of relaxation.

Exercise: Relaxation imagery

The students are read the following relaxation imagery script.

Sit comfortably in your chairs. Close your eyes and imagine yourself to be transparent and filled with your favourite colour of liquid. Imagine it to be exactly the temperature you find comfortable. If you are unsure of a colour, choose blue. Starting from the crown of your head, imagine this liquid draining slowly away through your body. As it does so, imagine each part of the body from which it has drained feeling lighter and relieved of tension. Imagine the liquid eventually flowing out through the tips of your fingers and toes, and you'll be left feeling relaxed. Move slowly when you have finished the exercise to avoid dizziness. (from Acres, 1994).

Homework

For homework, the students are encouraged to try mental practice and coping imagery. It is emphasised that if they are anxious about a situation, imagining themselves coping in that situation can be extremely helpful. They are encouraged to notice how they feel and act in situations they had previously imaged.

SESSION 10: REVIEW

The final session involves an informal review and discussion of the stress management techniques. The trainer provides a summary of how the different techniques impact upon the interacting response modalities.

In the school study we developed a short quiz to assess the group's knowledge of the concepts introduced. We also used this final session to reiterate the importance of continued practice of all of the techniques.

REFERENCES

Acres, D. (1994). *How to pass exams without anxiety: every candidate's guide to success.* Plymouth: How to Books Ltd.

Algaze, B. (1995). Cognitive therapy, study counseling, and systematic desensitization in the treatment of test anxiety. In C.D. Spielberger & P.R. Vagg (Eds.), *Test anxiety: Theory, assessment, and treatment* (pp. 133–152). Washington, DC: Taylor & Francis.

Alpert, R., & Haber, R. (1960). Anxiety in academic achievement situations. *Journal of Abnormal and Social Psychology*, **61**, 207–215.

Altmaier, E.M., Ross, S.L., Leary, M.R., & Thornbrough, M. (1982). Matching stress inoculation treatment components to clients' anxiety mode. *Journal of Counseling Psychology*, **29**, 331–334.

Bandura, A. (1977). Self-efficacy: Toward a unifying theory of behavioral change. *Psychological Review*, **84**, 191–215.

Barkham, M. (1989). Brief prescriptive therapy in two-plus-one sessions: Initial cases from the clinic. *Behavioural Psychotherapy*, **17**, 161–175.

Barkham, M., & Shapiro, D.A. (1990). Brief psychotherapeutic interventions for job-related distress: a pilot study of prescriptive and exploratory therapy. *Counselling Psychology Quarterly*, **3**, 133–147.

Beck, A.T. (1970). Cognitive therapy: Nature and relation to behavior therapy. *Behavior Therapy*, **1**, 184–200.

Beck, A.T. (1976). *Cognitive therapy and the emotional disorders.* New York: International Universities Press.

Benjamin, M., McKeachie, W.J., Lin, Y.G., & Holinger, D.P. (1981). Test anxiety: Deficits in information processing. *Journal of Educational Psychology*, **73**, 816–824.

Benson, J., & El-Zahhar, N. (1994). Further refinement and validation of the Revised Test Anxiety Scale. *Structural Equation Modelling*, **1**, 203–221.

Bernstein, D.A., & Borkovec, T.D. (1973). *Progressive relaxation training: A manual for the helping professions.* Champaign, IL: Research Press.

Bond, F.W. (1998). Using a case formulation to understand and treat a person with generalised anxiety disorder. In M. Bruch & F.W. Bond (Eds.), *Beyond diagnosis: Case formulation approaches in CBT* (pp. 81–102). Chichester: Wiley.

Bond, F.W., & Bunce, D. (2000). Mediators of change in emotion-focused and problem-focused worksite stress management interventions. *Journal of Occupational Health Psychology*, **5**, 156–163.

Borkovec, T.D. (1994). The nature, functions, and origins of worry. In G. Davey, & F. Tallis (Eds.), *Worrying: Perspectives on theory, assessment and treatment* (pp. 5–33). Chichester: Wiley.

Borkovec, T.D., Hazlett-Stevens, H., & Diaz, M.L. (1999). The role of positive beliefs about worry in generalized anxiety disorder and its treatment. *Clinical Psychology and Psychotherapy*, **6**, 126–138.

Brown, J.S.L., Cochrane, R., & Hancox, T. (2000). Large-scale health promotion stress workshops for the general public: A controlled evaluation. *Behavioural and Cognitive Psychotherapy*, **28**, 139–151.

Bruch, M. (1998). The UCL case formulation model: Clinical applications and procedures. In M. Bruch & F.W. Bond (Eds.), *Beyond diagnosis: Case formulation approaches in CBT* (pp. 19–41). Chichester: Wiley.

Bunce, D. (1997). What factors are associated with the outcome of individual-focused worksite stress management interventions? *Journal of Occupational and Organizational Psychology*, **70**, 1–17.

Cartwright-Hatton, S., & Wells, A. (1997). Beliefs about worry and intrusions: The meta-cognition questionnaire and its correlates. *Journal of Anxiety Disorders*, **11**, 279–296.

Culler, R.E., & Holahan, C.J. (1980). Test anxiety and academic performance: The effects of study-related behaviors. *Journal of Educational Psychology*, **72**, 16–20.

Davey, G.C.L. (1994). Pathological worrying as exacerbated problem-solving. In G. Davey & F. Tallis (Eds.), *Worrying: Perspectives on theory, assessment and treatment* (pp. 35–59). Chichester: Wiley.

Deffenbacher, J.L. (1977). Relationship of worry and emotionality to performance on the Miller Analogies Test. *Journal of Educational Psychology*, **69**, 191–195.

Deffenbacher, J.L. (1980). Worry and emotionality in test anxiety. In I. Sarason (Ed.), *Test anxiety: Theory, research and applications.* (pp. 111–127). Hillsdale, NJ: Erlbaum.

Deffenbacher, J.L. (1988). Some recommendations and directions. *The Counseling Psychologist*, **16**, 91–95.

Dendato, K.M., & Diener, D. (1986). Effectiveness of cognitive relaxation therapy and study-skills training in reducing self-reported anxiety and improving the academic performance of test anxious students. *Journal of Counseling Psychology*, **33**, 131–385.

Denney, D.R. (1980). Self-control approaches to the treatment of test anxiety. In I.G. Sarason (Ed.), *Test anxiety: Theory, research and applications* (pp. 209–243). Hillsdale, NJ: Erlbaum.

Ellis, A. (1962). *Reason and emotion in psychotherapy.* New York: Lyle Stuart.

Ellis, A. (1977). Rational-emotive therapy: Research data that supports the clinical and personality hypotheses of RET and other modes of cognitive-behavior therapy. *The Counseling Psychologist*, **7**, 2–42.

Eysenck, M.W., & Calvo, M.G. (1992). Anxiety and performance: The processing efficiency theory. *Cognition and Emotion*, **6**, 409–434.

Fletcher, T.M., & Spielberger, C.D. (1995). Comparison of cognitive therapy and rational-emotive therapy in the treatment of test anxiety. In C.D. Spielberger & P.R. Vagg (Eds.), *Test anxiety: Theory, assessment, and treatment* (pp. 153–169). Washington, DC: Taylor & Francis.

Flett, G.L., & Blankstein, K.R. (1994). Worry as a component of test anxiety: A multidimensional analysis. In G. Davey, & F. Tallis (Eds.), *Worrying: Perspectives on theory, assessment and treatment* (pp. 135–181). Chichester: Wiley.

Free, M.L. (1999). *Cognitive therapy in groups: Guidelines and resources for practice.* Chichester: Wiley.

Goldfried, M.R., & Davison, G.C. (1976). *Clinical behavior therapy.* New York: Holt Rinehart and Winston.

Goldfried, M.R. (1980). Psychotherapy as coping skills training. In M.J. Mahoney (Ed.), *Psychotherapy process: Current issues and future directions.* New York: Plenum.

Gonzalez, H.P. (1995). Systematic desensitization, study skills counseling, and anxiety-coping training in the treatment of test anxiety. In C.D. Spielberger & P.R. Vagg (Eds.), *Test anxiety: Theory, assessment, and treatment* (pp. 117–132). Washington, DC: Taylor & Francis.

Hembree, R. (1988). Correlates, causes, effects and treatment of test anxiety. *Review of Educational Research*, **58(1)**, 47–77.

Holdsworth, N., & Paxton, R. (1999). *Managing anxiety and depression: A self help guide.* London: Mental Health Foundation.

Hollandsworth, J.G., Jr., Glazeski, R.C., Kirkland, K., Jones, G.E., & Van Norman, L.R. (1979). An analysis of the nature and effects of test anxiety: Cognitive, behavioral, and psychological components. *Cognitive Therapy and Research*, **3**, 165–180.

Holroyd, K.A. (1976) Cognition and desensitization in a group treatment of test anxiety. *Journal of Consulting and Clinical Psychology*, **44**, 991–1001.

Holroyd, K.A., & Appel, M.A. (1980). Test anxiety and physiological responding. In I. Sarason (Ed.), *Test anxiety: Theory, research, and applications* (pp. 129–151). Hillsdale, NJ: Erlbaum.

Jex, S.M. (1998). *Stress and job performance: Theory, research, and implications for managerial practice*. California: Sage Publications.

Kennerley, H. (1997). *Overcoming anxiety: A self-help guide using cognitive behavioral techniques*. London: Robinson Publishing.

Keogh, E., & French, C.C. (2001). Test anxiety, evaluative stress and susceptibility to distraction from threat. *European Journal of Personality*, **15**, 123–141.

Kirkland, K., & Hollandsworth, J.G., Jr., (1979). Test anxiety, study skills, and academic performance. *Journal of College Student Personnel*, **20**, 431–436.

Kwee, M.G.T., & Lazarus, A.A. (1987). Multimodal therapy: The cognitive-behavioral tradition and beyond. In W. Dryden & W.L. Golden (Eds.), *Cognitive-behavioural approaches to psychotherapy* (pp. 320–355). New York: Taylor & Francis.

Lang, P.J. (1971). The application of psychophysical methods to the study of psychotherapy and behavior modification. In A.E. Bergin & S.L Garfield (Eds.), *Handbook of psychotherapy and behavior change* (pp. 75–125). New York: Wiley.

Lazarus, A.A. (1967). In support of technical eclecticism. *Psychological Reports*, **21**, 415–416.

Lazarus, A.A. (1989). *The practice of multimodal therapy: Systematic, comprehensive, and effective psychotherapy*. Baltimore, MD: Johns Hopkins University Press.

Lazarus, A.A. (1992). Multimodal therapy: Technical eclecticism with minimal integration. In Norcross, J.C. & Goldfried, M.R. (Eds.), *Handbook of psychotherapy integration* (pp. 231–263). New York: HarperCollins.

Liebert, R.M., & Morris, L.W. (1967). Cognitive and emotional components of test anxiety: A distinction and some initial data. *Psychological Reports*, **20**, 975–978.

Mahoney, M.J. (1974). *Cognition and behavior modification*. Cambridge, MA: Ballinger.

Matthews, G., Hillyard, E.J., & Campbell, S.E. (1999). Metacognition and maladaptive coping as components of test anxiety. *Clinical Psychology and Psychotherapy*, **6**, 111–125.

McIlroy, D., Bunting, B., & Adamson, G. (2000). An evaluation of the factor structure and predictive utility of a test anxiety scale with reference to students' past performance and personality indices. *British Journal of Educational Psychology*, **70**, 17–32.

Meichenbaum, D. (1972). Cognitive modification of test anxious college students. *Journal of Consulting and Clinical Psychology*, **39**, 370–380.

Meichenbaum, D. (1977). *Cognitive-behavior modification. An integrative approach*. New York: Plenum Press.

Meichenbaum, D. (1985). *Stress inoculation training*. New York: Pergamon.

Meichenbaum, D. (1993). Changing conceptions of cognitive-behavior modification: Retrospect and prospect. *Journal of Consulting and Clinical Psychology*, **61**, 202–204.

Meichenbaum, D., & Butler, L. (1980). Toward a conceptual model for the treatment of test anxiety: Implications for research and treatment. In I. Sarason (Ed.), *Test anxiety: Theory, research and applications* (pp. 187–208). Hillsdale, NJ: Erlbaum.

Meichenbaum, D., & Deffenbacher, J.L. (1988). Stress inoculation training. *The Counseling Psychologist*, **16**, 69–90.

Mischel, W. (1968). *Personality and assessment*. New York: Wiley.

Morris, L.W., & Liebert, R.M. (1970). Relationship of cognitive and emotional components of test anxiety to physiological arousal and academic performance. *Journal of Consulting and Clinical Psychology*, **35**, 332–337.

Murphy, L.R. (1984). Occupational stress management: A review and appraisal. *Journal of Occupational Psychology*, **57**, 1–15.

Murphy, L.R. (1988). Workplace interventions for stress reduction and prevention. In C.L. Cooper & R. Payne (Eds.), *Causes, coping and consequences of stress at work* (pp. 301–339). Chichester: Wiley.

Murphy, L.R. (1996). Stress management in work settings: A critical review of the health effects. *American Journal of Health Promotion*, **11**, 112–135.

Musch, J., & Bröder, A. (1999). Test anxiety versus academic skills: A comparison of two alternative models for predicting performance in a statistics exam. *British Journal of Educational Psychology*, **69**, 105–116.

Naveh-Benjamin, M. (1991). A comparison of training programs intended for different types of test-anxious students: Further support for an information-processing model. *Journal of Educational Psychology*, **83**, 134–139.

Naveh-Benjamin, M., McKeachie, W.J., & Lin, Y. (1987). Two types of test anxious students: Support for an information processing model. *Journal of Educational Psychology*, **79**, 131–136.

Öst, L.G. (1987). Applied relaxation: description of a coping technique and review of controlled studies. *Behaviour Research and Therapy*, **25**, 397–410.

Palmer, S., & Dryden, W. (1995). *Counselling for stress problems*. London: Sage.

Palmer, S., & Strickland, L. (1996). *Stress management*. Dunstable: Folens Publishers.

Prochaska, J.O., & Norcross, J.C. (1994). *Systems of psychotherapy: A transtheoretical analysis*. Belmont, CA: Wadsworth.

Reynolds, S., & Shapiro, D.A. (1991). Stress reduction in transition: Conceptual problems in the design, implementation, and evaluation of worksite stress management interventions. *Human Relations*, **7**, 717–733.

Reynolds, S., Taylor, E., & Shapiro, D. (1993a). Session impact and outcome in stress management training. *Journal of Community and Applied Social Psychology*, **3**, 325–337.

Reynolds, S., Taylor, E., & Shapiro, D. (1993b). Session impact in stress management training. *Journal of Occupational and Organizational Psychology*, **66**, 99–113.

Sallis, J.F., Trevorrow, T.R., Johnson, C.C., Hovell, M.F., & Kaplan, R.M. (1987). Worksite stress management: A comparison of programs. *Psychology and Health*, **1**, 237–255.

Sapp, M. (1994). The effects of guided imagery on reducing the worry and emotionality components of test anxiety. *Journal of Mental Imagery*, **18**, 165–180.

Sarason, I.G. (1984). Stress, anxiety, and cognitive interference: Reactions to tests. *Journal of Personality and Social Psychology*, **46**, 929–938.

Spielberger, C. (1972). Anxiety as an emotional state. In C.D. Spielberger (Ed.), *Anxiety: Current trends in theory and research* (pp. 23–49). New York: Academic Press.

Spielberger, C.D., Gonzalez, H.P., Taylor, C.J., Algaze, B., & Anton, W.D. (1978). Examination stress and test anxiety. In C.D. Spielberger & I.G. Sarason (Eds.), *Stress and anxiety* (Vol. 5). Washington, DC: Hemisphere/Wiley.

Spielberger, C.D., & Vagg, P.R. (1995a). Test anxiety: A transactional process model. In C.D. Spielberger & P.R. Vagg (Eds.), *Test anxiety: Theory, assessment, and treatment* (pp. 3–14). Washington, DC: Taylor & Francis.

Spielberger, C.D., & Vagg, P.R. (1995b). *Test anxiety: Theory, assessment, and treatment*. Washington, DC: Taylor & Francis.

Stiles, W.B., Shapiro, D.A., & Elliott, R. (1986). Are all psychotherapies equivalent? *American Psychologist*, **41**, 165–180.

Sweeney, G.A., & Horan, J.J. (1982). Separate and combined effects of cue-controlled relaxation and cognitive restructuring in treatment of musical performance anxiety. *Journal of Counseling Psychology*, **29**, 486–497.

Tallis, F. (1990). *How to stop worrying*. London: Sheldon Press.

Tallis, F., Eysenck, M., & Mathews, A. (1991). Elevated evidence requirements and worry. *Personality and Individual Differences*, **12**, 21–27.

Tobias, S. (1985). Test anxiety: Interference, defective skills, and cognitive capacity. *Educational Psychologist*, **3**, 135–142.

Turkat, I.D. (1979). The behaviour analysis matrix. *Scandinavian Journal of Behaviour Therapy*, **8**, 187–189.

Tyron, G.S. (1980). The measurement and treatment of test anxiety. *Review of Educational Research*, **50**, 343–372.

Vagg, P.R., & Papsdorf, J.D. (1995). Cognitive therapy, study skills training, and biofeedback in the treatment of test anxiety. In C.D. Spielberger & P.R. Vagg (Eds.), *Test anxiety: Theory, assessment, and treatment* (pp. 183–194) Washington, DC: Taylor & Francis.

Vagg, P.R., & Spielberger, C. (1995). Treatment of test anxiety: application of the transactional process model. In C.D. Spielberger & P.R. Vagg (Eds.), *Test anxiety: Theory, assessment, and treatment* (pp. 197–215). Washington, DC: Taylor & Francis.

Wells, A. (1994). Attention and the control of worry. In G. Davey, & F. Tallis (Eds). *Worrying: Perspectives on theory, assessment and treatment* (pp. 91–114). Chichester: Wiley.

Wells, A. (1995). Meta-cognition and worry: A cognitive model of generalised anxiety disorder. *Behavioural and Cognitive Psychotherapy*, **23**, 301–320.

Wells, A. (1997). *Cognitive therapy of anxiety disorders: A practice manual and conceptual guide.* Chichester: Wiley.

Wells, A. (2000). *Emotional disorders and metacognition: Innovative cognitive therapy.* Chichester: Wiley.

Wells, A., & Matthews, G. (1994). *Attention and emotion: A clinical perspective.* Hillsdale, NJ: Erlbaum.

Wine, J. (1971). Test anxiety and direction of attention. *Psychological Bulletin*, **76**, 92–104.

Wine, J.D. (1980). Cognitive-attentional theory of test-anxiety. In I.G. Sarason (Ed.), *Test anxiety: Theory, research and applications* (pp. 349–385). Hillsdale, NJ: Erlbaum.

Wolpe, J. (1958). *Psychotherapy by reciprocal inhibition.* Stanford, CA: Stanford University Press.

Zeidner, M. (1998). *Test anxiety: The state of the art.* New York: Plenum.

Zimmer, J., Hocevar, D., Bachelor, P., & Meinke, D.L. (1992). An analysis of the Sarason (1984) four-factor conceptualization of test anxiety. In K.A. Hagtvet & J.B. Johnsen (Eds), *Advances in test anxiety research* (vol. 7, pp. 103–113). Amsterdam: Swets & Zeitlinger.

CHAPTER 13

Preventing Counsellor Burnout in Brief Cognitive Behavior Therapy

Albert Ellis

Albert Ellis Institute, New York, NY, USA

Preventing and coping with counsellor burnout is often a problem in many kinds of therapy, especially when counsellors try to do therapy briefly. This may be less true when they use rational emotive behavior therapy (REBT) or other forms of cognitive behavioral therapy (CBT) because these methods of treatment usually spend little time on clients' past histories and focus mainly on the present. So, as I have pointed out previously (Ellis, 1996a), REBT is intrinsically brief, and CBT practitioners are used to short-term counselling.

Nevertheless, counselling that is specifically designed to be brief, and where counsellors are under some pressure to make it so, place unusual stressors on the practitioners. Thus, counsellors have to fulfill their own goal of helping clients quickly, have to meet the clients' expectations in this respect, and have to meet the requirements of possible supervisors, agency heads, and managers of national health services, HMOs, and other agencies that may scrutinize the length of their treatments. Some of their supervising agencies are permissive and will allow them additional sessions with severely disturbed or difficult clients; some of them are rigorous and will cut off their allowed sessions in short order. Quite a fix—even for counsellors who routinely practice forms of REBT and CBT and are relatively relaxed about doing so. The pressure on them to significantly help many different kinds of clients and to do so in few sessions may be relentless, even if they are healthy, little disturbed individuals who do not put extra neurotic pressure on themselves. If—!

Actually, of course, counsellors are often no better equipped to handle serious stressors than are some of their clients. Like the rest of the human race, they often have their own problems. My own therapy with people all over the world and my researches into the incidences of human disturbance lead me to hypothesize that virtually all people are somewhat neurotic—including the majority of counsellors (Ellis, 1976). To back up this contention, I have counselled, individually and in group therapy, hundreds of practicing practitioners over the last 60 years, and have intensively supervised several more hundred of them, and find my hypothesis largely confirmed. Of course, my observations are biased, but they are at least partially confirmed by several empirical studies of counsellors' disturbances.

What aspects of disturbance add to counsellors' stressors and contribute to their often reacting dysfunctionally and subjecting themselves to more burnout than the inherent

---

Handbook of Brief Cognitive Behaviour Therapy. Edited by Frank W. Bond and Windy Dryden.
© 2002 John Wiley & Sons, Ltd. ISBN 0-470-02132-2.

difficulties of their doing REBT and CBT would themselves produce? Let me discuss these aspects within the framework of REBT theory and practice. REBT is a constructivist or choice therapy that holds that people—and counsellors!—do not merely *get* disturbed by the stressors or adversities that happen to them and interfere with the fulfillment of their goals and interests. In REBT theory, adversities (A) do not usually directly cause disturbed symptoms or consequences (C). Instead, B, people's beliefs about or their *views* of A's, plus the adversities themselves that they encounter, lead to C's. Thus, adversities × beliefs = consequences, or A × B = C.

When neurotic counsellors, therefore, experience stressors or adversities (A's) in doing brief REBT or CBT, they frequently take their adversities too seriously at their belief system (B) and therefore produce neurotic distress at their consequences (C's). They largely do this by first telling themselves rational beliefs (RB's), which are preferences—such as, "I don't like these adversities of counselling and wish they would be eliminated. How annoying they are! But I can still enjoy doing counselling and helping my clients." However, when counsellors are disturbed and in danger of burnout, they frequently *also* tell themselves a set of self-defeating irrational beliefs (IBs)—such as, "I *can't stand* these adversities of counselling! They *shouldn't* be this bad, and *must* be reduced! They make counselling so hard that they may cause me to fail at quickly helping my clients. That would be terrible, and would make me an incompetent counsellor and an inadequate person!"?

In other words, counselling stressors and adversities may arise no matter how competent counsellors may be. But counsellors often create IBs *about* these adversities that help them react neurotically and make counselling more difficult. These IBs are usually unrealistic and illogical musts and demands, especially,

1. "I *must* be successful with practically all my clients and help them quickly, or else I am a rotten counsellor!"
2. "My clients and my supervisors *must not* be too difficult and impede my counselling, or else they are not worth helping!"
3. "The conditions of counselling *must* not be too difficult and demand too much of me, or else this profession is *too hard* and *awful* and I'd better seek another vocation!"

Counsellors, then, like many of their clients, often unrealistically and illogically *demand*, not merely *prefer*, too much of themselves, and create self-downing; they require too much of their clients and supervisors and make themselves angry; and they demand too much of the counselling profession, and make themselves unable to tolerate its stresses. As a secondary disturbance, they frequently blame themselves for being so self-downing, angry, and intolerant of frustration. They then feel doubly worthless and interfere still more with their effective counselling (Ellis, 1985, 1994, 2000b).

Actually, the REBT theory of counsellor's disturbance is more complicated than I have just presented it. I originally derived the theory from philosophers, including Gautama Buddha, Epictetus, Kant, and Heidegger, who clearly saw that people are natural constructivists who largely disturb themselves about adversities because they *choose* to add to these adversities their own irrational beliefs that their troubles must not be as bad as they actually are. These philosophers forgot to note, however, what I pointed out in my first paper on REBT in 1956 (Ellis, 1958) and in my first book for professionals on REBT, *Reason and Emotion in Psychotherapy* (Ellis, 1962). The nature of people is such that when they think, they also feel and behave; when they feel, they also think and behave; and when they behave, they also think and feel. Their thoughts, feelings, and behaviors strongly include and interact with each other. Moreover, their adversities (A's) affect their beliefs (B's) and consequences (C's), their beliefs (B's) affect their adversities (A's) and consequences (C's), and their consequences (C's) affect their adversities (A's) and beliefs (B's) (Ellis, 1994, 2000a, 2000b). Quite complicated!

This integration and influence especially go for counsellors' beliefs (B's), with which they frequently neuroticize themselves. They often exaggeratedly perceive the adversities of counselling that they encounter and also exaggerate the consequences that ensue when they have IBs about counselling's adversities.

Take, for example, Julie, a counsellor I supervised at the Albert Ellis Institute in New York. She knew REBT brief therapy well and did it more than adequately with her clients. But she had never had any personal therapy herself, and while she helped her clients to minimize their self-downing, she rarely reduced her own. She put herself down for her looks (which were distinctly above average), for her intelligence (which enabled her to get a PhD in counselling when she was only 25), and especially for her failing to help some seriously disturbed clients after she had seen them for only a few sessions. After two years as a counsellor at our psychological clinic, she was thoroughly burnt out and ready to quit counselling and be a researcher. That, she felt, would be a much safer profession for her.

Julie's main IB's were, "I *absolutely must not* fail to help some of my seriously disturbed clients after only a few sessions. My clinic demands that I must, my clients are expecting me to help them quickly, and I'm inept at doing brief CBT. I am therefore worthless as a counsellor and an inadequate person unless I cure my clients fast!"?

These were profoundly self-defeating beliefs, and in REBT (as I shall show later) would forcefully and persistently be disputed (at point D) to help Julie change them to strong *preferences* instead of insistent *demands*. But, first, let us look at these IBs more closely. Julie held them powerfully and convincingly: She not only believed but *felt* they were indubitably correct. So she held them *emotionally* as well as *cognitively*, *powerfully* instead of *lightly*.

Moreover, Julie's IB's included distinct behavioral or action-oriented tendencies. They were pushing her *compellingly* to obsess about her failures, to enervate her, and to practically drive her out of counselling and into doing research.

Julie's IBs, therefore, were really beliefs-emotions-behaviors—not merely cognitions that *made* her feel and act. They were in good part feelings and actions in their own right. Moreover, she could change her self-defeating beliefs not only by cognitively disputing them—as is done in REBT—but *also* by experiencing counterfeelings (e.g., letting herself feel the *pleasure* and *satisfaction* of helping her clients) and by *counteracting* against them (e.g., forcing herself to stay in counselling and expose herself to cooperative as well as uncooperative clients until she desensitized herself to seeing them and until she changed some of her ideas about feeling a complete failure).

As Epictetus said two thousand years ago, "It is not the things that happen to people that upset them but their *view* of them." But he forgot to say that a strongly convinced view includes important feelings and actions. Therefore, REBT has always disputed counsellees' irrational believing-emoting-behavings (IBs) by using strong emotional arguments and by also invariably using a number of important behavioral methods to uproot them. That is why it is called rational emotive behavior therapy (Dryden, 1995, 1999b; Ellis, 1994, 1998, 1999, 2000a; Ellis & Dryden, 1997; Ellis & MacLaren, 1998).

Let us get back to Julie. This chapter is limited to 6500 words, so let me *briefly* show how an REBT counsellor would treat clients like her who have (IBs) that lead them to damn themselves, do relatively poor therapy, and burn out so seriously that they consider quitting the career of counselling. What are some of the cognitive, emotive, and behavioral techniques of REBT that might be used with her? I will describe some typical techniques that an REBT or CBT counsellor might use with her.

CBT AND REBT TECHNIQUES THAT EMPHASIZE COGNITIVE ASPECTS OF COUNSELLING

In Julie's case of burnout, as well as with other counsellors who were burned out for similar reasons, an REBT counsellor would often use the following cognition-stressing methods.

Disputing Irrational Believing-Emoting-Behavings (IBs)

First the counsellor might show Julie her IBs and teach her how to dispute them. She would be shown how to dispute them realistically or empirically: "Why *must* I always do effective brief therapy with difficult clients? Where is the evidence that I *have to* do so?" Typical answer: "I do not *have to* do effective brief therapy with difficult clients, though that would be *preferable*. There is no evidence that I *must* do so, since if any law of the universe held that I *must*, I would be forced to do so—or else might die!"?

Julie would then be taught to do logical disputing of her IBs: "Does it logically follow that if I sometimes fail to help all my clients in a few sessions that I am therefore a worthless therapist and an inadequate person?" Typical answer: "No. If I fail in this respect, that proves that I am perhaps a poor therapist with *them* but hardly *in general*. If I were an *inadequate person*, I would fail at practically everything—and that, of course, is not true."

Julie would be taught to do pragmatic or heuristic disputing of her IBs: "What results will I get if I think that I *must* succeed with all my clients and that I am worthless if I don't?" Typical answer: "It will help me make myself very anxious and depressed and may contribute significantly to my burning out as a counsellor" (Dryden et al., 2002).

Using REBT, Julie's counsellor might also use some of its following cognitive-centered techniques:

Rational Coping Self Statements

She repeats rational coping self-statements to herself many times and shows herself that they are correct. "I never *have to be* effective with all my difficult clients, but I will do my best to help as many of them as I can." "I am never a failure or a loser but just a fallible human who fails some of the time."

Positive Visualization

An REBT counsellor might use positive visualization by showing Julie how to imagine how she helped some of her most difficult clients and could keep helping others. This might give her achievement-confidence or self-efficacy (Ellis, 1962, 1994), and, as Bandura (1997) and his associates have shown, self-efficacy might help Julie do better with some of her clients. Also, she could visualize herself failing with some of her clients, refusing to put herself down for failing, and otherwise handling a bad situation.

Modeling

Julie could be helped to see that other counsellors she knows suffer similar difficulties and do not awfulize about them. She could also discover that other people fail as much as she, but do not put themselves down for failing. She could model herself after them; and she could read biographies and view movies that show how many people suffer tribulations and failures and manage to cope with them quite well.

Julie could also be shown how to use comparisons of herself and others to prove that if one of her relatives or friends failed as much as she did, she would not deem them worthless; therefore, she can accept herself with her failings.

Psychoeducational Methods

Julie could be encouraged by her counsellor to read REBT and CBT self-help materials or to listen to tape cassettes and videotapes that describe some of the causes of self-deprecation and awfulizing and present methods of countering these feelings and the dysfunctional believing-emoting-behavings that accompany them. REBT and CBT materials, it has been shown, can be successfully used by themselves or to make counselling briefer and more effective (Ellis, 1993, 1996a, 1996b).

Using Cost-Benefit Ratio

Julie could be shown that the costs of avoiding counselling her clients and taking extra time off from work are outweighed by worse costs. The more she takes time off or cops-out by avoiding difficult clients, the more anxious she will tend to make herself. For she would then tell herself, "If I do avoid working with resistant clients, I will dread getting back to work when I am forced to do so and will consequently make myself more anxious." She also might be encouraged to see that the gains of copping-out, such as her enjoying reading and listening to music during her "rest" periods, are hardly worth the pains of feeling anxious when she thinks about resuming her counselling. Anxiety and burnout are worse than almost anything else in her life, and therefore she had better not avoid taking counselling risks.

Proselytizing

Clients of REBT therapists are often encouraged to practice some of its cognitive-oriented techniques with their friends and relatives. As John Dewey said a century ago, by teaching any subject to others, one usually learns it better oneself. Julie, being a counsellor, was already trying to talk clients out of their irrational believing-emoting-behavings, so her doing so helped her teach herself some of the best REBT disputing techniques. But since she avoided difficult clients and was anxious when forced to do so, her REBT counsellor would probably encourage her to take on more of these kinds of clients and to teach them methods of disputing their dysfunctional convictions. She would, in the process, help herself see her own believing-emoting-behavings and be able to dispute them actively.

Cognitive Distraction and Relaxation

When people are anxious or depressed, they often use cognitive distraction, such as reading or watching TV, or specific relaxation techniques, such as yoga, meditation, or Jacobson's progressive relaxation method. They thereby temporarily focus on using these techniques and block out some of their anxietizing. Julie sometimes taught her clients relaxation methods but used them only moderately herself. Her REBT or CBT counsellor might therefore encourage her to use them more frequently, to achieve palliative relief from her overwhelming anxiety. But her counsellor could also try to persuade her to use strong disputing of her IBs, and this would not merely interrupt but truly minimize her anxiety-producing believing-emoting-behavings.

Practical Problem-Solving Techniques

An REBT or CBT counsellor would usually first try several methods that would help reduce Julie's panic and her avoidant actions, because while she is panicked she is not likely to employ effective problem-solving. As she seemed ready for more effective problem-solving, her REBT counsellor might show her how to use more practical methods of tackling her counselling and other problems. Thus, she might be taught to experiment with many methods of problem-solving, to check out their effectiveness, to persist until she discovered better methods, to look for alternative solutions, and to use various self-instructional techniques that Meichenbaum (Meichenbaum & Jaremko, 1983) has described.

REBT AND CBT TECHNIQUES THAT EMPHASIZE EMOTIONAL ASPECTS OF COUNSELLING

While employing the foregoing and some other REBT cognitive-oriented techniques with Julie, her REBT counsellor would often use them and encourage her to use them quite vigorously and emotionally, as well as behaviorally, so that they would maximally help her overcome her counselling anxieties. In addition to these cognitively emphasizing methods, her counsellor might encourage Julie to use several emotive-experiential methods of REBT if she was not already using them to help herself. Here are some of these main methods.

Unconditional Other-Acceptance

Julie's counsellor would especially give her unconditional other-acceptance (UOA) and show her that she was always acceptable to the counsellor *whether or not* she performed well as a counsellor and *whether or not* she won the counsellor's approval. She would also be taught the personal and social value of UOA and its desirability in her professional and personal life. She would be helped to see how *all* people can be accepted as worthwhile *humans* in spite of their failings and lack of good relationships. She would be taught how to accept sinners—including her difficult clients—in spite of their sins.

Unconditional Self-Acceptance (USA)

Julie's counsellor would not only give her UOA and show her how to model it for herself, but would specifically show her how to acquire it emotionally and philosophically. Thus, she would be shown that she could decide to accept *all* people, including herself, just because they are alive and human—and therefore "deserve" and can *choose* to accept themselves whatever their behaviors. Or she could be helped to decide—yes, *choose*—to rate her own behaviors as "good" when they led to healthy personal and social results and to rate them as "bad" when they led to unhealthy or destructive personal and social consequences. But— and this is quite a *but*—she would decide not to rate globally herself, her being, or her personality *at all* (Dryden, 1999a, 1999b; Ellis, 1962, 1996c, 1999, 2000a, 2000b; Ellis & Blau, 1998; Ellis & Harper, 1997; Hauck, 1991).

Shame-Attacking Exercises

Julie could be shown how to use my famous shame-attacking exercises (Ellis, 1973, 1994, 1998, 2000a, 2000b) to help her remove her guilt and self-damning and achieve unconditional self-acceptance (USA). Thus, she could deliberately do some foolish, ridiculous, or silly acts in public and make herself feel healthfully sorry and disappointed if she was criticized for doing them but not make herself feel ashamed or self-downing. For example, she could wear outlandish clothing, tell some people "shameful" things about herself, or walk a banana on a red leash and feed it with another banana. While doing these shame-attacking exercises, Julie would work on *not* feeling embarrassed or ashamed!

Rational Emotive Imagery

Julie could be shown how to do Maxie Maultsby, Jr.'s rational emotive imagery (REI) (Ellis, 2000c; Maultsby, 1971). To do this, she would vividly imagine some "terrible" thing happening—such as her failing with a very difficult client and having that client attempt suicide—and let herself feel *unhealthily* anxious and/or depressed about this image.

She would fully get in touch with her unhealthy feelings and even implode them. Then, keeping the same dismal image, she would make herself feel only the *healthy* emotions of disappointment, regret, and frustration. If she did this at least once a day for a few minutes for 20 or 30 days, she would probably train herself to feel healthy disappointment automatically instead of unhealthy anxiety whenever she thought about failing, or when she actually did fail, with a difficult client.

Strong Rational Coping Statements

Julie might be shown how to use strong, vigorous rational coping statements to undo her anxious reactions, such as, "I *never, never* have to put myself down—even if I fail miserably with some of my clients!" and "I am *not* a miracle-maker and can only do my best to quickly help my difficult clients!"

Forceful Disputing

Julie might be encouraged to very forcefully put her irrational believing-emoting-behavings on a tape cassette, to try to dispute them powerfully on the same tape, and then to let some of her friends listen to the tape to see whether her disputing was accurate and truly vigorous and convincing.

Role-Playing

Julie could have a friend role-play her supervisor telling her she was doing very badly with difficult clients while she, role-playing herself, responded to the supervisor. Onlookers could then critique how well she did in the role-play and get her to play it over again to improve her handling of the situation. If she became anxious during the role-play, it would be stopped temporarily and she would be asked what she was telling herself to make herself anxious and how she could dispute her dysfunctional self-statements and make herself less anxious.

Reverse Role-Playing

Julie could be asked to give one of her core irrational believing-emoting-behavings to a friend or partner who would rigidly hold it and resist giving it up. She could then get practice in strongly disputing it herself.

Humor

Because anxious people take things *too* seriously, and often lose their sense of humor in the process, Julie's REBT counsellor might encourage her to take some of her problems more lightly and see them in a humorous vein. She might also be encouraged to sing to herself some rational humorous songs (Ellis, 1987, 1999) to interrupt and help to change her anxiety-provoking attitudes. Here are some REBT humorous songs she might use.

Perfect Rationality
(Tune: *Funiculi, Funicula.* Music by Luigi Denza)

Some think the world must have a right direction,
And so do I—and so do I!
Some think that, with the slightest imperfection,
They can't get by—and so do I!
For I, I have to prove I'm superhuman,
And better far than people are!
To show I have miraculous acumen—
And always rate among the Great!

Perfect, perfect rationality
Is, of course, the only thing for me!
How can I ever think of being,
If I must live fallibly?
Rationality must be a perfect thing for me!

Love Me, Love Me, Only Me!
(Tune: *Yankee Doodle Dandy*)

Love me, love me, only me,
Or I will die without you!
O, make your love a guarantee,
So I can never doubt you!
Love me, love me totally—really, really try, dear;
But if you demand love, too,
I'll hate you till I die, dear!

Love me, love me all the time,
Thoroughly and wholly!
My life turns into slushy slime
Unless you love me solely!
Love me with great tenderness,
With no ifs or buts, dear.
If you love me somewhat less,
I'll hate your goddamned guts, dear!

You for Me and Me for Me
(Tune: *Tea for Two*, Music by Vincent Youmans)

Picture you upon my knee,
Just you for me, and me for me!
And then you'll see
How happy I will be!
Though you beseech me
You never will reach me—
For I am autistic
As any real mystic!
And only relate to
Myself with a great to-do, dear!
If you dare to try to care,
You'll see my caring soon will wear,
For I can't pair and make our sharing fair!

If you want a family,
We'll both agree you'll baby me—
Then you'll see how happy I will be!
(Rational Humorous Song Lyrics by Albert Ellis,
Copyright by Albert Ellis Institute.)

CBT AND REBT TECHNIQUES THAT EMPHASIZE BEHAVIORAL ASPECTS OF COUNSELLING

An REBT or CBT counsellor would also use some of the major behavioral-emphasizing techniques that are frequently used with anxiety-prone clients like Julie, including some of the following methods.

In vivo Desensitization or Exposure

Julie might well be encouraged to stop avoiding taking on difficult clients and perhaps even risk taking on additional ones. If, while doing this kind of risk-taking, she vigorously disputed her irrational believing-emoting-behavings, she would be better able to see that nothing "horrible" would happen when she failed with some clients, and that she was then neither an "inadequate counsellor" nor a "total failure" as a person.

Staying with "Terrible Situations"

Julie would be encouraged, if she were stuck with some difficult clients or critical supervisors, to stop herself from copping-out. Rather than try to leave the situation, she would force herself to stay in it awhile, to work actively to reduce her anxiety, depression, or anger about it, and, after doing so, she could decide whether to leave or stay in the stressful situation. She then would have a chance to work on her disruptive feelings and behaviors under difficult conditions and to refuse to allow these conditions to upset her.

Reinforcement

Julie might be shown how to use contingency management and operant conditioning to help herself do her cognitive, emotive, and behavioral homework and to confront difficult counselling tasks on which she procrastinated or copped-out. She would be encouraged to reward herself with some pleasurable activity only *after* she ran some risk that she commonly avoided.

Penalization

If Julie consistently refused to change her thinking, feeling, and behaving in order to make herself less disturbed, she might be encouraged to take some real penalties to discourage her resistance. Thus, she might be induced to burn a hundred dollar bill, contribute money to a cause she hated, or do some very unpleasant task when she stubbornly refused to do therapeutic activities. If she agreed to such penalties but refused to enact them, she could be monitored by a friend, relative, therapy group, or counsellor.

Skill's Training

If Julie lacked certain personal or social skills that would help her combat her anxiety and function as a better counsellor, she could be helped to acquire these skills by an REBT counsellor, or by encouraging her to take some special training workshops or courses. Thus, she could, if relevant to her basic problems, be helped to become more assertive and to communicate better with her clients and supervisors.

Relapse Prevention

If Julie made some progress with an REBT counsellor and then fell back to becoming more anxious and avoidant again, she could be helped with several relapse-prevention techniques. To this end, an REBT counsellor could show her how to reuse some of the methods she was then neglecting. She could be shown, for example, how to identify high-risk situations, to have realistic expectations about slipping, to monitor her urges to fall back to anxiety-provoking thinking and acting, to monitor her irrational believing-emoting-behavings, to review the disadvantages of relapsing, to distinguish her wants from her "shoulds", to strive for long-range goals, and to use other relapse-prevention methods (Ellis & Velten, 1992, 1998; Marlatt & Gordon, 1989).

As noted above, REBT counselling with Julie would particularly focus on the fact that she herself is a counsellor, who might already be using—though perhaps not too effectively—REBT and CBT theory and practice with her clients and with herself. Her counsellor would therefore determine whether she truly understood the theory and practice of REBT and CBT, and how frequently and intensively she used it with others and with herself. In some instances, the counsellor would largely be reminding Julie of the REBT that she presumably knew, urging her to use it more vigorously and often, and monitoring her usage of it. In other instances, however, the REBT or CBT counsellor would act as if Julie were a neophyte and would give her some primary education in cognitive-behavioral theory and practice.

In any event, since Julie is a counsellor, the REBT practitioner would emphasize how the methods they discuss could primarily be used to help Julie herself, but also be employed to increase her therapy skills—with the difficult clients with whom she has trouble as well as with other clients with whom she has relatively little difficulty. So the counselling would tend to be more theoretical and more practical than it would be with, say, a client who was anxious about her job as a computer expert or as an attorney.

For example, I saw as a client a CBT counsellor who came to therapy mainly because he felt inferior to his highly intelligent and literate wife, and about his being an inadequate and angry father to his seven year-old son. Although he seemed to have little difficulty in doing counselling, I kept pointing out, while showing him how to use REBT with his feelings of inadequacy and his rage at his son, how the counselling techniques we were discussing for these problems could also be applied, apparently more intensively than he was doing, to his own clients. At the end of 12 sessions of therapy, he said that he had greatly benefited from the therapy, but especially thanked me for helping him work more successfully with his clients. I was gratified to hear that.

In the case of the counsellors with whom I do therapy, I particularly stress what I call "elegant" REBT—that is, helping them feel better *and* get better. This includes their achieving the following therapeutic results:

1. minimizing the presenting symptoms for which they came to therapy
2. minimizing other symptoms of which they may not have been too aware when they started therapy
3. maintaining their progress and only occasionally making themselves disturbed again
4. When they do fall back, quickly and strongly using the REBT techniques that helped them before
5. making themselves little disturbed when really adverse situations occur in their lives
6. fully realizing that they largely control their emotional destiny, and actively committing themselves to keep working at REBT and using it to accept the *challenge* of making themselves less disturbed *and* considerably less disturb*able* (Ellis, 1999, 2000a).

I try to help most of my clients achieve this ideal state of feeling better *and* getting better, but I find that they only achieve it in relatively few cases because they mainly work at overcoming their presenting symptoms and are highly satisfied when they do so. But I especially stress the achievement of this "elegant" kind of less disturbability with counsellors that I see as clients. They are more likely to do the persistent cognitive, emotive, and behavioral work of committing themselves to this therapeutic goal and thereby maximally helping themselves and their own clients.

If you, as a CBT or REBT counsellor, would strive to help yourself elegantly feel better and get better, here are some steps that I recommended in a recent paper I presented to the Evolution of Psychotherapy Conference in Anaheim, California (Ellis, 2000c). The references that I give in the following section are taken from 15 articles in the January 2000 issue of *The American Psychologist* on positive psychology, edited by Seligman & Cziksentmihali (2000). In these articles, many outstanding psychologists and researchers describe their findings on positive psychology and the minimizing of cognitive-emotional-behavioral dysfunctioning. I was pleased to discover that these authorities on the psychology of human happiness largely agreed with the main therapeutic points of REBT, which I had coincidentally summarized just before I read their papers. Anyway, here are the main REBT recommendations that you can consider in treating any of your clients that you would like to help feel better and get better, and that may be particularly useful with therapists and counsellors who are anxious and depressed, and in danger of burnout. I suggest that these clients be taught—yes, actively, directively taught—the following:

1. To be distinctly aware of the important role that their believing-emoting-behavings contribute to their emotional dysfunctioning and possible improved functioning.
2. To see that they have the power to change their IBs to rational ones (RBs) *if* they work persistently and strongly at doing so with several cognitive, emotive, and behavioral methods.
3. To realize that after working for several weeks or months at their irrational believing-emoting-behavings, they can turn from automatically and unconsciously dysfunctional ways of holding them to automatic and unconscious functional ways of thinking, feeling, and behaving; that is, after some persistent work!

4. To see that they had better have strong *intentions* to change along with the *will* to change. Will*power*, as I have noted (Ellis, 1999, 2000a), includes the intention, the decision, and the determination to change—and, particularly, the *action* required to do so. Will has no power without action (Baltes & Staudinger, 2000; Missimini & Della Fava, 2000; Ryan & Deci, 2000).

5. To recognize that changing to get better as well as feel better usually involves deep, dedicated, conscious *commitment* to do so. The action required for their will*power* involves strong, persistent commitment to act and to keep acting until their changing becomes solidified (Baltes & Staudinger, 2000; Ryan & Deci, 2000; Taylor et al., 2000; Vaillant, 2000).

6. To see that intending, determining, and acting to change had better be taken in advance of changing, during changing, and after changing—constantly and ongoingly! (Baltes & Staudinger, 2000; Ryan & Deci, 2000; Taylor et al., 2000).

7. To be taught that they had better work at using a cost-benefit ratio to determine whether to try to maintain or change some of their behaving and to keep calculating the personal and social advantages and disadvantages of doing so, particularly in regard to their harmful compulsing and avoiding (Baltes & Staudinger, 2000; Buss, 2000; Schwartz, 2000; Vaillant, 2000).

8. To be shown that changing can be plotted and schemed in advance by their imagining that the worst things—like the death of several family members or fatal disease to oneself—*can* happen, and by working on how they can think, feel, and do if it *did* happen. They had better imagine and plan to work through real adversities several times, until they automatically believe, feel, and prepare to act on any grim possibilities (Baltes & Staudinger, 2000; Taylor et al., 2000).

9. To take the *challenge* and *adventure* of creating and maintaining a profound attitude of unconditionally accepting themselves, other people, and world conditions, no matter what occurs in their life. They had better strongly, determinedly commit themselves to this challenge and adventure and make it an integral, unforgettable part of their living (Peterson, 2000; Ryan & Deci, 2000).

10. To acknowledge that their strong desires, preferences, and goals usually add to their life, health, and happiness, but that their escalating their desires into absolutist and rigid musts, shoulds, demands, and necessities frequently leads them to dysfunctioning (Baltes & Staudinger, 2000; Ryan & Deci, 2000; Schwartz, 2000; Simonton, 2000).

11. To see that having an optimistic rather than a pessimistic view of themselves and their future is highly preferable—as long as they do not take this view to overoptimistic extremes (Peterson, 2000; Taylor et al., 2000).

12. To see that they can think, feel, and function better if they have some central meanings, purposes, and values that they create in their lives and keep maintaining on an ongoing basis (Baltes & Staudinger, 2000; Ryan & Deci, 73; Taylor et al., 2000).

13. To see the stressors or adversities of their lives often humorously instead of too seriously and thereby create more functional believing-emoting-behavings (Salovey et al., 2000; Vaillant, 2000).

14. To give due regard to their individualistic and competitive goals and strivings but to work clearly for them within a social and societal context. Their personal and social functioning and happiness had better include helping others thrive with minimal pain and maximum happiness (Baltes & Staudinger, 2000; Buss, 2000; Diener, 2000).

In conclusion, let me say that REBT and CBT counsellors can use, with members of the counselling profession who are contributing to their potential burnout with their own emotional problems, similar techniques to those they would use with regular clients with burnout problems. Burnout tendencies largely result from strong irrational beliefs leading to self-downing, condemning others, and low frustration tolerance. By focusing on the important issues of unconditional self-acceptance, unconditional other-acceptance, and high frustration tolerance, counsellors can help other counsellors to ward off the feelings of anxiety, depression, and rage that often lead to burnout. The techniques of REBT and CBT will not, of course, prevent burnout in all counsellors. But they may help appreciably!

REFERENCES

Baltes, P.B., & Staudinger, V.M. (2000). Wisdom: A metaheuristic (pragmatic) to orchestrate mind and virtue toward excellence. *American Psychologist*, **55**, 122–136.

Bandura, A. (1997). *Self-efficacy: The exercise of control*. New York: Freeman.

Buss, D.M. (2000). The evolution of happiness. *American Psychologist*, **55**, 15–23.

Diener, E. (2000). Subjective well-being. *American Psychologist*, **55**, 34–43.

Dryden, W. (Ed.) (1995). *Rational emotive behavior therapy: A reader*. London: Sage.

Dryden, W. (1998). *Developing self-acceptance*. Chichester, England: Wiley.

Dryden, W. (1999a). *How to accept yourself*. London: Sheldon Press.

Dryden, W. (1999b). *Rational emotive behavior therapy: A training manual*. New York: Springer.

Dryden, W., DiGiuseppe, R. & Neenan (2002). *A primer on rational emotive behavior therapy*. Champaign, IL: Research Press.

Ellis, A. (1958). Rational psychotherapy. *Journal of General Psychology*, **59**, 35–49.

Ellis, A. (1962). *Reason and emotion in psychotherapy*. Secaucus, NJ: Citadel.

Ellis, A. (1973). *How to stubbornly refuse to be ashamed of anything*. Cassette recording. New York: Albert Ellis Institute.

Ellis, A. (1976). The biological basis of human irrationality. *Journal of Individual Psychology*, **32**, 145–168. Reprinted: New York: Albert Ellis Institute.

Ellis, A. (1985). *Overcoming resistance: Rational-emotive therapy with difficult clients*. New York: Springer.

Ellis, A. (1987). The use of rational humorous songs in psychotherapy. In W.F. Fry, Jr., & W.A. Salameh (Eds.), *Handbook of humor and psychotherapy*. Sarasota, FL: Professional Resource Exchange.

Ellis, A. (1993). The advantages and disadvantages of self-help therapy materials. *Professional Psychology: Research and Practice*, **24**, 335–339.

Ellis, A. (1994). *Reason and emotion in psychotherapy*. Revised and updated. Secaucus, NJ: Carol Publishing Group.

Ellis, A. (1996a). *Better, deeper, and more enduring brief therapy*. New York: Brunner/Mazel.

Ellis, A. (1996b). *How to maintain and enhance your rational emotive behavior therapy gains*. Rev. ed., New York: Albert Ellis Institute.

Ellis, A. (1996c). *REBT diminishes much of the human ego*. Rev. ed., New York: Albert Ellis Institute.

Ellis, A. (1998). *How to control your anxiety before it controls you*. Secaucus, NJ: Carol Publishing Group.

Ellis, A. (1999). *How to make yourself happy and remarkably less disturbable*. San Luis Obispo, CA: Impact Publishers.

Ellis, A. (2000a). *Feeling better, getting better, staying better*. San Luis Obispo, CA: Impact Publishers.

Ellis, A. (2000b, May 28). Profound therapy: Helping clients to get better rather than merely feel better. The Evolution of Psychotherapy: A Conference. Anaheim, California.

Ellis, A. (2000c). Rational emotive imagery: RET version. In M.E. Bernard & J.L. Wolfe (Eds.), *The RET source book for practitioners* (pp. II, 8-II, 10). New York: Albert Ellis Institute.

Ellis, A., & Blau, S. (1998). (Eds.). *The Albert Ellis Reader*. Secaucus, NJ: Carol Publishing Group.

Ellis, A., & Dryden, W. (1997). *The practice of rational emotive behavior therapy*. New York: Springer.

Ellis, A., & Harper, R.A. (1961/1997). *A guide to rational living*. North Hollywood, CA: Melvin Powers.

Ellis, A., & MacLaren, C. (1998). *Rational emotive behavior therapy: A therapist's guide*. San Luis Obispo, CA: Impact Publishers.

Ellis, A., & Velten, E. (1992). *When AA doesn't work for you: Rational steps for quitting alcohol*. New York: Barricade Books.

Ellis, A., & Velten, E. (1998). *Optimal aging: How to get over growing older*. Chicago: Open Court Publishing.

Hauck, P.A. (1991). *Overcoming the rating game: Beyond self-love—beyond self-esteem*. Louisville, KY: Westminster/John Knox.

Marlatt, G.A., & Gordon, J.R. (Eds.) (1989). *Relapse prevention: Maintenance strategies in the treatment of addictive behaviors*. New York: Guilford Press.

Maultsby, M.C., Jr. (1971). Rational emotive imagery. *Rational Living*, **6**(1), 24–27.

Meichenbaum, D., & Jaremko, M.E. (Eds.) (1983). *Stress reduction and prevention*. New York: Plenum.

Missimini, F., & Della Fava, A. (2000). Individual development in a bio-cultural perspective. *American Psychologist*, **55**, 24–33.

Peterson, C. (2000). The future of optimism. *American Psychologist*, **55**, 44–55.

Ryan, R.M., & Deci, E.L. (2000). Self-determination theory and the facilitation of intrinsic motivation, social development, and well-being. *American Psychologist*, **55**, 68–78.

Salovey, P., Rothman, A.J., Detweiler, J.B., & Steward, W.T. (2000). Emotional stress and physical stress. *American Psychologist*, **55**, 110–121.

Schwartz, B. (2000). Self-determination: The tyranny of freedom. *American Psychologist*, **55**, 79–88.

Seligman, M.E.P., & Cziksentmihali, M. (2000). Positive psychology: An introduction. *American Psychologist*, **55**, 5–14.

Simonton, D.K. (2000). Creativity: Cognitive, personal, developmental, and social aspects. *American Psychologist*, **55**, 151–158.

Taylor, S.E., Kemeny, M.E., Reed, G.M., Bower, J.E., & Gruenewald, T.L. (2000). Psychological resources, positive illusion, and health. *American Psychologist*, **55**, 99–109.

Vaillant, G.E. (2000). Adaptive mental mechanisms. Their role in a positive psychology. *American Psychologist*, **55**, 89–98.

Author Index

Index compiled by Fiona Smith

Subject Index

Added to page number 'f' refers to a figure.

long-term outcome, assessment of, 29–30
low-back pain, research supporting brief
    CBT, 15

maladaptive worry, 102
manualized treatments, 24–5
medical disorders, link with anger, 78, 83
medication, use in PDA, 59–60
mental imagery techniques, 279–84
mental rehearsal, 283
mental videos, 152
Meta-Cognitions Questionnaire (MCQ), 105–6,
    108, 246
meta-cognitive model of GAD, 103–5
    relevance for treatment of evaluation strain,
        246
meta-worry, 102, 246
metacognitive focused CBT
    treatment of GAD, 107–113
        application to TA, 246–7
milk, milk, milk exercise, 132–4
mismatch strategies, 112, 247
modeling, 293
monitoring charts, 217, 218f, 219f
motivation, of patients, 25–6
motivation imagery, 282–3
motivational interviewing, 169
multimodal therapy (MMT), 244
muscle relaxation exercises, 225–7, 229f

National Institute on Drug Abuse's Treatment
    Outcome Study, 164
natural recovery, 178–9
negative meta-beliefs, 104, 105, 246, 270–71
    modification, 111–12, 272, 273–4
negative mood states, monitoring chart, 217,
    219f
negative thoughts, 259
    challenging reality of, 259–61
    in social phobia, 143
        evidence for, 145
        modification, 155
    suppression of, 37–8
network analysis, 207–9
network members, 208–9
non-compliance, management of, 235
Novaco Provocation Inventory (NPI), 82

obesity, research supporting brief CBT, 12
observation, behavioral, 200
observer exercise, 131–2
observer perspective hypothesis, 143
    evidence for, 145
obsession, 102
occupational stress see work stress
open-ended couple therapy see CBCT

operant conditioning, 1–2
organisational stress, 121
outcomes, assessment of, 28–30
overt avoidance behaviors, 69

P-E-T-S protocol, 153
pain management, 14–15
panic attacks
    maintaining mechanisms for, 61
    presentation in context of social phobia, 157
    problems of relaxation exercises, 226–7
panic disorder with agoraphobia see PDA
partners' standards, assessment and
    intervention, 197–8
passive aggression, 83
patient selection, S-FIT for PDA, 59–60
patients, assessment of, 25–7
PDA, 55–6
    research supporting brief CBT, 6–8
    S-FIT
        case example, 60–74
        description of, 56–9
        patient selection, 59–60
penalization, 298–9
person, separation of problem from, 216
phobias see PDA; social phobia; specific phobia
physical aggression, 83
planning, child and adolescent brief CBT,
    207–10
plans
    development of workable, 173–5
    experimental, 172
PMR, 264
    shortened versions, 264–7
points chart adolescent reward system, 225f
positive data logs, 155
positive meta-beliefs, 245–6, 270
    modification of, 112–3, 272–4
positive target behaviours, monitoring chart,
    217, 218f
positive visualization, 293
post-event processing, 144
    dealing with, 154
    evidence for, 145
post-mortem see post-event processing
post-traumatic stress disorder see PTSD
power standards, 198
preparatory phase, for anger treatment, 91
primary distress, 194
    developments in CBCT, 197–9
    implications of brief CBCT, 197
private events
    control of, 42–3
    self as distinct from, 45–6
privileges and fines system, 218f, 225
problem drinking see alcohol abuse

Index compiled by Fiona Smith